Caroline Chesebo

Peter Carradine

The Martindale Pastoral

Caroline Chesebo

Peter Carradine
The Martindale Pastoral

ISBN/EAN: 9783744666091

Printed in Europe, USA, Canada, Australia, Japan

Cover: Foto ©ninafisch / pixelio.de

More available books at **www.hansebooks.com**

PETER CARRADINE

OR THE

MARTINDALE PASTORAL

By CAROLINE CHESEBRO'.

> "For Love, methinks, hath power to raise
> The soul above a vulgar state;
> The unconquer'd banners he displays
> Control our fears, and fix our fate."

𝔑𝔢𝔴-𝔜𝔬𝔯𝔨:
SHELDON & COMPANY, 335 BROADWAY.
BOSTON: GOULD & LINCOLN.
MDCCCLXIII.

Entered according to Act of Congress, in the year 1863,

By SHELDON & COMPANY,

In the Clerk's Office of the District Court for the Southern District of New York.

J. H. TOBITT, *Printer and Stereotyper*,
1 Franklin Square.

C. S. WESTCOTT, *Printer*,
79 John Street.

CONTENTS.

	PAGE
CHAPTER I.	
The Bomb-Burst	7
CHAPTER II.	
Looking for a Substitute.	22
CHAPTER III.	
The Advent, with Results	33
CHAPTER IV.	
Morning Glory	42
CHAPTER V.	
Nature and Grace	47
CHAPTER VI.	
One Kind of Sympathy	55
CHAPTER VII.	
Thirty Miles, and More	61
CHAPTER VIII.	
The Elder's House	69
CHAPTER IX.	
The Gathering	86

CONTENTS.

CHAPTER X.
In the Woods 106

CHAPTER XI.
Miranda's Changing Heart 117

CHAPTER XII.
What is a Cousin Good For? etc 123

CHAPTER XIII.
Correspondence 136

CHAPTER XIV.
What an Inkstand Cost 147

CHAPTER XV.
Divers Gifts, and Ways of Receiving 154

CHAPTER XVI.
What is Small and What is Great 166

CHAPTER XVII.
The Letter 176

CHAPTER XVIII.
The Friends and the Lovers 183

CHAPTER XIX.
The Declaration Read 193

CHAPTER XX.
The Fourth of July in Prospect 198

CHAPTER XXI.
The Fourth in Fact 204

CHAPTER XXII.
The Fact Continued 206

CHAPTER XXIII.
By the Way 214

CONTENTS.

CHAPTER XXIV.
The Fact Concluded.... 222

CHAPTER XXV.
Mr. Carradine Consults with Mrs. Johnson...... 230

CHAPTER XXVI.
The Progress of Affairs.... 239

CHAPTER XXVII.
A Financial Crisis.... 249

CHAPTER XXVIII.
The Desperate Remedy...... 254

CHAPTER XXIX.
The Courage of—Love?...... 259

CHAPTER XXX.
The New Home...... 265

CHAPTER XXXI.
The Cousin 273

CHAPTER XXXII.
For Nature, or Against?...... 281

CHAPTER XXXIII.
Death in Life.... 292

CHAPTER XXXIV.
For Better, for Worse...... 302

CHAPTER XXXV.
Till Death Us do Part..... 307

CHAPTER XXXVI.
Old Things becoming New.... 315

CHAPTER XXXVII.
A New Nick in the Circle.... 322

CONTENTS.

CHAPTER XXXVIII.
Sally's Liberation 329

CHAPTER XXXIX.
The Wedding-Day, and Place 337

CHAPTER XL.
Home 347

CHAPTER XLI.
Randy under the Spread Eagle's Wings 353

CHAPTER XLII.
Walking among the Tombs. 363

CHAPTER XLIII.
Oliver's Return 381

CHAPTER XLIV.
Light in the Valley 386

CHAPTER XLV.
A Day of the Lord. 395

Peter Carradine.

CHAPTER I.

THE BOMB-BURST.

There was a great uproar in the red schoolhouse under the hill, whose rod was swayed by Miss Miranda Roy.

Every little tongue not paralyzed by fright was wagging, and every youthful brow discernible, for there was much hiding of faces among the boys, whose prudence exceeded their curiosity, and the girls, who were ashamed of their tears— every brow discernible, I say, was knit with displeasure or with rage, and a desire for vengeance was eminent.

The weight of the teacher's displeasure had fallen, this warm spring morning, on the shoulders of little Harry Johnson, who, after a violent struggle, had escaped from her hands, and now was flying up the hill, blazoned with fiery impressions—the herald of his own wrongs and humiliation.

Having restored the school to something like order, the teacher continued her tasks. But, though she could secure quiet, she could not command feeling. Grief and indignation, and a desire to get out where they could express emotion without danger, all this might have been evident to Miranda had she looked with questioning along the rows of little faces. Her own face seemed, to the young eyes that secretly made their observations, quite awful in its rigidity, and never before did her voice sound so harsh.

She would have the children of Martindale know who reigned in this school-room. But, secretly, she was very uneasy; not because she saw that she had been unjust. She remembered that little Harry Johnson had not merely run home to his father and mother. In comparison with the whole reality, that fact was a trifle. She and Mrs. Johnson understood each other so well, that it would be an easy matter to explain this difficulty. But Harry had likewise gone home to Peter Carradine, who lodged with his tenants. Peter Carradine, most impetuous, self-willed and headstrong of men, whose sole plaything in this world was Harry Johnson!

This recollection calmed her—but the calmness was that of the ominous lull which precedes the furious storm-break. She anticipated the worst of possibilities. At the very least, disgrace. Her flushed face paled, and it was not merely by supple bending before the authority of her own imperious will that she went through the next hour without exposing to the children her troubled state of mind.

The hour had hardly ended, when she heard voices in the path that led to the school-house, and she needed no one to announce the approach. She knew that Peter Carradine was coming on, leading Harry Johnson, but what would follow his arrival, she dared not conjecture. Hardly knowing what she did, she dismissed the class reciting, and the children huddled back into their places. Then was heard the quick, firm tread of the approaching man, and the teacher's apprehension was swiftly realized.

Carradine was a tall, strongly-built man, of swarthy complexion—features expressive of power and resolution—eyes specially remarkable for their revelations of the rich, rough nature of the man. They were now filled with wrath to overflowing.

He came with rapid strides, leading Harry Johnson by the hand, and Miranda Roy need not ask herself whether explanation were not possible that would justify her discipline. But though, just now, really afraid of Peter Carradine, she was not the woman to betray her fear. Self-possessed, determined on civility, she stood to learn the meaning of this intrusion. So much was expressed by her attitude as she awaited the outbreak.

Up to this day and hour, a very different relation from that now having ominous suggestion, had been maintained between these parties. The teacher and the patron were on the best terms possible—but at this moment he was not disposed to abate his wrath for the sake of her father, the neighborhood, or herself. Old acquaintance, and friendship likewise, went for nothing when his sense of justice became passionate.

"Randy," said he, "Miss Roy!" with a glance around the room, he fixed his stern eyes upon her; eyes in which now, judgment only was conspicuous. "When I nominated you to teach here in this district, I thought you was fit for the place. I've had my suspicions since then that I made a mistake. But I said nothing before—for your sake and your father's—but other folks have fathers, beside you. You may take your things now, and go home. And don't ever ask me to recommend you for a teacher!" Then, turning shortly from her, and addressing the school, "Children, you are dismissed! Go home and tell your folks what has happened. Tell the truth about it. Before another week goes over, I shall have a teacher here for you. Take your books and go off, all of you."

There was some stir among the children, but the teacher, not fearful of risking anything now, when she saw that all was lost, said, in a voice not elevated above its usual tone, with unusual dignity, that commanded attention and produced a hush:

"Children! I'm your teacher, and I have not dismissed you. Keep your places! Mr. Carradine, it is like you to hear only one side."

"I won't take that, ma'am. Seeing's believing. What does a man need to hear, when he can see that boy's back, done by a woman's hand too? That don't need an argument."

"I punished Harry Johnson for his disobedience, any boy or girl here will tell you that." She looked around, but every boy and girl was looking straight at Mr. Carradine, evidently anxious to evade the appeal.

"Well, Randy," said he, speaking more quietly, for her self-control had its influence on him, "your ideas about punishment won't do for me, that's all. There's ways of managing children—I should think a woman would know it without a man's telling her—short of waling flesh like that. You're through here! Children, what are you about? Well, stay we'll put it to vote. That will be according to order! Shall Miss Roy go on teaching you, or shall I look about this afternoon and see if I can find a new teacher? Go or stay? Put that to vote."

1*

"Go!" cried one of the elder boys, and every little voice echoed, or seemed to echo, that decision.

"Well," said Mr. Carradine, for the first time smiling, and he wiped the great drops of sweat from his forehead as he added, addressing Miranda, "do you want anything more?"

What right had a woman who could beat a child to any other treatment? He was at that moment as triumphantly victorious as if he had carried a point against an opponent at the polls on an election day.

"I am sure," answered Miranda, more agitated than she had seemed to be at any moment since he came into the school-room; "I am sure I ought to be glad to be rid of a nuisance. Your way of interfering don't agree with me When you get another teacher, recollect that."

Mr. Carradine did not reply, except with a grim smile, and she now gathered her books together and left the room.

Finding himself alone with the scholars, who had shown no disposition to move while the discussion lasted, Mr. Carradine questioned them again, and satisfied himself that he had done wisely; then he repeated his promise that he would at once supply the school with a new teacher. The children generally, as well as Miranda, supposed that he was thinking of Sally Green, the Elder's daughter. They knew of no other person eligible to the office.

But Mr. Carradine was looking beyond Martindale, even as far as Brighton. He calculated always on finding the very thing he wanted. His "Do this!" was generally answered by a "Done!" and most of the scholars were so impressed with the notion of his authority, that not one of them now doubted his ability to perform what he had engaged to do. So they ran out in various directions to tell their folks, as he had enjoined upon them.

It was an event to talk over that afternoon—and every farm-house round about was vocal with the various versions —and not every woman, neither every man, endorsed the deed of Mr. Carradine. Indeed, the fact that it was Carradine who had taken upon him to administer justice, was enough to throw suspicion on the verdict rendered; few persons had such confidence in him as to agree willingly to his taking on himself the duties of counsel, judge and jury. Yet such was his position in the neighborhood, and especially towards the school-house, that any person might safely have prophesied that his decisions, however aggravating, would not be really interfered with.

Two brothers, named Jobson, lived opposite the school-house, some distance from it, down the road. The elder brother was a bachelor and kept the Martindale tavern, this same little, low frame house, you see of what humble pretensions. But it is a marvellous corner; a glorious place to gossip round and drink at—there is also, close at hand, a spring, whose bright, pure water ever flows into the trough, where travellers can give their horses drink—so all the purpose an inn could serve in Martindale is answered. Jobson, the blacksmith, is the inn-keeper's younger brother, and between the two the mail is distributed three times a week to the town of Martindale, for one or other of the brothers is postmaster—the inn-keeper, it is generally supposed, but the blacksmith appears to be the more reliable man of the two, and it is he who generally opens the mail and makes it up at stated intervals. The blacksmith's shop adjoins the tavern, and idlers seem to be as fond of loitering round its door as on the tavern steps, especially if they are under no immediate necessity for grog—for Senior Jobson's aspect does most conspicuously proclaim his belief that self-indulgence is the end of living; so that a wretch whose credit was declining, pockets empty, stomach craving, really manifested no mean degree of courage when he showed himself on the tavern steps. "What will you have?" was a question as startling and confounding as could well be proposed under such circumstances; especially when it proceeded from a person of Senior Jobson's aspect, whose fullness and unbroken self-possession seemed so scornful of all emptiness and want.

The brothers were sunning themselves on the tavern steps, Senior Jobson portly, glowing, jocose. Junior Jobson, the likeness of his elder brother as he was in his prime, before he took to drink and idleness, (I mean not to drunken laziness,) a fair-faced, light-haired man, irascible, but withal kindly in his aims, and as good a blacksmith as ever managed bellows. Oliver Savage was cutting initials in one of the posts of the rough stoop—besides these, the Indian Doctor, famous for his root remedies, sat on the steps, to rest after his long foot journey

Towards this group came the blacksmith's boy on a run; but, instead of halting as he approached the house, he made past at full speed.

"Holloa there!" shouted Junior. "What are you home this time of day for, sir? Didn't I say I'd flog you, Ethan Allen, if I caught you again out o' hours?"

"They aint no school. We've had a row. Teacher's gone home. Mr. Carradine sent her!" cried the boy, as if he saw the phantom of a raw-hide flourishing above his head.

"What's that? Come here, sir!" The men's ears were well set when the child came nearer. Every one of them got up, and they stood round the reporter, after the fashion of idle men hungry for news, the most incorrigible gossips in the world, by whom scandal thrives. Let the obloquy fall no longer on tea-drinking old women. Lift up your heads, dear, venerable dames, and take an extra cup, while the unbelieving go to prove my words at the next corner.

The blacksmith's son, feeling himself quite secure now, for he understood, child though he was, the expression of the company, that he stood high in favor at this moment, gave his version of the occurrence in the school-room.

Then said Oliver Savage:

"That's like Pete Carradine. A devilish old tyrant, any how you can fix him."

"Six of one, half dozen of 'tother, it's my opinion," said the blacksmith. "Randy's pretty stiff, let her be sot once in her way. You must fight or go round. How d'ye 'spose Roy has got on with her all by 'mself so? He's a meek, peaceable man, Roy is."

"Roy—he's a chicken. Thank'ee! thank'ee! I'm beholden to ye, sir, for letting me live, ye know," whined Senior Jobson. Then he broke into a loud laugh. "Lord! such a toad; I wonder if he won't set to praying off this great evil."

The Indian Doctor, a tall, slender fellow, yet powerful and wily—famous for his cures of the sickly and the weakly, and, above all, the credulous, now spoke:

"Such a girl is managed easily enough; it's only to know the way. You might lead her now, like a lamb—but as for driving of her, or even interfering—bless your soul! know better! Old Roy knows a thing or two besides praying

Senior. By George, though, I'd like to have seen that fight! I'll be bound she went off dry-eyed from it."

"Did she, Ethan Allen? Did Randy? Did she cry any, you know, sonny?"

"Yes, you young screamer, you does, if any one," said the uncle. "He's got an eye in his head for seeing, Ethan Allen has."

"Cry!" exclaimed Oliver Savage, and he turned on his heel, apparently disgusted with the ignorance that could propose the question.

"No, she didn't cry none," replied the child.

"But they talked out pretty sharp and brisk, pretty loud, I guess?" asked the doctor.

"No, it was as still as anything. You could a'heard a pin droppit."

"He's got 'em under his thumb," said the innkeeper.

"Yes, sir, there couldn't be a tighter squeeze," observed Oliver Savage, with a knowing look at Senior Jobson. "If he's the mind to do it, they'll have to look up new quarters before they're a week older. I shouldn't wonder."

"*I* would, then, Oliver," said the blacksmith. "Carradine's ekel to anything, they say; but there's p'ints where he stops short. I've seen that man go on tippitoes all for to save ant-hills. If he's that keerful for to save a vermin—"

"That isn't it," interrupted the doctor. "The thing is n't whether he'll turn 'em out, d'ye see, but whether they'll be willing to stay in. I'd hate to have old Roy and Randy moving out of the district at the bid of any man."

"Don't borry trouble, Tom; Martindale ground will be under old Sam's feet, till Martindale grass grows over his head. You couldn't root him out with a lever short of the one that pries the old world up when it gets stuck among the stars."

"It's a dodge that won't be come, that won't," exclaimed Oliver Savage, walking up and down the stoop, that was well marked with tobacco juice, owing to the unremitting efforts of the four men, half an hour ago, spitting at a mark. "The town of Martindell wouldn't allow it, sir—it would rise up against it."

"You talk like a fool, Savage; what's Martindell got to do with old Sam Roy and his doings? I don't see."

"You don't! Then try to get up a dance here in your old tumble-down, without Randy. You wouldn't want another proof."

"George! you ought to know what girls are good for!" said Senior, with a vast deal of contempt in his retort. "You young carpetty knight!"

Junior, perhaps, heard a quarrel in the distance, for his brother was in one of his provoking moods this afternoon; and he asked a question which he could as well have answered as any other man.

"He's got a moggage, has he, Carradine has, on old Samuel's place? I'm sorry—I'm right sorry."

"Sorry!—I wish I had your money!" exclaimed Oliver. "I'd pay the old curmudgeon afore he was half an hour older, and take the moggage myself. But he wouldn't give it up! He's swallering everything in his reach, and Roy's land just fits into his farm. He wants it, and he'll have it. That's so."

"Lord! Oliver, you're getting tremenjus. There won't be any living 'long side of you when your turn comes. Oh! you needn't fire up that way. I expect, for one, you'll be rolling round in your chariot yet, like old Squire Martin and the best of 'em. What was you cut out in your shape for, if you wasn't born for a gen'leman?"

Apparently doubtful as to how Senior intended these words to be taken, Oliver was dubious how he should take them. He concluded to believe the prophecy a true one, and was confirmed in his choice when, on looking down the road, he saw Sally Green.

He pointed towards her, and was about to speak, then he changed his mind, leaped over the steps, and took the road, walking with rapid strides.

"Puppy!" said the innkeeper.

"But the girls think there's nobody like Oliver Savage," said his brother.

"Of course they do. There's Sally Green! Suppose she didn't know he stood here on the steps, ready to follow her lead?"

"Don't be hard on 'em," said the doctor. "We've been young, all of us—"

"You! when Adam was a yearling! But, the devil's in it, you haven't a gray hair yet, and you never will have. I believe you're the wandering Jew! Come, take something, Boneset."

"I'm your man for that," said the doctor, with a laugh, and he followed Senior to the bar-room, and there they sat drinking till night. It was a rare time, that, for hearing the secrets of the country round about. Boneset had them at command, and Senior Jobson was a receptacle for such things, to be sure! When ships go down with all their treasure into the ocean's depths, the grandeur of the sepulchre is at least equal to the horror of it; and divers have our honor; but how is it when we know that scavengers fish out from the sewers some fair woman's plain gold marriage-ring, or the diamond witness of betrothal, the jewelled miniature, the baby's coral, manifold pledges to be redeemed, or forever unredeemed! There should have been misgivings in the hearts of women while this doctor sipped his brandy and water, since pitch defiles. But no! they trusted him, because his office was a sacred one—the priest commands confession, though vilest of animals he be.

Junior Jobson, meanwhile, had returned to his shop, and was working at his forge, and meditating on the hard case of Samuel Roy, when the old man rode up to his door and startled him by a little familiar laugh, with which he prefaced what he had to say whenever he was pleased—and he was particularly pleased just now to find the blacksmith in his shop, for he was in a hurry to get home, and the bar-room was the last place he liked to visit, even though looking for a man; necessity seemed hardly to justify the crossing of that threshold.

"Junior, here's a little job for you, if you've got the time. Robin took to limping a mile back, down there by the bridge, a stun maybe, or a nail—I can't see—I left my eyes to hum; feel there, **that** makes him wince," while he spoke he handed Robin's **right** fore-foot over to the blacksmith's inspection.

"**Yes'ir**—that's **a stun**—sharp as glass too—wait, I'll fetch him. There, sir! Now, old Robin!" Honest Junior having rendered this swift service, stroked Robin's neck with kindly hand; then he looked at Samuel, dubious and uneasy. "You won't be limping any furder, old Robin! You don't come from home direc, then?" he said, turning from the horse to the master.

"I've been down to Brighton," answered Roy. "Beats all—to think that the houses of the Elder's stood there—and them popples all growing fine—ere a tree was cut on Brighton ground! And I've seen it all done—canal dug—railroad built—and, this afternoon, what was it but a balloon going up, with a party aboard! We're getting hard on, Junior. I shan't see it—but your boy may. Says I to Randy, says I, be keerful, you're a trainin' up the childern for a great day of the Lord; and I say the same to you, be keerful. It's a resk you run, Junior, bringing up your boys among whiskey barr'ls."

Speaking thus, Samuel mounted his horse again, not doubting that his warning would be taken kindly. Whether it would be so taken or not, there were times when the old man felt free to speak his mind in warning and counsel as a privileged person, and this was one of them.

"Hold up, there!" cried Junior, flashing fire he would repent of in five minutes. Roy's reflections on the house seemed to him an insult to his elder brother, of whom he was so proud. "You brung up your girl 'cording to your notion, I reckon; what's the reason, then, she must git into a row all of teaching in a quiet room, some consid'able distance from the smell of whisky barr'ls?"

"What's that, Junior; what's that you're saying?" asked Samuel—and the blacksmith thought that the voice of the old man trembled, that his face grew pale, and he was sorry he had spoken.

"Nothing," said he, dropping Robin's bridle, and turning half away.

"You said a row—what? Who's?"

"Nothing; only she's had a misunderstanding time with Carradine—'twould take a angel to get on peaceable with him. Yes, sir, it would! And if Randy' couldn't take it from him, there ain't the man or woman in *this* town 'll wonder. So she's gone hum, and there's to be a new teacher. That's what Ethan Allen said, but they don't know nothing, these children, and I'm thinking you'll find it all right when you get up to the farm. I'm a blasted fool for trying to give you information I ain't got myself! That's all Mr. Roy."

"I'm beholden to you, Junior, for setting Robin right. Get up, Robin—we'll be home now, sudden," and under the tightened rein and the mild voice's injunction, the old gray trotted off.

"It's a tongue," said he, while his visage lengthened, "that never wagged to purpose but once, or I disremember. That was when I telled old Carradine to take his horse to the devil to be shod, then he'd be sure to get his work well done. But he's a curious critter. He took it for a compliment, I do believe. And it's certain I've had more dollars from him than quarters from another farmer round. It's fair to hear both sides! I wouldn't want any one chastising of my boy like as I would myself, or mother. Randy's overly quick. But, there! it's none of my business. I'm sorry for old Sam."

Robin's gentle trot brought the rider duly up the road and down the lane. Randy had been waiting the return with an anxiety from which she vainly sought to rid herself. She had rehearsed again and again the story that must be told, and, while adhering to the truth, she had modified and rearranged the statement of ugly facts which any showing must prove ugly. The sound of Robin's hoofs, striking against the stones in the lane, would have disturbed any meditated version of the story. She knew, as well as her father, that peace with Mr. Carradine was all-important— that dismissal from the school, under these circumstances, was not only disgrace to her, but might be ruin also. And she must tell him that war had been waged, and that Mr. Carradine had punished her for her school discipline. Her pride was outraged and resentful; and yet that did not hinder her from seeing other results that could not fail to move her more than even the displeasure of the neigborhood, and her own humiliation. She knew how painful to her father was all strife and misunderstanding, her work in this world had never been that of a peacemaker, but no disturbance in which she had ever taken a part had an aspect serious as this. Sick at heart, she turned away from her reflections as her father rode past the kitchen window, on his way to the barn; the tea-kettle was boiling, she had only the tea to make—all would be ready for him when he should come in. And now he came in his usual slow, cautious way, that left nothing unheeded or undone; at the spring he stopped to drink, in the shed to wash his hands— this ceremony seemed to be almost a rite with him, at least he performed it with an Israelitish scrupulosity—but at last he was sitting in his usual place, and Miranda was pouring tea for him, as she had done now these ten years, since her mother died. But never had the father and daughter sat down at that board under such constraint as at this moment oppressed them. The one thought that stood out conspicuous beyond others, in the mind of Samuel, was Junior Jobson's reproachful taunt; certainly he *had* brought up Miranda since her mother's death; he had not lived unforgetful of his obligations as a Christian man, and the child's conversion had been the burden of his daily prayers. Jobson's words seemed to show him that Miranda did no credit to his teaching. He knew her faults—knew they were many—and that they were precisely such as would expose her to suspicions; he knew, besides, that she was greatly better than she seemed; but, perhaps he had been to blame; maybe he had not done for her what he might—this thought it was that made his gravity so solemn that Miranda, from moment to moment, was persuaded more and more that what she had to confess was no secret from him.

"Father," she said, "did you hear any bad news down in Brighton?"

"No—no. It was a stirring time down there—noise enough, and crowds o' people. To see the balloon, of course—to see the balloon."

"I didn't know about it. What balloon?"

"The mammoth, they called it, some such name. There was a party went up in it. I wish you had been with me, Randy. It was a sight to see."

"It wasn't to be," she answered with a sigh. "I had to stay home, and quarrel with Mr. Carradine! First or last, it's got to come—and there it is! We might have expected it—but if we didn't, there it is, just the same."

"Have you quit the school, then, Randy?"

"Quit the school!—he put me out of it! He's going to get a new teacher!"

Randy's face turned red and pale while she spoke thus, but she did not for an instant shrink from her father's steadfast gaze.

"Put you out of it?" asked he. "And did he do it, Randy?"

"Told me to go, to be sure—"

"Oh—I thought, if he laid hands on you," said the old man, and it almost seemed as if something like anger and threatening were in the tone of his voice, but the hint at passion was so very remote and vague, that it hardly thrilled the heart of Randy.

"Oh, as to that," said she, "he knew better. I don't think there's danger of that from any one. I'm safe so far. But they'll all *say* what they like. Because I punished Harry Johnson."

"Randy, it's good to bear the yoke in your youth."

"Father, what's that to do with it? Mr. Carradine—you know what he is. It isn't for myself I care. There's the mortgage, and living right here under his feet, and him to trample on you if it suits him; and there's nothing would suit him better than to worry old age and insult women!"

"There! don't!" exclaimed the old man, terrified at the spirit with which Miranda spoke, obliged as he was to own that there was some truth in what she said. "You know, daughter, what we talked about 'tother night, and what you owned and promised. It's getting the upper hand—put it down—put it down."

Miranda drank a cup of tea, and filled it again before she spoke. Her voice trembled when she said:

"If it's got the upper hand so as to make a ruined man of you, father, I'll never expect nor ask forgiveness in this world."

"Oh, it's little odds, then, where we be, if our hearts are right and we're together, Randy. It won't be as you're fearing, I'm led to believe it won't. I'm free to say it won't. I have been young and now am old, yet never saw I the righteous forsaken, nor his seed a begging bread."

"He's going to get a teacher up from Brighton."

"He is. A teacher up from Brighton to teach in the red school'us?"

"So that's all," said Randy, much relieved now that the whole business was before her father, and that he took the intelligence so quietly, for though assured in her mind that he would take it thus, she had no peace until she saw the proof.

Having spoken thus, she fell back on her own reflections; and her father seemed to be absorbed in his, for they finished their meal in silence; then he went and sat down in his arm-chair, by the door, according to his evening custom, when the farm work was not urgent.

Between her doubt as to whether Mr. Carradine would carry out his indignation against herself into persecution of her father, and her doubt as to whether, if he showed no such disposition, it became them to remain in their present position quietly, his debtors, the daughter was sufficiently disturbed.

Serene as the course of her father's reflections seemed to be, the old man was, in fact, greatly troubled. Most of all by the impression made by Junior's run at Randy. The father needed no such testimony as the day past had afforded; he knew what Randy's temper was. Its flashings and fires had alarmed and troubled him too many times to admit a doubt of the blame under which she stood at present. But he knew moreover, the swift repentance that generally followed any over-hasty word, or act; he believed, with all his heart, in her kindliness and generosity, and uprightness—he knew that she was never cruel, nor deliberately unjust, and the wrong she did herself in these explosions always appeared to him far greater than she could inflict on others. He had, moreover, the most delightful confidence in her ability to teach. He could not imagine a kind of work to which she would be incompetent. Of late, he had thought that he could see some evidences in her of awakened religious feeling, and he had great hopes of Randy—let her once put on the "easy yoke of a profession," and all would be well. The ardent spirit that in any service must make itself evident, would be a shining light if it but once caught the flame of a holy fire. Let him once behold that alive, generous and courageous spirit serving in the temple of the Lord, he would close his eyes in peace. Sitting there at rest in the mild spring evening, looking over the fair landscape, the woods and fields, and the long road, winding as a river, his faith and hope did not forsake him. And he prayed silently, what he repeated afterwards in the evening supplication with which he ended each day, " Oh! Lord, let no witness go forth out of us distracting to thy cause! Let not the ungodly rise up agin thy servants to say, 'There! there!' and shame our profession. If we have offended thee, oh! give us to repent, and confess, and make peace, wherever we go. Don't forsake us! don't let us forsake thee! Don't let our pride or our wrath turn into hate agin any human creetur, for whom thou sheddest precious blood."

And thus only he could find it in his heart to reprove her, by a confession of sin, and prayer for deliverance to ONE so high above them, so mighty above all men, that the heart must have been harder, and the will more perverse than Miranda's, to listen without joining in the amen that came from the old man with a deepened sense of his helplessness, and a stronger grasping at the sacred promises.

So the night closed over them. Over the old log-house with its framed additions, whose corners were decorated by hop-vines, whose windows, ornamented by a lattice work of twine, through which the stems of the sweet-brier were woven. Over the fine broad field, in whose midst stood the comfortable, homely dwelling. How quietly over all animate things within the ownership of Samuel Roy;—good, patient, humble man, proud of but one thing in this world, his daughter, how sadly over him!

CHAPTER II.

LOOKING FOR A SUBSTITUTE.

Mr. CARRADINE was a man of authority, so far as the school was concerned. The building had been erected at his expense, on his own land, and he had given the grove in the rear, including the spring, for a play-ground; and the farmers round about seemed so willing that he should take the burden of the expense upon himself, that they could not in reason object to his show of authority in that regard. Neither was it surprising that he should sometimes assume as much authority in the management as others would allow. He was one of the money powers of Martindale; the most liberal among them, and as he was not disposed to make himself obnoxious, he had not to complain of any reasonable opposition to his plans and management. No charge of interference had been brought against him up to the opening of this record.

Dexterously and promptly the man's judgment had served him in this instance, and he came from the conflict with a sense of justice done, not at all with the consciousness that the greater had subdued the weaker; that the man had managed the woman.

Always a man of few words and prompt action, he harnessed his team that afternoon and drove down to Brighton. Mrs. Johnson went with him, but not as an assistant in the business. Neither (for she liked Miranda,) was she quite easy at the turn the day had taken. But she knew better than to interfere with Mr. Carradine in his present mood—she thought she knew better, and held her tongue, even when her mother-heart had the generosity to suggest that possibly he had been over hasty. Randy had been strict and stern; but if she had been cruelly unjust, she would certainly have been quick to own it. So, between her conflicting conclusions, Mrs. Johnson, like a prudent woman, modified her sense of injury, and rode to town in quiet. Not as an assistant in the business, as I said; Mr. Carradine felt his competence to conduct that alone. She had her shopping to attend to, and he left her at the grocer's before he drove on to the house of Brown, the School Commissioner.

Now the Commissioner's daughter had graduated but a few weeks since at the Brighton Academy, as also had the daughter's friend, one Mercy Fuller, who was spending part of the vacation in the family.

No sooner had Mr. Carradine made known his wish than the Commissioner struck his hands together and exclaimed:

"Here's a circumstance! The girl you want is within beck and call, asking, not an hour ago, for a situation; they want her at the Academy, but she's tired, and needs rest, and if she could get some place in the country, that's what she was saying. I'll call her! she'll answer for herself."

"Wait," said Carradine. "You've seen Sally Green.— Is your young lady like her?"

The Commissioner laughed.

"Is that the kind you want?"

"Do I want to breed a murrain up in Martindale? But, look here—she came out of the Academy too!"

"What's bred in the bone, sir, will come out in the flesh. Cure a gangrene, will you, by a plaster? But if you can get Miss Fuller to say she will teach your school, don't you stand for the price, that's all."

"Bring her round," said Carradine.

When she came into the office, Brown, explaining by the way the nature of the business on which he had said he wished to talk with her, she seemed to be surprised, as people given to wishing usually are, when they find themselves on a sudden taken at their word.

But, quickly coming to an understanding with herself, Miss Fuller decided that, if she found, on going over to Martindale, that the place satisfied her, she would at once accept the situation; pleasant scenery, comfort, independence, and reasonable wages, were the conditions for which she stipulated, with a clearness and a promptness, which led Carradine to conclude, "There is a woman of business—she don't look like it neither."

When he had given his explanation of the needs of the school, omitting, however, to state the reason of its need

Mr. Brown promised that he would, the next day, drive over to Martindale with the young ladies, and Miss Fuller should then give her final answer.

Thus easily matters were arranged, and Carradine drove away from the Commissioner's door, feeling a tolerable assurance that the business was as good as settled.

"Did you ask the questions you said you would of Brown?" inquired Mrs. Johnson, curious to know greatly more concerning this interview than Mr. Carradine would be likely to communicate.

"Why, no," he answered, as pleased at the reminder as positive people usually are when their deeds have fallen short of their promises. "I asked Brown if—" here his prudence suggested that he had best withhold the name of Sally Green, "if she was like the rest of the city girls. You see what they are, Mrs. Johnson; made up for a show, like them paper flowers you talked about."

"That Sally Green made? Very pretty they be, on the mantel-tree piece; the Elder says it's going to be their winter garding."

"Yes," said Carradine, thoughtfully, "a winter garding. I'd prefer what grows natural in the summer. You can live on that! But, I tell you, a young woman with her ribbins and prinking, what's she good for now?"

"Don't be hard, sir; it ain't long we keep young, try our best. Sally is a unly child, and if she was an orphan to-day, she's money enough to take care of her," said Mrs. Johnson. "They've brought her up tender—she ain't meant to be a farmer's wife. There's men in the world that can do without farming. Good for Sally Green and such as have edication."

Mrs. Johnson was not half satisfied with her apology for the Elder's daughter, but she derived a little satisfaction from the expression given to the distaste hinted for the slaving life herself led. She was born and brought up in a town, and to this day looked back with longing regret to its dust and clatter, its novelties and shows. But these retrospections were never indulged in, except at a cost. Conscience stood ready to reproach her for all that was involved in this regret and discontent. Would she, indeed, renounce Johnson, and little Harry, and her religion, to be a girl once more and live a lady's maid, as she was doing when

Johnson caught her in his toils and carried her away into the lonesome country? Well, at least, she could feel for Sally Green; and, though it might be accounted a sin in a professor, could admire and flatter Sally's flashing, flimsy show of dress, and pity her for the accident that had cast her lot on a farm, when she might have shone in town.

Mr. Carradine was perhaps musing over her defence of Sally—he did not speak in some time—when he did, he said :

"I had my answer to those questions without asking. You wouldn't be afraid to trust children to the care of the young woman, Mrs. Johnson ?"

"Well, give us a bit of a pictur; how you saw it," she said, glad to have escaped the argument which she had invited.

"A peaceable looking young woman. Smart, and great for learning. Brown recommends her. No gadder, says he ; and no gossip ; but as firm as a rock."

"Like enough to Randy, for all I can see."

"Not a bit, ma'am. Randy isn't firm; she's like tow to take fire."

"But you let her alone, and she goes out, of herself. If she ever gets broke in—why, what do you think of your Bill there ? You wouldn't sell him for *love* or money ; but I guess you had a time of it bringing him round ! You ain't nearer to your horse, Mr. Carradine, than the Lord is to Randy. It will take him to do it; but it'll be done. Firm as a rock—you like that ?"

"Yes," said Carradine, "in the right kind of woman."

"Oh, dear—the right kind of a woman ! Is there such a thing as that, now ?"

"Maybe," he answered quietly.

"I've tried to pictur her," said Mrs. Johnson, who seemed to be speaking for all Martindale—and, indeed, she had in view the occasions on which she must hereafter make satisfaction for the event of this drive to Brighton, and she must be able to say with a clear conscience that she had stood up against 'foreigners.' "I've tried to pictur her, thinking of what she could be like; but it's allers a flying image I get, like them pictures of angels in the big Bible. Where did you get your notions ?" She asked the serious question quite playfully ; but he answered gravely :

"Out of my conscience."

"Conscience! Out of your conscience, sir?"

"Isn't that what you steer by? Do you think I'm like the Pagans you hear so much of in your Herald? Though, for the matter of them, they've got their own light to walk by, to my mind."

"Oh dear, no!" answered Mrs. Johnson, somewhat flurried, in spite of the smile that succeeded this rather sharp questioning. "But what can your conscience tell you, sir, about womankind?"

"It remembers me of my mother." Here Mr. Carradine drew the reins, and Bill went on with extra speed for half a mile. Then said the master:

"It isn't to be expected she will be our teacher long. It's the country air she wants for health, and for rest. I hope she will get both; I do indeed. She don't look over-strong."

"Sickly?"

"Sickly!—No; but not as strong as an ox. Not weak neither. This is a pretty country—don't you think so, Mrs. Johnson?"

As he said this, Carradine looked around him and took in the pure air and the bright prospect, as if with renewed senses.

They were just entering the "black forest," through which the straight country road ran on a level for three miles. He was thinking that, when they had passed through this shade and silence, they would come upon the fine farm lands, the broad prospect. And would the young woman find the country fair? How would these great meadows strike upon her eye, these beautiful broad meadows, dotted here and there with fine forest trees, left for the shelter of cattle by the thoughtful care that tilled the lands? And the fields of clover, and the windings of the river, by whose side the road ran full ten miles? What would she think of the tulip trees? and the great pines? and the pine grove? What might her notion of a pleasant country be? He was curious to know.

And he looked at Mrs. Johnson, who was slow to give her answer.

"Maybe—yes—for farmers." Then she pinned herself fast to this acknowledgment by a text. "The earth is the

Lord's and the fulness thereof." But this kind of vengeance on herself did not change the fact that she was going back to duties which she did not love, to a retirement that had no charm for her.

As he drove along among the farm-houses of Martindale, Mr. Carradine was tempted to stop and communicate with his neighbors the measure of success he had met with in seeking a teacher for their children. But caution prevented him. Time enough when he should have settled the business—under provocation even, he was not a boaster.

So he drove past the blacksmith's shop and tavern; past Elder Green's; past the lane that ran down to neighbor Roy's; and up the hill to the red farm-house occupied by his own tenants, with whom he lived.

The most that Carradine could say was, that he felt satisfied with his day's work, and every moment less disposed to construe charitably the act he had so speedily avenged. All was indeed over with Miranda when he sat smoking his pipe in the corner of his piazza, and reflected on the day's eventful passage. In comparison with Randy, dark-haired, energetic, swift in thought and deed; handsome, and so proud that she seemed to be defiant even in ordinary dealings; impetuous and self-willed; and withal a chivalrous, brave-hearted girl, both generous and loving; in comparison with her, how strangely attractive to his fancy the face of the young lady he had seen at Brighton!

"Such flowers don't grow wild," he concluded; "you must graft the tree that bears such fruit." It was certain also that no woman had excited in him equal curiosity. Her fair face haunted him. When he had spoken to Mrs. Johnson of her desire for the country and for rest, and she had suggested the notion of sickliness and weakness, he seemed to receive a new idea of strength, as attractive as it was novel. The young woman was *not* as strong as an ox—but—she wasn't born to do the work of oxen. She seemed to be cautious, and yet ready—and well assured of her ability to perform what she engaged to do.

And yet almost any person knowing Mr. Carradine would have pronounced this teacher incapable of filling the situation to his satisfaction.

To what purpose—yea, let the items be given; there she was, then, in the house of Commissioner Brown, or before the eyes of Peter Carradine musing in his piazza—a stature slightly above medium—demeanor untroubled, aspect cheerful—eyes light gray and far-seeing, face fair and good, hair brown and curling—voice clear, distinct, deliberate, outspoken, as if the heart had nothing to conceal; as if the woman had something to do for herself and others, and was conscious of it; had a being to sustain, and knew the worth of speech. Yet her words were not many.

I find in her nothing coarse or tawdry; nothing mean or base, now that it seems some definite report is to be given. She expresses a thoughtful, kindly nature. Her cheerfulness is active, does not betray ignorance, neither senseless content. She has had some sorrows as well as some true joys; and her conviction, that by which she lives, seems to be that it is a pleasant thing to see the sun.

And Mr. Carradine, wise in cattle breeds, and crops, and lands, careless of women, too hurried for every thing in this world except business, is pleased to think of her. And he is somewhat anxious—thinking, what if she comes up to-morrow and finds the country not agreeable, the school-house uncomfortable—nothing to her notion?

If she turns her back on Martindale—she is a free agent; no one can constrain her to see what she may not be able to see in the district, (and that is a vexation,) will he regret anything besides the children's loss, and the mortification of failure?

He does not even ask himself that question. But if there is anything objectionable in the school-house, he would not oppose improvements she might recommend, if within the bounds of reason.

He sat there, thinking of these things, long after he had smoked his pipe out. At last a sudden recollection brought him to his feet. He had forgotten to speak to Johnson about Bill. But so accustomed was he to carrying out all plans and purposes with prompt despatch, that he had not walked the length of the piazza before he had determined that it might be wise to defer Bill's shoeing until daylight This reflection, however, did not satisfy the unconscious desire that deftly suggested Bill's need of shoeing—and the tavern stand. He remembered now that he had a little business to transact with a neighbor, and where so likely to find him as in Jobson's bar-room?

Carradine could deceive himself as readily as another man. What he really went down to the tavern for was to satisfy his curiosity in regard to public opinion in Martindale. Very rarely was he seen in that part of the house superintended by Senior Jobson. He never was invited to "take something" by that genial proprietor, though whenever they met they were friendly enough, and there was probably no danger that either would ever cross the other's path, or interfere with his interests.

Olmstead, the man whom Carradine was in search of, sat in the tavern porch with half a dozen of the usual hangers-on. As he approached, not a soul of them could mistake the man, his figure, or his bearing. Senior Jobson said:

"Lord! there's the devil himself, come to see what ye're making this rumpus for about him. I'll expose the lot of you."

Junior retorted, with a laugh:

"There's two can play at that game."

"Yes—what started Senior up so, I wonder; haranguing us by the hour. I say it's Randy!" exclaimed Olmstead, a burly, happy fellow, who came down for his newspaper two hours ago, and forgot his errand the moment he arrived in sight of the Spread Eagle.

"Randy be sunk!" muttered the bachelor—but he walked off to the other end of the porch, and by the time he could pace back again, Mr. Carradine had come nearer, and called out:

"Is Joshua Olmstead anywhere about?"

"Here!" returned Olmstead. "What's i' the wind?"

"You're the man I wanted," said Carradine, and he ascended the steps and took the seat by his neighbor, which Junior had vacated but now. Their conference was brief—then Senior, who had observed them from a distance, said, approaching:

"What's the row up t' school-house, captain? You scattered the young ones like leaves blowing about afore the wind."

"What's the report?" asked Carradine, not disappointed to hear the interrogation.

"Randy's quit, and a new teacher coming. So?"

"If one can be got. Yes; Miranda Roy has left."

"Randy's a smart girl," said Junior Jobson; but it was a remarkably small voice of vindication.

"The devil's in her, though," answered his brother, the innkeeper. Beyond hearing, there was interrogation in this assured assertion.

"Oh, ay—she's well enough. Miranda's a good girl in her place—but that isn't in th' school-house. And so, there are others in want of a good place, I expect. We'll not have to go begging," said Carradine, with magnanimity.

"But she—ha! ha!—Rand's a tiger if you get her roused up, captain. Tooth and nail! I'd as lief have a wild-cat after me."

"I wouldn't then. You don't know what you're talking about, Olmstead."

"Don't I? Well, I'd like to keep a school once, any way, with her for a beginner. I'd take the mischief out of her, or die a trying!"

"Leave her alone; leave her alone," said Carradine, pleasantly.

"'Tisn't all of us that's fit for every kind of business that's going. Put that girl in her right place, and she'd fill it full. I believe in Randy Roy; but I don't blame you, neither, Mr. Carradine." It was Junior who said this.

"Who does?" exclaimed the brother, as if the very notion were preposterous.

"You think it's the thing, then, all of you—a new teacher?" asked Mr. Carradine, not a little pleased at this report of the general opinion.

"I don't know what a man could a done different. If a woman takes to 'busing the children, time the men took 'em up," said Olmstead; he was a husband and a father; his house was full of little ones—he spoke feelingly.

"Yes, yes," said the Junior, endorsing the proposition without clearly seeing its bearings, for he regarded himself at the present time as Miranda's defender. "Yes, yes; that's so, neighbors."

"I'm glad to have your opinion, friends. I knew I was in the rights of it; but a man likes to have his friends see what he sees; and that's rare—it's rare! Olmstead, you'll recollect, will you? Nine o'clock, sure. Good night, all round."

So Mr. Carradine departed; but he had taken scarcely

a dozen steps beyond the road, when Senior Jobson started after him. It seemed to be a sudden movement on his part, but it followed after the coolest deliberation.

"I say, captain," he called out, and those whom he had left behind him heard as distinctly as Carradine, and every strained ear listened for what should follow, but the two men moved on beyond hearing before they spoke again. This was the conversation that then passed between them:

"Captain, I've been thinking more about that farm land. I want it this spring; I want it the worst way."

"What farm land? You don't mean Roy's farm, Jobson?"

"Why don't I? It belongs to me of right—never ought to have been sold; cut up the best strip ever was for barley—and that's the kind o' grain that pays me best."

"No doubt. But I told you, Jobson, I'd no sooner give that mortgage into another man's hands than I would sell my eyes. It's what I said to Roy when he got into that cramped corner of his—you know how he got there—helping his brother Edward. No, no; can't be done, Jobson; can't be done!"

Whenever Mr. Carradine spoke in this tone, it was well understood that further discussion of a subject with him would not only prove vain, but also vexatious. Jobson, knowing that he should gain nothing by any kind of argument, ended the conference by saying:

"If ever you change yer mind, then, you won't be favoring another man afore me?"

"No, no; you shall have as good a chance as another when that time comes. Be sure of that, Jobson."

"That's all. Good night, then."

"Good night to you," said Carradine, and the two went their separate ways—Carradine indulging himself in this outbreak when he found himself alone:

"Beast, talking of barley! He wants the mortgage so he can choke the old man and badger Miranda. He'll wait awhile then."

"Come, boys, let's drink to the new school-ma'am," said Senior Jobson, as he returned to the tavern.

So the party went into the bar-room and drank to the health of Mercy Fuller!

Privately, Junior's wife joined in the drinking, and went to bed. Overburdened with children, work and care, this was her rest and recreation. She had overheard Senior's invitation, and the merest suggestion of that " invisible spirit" he had invoked in behalf of the coming teacher, was enough.

CHAPTER III.

THE ADVENT, WITH RESULTS.

Mr. Commissoner Brown came up to Martindale next day, with his daughter and Miss Fuller, and the party visited, together, the little red school-house under the hill, at whose door Mr. Carradine stood waiting.

It needed but a glance to assure him that he might throw aside his fears, such a look of pleasure was on the face whose satisfaction he had most desired to witness, that he, a man never disposed to burden himself with any unnecessary care, quickly assured himself with an inaudible "all right!" and led the inspectors into the school-house, which he had taken the pains to bring into order while he waited their arrival.

The place seemed to answer Miss Fuller's wish. She had anticipated nothing so comfortable; she found nothing to disapprove, but much to be glad of. And Mr. Carradine showed the party with pride, encouraged by her praise, into the wood-shed, and to the spring in the grove, back of the house, but without a suspicion that Mr. Brown would add:

"Carradine, you did as good a public work as ever was done for Martindale when you gave the land and built the school-house."

Yet he felt a little honest pleasure in that kind of endorsement, though he answered modestly:

"How could I help it? Nobody else would undertake the job. I should think we had half a dozen meetings before a man of them would say what he was willing to give towards it. Finally, I told them they might as well save their time and breath, as well as their good-for-nothing money, and stop talking. They consented, all round."

"Then you have a right to find your own teachers, certain. I wonder they don't object to that, though," said Mr. Brown.

Carradine appeared more anxious to learn what Miss Fuller thought of the country, than even to establish his right to supply the school with teachers; for he said nothing in particular about the present vacancy, or the sudden transfer he was making of the pupils from one instructor to another. He seemed delighted to hear Mercy praise the drive from Brighton. Nothing apparently had escaped her notice; woods and fields, those fertile fields where cattle grazed, the tulip trees, the pine trees, the river, the hills, and the broad meadows, she had observed, and she admired all. He was quite satisfied. And if he had now thought of Miranda, it would have been as we are too apt to think of the victims of other modes of progress in the world. Every blessed sewing machine! must we darken and lessen benefit with thinking of the inefficient and the incompetent who will perish under the wheel of that domestic Juggernaut?

During the hour of their visit it was arranged that Miss Fuller should come up next day to Martindale, and that her summer career of "boarding round" should begin with Mrs. Johnson.

In the course of that same hour Mr. Brown and Mr. Carradine drove about among the farmers, notifying the various families that the school would begin next day, and that under most favorable circumstances. The children were expected to muster in full force, and promptly, for it was not likely that Martindale would ever again have such a teacher as the lady who had engaged to serve them for the summer.

This business now accomplished, Mr. Carradine might rest —if he could.

He went into his room on the north side of the house, dressed himself in his working-clothes, and walked down to the field where Johnson was plowing, and stayed there until dark. He was, therefore, probably at work. Why not! There was not in the town so diligent a man as he, nor a man who had so signally prospered by industry. Work was his chief business in life, apparently; and this little episode recorded above must have sent him back to his toil with an increased zest. He had a hundred things to think of. Why did he think of but one?

Mercy Fuller returned to Brighton smiling and satisfied, packed her trunk and sent her answer to the Principal.

Brown said to his daughter, " Carradine is an odd stick, but a bachelor, and rich." To which the daughter answered, " Father, how absurd."

Sally Green walked down the lane that led to Samuel Roy's house. She had not seen Miranda since yesterday's disturbance, and she had heard, meantime, many versions of the story besides that delivered last night by young Savage. Public opinion justified neither of the parties concerned in the quarrel, but all the sympathy Sally had to give was given to Miranda; and when she came fairly to discover, and speak her mind, Peter Carradine would not be spared.

All day Miranda had been expecting this arrival; and if Sally had only to run up in the morning with a single word of trust and love, beyond all things her friend would have valued such a testimony—one expression, impulsive, ardent, believing, would have outweighed scores of more deliberate utterances. But up came Sally, late in the afternoon; a smooth-faced, pretty girl, who wore her black hair combed straight back from her forehead, with a curl plastered against either temple—and her eyes, large, bright and black, wide opened to the world; her complexion clear and dark, was without a blemish. There was not an evidence in that showy beauty of either strength or wisdom, but those who loved the girl made no requirement of wisdom or of strength. Wilful, and selfish, and vain, she had made her way thus far in life, so pleasant and so charming, it was a rare thing for any one to oppose her. Such as attempted opposition did it to their cost, and never to her benefit.

She had on her a flat straw hat, trimmed with pink ribbons, and a pink dress made for her while she was at the boarding school, whose deep folds were well trimmed with fringe. She wore, likewise, ornaments on her hands, and wrists, and bosom; and the chain round her neck secured a gold pencil, with a number of pretty and curious charms, tokens of the undying affection of schoolmates, with whom she was just now in the close communion of a constant correspondence.

Curious though she felt in regard to Randy's state, Sally was mainly urged to this present visit by her grandmother's anxiety—and when they had watched the Commissioner's democrat till it wheeled out of sight, returning to Brighton, she put on her hat, and started for Samuel Roy's.

Randy was busy sorting the garden seeds, which must be planted to-morrow. She had arranged the papers of flower-seeds, and was deep among the shadows of future garden treasures, when she looked up and saw Sally Green.

"Don't get up," said Sally, as she stepped across the parcels ranged round the door-sill, on which Miranda sat.

"I can't," said Randy, looking a little disturbed, but speaking out strongly, fluently—"take a seat. I'm getting ready for gardening. It's late for planting, I think, but I couldn't get a minute of time before. I won't have that to complain of any longer. You've heard it all, of course?"

"You ain't killed any way," said Sally. "I expected to find you in bed sick—not able to see out of your eyes for crying. That's the reason I didn't come up this morning."

"Thank you, kindly," answered Randy; but she looked indignant. Sally's fine dress, or the perfume she carried, so dainty and rich, had an indisputable effect in controlling the speech of an angry woman at this present moment. "What do you think of the business?" she asked.

"I think it might have been expected. Cruel and mean —I never changed my mind yet about him. I wouldu't like to have to thank him for a favor."

Randy winced at that. If her face lightened during the first part of Sally's remark, it darkened at the last words.

"It's desperate!" said she. "I'm done with him, though; and I'm glad of it."

"Never mind. So'm I. But I wish you could have seen him flourishing about, you know, with the folks from Brighton city, this afternoon."

"What folks?"

"Why, the new teacher. Haven't you heard? Yes, he's got a new teacher—went over yesterday afternoon to see about it, and to-day they came to look! There was Mr. Brown and his daughter, and this young lady. A dreadful common looking affair, too; milk and water. We've got to have her boarding round next. She's going to Johnson's the first week. And we shall have to take her in our turn, I expect. But it will be as cool a week as ever she spent, I promise you. Of course she'll be treated well, but she might better be cast off on Robinson Crusoe's Island. I've seen city folks before! And Mr. Carradine needn't think he can come any of his games in this district. You know grandma don't believe in him. Neither do I. So you've two on your side, Randy, if you hadn't the whole town, as you have, you know."

Sally had fairly talked herself round into full belief in sentiments which by no means actuated her when she left her father's house. Indeed, at home, where Mr. Carradine met with no manner of favor, she had seemed to be disposed to regard Randy's temper in the fullest and worst light.— What she had said of the arrival in Martindale that day, and the departure therefrom, had greatly excited Miranda, but she took the tidings with apparent composure.

"When does the school begin?" she asked.

"To-morrow."

"That's sudden—his way!"

"And that's all you care! You're as queer as he is. I would have liked to see you two. I don't believe he had the best of it."

"Nor I."

"So he was just mean enough to start off on the other track and get another teacher. I didn't think he'd do it— though he said he would."

"But it was dreadful to get roused so. I think I would rather die, Sally, than go through with anything like that again. Besides, father is so troubled, though he don't say much. He's in debt to Mr. Carradine. If it wasn't for that it wouldn't be so bad. To have business with a man that's served you so—right or wrong—it wouldn't be agreeable to a saint, and it isn't to him. When uncle Edward got into his difficulties, father borry'd money of Mr. Carradine, and he never's seen the time when he could catch up with himself since. That's the only thing. If I have done wrong, how 'll I forgive myself for bringing a new trouble on the poor old man?"

For the first time that day Miranda burst into tears—but the storm was brief as sudden. She would not allow herself to lament what had happened in any useless way What could she *do*?

Sally consoled her, after her fashion, innocent of a suggestion.

"Oh, dear—*can't* it be done, somehow? Can't the

money be raised? I don't wonder you feel so. If it wasn't for that debt!"

"Maybe it might be raised; it might—yes; easy enough. I'm all that stands in the way to that, too! You don't see how I can be such a stumbling-block to myself as I am! Oh! Sally, I suppose I am a dreadful wicked woman. And I know I'm a terrible fool. Always getting into trouble. When I see how quiet father goes along, I wish I was a Christian, if for nothing else. I expect it's a spirit they get, that makes it easy to live; and it's always been hard, up-hill work to me."

"Don't talk that way; you'll come out of it somehow, Randy, and light on your feet, like the cat thrown out of a window; I can see that." Sally laughed, as she rose from her seat. Her business here as a consoler was now done, and somehow, Randy's company was less agreeable than usual.

"What is the young lady's name that's coming up from Brighton?" asked Randy, rising also. She would not invite Sally to remain longer; it was a presence that only seemed to aggravate her present depression.

"Fuller. She's nothing. You needn't bother about her. I'm going. I shall tell grandma that Randy's Randy yet. Come home to tea with me!" This sudden invitation seemed to be an unlooked-for escape of sympathy. It claimed Sally's subsequent admiration.

"And leave father?" said Randy—she appeared to hesitate.

"No—I suppose not, as long as he lives! Come and walk a little way, then."

So Randy got her green checked sun-bonnet and walked with her friend along the road toward Elder Green's.

On her return, Miranda met Senior Jobson, who came out of his barley field, which adjoined her father's farm. He said:

"Miss Randy, will you tell your father if he wants my span to-morrow, for breaking up, I won't be using of em? It's going to be a good season, and I want the old man to have a fine summer harvest."

She thanked him, and thought her father would be glad of the horses, if Mr. Jobson was sure he had no use for them.

As to that, he answered, walking along beside her, encouraged to do so by her civil speech, he should not mind being put out in order that he might serve Neighbor Roy before he served himself. The old man was not as strong and able to work as he was once. It would be strange if neighbors who had always known him, couldn't sacrifice a point or two on account of so good and peaceable a man!— He expected some new farming machinery this summer, and he believed it would save her father the expense of employing harvesters and threshers, in the way he had always been obliged to do. He thought he could just mention it to her, and she could speak of it to her father and it might encourage him, for he thought that Samuel looked more infirm than usual this spring. And he knew that *he* was no great favorite ; so, if he would manage it for him, he would thank her kindly ; or, if she would call on him any time, for he supposed that she would be a farmer like the rest of them, and beat 'em all, maybe—he shouldn't wonder.

She thanked him—she more than thanked him. What he had said about her father's failing health, this friendly and kindly observation of what she had hardly dared acknowledge to herself, the offers of assistance in the farm work, coming in such a shape, above all at such a time, softened the heart of Randy, caused her to judge kindly of Senior Jobson, and she spoke out the impulse she felt.

"I wish you had the mortgage in your hands, Mr. Jobson! I'd sooner be thinking that the debt was owed to you than to Mr. Carradine."

"Carradine don't trouble you about it, does he, Randy."

"No, but it's the owing of it to him that I hate and despair of."

"Yes, yes," said he, thoughtfully, and none of the bar-room swagger was perceptible now ; very quietly he was walking by Miranda's side, a much-abused man she took it into her head at this moment to think. The old process was going on again. She, like all the rest of the world, was seeing in him what she desired to see. "Yes, yes ; there's none of us lives quite free of others. If it isn't one kind of, debt it's another. Money or affection! If I *had* that mortgage—I wish I had! that should be the last of it. All the interest I'd ask for it wouldn't trouble you to give. You understand me, don't you ?"

"Well—but—Senior, don't talk that way, if you please."

"I know," said he, "you are a deal too good for me. I wasn't thinking my taking of that debt would be as if you was obligated to seal the bargain. I know you're too good for me."

"Too good!"—She looked at him, and seeing that he was in earnest, that he really meant what he had said, shook her head. "Don't say that again; I don't know what the meaning of good is, but I'm certain it isn't me."

No man would have credited that Senior Jobson approached Miranda Roy with a confession of this nature. But he probably believed, for the moment, that what he said was true, though the belief may have sprung from the knowledge of the girl's pride and spirit, and of her present humiliation.

Her exclamation, which expressed a rare, self-depreciating mood, encouraged him now to urge his suit on other grounds besides those of expediency.

It could not surprise her, for in divers ways before now he had presented the cause to her mind. Never in so many words—never openly, as now. And never until now could he have trusted his cause to her with confidence, for beneath the seeming doubts with which he pleaded for himself, was a strange assurance of a verdict that would leave him no longer a prisoner of hope. While he spoke on, distinctly up rose before him the Spread Eagle lifted into a second story, newly winged and enlarged—a thriving tavern, with a landlady who should do the honors of the house to the admiration of all travelers. There too, he seemed to see—oh, triumph of common sense!—the form of Samuel Roy reposing on the shady side of the new piazza, with a handkerchief over his head, and his pipe in the hands of a mischievous urchin, whose name was not Ethan Allen. It was a flight of imagination by no means uncommon to the mind of Senior Jobson, and it did not embarrass him when he spoke, nor when he waited for Miranda's answer.

By a rapid mental process, she had surveyed this business from beginning to end. Her pride and her filial love decided it. She looked at Senior Jobson; he was not offensive to her. His person was not contemptible, but, on the contrary, he was built in quite a noble style of manhood, and she had never seen him except in his better moods. It was said that he could storm, and exact, and tyrannize, and that he was cruel; but to her he seemed a good-tempered, amiable man, and the contrast of his disposition to frolic, with the grave and quiet life to which she, a girl so spirited, was born and bred, was not entirely distasteful.

He was not the man she would have chosen, maybe, had all things gone well; but now, without misgiving, she said:

"You have a mind to give up the tavern, then?"

"No I haven't. I've a mind to build a big, fine mansion on the corner opposite the Elder's, and take a mate that the Spread Eagle may be proud of."

If he had spoken out his purpose with less precision, it would have pleased her less, this was not an hour when she wished to rule. The deliverance she longed for left her incapable of a wish to direct or dominate. The strong man's strong speech, that left no room for a compromise, seemed to be just what she needed to hear.

"It isn't a dove, then, you liken me to," said she, "If it had been a ground-sparrow, I wouldn't have wondered."

"None o' them for me!" he answered. "Randy, have you given me your consent?" He looked at her with admiration —he spoke with tenderness.

"Yes." Her lips closed firmly on the contract. She knew its nature; she would keep her word.

"Then I'll go in with you, and talk it over with your father. If Randy's willing he'll be," was Senior's prompt decision

"I don't know." She hesitated, then her part became clearer—she said plainly, "You must let me manage that! He's old and feeble, and crotchety, you know. No—let me talk round him and clear the road for you, Senior. He's fond of me—I wouldn't ask him, anyway, to give me up just now."

"Well—so," consented Senior; "I can trust Randy out of sight."

They separated, a courageous pair, without the least misgiving. Senior was well aware that a tolerably desperate cause might be trusted with Miranda for management, if a resolute will could determine the winning.

CHAPTER IV.

MORNING GLORY.

Mightily excited were the young people as the hour approached for the opening of school. Not one little white head and red face was missing. Curiosity and self-interest were alike urgent in deciding the parents of the neighborhood as to the course they must take. They could express their sympathy for Miranda when the time came for that, in another way than by keeping scholars from the school. When the children came into the school-room at the sound of the bell that called them from the grove and the wood shed, where they had congregated, not for sport, but for mutual encouragement, curiosity struggling with timidity, a glance at the desk, where the lady stood with Mr. Brown and Mr. Carradine, seemed to reassure them.

Certainly there was nothing to fear in the mild eyes turned toward the door, quietly observing all who entered; and as the confidence that belongs to numbers increased every moment with the entrance of one and another scholar, till the benches were nearly filled, the children's eyes became fixed on the teacher's stand, and, for the first time in their lives, they saw, by deliberate and permitted observation, a well dressed lady.

Do I mean a fashionable woman? Have I even on my hands here a girl who has spent her time, and thought, and money, on a toilet that shall somehow enchant the beholder? Not exactly. Far costlier dresses *have* been worn, and rendered less imposing, by a less serene grace. All ladies in blue muslin, and lace and ribbon decorations, do not look as well as Mercy thus attired. Costlier head-gear has been less becoming than the curls Mercy wears. She is not negligent of her dress, but gracefully heedful. The first glance does not repel you, but attracts, which surely is well.

And this is what the children see, and note with more or less keen observation.

When the roll whas called, every name was answered by a "Here." Then Mr. Carradine announced to the scholars that Mr. Brown had been so fortunate as to procure Miss Fuller's services, and with that announcement his speech ended.

Mr. Brown then addressed the children, and the gentlemen withdrew, leaving Miss Fuller to her fate.

With satisfaction, tempered by reluctance, Mr. Carradine retired, leaving her mistress of the ground. He felt so curious to know how the teacher would proceed, and what the result of the afternoon's experiment would be.

He must content himself with his imagining till he should hear Harry's report. And the flight of fancy was both easy and agreeable; though it was so novel an occupation for him to speculate in matters so uncertain as a woman's ways and looks in managing a common school. He could guess exactly Miranda's procedures, but the probabilities in regard to Miss Fuller were really beyond Mr. Carradine.

He had some notions of his own as to how the school should be conducted. And it spoke well for him that he was so much interested in the children. But he would be misunderstood—he expected that; that was the difficulty under which he said (to himself) he labored always. Indeed how such a man could have expected a reputation for gentleness and courtesy, was a mystery. That he should have desired the confidence that is accorded to the gentle and the courteous seemed incredible. People said that he rode rough-shod over the neighborhood; cared nothing for the wishes of others; was scornful of their opinions. That to crush and to discourage others was the principal effect of his "honest," "plain" speaking. The timid liked not to encounter Mr. Carradine. Some, every way his equal, hated him. Persons of cooler temperament and superior fortunes appreciated him for what he was, and smiled at his infirmities. To my mind, his great lack in those days was a lack of sympathy, and for that lack the neighborhood may not only blame him; but it also shall be summoned to the bar, and tried on the charge of guilt in helping to aggravate this sin of omission in a strong and not unjust character.

Peter Carradine was by no means a person whom ordinary contact would discover to be agreeable, or generous, or tender-hearted. He had not the voice, nor the eye, nor the mien, nor the purpose of the charmer. He spoke bluntly, sometimes coarsely, sometimes rudely; he dashed right or left, according to the course on which he had determined, and in his desire or endeavor to obtain an end, it was himself, not others, he was serving. Then let others see to it. He was a man of strong passions. Those who disliked him told hard stories of his past; reported that he was a miser in his mature years as he had been a spendthrift in his youth. That he was revengeful—never forgot injuries. Churlish, close in bargains, strict in abiding by the *letter* of a contract. Hardly a man in Martindale but had come into collision with him on one occasion or another. Does the reader see a quarrelsome, overbearing, disagreeable cynic? That was not Peter Carradine. Yet his conspicuity in the region was unenviable; he was an isolated man, whose intercourse with the people around seemed to terminate with the conclusion of business transactions. Never in any social gatherings—seldom in any public service, except that of the government, was he known to take his part. Yet the people of Martindale, on the word of Mrs. Johnson, were assured that he could enjoy his joke and a long evening chat, and could make himself agreeable, if he would but take the trouble. It was an assurance, however, that was not calculated to secure him favor. The inaccessible being loved none the better if we feel that contempt and scorn are the barriers of access.

"He's a curious man, a dreadful curious man," said Mrs. Johnson to Mercy, who was helping her to tie the cord which should by-and-by support the morning-glory vines, when they aspired toward the top of the high picket fence that separated the yard from the road-side.

Mrs. Johnson had determined that she would pre-occupy, with her report of Mr. Carradine, the verdict Miss Fuller would be sure to hear of him, and the late transaction, from the neighborhood. She was kindly disposed towards Mercy, and could see that it was in her power to save her from doubt and annoyance, by saying what she had to say at once, before any gossip reached her.

"A dreadful curious man, and high-handed. But when all's said and done, as my man says, says he, Mr. Carradine is just. He's in the right. He don't leap till he's looked. You may be put to it now by his way of speaking."

"Not in the least," said Mercy; "he is not a man to deceive any one, you can see that; he says just what he means—and I suppose it isn't likely I shall give him occasion to say anything to me that would be offensive."

"Likely not. But he is queer. When we first come up here—oh, that's many a long year since, Miss Fuller!—and he come to live with us, I tell you it was difficult to know how to manage to get along peaceable sometimes. If it hadn't a been for Johnson, I couldn't a done it. But Johnson is another for making peace, if Mr. Carradine is going for unmaking it. And he isn't—not exactly. I like Miranda Roy; I always liked Randy, and it'll allus go hard with me for thinking it was my boy that brought round the difficulty that broke up the school."

"What was that?" asked Mercy—the very question Mrs. Johnson had gone all this way to induce her to ask.

"She chastised him over severe. I don't doubt he provoked her to it; though he's my only son, I'll say it. It wasn't right. But if I'd knowed in time, I wouldn't a had the disturbance, for Randy's sake, for she's a dreadful proud and high-strung girl, and 'taint the way to deal with such, I feel to say; and for her father's sake, for he's a saint in Israel, Miss Fuller, if 'ary one is left. So he took Harry back to the school'us, Mr. Carradine did, and just shut up the hull concern. And that's how you came to—how it happened that there was need of a teacher for Martindell school'us. I rode down with him to Brighton city that same afternoon, and he seemed pleased, I tell you, coming back, to think of the new teacher."

Mrs. Johnson, having lightened her mind of the burden of duty that had weighed on her all day, felt at this moment equal to all manner of farm affairs, and every emergency of her rural estate. Nor was she displeased to see how gravely Miss Fuller took the information she had given.

"Miranda, did you say her name was? I must see

her," said she. "I must tell her. Perhaps I can bring her and Mr. Carradine to some understanding, and get her back into the school again. I am so—so sorry!"

"Yes,—yes—I know you are! I thought you would be! But I'm surpised to hear't—I be; as much as I was last night, when I dreamppit being drawn out of my winder. I thought it was the resurrection morning, Miss Fuller—but they said we must get acrost the creek first, afore we could go up—and that's what all the people was running to do, but of a sudden, afore I could stir, I was drawed out of my winder, that one you see there with the white curting drawed back an inch or so, and I went up, and up, like an arrer, till the pure joy woke me up. And I had dreadful pleasant thoughts, lying wakeful after that. It seemed to be a promise, and I couldn't help of taking Johnson and Mr. Carradine into it. But you don't know Randy, and you don't know Mr. Carradine, if you think you could get her back, or him to let her come. But, oh! I'm so uplifted to think that you wanted to do it! I'm sure, now, I can say ye'r welcome to Martindell. Ye'r welcome, Miss Fuller, to the best't can give ye!"

Then she went on speaking a little louder, for she saw Mr. Carradine coming from the road.

"Yes, they're very purty when they're all blowed out. When I was a girl—it was a long, sweet time ere I come to Martindale, Miss Fuller!—I used to have mornin' glories all round the fences to my father's yard; that was such a long while ago. Blue! and purple! and pink! and white!" —She enumerated with an emphasis which Mr. Carradine, who stopped as he came within the gate, smiled to hear, and he went on to the house with the smile still on his face, as if he had looked into the heart, just then of a white morning glory.

CHAPTER V.

NATURE AND GRACE.

The next day, being the second day of Miss Fuller's reign, the afternoon school was broken up at an earlier hour than usual, and the little people went flying along the roads, and meadow, and wood-paths, in various directions, hasting homeward, in order to escape the violent storm that was approaching.

Mercy also was on her way up the hill, thinking she should reach the red farm-house ere the down-pour. But she had not calculated well. She had not gone half-way when the clouds met, with the shock of lightning and a swift and keen report. As, with flying steps, she approached the lane that led down to the house of Samuel Roy, the old man, half blinded by the dust, and struggling with the wind, advanced from the opposite direction; they laid their hands upon the gate at one moment, and with one purpose, and it required the strength of both to throw it open.

It was enough for Roy to see that a woman was caught in the storm.

"Come in! come in't the house!" he said, and they ran together down the lane.

"Beats all!—Beats all!" cried the old man, as he came up panting behind the stranger, who had thrown open the door of the house, and stood now dripping like a mermaid, under the shelter of his roof,

"Step right in, right in!" said he, gaining the landing. "Step in till I shut the door," but it required again the united strength of both, the wind blew with such violence. "Thank ye; I ain't ekel to anything as I was once," and he slipped, panting and pale, into his high-back rocking-chair. When he called for his daughter:

"Randy!—where's Randy?"

Her work was on the table, the patch-work she was sewing; she had only left the room the moment before, to see if there was anything about the house exposed to damage of the storm. She had been sitting there in the dead silence, thinking of Senior Jobson, and devising methods by which her father might be won over to his side; recalling whatsoever would be likely to lessen his prejudice against Senior; thinking of the *Spread Eagle's* new wings, and satisfying herself that she had done, and would do, well and wisely, when the rising of the storm broke up her meditation, and summoned her from her work.

When she heard the voices and her father's call, she came into the room, hoping that it might be Mr. Jobson who had brought her father home, and himself sought shelter in the house; but when her eyes fell on a stranger's face, it was evident to that stranger that she was not warmly welcome. The kind and friendly face was not an agreeable sight to Miranda. She knew, of course, that this could be no one but Miss Fuller, and she was not a cold-blooded philosopher, but a warm-blooded woman, and that there was no reason in her present indignation, had nothing to do with the matter. She was indignant to see Miss Fuller standing there—indignant to perceive that she was such a person; for how was she to see an enemy in one whose aspect was so mild and friendly?

Miss Fuller was the first to speak.

"I am ashamed to spoil your white floor. But you see how it is—and this gentleman was so kind as to let me in." She smiled as she looked at herself and saw the plight she was in.

"You've spoiled your dress," said Randy, "It don't matter about the floor. Father, your dry clothes are hanging up in the entry. Sit ye down." She pushed a chair towards Mercy as she spoke. The noise she made in doing it seemed to shame her ill manners, and with a flushed face she took up the chair and carried it to her guest. "Father, remember your rheumatis."

"Yes, yes, Randy I'm going. But I'm so beat—beat," said the old man, looking anxiously from his daughter to the stranger, whom he also by this time was persuaded could be none other than the new teacher. "She never'd a' lived to clumb the hill. I look on it as a Providence she'd got by our gate as I came from the lot;" his explanation sounded like an apology for bringing the stranger into the house, and he did intend it for one. Miranda understood it, and said quickly:

"It would a' been a pity if she'd tired in such a storm, with Samuel Roy's house near by. Time the girl knew where she is," thought she.

"Then you are his daughter?" said Mercy. "You are Miss Roy?"

"Yes, that's Randy," said the old man, looking still anxiously from one young face to the other; speaking quickly—so anxious for peace.

"My name is Mercy Fuller," she said, and she offered her hand to the old man. He took it into his hard palm and said, looking at her in his serious, steady way:

"It's a good name."

"It was my mother's," she answered. "There could not be a better name."

"She's a living yet, I hope."

"No; not these many years."

"Oh, then, that's a long time for you to be remembering of her."

"But we never forget those we love."

"You've got the rights of it! Randy and I know that's true. *She's* been dead now this ten year; it's long to live after her; but it might a' been yesterday, for the fresh feeling when we think of her. You—you ought 'o have a dry gownd, Miss." So saying, with a look at his daughter that was urgent, the old man went into the next room.

"I'm not afraid of the wetting," answered Mercy to this hint, for she saw the perplexity into which Miranda was thrown by it. Then said Miranda:

"I can get dry clothes for you, ma'am, but I won't speak for the fit."

The decision with which the offer was declined set Randy's mind at rest.

"I never saw a storm come up so rapidly," said Mercy.

"I watched it for an hour—the sky was looking awful," answered Miranda.

Then there was a pause, and an awkward silence, broken presently by Mercy, who said:

"I was coming in to see you very soon, Miss Roy; I would have chosen to come when the day was fair, instead of such a storm as this, when I seem to have been driven in. I wanted to see you."

"What for?" asked Miranda.

"Mrs. Johnson told me about you and the school."

"I expect she did, of course."

"She likes you well. I think no one could regret more what has happened. If I had known the circumstances, I would not have come to Martindale. If you will try to come to an understanding with Mr. Carradine, I promise to help you; you shall have the school, and I will go back to Brighton."

"I wouldn't have you for the world!" exclaimed Randy, surprised beyond measure that the stranger should have taken up the business in this spirit. She had banded together all who had to do with Mr. Carradine—Mrs. Johnson, the new teacher, and the rest—as a company in league against her. But it seemed the fact was something different

"There are a hundred places I might find," returned the teacher; "vacancies, you understand, which I could fill without exciting any unpleasant feeling. I never could forgive myself if I had come here knowing all the circumstances. I can say that without deciding your difficulty with Mr. Carradine, one way or the other. But now let me be a peacemaker between you."

"Don't!" said Randy, as if she feared that, without her consent, against her wish, the reconciliation might in some unforeseen way, be effected. Then she added, "You couldn't manage it; you don't know Mr. Carradine. And if you did, I wouldn't go back. As long as I live, I'll never teach in Martindale school-house! But," she continued more quietly, "I am obliged to you for not being my enemy."

"I hope we shall be friends. I wanted an opportunity to explain this to you. It would be pleasanter to me to know that you liked to have me in the neighborhood all summer."

"I don't know," said Randy—she was going to say that

she didn't know what she had to do with Miss Fuller's staying anywhere—but she checked herself, and Mercy said:

"We ought to understand, by what we feel ourselves, that it is not right to make up our mind suddenly about anybody's actions."

"That's so!" said Mr. Roy, who, standing clad in his dry garments just outside the sitting-room—within his bedchamber—had heard these words with remarkable satisfaction.

"One who could see both sides and all sides of every question would pass very different judgments from ours, many times."

"The Almighty is the only one who can do that—the only one who can be trusted to the full, for perfec justice. So I tell Randy, here. But she's wonderful tried about Carradine's going on in the school'us. And p'raps she was hasty. And maby he was hasty—wrong't both sides. I shouldn't wonder, ma'm. But it come hard, old neighbors so. I never was much for chastising; she was all I had. But there's some that needs it. Spare the rod and spile the child. I'm agin letting 'em run over you roughshod; but it's dreadful difficult dealing with children, and I'm not overly sorry it's come, though I'd liked it to come different. For what with it all, she was wearing out."

"That's what father thinks," explained Randy, as if she was not to be confounded with the old man in his expression of sentiments.

"A wearing hard," he repeated with decision. "What with getting up afore the break of day, to get the hum work done, and a hurrying time at noon, and work agin till nine o'clock at night, I say 'twas too much. It would 'a broke her down."

"A great deal too much," said Mercy; "and if that was the way you went on, we ought not to be sorry that another person does your work with the children. It makes me more content to stay here."

"I'm through with teaching, nothing's surer," said Miranda. "As long as I live I'm through with it. All the Carradines in creation couldn't bring me back."

"It ain't the work for her; but now tell us, do you like school-teaching, ma'm?" asked Samuel, nervously, so desirous to smooth away the possible results of his daughter's hasty speech, that he trembled from head to foot.

"Yes; that's my business in this world. I expect to be a teacher always—of course I must like it ; and I do."

"It's good to set hand to work with that mind in ye for it," said Samuel. "When I come into Martindell it was a big piece of forest all through the valley ; heavy timbered land. But there! I'd paid my money down, and got my papers—nothing for't but to go straight through. Here I've been now over thirty years, and the capital I started with is what's kep me gwine. And that's good courage! as I tell daughter. Straight ahead, sez I. No looking back. Fits and starts won't do the business. It's straight ahead does that. We had a young man up here preaching. What's his name, Randy. I'm dreadful forgetting of names."

"Mr. Collamer."

"Collamer—Mr. Collamer. He says it's so in religion, as in everything else. It's the old straight way. You get out o' that, and you're lost, sez he. Jes so with everything else. It's a keeping to one thing. So, ma'm, it's my opinion, if yer going to school-keeping, you'll make the first-rate of a teacher. But Randy's call ain't that way."

"What way is it, father?" asked she ; and she spoke pleasantly, though she was not wholly pleased.

The old man heard more in the words than Mercy did ; he looked at his daughter with his steady serious gaze, and answered slowly:

"It's to be a poor man's daughter—cause that's what you be ; and whatever else He pleases, as I humbly hope."

"Whatever happens," she said, as if amending his expression.

"We won't argyfy it," he replied. "Randy and I don't agree yet about that. But I'm free to believe we will ; and I'm bound to believe what's writ, not to be wise above it. Scriptur's scriptur for me. But she isn't settled yet about natur and grace."

"I don't think Providence's going out of His way to favor me. I don't expect He will bring things to pass because I want, that's all," said Randy, explaining her position in a spirit of self-depreciation, that equalled the haughtiest pride in its offensiveness.

"She puts Him fur off," said the old man, "He don't

seem so to me. Not so fur as you be, Miss Fuller. For what does the Record say? God is greater than our hearts, and knoweth all things. He's a living in us. She's for thinking Him far off, a'yond the Rocky Mountains, I'm afeared. But it 'pears to me He is quicker to hear when I speak than she is, for the reason that He knows afore I ask what I am longing fur; and put the wish into me, if I live by faith. Yes! yes! glory to God! nearer to me than my child, for He's my God! Now, I'm free to say, I was took back about that school business, ma'm, but I've seen since, it's right. It's all right. Bless your soul, all right."

A feeble creature was old Roy; utterly contemptible if brought into the glare of worldly illumination. Feeble, wavering, patched and poor. His faith was the sum of him. But look what it did for him. Any text of Scripture in which was any Divine healing or uplifting power, could save him in temptation, in despondency, in pain, in poverty. And his mind was wrapped up in these sacred balsams. His life was covered with these sacred " charms."

His daughter seemed to have heard and seen too much of this; she was unlike him—bolder to wish and long for, to plan and to attempt. She was more ambitious, and more headstrong, than he had ever been. But her conscience was as sensitive as his, and set to watch and guard in the midst of such opposing forces as made up her character!

She turned now to Mercy, with intent to change the conversation, and asked:

"How do you think you'll like living in a farming country? Won't you find it lonesome?"

"It is delightful to me—it is a great while since I had anything like the rest I know I shall have here; and if I stay, it will be because you wish it—because you are friendly towards me," she said returning to that point.

"I've nought against you, I am sure," said Randy. "It's agreeable to me to know what you are here for."

The old man, delighted to hear this polite speech, hastened to deepen its impression.

"It's a purty valley as you'll find," said he. "I've been through all this section; there's nought goes ayond Martindell. You wouldn't find it lonesome, I should think. There's no purtier meador land. And the woods and brooks you've got to find out yet. Martindell isn't the worst place in the world."

Old Roy was not a Captain Cook, neither a Bayard Taylor, to be sure. You might perform on foot all his journeys without making yourself famous. Love gave him the knowledge he assumed in this decision; and his listener did not object to his conclusion. That pleased him, and while the storm was expending its strength she listened to all he had to say of Martindale.

CHAPTER VI.

ONE KIND OF SYMPATHY.

The evening sky was without a cloud. The sun, at parting, thrilled the heavens, as your soul is thrilled in an hour of separation. The pink flush changed to purple, and light that seemed impassioned throbbed through the firmament; but, at length, through the depths of emotion, came tremulous, and yet assured, the evening star; and a divine calmness overspread all things.

Miranda walked from the house up the lane, and looked over the great farm gate. As she came along, she noticed the print of Miss Fuller's steps, and she was thinking of Mercy, when, looking down the road, she saw the Elder's daughter coming, and knew of course, that Sally's errand concerned her, whatever it might be.

It was of Sally also that she had been thinking when she left the house and walked up to the gate; she hoped that some lucky chance would bring them together.

"I had a feeling you would come," said she, as Sally drew near. "You always send a warning beforehand." Randy's eyes were full of admiration as they fixed on Sally, and that Sally could plainly see; it made her more complacent.

"How is that?" she asked, as she passed through the gate.

"I begin by wanting you, and then you come."

"Always? Every time? Don't it fail sometimes? Don't you ever want me except when I come?" Exacting even here by force of habit, what proof should she require of Randy's love, expressed a hundred times, and after every fashion?

"Maybe. Who do you think I had for a visitor all through the storm? Come, now!"

"Mr. Carradine, I guess."

"No. Mr. Carradine!—He don't come this way, mind you, to his farm."

"It would be a short cut by the west road," said Sally.

"He don't take such short cuts."

"Miss Fuller?"

"Yes."

"No."

"Miss Fuller. She came flying down the lane with father, and if they had been both dipped into the creek, they couldn't have looked more dripping. I had to laugh."

"I should have thought she would have kept the road, and took the drenching before she would come in."

"Father asked her. She didn't know who he was—and, as near as I understand, she helped him—he was half blinded by the rain, and the lightning was terrible."

"It struck the big elm in our wheat lot, and tore it open like a sheet of paper. Grandma saw it, and I heard her saying, what if the Millerites was true? Wasn't that queer for grandma?"

"She said she would have come down anyway if it hadn't a rained—some time. And she was sorry to have it seem as if she just come for the shelter. I think she *would* have come. She wants we should be friends."

"Oh, yes—of course."

"I think she means it."

"Why shouldn't she mean it, Randy?"

"I didn't expect it of her."

"I expect anything. Didn't you say you supposed Mr. Carradine had it all in his mind, and trumped up the excuse to get her in?"

"Make me eat my words; that's right! Well, I will. I said so—but I don't believe a word of it. She's of a mind to go away from Martindale if I only speak the word. She wants to make peace between us, and get me back into the school."

"It's likely! Peter Carradine won't be a bachelor six months from now," returned Sally, coming out with the result of her day's reflection—unchanged in her conviction by Randy's present mood and statement.

"You think she would marry him?"

"Yes—I believe it."

"Just as soon as she would marry a—a—a hedgehog."

"Well, now you've said it!"

"I mean she couldn't in the nature of things. Why, have you seen Mercy Fuller?"

"Yes; I called up there with grandma, yesterday. I couldn't help it; I didn't want to go. She's to come to our house next. I think I'll come over here and stay that week."

"No you won't; you'll stay at home, and before next Saturday night you'll be repenting in dust and ashes for what you have said. I know you, Sally; better than you know yourself. I don't much like her, and that's honest; but I can see how it stands. She isn't to blame for having my place. She wanted a situation—that's what she's got. She's well enough. We won't be running across each other's path, I reckon."

"How do you like her looks, Randy?"

"She's good-looking. Very pretty, I expect," answered Randy, flaring out into a little generosity, for with her, just now, mere justice was real generosity. "She has a pleasant voice—father liked to hear her talk. But I didn't seem to agree with them, you know. She never lived in a farming country like this; but in a school-house pretty much; seminary, she called it. She expects to be a teacher always—of course that don't mean in such a school-house as ours."

"What did you say, Randy?"

"I said I was glad she had come. And I am! She came for her health, and I hope she'll find it. There! I do. It wasn't her, but Mr. Carradine that was to blame. Maybe he wasn't! I expect nobody is much to blame for anything. Only I hope he will just keep out of my way, you know."

Randy's lip quivered as she spoke thus, and she slowly closed and opened her eyes, that the tears gathering within the lids might have opportunity to disperse in secret.

"Nobody minds what Peter Carradine says, I should think," said Sally Green. "Don't *you* mind him, Randy."

"*I?*"

"Yes. No wonder you called him a hedgehog."

"I didn't, Sally! I never called him so. I said—"

"Oh, well—I know. It's all the same. If you just look at him, and then Mr. Collamer! And he's your friend. And so is all the rest of Martindale, I'm sure."

"Do you suppose that Mr. Collamer will come up before the Camp Meeting?"

"He's coming next Sunday, for sure. Yes; he's going to Camp Meeting too. You won't have the school to hinder you now, Randy, and you can stay a good part of the week. You can tell your father there'll be room for him too. 'I want to go—I want to go—I want to go there too!'" she ended by singing this line of the refrain of a sacred old song.

Very sweetly the young girl's voice sounded in the stillness of evening. Old Mr. Roy heard it, and it set him to singing by the hour in his kitchen.

"I suppose," said Randy, "that Mr. Collamer will be the man worth hearing; but it will be pleasant to go to the meeting. To get away from work a little while, and have a change—I am sure I shall enjoy it." She spoke wearily, and her face was sad.

"I can hardly wait for the time to come," said Sally.

"He makes you want to believe what he believes, he seems so sure of every thing he says," said Randy, seriously.

"Grandma told him your case, Randy."

For a moment it seemed as if the reception of that intelligence had produced a result in Randy far beyond either Sally's anticipation or her own; but she rallied before Sally could speak, and said:

"She couldn't—I couldn't, no one could! But father says it's all right—and he is a happy man in his religion, if ever anybody was. And so I try to think with him; but grandma Green couldn't explain it. What did he say when she told him?" she added, trying to conceal the timidity with which she proposed so simple a question.

"I don't know," said Sally.

She did know, however. She remembered that the minister had quoted the lines of Cowper's hymn:

("God moves in a mysterious way,
His wonders to perform."

And when Randy acknowledged, "I don't know, but there isn't a person I'd rather have think me an unbeliever. But it don't seem to me I am." Her friend did not explain what she had seen quite clearly, that the minister had not considered Randy's case so very dark and strange as grandma seemed to do. "Anyway," continued Randy, "I wouldn't miss of hearing him preach in the woods."

"He preaches at you so it's terrifying, though."

"That's what I like. He is speaking to you. And he has enough to say."

"Dumb as a door-nail in the house though."

"You don't like him, that's plain."

"You do; that's plainer."

This charge occasioned an incredible disturbance. It vexed and troubled Randy to an extent that surprised her who brought it. Astonished at herself, Miranda said:

"I like him, yes—as you say, I do. I like him better than any preacher I ever heard in meeting."

"Yes, pretty good. He's young, though," said Sally. "I've heard better; but he's good enough, to be sure, for folks here in Martindale."

I am ashamed of Sally Green; but from her cradle the girl had learned to conceal herself—to circumvent, connive, contrive—to have her own way. To conquer herself; to choose the will of another; to prefer another's pleasure to her own in insignificant matters, which her choice could have rendered significant, which her choice *did* render so, she no more aimed at such a course than will the child your neighbor trains up to believe that the universe waits his pleasure. Fortunately for the neighborhood, she was destitute of the energetic will that would have carried into operation the tendencies of her nature. Martindale was thus delivered from a fiery scourge.

Up to this hour she and Randy had supposed they understood each other. The way in which, suddenly, new paths opened before each, the way in which the light fell on those paths, had taken both by surprise. Those paths would carry them far away from each other. Would they enter them?

They stood talking till dark on these matters of common interest; then Randy let Sally go, without betraying Senior Jobson's secret.

She fully intended, however, when she went back to the house, to speak to her father about Senior Jobson. She had one or two acts to relate that were to the innkeeper's credit; facts calculated, she thought, to lessen the old man's prejudices; but, though the opportunity was not unfavorable, she lacked the will to make good use of it; they talked a little about the weather, and the prospects for to-morrow; arranging the order of the farm-work; and then the short evening ended, as usual, with a prayer.

"But," said Randy, lying wakeful long after her father's heavy breathing announced from the next room his heavy sleep, "I'll speak to him to-morrow. I must bring him to see it. Once that debt's paid, I'll be able to rest again. If it wasn't for father, I'd know what to do. I'd get out of Martindale. But that's a Providence, he says. He would be able to take Senior for a Providence too, I should think. I could keep a good tavern; it wouldn't be so lonesome down there. Senior would take a new turn if he was married. He has money; he could do what he promises. I should think myself lucky to be able to help father; he's too old to work, and the farm going to ruin for want of a man to manage it. To live here under Carradine's feet too. Senior always liked me—I can remember, so long ago, when he set me up on the bar and kissed me, and asked me if I wouldn't come to be his wife, and help him keep the tavern—I wonder if he was thinking of it then—I don't suppose he could be brought to keep a temperance. This would suit father, though."

So, unconsciously, the thinking woman passed into a dreamer, and was at rest.

CHAPTER VII.

THIRTY MILES, AND MORE.

AMONG these green fields, then, the fine farm lands of this broad and pleasant valley, there was unrest and suspicion, deceit and passion, greed and trouble! The human heart was there—and the human voice! Speech, which emerges from the heights and depths, an inefficient messenger, whose trumpet seems pledged to give forth an uncertain sound.

Let Miss Fuller descend from Mr. Carradine's farm-house to the house of Elder Green.

She has been four days in Martindale, and Mrs. Johnson says :

"Yes, Huldy Green wants to begin the reg'lar way—and that is right. More or less, we don't make nothing of the teacher's stay with us, but the rest is dreadful partik'lar. So you'll begin the Saturday night in a new place. You needn't mind it. You can't feel strange at the Elder's after half an hour. You will like Sally Green. She's more a companion like, for Sally's been eddicated. She was sent to town a good many quarters. The Elder, he hasn't but one ; and he's great on eddication. And mother Green, and Huldy, and the Elder, all of 'em, they're the best of people."

So it was that Mercy Fuller would go down to Elder Green's, to the old brown farm-house, surrounded by poplar trees, conspicuous from whichever direction you chose to approach Martindale.

Encouraged by Mrs. Johnson's assurances in regard to the inmates of that dwelling, Mercy said "Good-bye" to Mrs. Johnson, but she had taken only a few steps down the road when she recollected what Johnson had told her, that a little distance beyond them, further up the hill, she could get a view " of thirty miles of country straight ahead !" A desire to look that far this evening drew her back, instead of forward: she had plenty of time—soon enough, at least before dark, she should arrive at Elder Green's. Backward, therefore, until she came near to a little enclosure, surrounded by walls of evergreen, cedar, and young pine trees, within which were two white and two gray gravestones, for this was the burial-place where slept Mr. Carradine's dead. Surprised by this discovery, Mercy stood hesitating whether she should cross the fence and read the inscriptions, when Mr. Carradine, who had been at work in the enclosure, came out, bringing an armful of dead branches he had cut from the hedge.

He, too, seemed to be surprised, mainly that she should be walking in the road alone, merely for the pleasure of it. True, he was never lonely in his lonely toil—he had not for years known what it was to *want* companionship, though he had little of it. But he could not see that solitude was the best, or most natural thing, for the young teacher. When he found that she was going further up the hill, he dropped the rubbish he carried, brushed the dust from his coat, and was ready to accompany her; not because he thought his company would please her—he argued from the opposite postulate.

"Yes," said he, as they walked along together, "you'll get a noble view to-night—a broad thirty miles. If it was only morning, you could see Mr. Martin's house quite plain —you might think it was on fire. I have seen Camden Lighthouse many a time when the sun was rising. That's on the sea-coast, forty miles, they say."

"The sea-coast? Can you see it from here? I wish it were morning!"

Carradine just glanced at her as she walked by his side. "Home-sick!" he mentally commented. "No wonder." But he was mistaken.

"You're not getting tired of us, I hope," said he.

"Oh, no—it is quite pleasant. I have what I asked for a pretty country and a quiet life. But it seems, since you speak of the sea, as if I were nearer home than I thought. This is a ruin, it seems."

She spoke the last words carelessly, and was looking over the field at her left hand as they walked along.

He answered with hesitation:

"That's where the old house stood. Thirty years ago, my father lived there."

"No one since his time?"

"No one. I could not make up my mind to tear down the old chimney and fire-place. They've crumbled, as you see."

"I understand," she answered; and they continued walking up the road together.

In all his life, Carradine had heard no words that thrilled him as did this simple expression from a good and kindly woman. Her acknowledged appreciation of the feeling she supposed he must have had in leaving that old ruin on the ground of the old home, seemed to place them for an instant on a level, as like human beings.

Though the instant after he felt that she was exalted to heaven, and himself abased to hell, by his convictions and his consciousness; still, for a moment, she had "understood" him—and she had acknowledged that she did, with a frankness that won his instant gratitude. Why, this was compensation enough for a lifetime of Martindale misunderstanding!

If indeed he, Peter Carradine, could deem that he had been misunderstood!

Often his recollections had burdened him; he had felt them to be a disgrace. He had longed to be delivered from them. Had felt that there would be a chance of happiness for him could he blot out the past, whose shadow fell on all the present time, and would doubtless stand through every future. And yet, here he was, revolving in his mind the story of this past—thinking to repeat the story that had never yet had utterance from his lips, to Mercy Fuller!

Not actuated chiefly by the thought that she had heard the tale from others, and the desire to give her the best version! But because—how far was it from him to prate of himself! How unusual to allude remotely to those who were gone. What is it that makes a soul in its consciousness of a near presence of Divine purity, rejoice even in the midst of self-abasement, that it can at least take part with the Almighty against itself without any treachery, but with truest loyalty to that self. It was precisely the same impulse that held him now in the posture of one who voluntarily seeks a confessional.

"You think you understand me," said he, in answer to that simple assurance of hers. "Do you?—are you sure?"

"I remember a place," she said, "that I am weak enough to think I could not endure to know was removed from the face of the earth. And yet, of course, I could endure to know it, and I have no assurance that there is a trace of it still left. It cannot be *destroyed* as long as I can remember anything. And age, it is said, remembers more and more distinctly, all that belonged to youth."

"If that is so," he said, "I shall fear to grow old."

"Perhaps you will find, when the time comes, that you had little cause to fear."

He smiled grimly, that she should attempt to soothe him; and answered:

"I can't look back to any time so pleasant that I should like to be visited by its ghost. You might guess that." Here he paused, resuming in a changed voice, "It is from this point you can see so far. But it is too late to-night. Just after sunset, or early in the morning, is the best time. You can hardly see beyond Elder Green's to-night."

"I ought to be there this moment; and I must go at once," said Mercy.

But as, returning, they passed the burial-ground, both walked slowly, while Carradine told of the changes in the landscape since he could remember. Then he pointed out to her the several clearings, their progress, and their history, for she seemed interested in the relation; of the fortunes of the neighborhood he spoke—and last of all of Peter Carradine.

He was an amusing as well as a veracious chronicler. Not more conspicuously does the lion stand in the sheep pasture than Carradine stood in the neighborhood; he was that capable in the comparison.

He could well afford in this speaking to a general lenience in judgment—and it made an impression on his listener that he passed so mild a sentence. That he was considerate, that he was just, that he restrained now his natural impetuosity of speech, and was mindful, in making up his estimates, of facts which those he judged would hardly suppose could find place in his computation. He was in a beautiful mood. And when such a man is subdued to mildness of feeling, as well as of speech, there is occasion for observers to draw near and listen with respect, for it is a great hour in his experience. Who can tell what issue it may have? For his audience, Carradine could not have desired a better than this present. Irresistibly, it seemed, she impelled him to speech. He spoke to her of matters which had never before escaped his secret mind. The remembrance and recital stirred him, strong man that he was, as a storm stirs the oak's great branches and tears away its crown.

He told her of his mother; of her pinched, starved latter years—of her face as for the last time it appeared before him! Of her life of hardship, and privation. How the recollection of that dreadful experience had power in her death; how it had changed his life; how he had sought, from that day of bereavement, no consolation, no excuse, but had said *I am a man*, and resolved on doing a man's work. He said he had another life than that his neighbors gave him credit for. He wondered that they could suppose a man would turn from wild ways to those of honesty, sobriety and labor, unless the heart in him was changed.

To nobody but Miss Fuller had he ever acknowledged what vows he had made, and how hard they were to keep. But there were witnesses he would dare to call on in his last moments, who must testify that he had not merely become a changed man for the sake of profit. It was from his mother's death-bed that he had turned to a new life. He had been his own worst enemy. But he had fought his way clear of the past, seeming to be cheered on by all the dead; from beyond the grave their voices had encouraged him. No living voices said, "Bless you!" "Go on!"

He stood now, he said, a freer man than he had ever hoped to be. He had fought a fight such as he did not believe was common to men. And he had been victorious. Yes, on the whole, victorious.

Could Miss Fuller doubt this when she saw how these memories moved him?

Brief was the story, simply told. But its eloquence, pathos and power, moved her to pity even beyond her knowledge. She stooped ready to justify the man who could speak *thus* of fortunes such as his had been.

True deference toward woman, tenderness toward childhood, horror of wrong-doing, and manly scorn of oppression and baseness, came out in this wonderful utterance. For it was wonderful! Deductions might have been drawn from his speech which would have surprised him; but he would have been certain to abide by it. And withal there was revealed a sense of justice, a desire to vindicate himself, and yet not to deceive the woman to whom he spoke, that could not fail to win his listener's interest. The satisfaction with which Carradine yielded to his impulse in this speaking was significant. Hitherto the past was as a haunted chamber, whose doors were locked and barred. He might pass them alone, but not without a shudder—because of his recollections, not chiefly from fear of exposure. Voluntarily, he had deemed, he could never open those doors that others might enter to inspect what was therein hidden. But it had come to pass that he feared the exaggeration of suspicion and the reports of the neighborhood, much more than the exposure of reality. And here he was speaking of these things to the purest, wisest, loveliest woman he had ever seen! He found comfort in the thought that, with sympathy, even with pity, Miss Fuller would learn of a youth that must be without one ray of beauty, as she inspected it. He seemed to have discovered that, beautiful though she might be, and was, to his sight, such a story as he told would have a different meaning to her than others. She would not be lenient and charitable because that was her duty, but because she would see a deeper necessity than the constraint of duty leading her to judge his past and present, in a way beyond the power of Martindale.

While he walked with her down the road, even to the poplars surrounding the brown farm-house, their talk was of matters immediately connected with the facts he had related.

When they separated, it was not to forget this confidence. Neither to regret it. Mercy said to herself, "The man is better than he seems—but a very remarkable person. I wonder how much of his strangeness comes out of the fact that people seem to be afraid of him." Then she dismissed that thought, and recalled another, brought up so forcibly when he spoke of the Camden light-house, forty miles away. By the sea that light-house stood—for mariners were its beacons. She seemed to hear the roar of the great flood, the rushing of the breakers, and she was lifted aloft by a memory that bore her to and fro, till her thoughts kept time to the great anthem of the deep. So, in a lofty mood that would have become an entrance into majestic presence, she ascended the steps that led to Calvin Green's front door.

Carradine sat in his corner of the piazza that night and smoked to a much later hour than usual.

Johnson and his wife sat on their side of the house expecting that he would come, according to his custom, to talk over to-morrow's work. But he was not thinking of to-morrow's work. And he had forgotten Johnson and his wife. Even the voice of Harry did not allure him, though now and then he heard the child repeating his evening hymn. And neither was he disturbed when he heard the little fellow rounding the corner of the piazza and hurrying towards him. Still the boy approached quite to his side before he seemed to be aware of his coming, and even said, "Good night, Uncle Carradine," ere the piercing eyes turned on him.

"Good night, my lad," said Peter; but now he detained the boy, who would have run off, in obedience to his mother's injunction—he was not to stay and trouble Mr. Carradine.

"I heard you reciting some pretty verses. Are you asleep, Harry?"

"No, sir, wide awake;" and the child opened his eyes to show how very wide awake he was.

"Let me hear the verses then." He put off the boy a pace from him; forthwith Harry straightened himself and recited promptly, for he had learned one thing well—never to contradict or deny Mr. Carradine.

"Well done!" said Peter, in the end. "Miss Fuller will make something of you yet."

"Yes, sir," said the boy, and his face brightened with pleasure because of the novel praise. Then came his mother's voice:

"Harry! Harry! What did I tell you, sir?"

"One minute. There—kiss me, Harry," said Carradine quickly. He stretched out his great arms, drew the boy towards him, kissed him, and let him go.

It was an act Harry Johnson would remember through a hundred years. It had never occurred before, might never occur again. But when Harry Johnson should become a man, and must needs judge the character of Carradine, that kiss would have weight in the evidence.

Surely it was significant that the man's first kiss—a voluntary kiss, conferred as a king's amnesty, should have fallen, such a night, into possession of a child!

CHAPTER VIII.

THE ELDER'S HOUSE.

They were looking for Mercy Fuller's arrival at Calvin Green's.

There was the Elder's little and lean self, whose feeble eyes and scanty hair, and obsequious nose, were libels, every one, on the timid man, who was as good, in fact, as a timid man can be. A hard-working, honest farmer, with a good deal more heart than brain, and conscience sufficiently intelligent to keep him tolerably miserable his life long. Nothing but death could deliver Elder Green from the bondage he was in. Oh! for such a man, what a wonder in the ultimate revelation of the glorious liberty of the children of God!

Calvin loved, with a worshipping fondness, his daughter Sarah. She was his only child—the most beautiful of womankind; and probably the best. That he had loved her blindly and unwisely from the outset I need not be harsh enough to say. What he and the rest of them had helped Sally to become, was of itself a sufficient testimony. If there was any one in this world to be satisfied and pleased at all cost and hazard, it was Sally Green. If folly, and ingratitude, and selfishness, and vanity, ever had the power to throw dust in the eyes of tenderness, and generosity, and love, they conferred it on Sally Green, and she used it as perhaps one girl out of a million would refuse to do, under the same circumstances.

There was Esther Green, the Elder's mother, whose brain was larger than her heart—and it was she who had given her good-tempered son his unfortunate bias, and fostered it by all subsequent education. He held his mother in great reverence, and was grateful to her for her work in him.

Grateful too for precisely that which discredited her ability to do the thing she had attempted. / Let not the cedar-tree boast loudly of the power that has pruned and trimmed it to the stature of a shrub. Never shall the free winds of heaven shout for the quickening answer of the mighty limbs! Never shall cattle gather under the incompetent shade! Never shall the tired traveller look forward to it, on his hot and dusty journey, for the rest of noon! Nor the birds sing, where might have waved the giant cedar branches!

Oh, Esther! a little truer sight would show you that, instead of priding yourself on Calvin Green, you had better call on rocks and mountains to fall and hide you from the vengeance of the world you have cheated of a full-grown man.

Her brain was larger than her heart; and neither had been trained to any noble proportions. She was a thin, erect, proud woman, who called herself a Calvinist; but the great John Calvin must marvel much to hear it; repudiating, beyond question, with some terror and some grief, every sentiment by which the woman, in her age, linked herself to the teaching of his youth; every doctrine by which her amazing littleness claimed oneness with him. Conforming her starved life to *her* perception of his doctrine in the world's present age, she exhibited in herself the meaning of one Paul, who deprecated any advocacy of *his* version of truth, proclaiming that Eternal Truth was Christly, in all needful demonstration.

Esther was quite old, yet her vigor manifested none of the signs of age. Her hair was white—her face was brown and wrinkled—but her blue eyes, bright and cold as the winter sky, needed no aid of spectacles. She was a living chronicle, and she had as proud a heart as could well beat within such a compass. She was proud of being the first settler of Martindale. Yes, her family was the very oldest of that town. Inestimable distinction! There were men who had come in later, and who had grown rich faster—but, they were new comers; a misfortune, if not exactly a crime.

In chief, she was proud of her piety. Proud of having endeavored to subdue her pride, and "neighbor" with her neighbors, and submit to the necessities of a new country, for she was a town-bred girl herself. She never gossipped with these neighbors, and she was proud of that. The Elder's first wife, Sally's mother, was a city girl, according to Esther's counsel, and she was proud of that. Sally had been at school in town two years, and was "accomplished," besides very pretty; incredibly proud of these facts was poor Esther. And I am afraid to tell you all her ambition for dear Sally. The impression Esther made was deep and peculiar; one felt quite sure she must have been born so— if not really in the neat white cap, and the white neckerchief, and old and rigid, yet in complete possession of the infantile correspondents to these things. Such a woman never comes by chance. She is born, as they say poets are; and as are all persons who prove in the end to be anything in particular. A fact for dolts to laugh at, and the whole world to weep over; according to the last clause of the second commandment, twentieth chapter of Exodus.

Then, there was Huldah Green, the Elder's second wife, a comely, kindly woman; a trifle deaf, and chief illustrator of the Abrahamic hospitality. You could never find her amiss; she would smile on you across a wash-tub, with an apology that " washing days *would* come, and she thought she would help Nancy," which you were by no means to construe into a hint that your presence was unwelcome, or your visit ill-timed.

Such a woman as looked at work as if it were a pastime. And some imbecile persons were in the habit of averring that she did thus regard it! There is no end to the credulousness of self-love. Spirit no doubt can act like magic upon matter. Its willingness works wonders though the flesh be weak. But the probability in regard to Huldah Green was, that back and limbs grew weary sometimes, through obedience to the kindly impulse of the heart.

But as yet there was no noticeable faltering of the quick light step—in the face no indicated impatience of languor, or sadness of pain, and bright her eyes were as in youth.

Huldah was kind to Sally Green with an unchanging tenderness. The feeling with which she took the motherless young child in her arms when first she came into the Elder's house; the wife of Calvin Green had never under any provocation failed her.

She lived in peace with her exacting mother-in-law.

She never troubled herself about doctrines.

But she enjoyed a good sermon, how much! If it was

preached out of one of St. John's epistles, those Love Letters to the Ages, all the better.

I think of her by some strange mischance engaged in theological disputes! Disastrously prevented in the boundless charity with which it was her nature to meet every threatening aspect—hindered in that generous impulse that constrained her to take herself out of every mortal's way—compelled to breathe the air oppressive and impure, which is the breath of life to worldlings. Such spirits have ere now been so compelled. There have been many martyrs during these six thousand years.

Here, in Martindale, the Elder's wife—Sally's mother—Esther's daughter, she had so much to think of that pleased her—to do, that interested her! She turned her deafness to such good account—she smiled her way from shadowy paths into the sunshine with such a hearty good will—you could not think her sadly out of place.

How many such women, brave as veterans, all underrated, beautiful as sunflowers, and as constant to the sun, you and I have seen! How they blossom by the roadside, in spite of dust and storm! God shields all their exposure, and makes their memory as a rock in a dry and thirsty land! Love, at last, shall lave the feet that never wearied, running on love's errands.

And a great vision shall at length arrest the eyes so restless in their watchful care.

There was already a guest in the house of Elder Green. Mr. Collamer, the preacher promised for to-morrow's service, had arrived.

His satchel had been carried into the principal guest-chamber of the house—and his person sat composedly in the best parlor, that formidable room from whose small windows the heavy-boarded blinds were now thrown open for the admission of rare daylight and sweet air.

The large room opposite the parlor, across the entry, answered all ordinary family or hospitable purposes. No one could dream of questioning whether the household felt more at ease in one room than the other. There is something in this showy furniture, the gay carpet, the polished mahogany, the look and smell of newness, that indicates an abrupt change in the family drift; incongruous the manifestations of such change must be; the present seems to have grown with a not quite graceful naturalness out of the past. Sally, of all Martindale, harmonizes best with the modern style of the new furniture, but Sally is in direct antagonism towards the state of things among which she was her being.

It is curious to see how a man like Elder Green can stand affected by such signs and shows. He had an interest in this fine upholstery, and the skillful work from cabinet warehouses. These things had cost him money, they represent their value—it was not the unfitness of the low ceilings and the long narrow room for the reception of fine furniture that might have decorated any gorgeous steamer's magnificent saloon, but another kind of unfitness that troubled him when he stood in the doorway and looked around on the completed arrangements. He was only Calvin Green, and pine furniture, grained neatly, walls whitewashed, floor covered with one of industrious Huldah's nice rag carpets, served his purpose to all conceivable intents.

And yet, when he became accustomed to the new parlor gear, recognized that he could well afford the outlay, saw Sally's satisfaction, heard the neighbors' wondering admiration, the strange shyness that he felt on account of his new splendors passed away; above all, when his mother took to knitting tidies for the arm-chairs, and the sofa, with a serious proud satisfaction, and Sally occupied herself with leather-work and wax flowers, for the "mantel-tree-piece" and the walls of that best room, he was a kindly man, and he had a little pride—he could not find it in him to mar the women's satisfaction.

In this room sat Mr. Collamer. He was quite a young man, having much more learning and enthusiasm than experience; and he had entered the service of his choice with a spirit that gave assurance of his power to prove himself. Though fearless (not insolent) in speech, when not called out by occasion or real interest in a topic, he had the appearance of timidity; his taste might have made of him a student, not a public speaker; but his convictions had proved stronger than his apparent inclination, and in almost every struggle they had carried their point. Rarely is so much gentleness of manner and of heart united with a spirit so valiant and determined. Since he came from his retirement to active life among working-men, he had continually surprised himself. Long would he continue to surprise himself.

There was nothing in his personal appearance so striking as to command immediate attention. His slight figure was well and strongly fashioned; no passing breeze, no day's toil would demolish him. If the signs were to be credited, long life was before him. His countenance was beautiful by virtue of expression—paled just now by over-work, and one would not at a glance suspect, much less discern, the fiery glow of the heart within. His blue eyes and light hair completed the veiling, for, in fact, here was a spirit in disguise. Ordinary people, to whom he came so quietly, how should they suspect the power, or anticipate the flashing of those eyes, or the thunder of that voice, in the great storm-gathering of feeling, and the storm-break of truth?

In this room, with him, at twilight, Mercy Fuller sat and talked, with Sally for an auditor, while Saturday night's work on a farm demanded busy hands and feet of other members of the family.

To the great relief of Huldah, Mrs. Green, the visitors were thus disposed of. As yet, she had been merely able to pay her welcoming respects to the school-teacher—how sincere the welcome was her meditative comment, as she walked about from cellar to bedroom, from dairy to kitchen, overlooking all things, proved.

"Randy said she had a pleasant face, and Randy's right about it. I'll give her of the best—but she's not your kind that complains, and find nothing good enough, do your best and die of trying. I don't hear nought of her but good, and sure her face don't belie it. I'll set as good before her as I would to the President. If she'll only take to grandma, and Sally! Sally, where's your grandma?"

"In the parlor. I came to find you. Everything is done twice over. Do come in!" said Sally, with unusual kindliness, as, looking about the kitchen, (for she thought as she sat in the parlor that she heard the voice of Oliver Savage,) her eyes fell on her stepmother's anxious, heated face.

"It's Saturday night, you know," Huldah answered, feeling that a little apology was due for occupying herself with what must be done, because secretly she felt happy to escape from the parlor constraint into the freedom of the kitchen. "It's Saturday night, and things must be done up strong, or they'll come undone ere Monday."

"They couldn't if they tried, with you to oversee. Come

now, mother, you'll like Mr. Collamer." In the mere kindliness of Sally's voice was a mightily soft persuasion to the ear of Huldah Green, for Sally, her step-child, was not always considerate—nor generally mindful of another's pleasure; was not even now—but Huldah, happily, was not given to any peace-destroying analytic mental operations.

"How is it with the teacher, Sally?" she asked, hesitating still to leave her scene of action.

"Come and see."

"Oh, you won't say; but she looks pleasant—good and kind—harmless like, I think."

"But come and see—such a remarkable gathering, it's worth your while," urged Sally, standing in the kitchen door, and looking out into the yard, that was filling fast with shadows.

Sally carried her point—Huldah smoothed her front hair, brushed off the imaginary dust from her person, and then stepped lightly towards the entry through which, Sally following, they passed to the parlor.

The gathering in the parlor, all assembled, was, in fact, "remarkable." Man and woman, age and youth, purse-pride and vanity, intolerance, recklessness, charity, religious enthusiasm, had expression within those walls; had full-blooded life there.

Elder Green sat on one corner of the sofa, whereon Mr. Collamer was also seated. Conspicuous, and separated from the remainder of the company by the arms of the easy chair, whose covering was of purple velvet, sat the Elder's mother; by the table that stood under the looking-glass, between the two front windows, sat Mercy Fuller, busy with some trifling thread-work that occupied her fingers merely. Sally sat down near the door, instead of following her mother to the table, least at ease, perhaps, of any person of the group, but not on account of the unusual company. Here, on this occasion was an unmarked failure on the part of Sally Green to occupy the place that seemed naturally hers. A failure that was not made significant to any one, nor clearly to herself. It would not have become her, in the presence of elders, to take upon herself the conduct of the evening's conversation, but a woman so well-dressed, with whose education so much pains had been taken, in whose behalf at least no expense had been spared, ought not to have sat there by the door, so desirous to avoid responsibility as even to long for that voice and step in the kitchen, which, on the pretence of summoning her mother, she went out just now to greet. But don't think it was her fine surroundings that embarrassed Sally, or a sense of incompetence to take part in such conversation as passed an hour ago between the minister and school teacher; at which time she revised a little —on compulsion, and unwillingly—her opinion of Miss Fuller, and determined henceforth to avoid her. Prosperity in temporal things—ambition to eclipse her neighbors, to be looked up to by them, to be courted by them, for personal beauty and the show of perishable circumstance, for the position of money and family—this was Sally Green. What was there within or without her that could draw this nature forth to any exalted aspiration! What is it that sustains any such nature in the world? Accident. The good it craves for, and aims at, is beneath it, and unhindered in obtaining that, it will descend for the possession. This is the way they take to reach "the Blessed Life."

When Huldah came into the parlor, Elder Green had just asked Mercy about her long walk that afternoon; she told him the direction she had taken, and now he remarked:

"Past the old Carradine place then. Yes, it is very sightly up there. Then you saw the ruins."

The next moment he had occasion to repent that suggestion, for his mother never lost occasion to rigorously, and, as she deemed, religiously condemn the Carradine history— quite the most profane within her knowledge. Carradine was the name by which, as a social being, Esther hated sin, and the show of sin's prosperity. Carradine was the token by which she knew that the feet of the unrighteous were set in slippery places. The theme on which she mused until the fire of—shall I call it envy?—burned. Envy and malice, and uncharitableness, are harsh words, and one feels compunction using them in reference to a woman, above all an old woman—and above everthing a "professor," who had read her Bible so much and prayed night and morning for so many years.

She spoke up now with the promptness of one who is prepared.

"The old ruins must be gone by this time, Elder. It was long ago that I saw only the stump of the chimney left.

Never a house dropped out of sight so sudden as that one. Never vengeance made a cleaner work."

"There are a few traces left—not many," said Mercy, now curious to hear the traditions in regard to the Carradine fortunes. His own words, and his attitude and aspect as a dweller in the town, excited her curiosity. The tone of Esther's words increased it.

"I've often wondered at the man for leaving sign or token on the ground. It wasn't a home that ought to stand, and it couldn't stand. But that's his pride. He'd never cover up the rubbish, somebody might think he wanted to put out of mind what the town of Martindale never could forget. When I was young, it was reckoned a good deal of a house. Old Mr. Carradine brought more money with him to this country than any other settler that purchased of my husband." Here Esther paused, from her manner of speaking you might almost have thought that she saw no difference between the Maker and seller of land.

"But that was the prime difficulty," explained her son, the Elder; "he had more money than faculty to deal with a new country. So it was all waste and want."

"Waste and want and sin. You can see it all when you look at Peter Carradine—such a dreadful man. There was never another like him."

"But a quite successful farmer, is he not?" asked Mercy.

Sally wished for Randy to stand by and hear this conversation. She smiled to think of Carradine's prosperity as here adverted to, in the hearing of grandma, Esther Green.

Mr. Collamer turned and looked at Mercy when she spoke. A smile seemed to be somewhere hidden in his face, but it may have been a mere beam of benevolent pleasure, excited by the hope that possibly there was some redeeming point in the character of this notable man of Martindale.

Esther's surpise to hear a stranger even associate the words prosperity and Carradine was great, evidently—her cold blue eyes expressed it.

"I suppose," answered the Elder, in a tone that did him credit, "I suppose that Mr. Carradine is the richest man in the town of Martindale. I mean for a working man. Of course there's Mr. Martin. But we don't take him into account."

"My son," said Esther Green, in a sharp and pained surprise, "whoever thinks of Peter Carradine as a *rich* man."

"I know, mother. Maybe it's wrong—but folks don't always see things as it's right. Carradine is active and sharp, a good deal of a man in business. It isn't anything beyond that the most of folks will care about. He's prosperous, as you said, Miss Fuller—you're right. He owns a deal of land—and he's a careful farmer. 'Cause he put himself to it—and he'd carry anything he tried to carry. By-and-by, sir, when we old people are gone, and there's a new set in Martindale, these things will be forgot. It's right they should be. He's a sober man, and honest in his dealings—as honest as a man like him can be. There's no cheat about him. And money goes a long way. If that man was to marry, sir, and raise up children to his name, they'd ride prosperously over all this region. I can't speak agin light and knowledge—he isn't the the kind o' man that it's good for *me* to be with; but he's prosperous."

At this unwonted speech, delivered with a spirit that nothing short of an exacting sense of duty could have inspired, Elder Green sat back in his seat. Through the shadows, Sally Green looked at Mercy Fuller. A silence that could be felt was upon the company; the Elder seemed to have controlled it, as sometimes, on larger occasions, a church full of people, apparently silent, becomes suddenly electrified by the speaker's sentiment or thought. Then the *feeling* of silence has been understood; as it was in this dim parlor, at the present speaking.

Esther Green's voice broke the charm.

"If it had been religion that brought about the change in him!—but it wasn't, it was pride. He was too proud to be a drunkard and a vagabond."

"That may be the cleanliness that's next to godliness, that pride," suggested Mr. Collamer.

"I can remember when he lay in the old barn, a week at a time, no better than a—"

"He did drink pretty freely in those days," said her son, speaking hurriedly, as if he would prevent his mother's severe judgments. "He was quarrelsome, too, when he was in liquor—better tell the story, and make an end of it—until he had taken so much that he lost his wits entirely, he seemed crazy-like. It wasn't safe to be with him. They led a dreadful life up there at Carradine's, I do suppose. I have brought Peter home with me, many's the time, when he was so crazed with drink it wasn't safe to leave him with those that would be ha'sh on him. He was difficult to deal with when he got to going—obstinate, sir; you couldn't drive him! He hain't touched a drop of liquor now for years. I don't suppose he could be persuaded into it. He might keep a tavern, for all the harm 'twould do him. After his brother died, it was, that he changed so entirely. And he was very kind to his mother. But it wasn't for long. After the two little boys died, she was carried off. He seems like a hard man, Peter does—but it's made, half of it." [Well done, Calvin Green!] "He earned his first twenty dollars working on my father's farm. Never such a man in the county for work. Land was for sale cheap—and when he took it into his head, sir, that he would have possessions, it seemed impossible for the land he set his eyes on to keep out of his reach. What he wanted, that he got. There's no double-dealing and no overreaching to him either."

"But what's the reason, then, that everybody's feared of him?"

"There, that's it," said the Elder, as if now he and his mother might come to an understanding; "he's forbidding, proud, he don't like to remember. He's afraid that others do remember—and he wouldn't have a body think he cared, not for all the land he owns."

"Close and careful, but honest, isn't that what you mean, Calvin?" asked his wife.

"Just so, Huldah;" by the tone of the Elder's voice it seemed as if he would bestow a look of full approval on his wife. Instead of that he looked out of the window.

Mr. Collamer seemed now disposed to take part in the conversation.

"If I understand, Mr. Carradine is what we call a worldly man."

"Just so, sir," replied the Elder.

"A very scoffing man," said Esther, determined that, at all hazards, religion should be honored, and perfectly unconscious of a fear that her hatred to sin might deteriorate into hatred of the sinner. "I was thinking you might just as soon look for our gravelly hill to be converted into pasture land."

"Oh, mother," said Huldah.

"Just!" reiterated the old woman; "or into a garding."

"With God all things are possible, you know," reminded the minister; "and it is the great glory of the Gospel that it has converted, and can convert, just such men."

"And there are many ways to heaven," Mercy assured herself with tranquillity.

"I never saw the person who minded me so often of the text, 'Ephrim is jined to his idols—let him alone.'"

"But Divine truth is sharper than a two-edged sword," argued the minister.

As if by common consent, the theme of conversation was now changed.

Sally, unnoticed, except by her mother, had slipped out of the room while Carradine was yet under discussion. She was certain that she heard footsteps in the kitchen, and this time was not mistaken; young Savage was just going out.

"Oh," said he, and he stepped back, his eyes full of greed's worshipping devotion; his face all smiling. "I was just going to give it up."

"I thought I heard somebody," she answered. "There's company in the parlor, I can't stay a minute. Did you want anything, Oliver?"

"No—No—" how could he be so audacious as to want, or be conscious of a want, in such a presence! He seemed abashed before it, and only stammered, "You'll be going to the preaching to-morrow?"

"Yes; you must be there too. It is better than hanging about the tavern on Sunday," said the Elder's daughter. "Besides, it is a preacher such as don't come to Martindale every day."

"I'd go," said he, "for one thing. I don't care who preaches—I'll sit where I can see you."

"Yes—well—you will see that I wear a veil then, a thick green veil. So you will be obliged to attend to something besides me, you silly fellow."

"If I know you are there, you may wear a hundred green veils. You know I could see through 'em."

It made no difference if she called him silly, and little, and a boy, and a wicked one. He knew that she liked to hear him praise her beauty; and he thought that the pleasure was excited because the praise came from him!

"Who is the preacher, though?" he asked, anxious to detain her.

"Mr. Collamer, you remember? He can tell you some things you would be wise to believe."

"I shall ask you to say them over for me sometime, and then I shall be sure to remember. I never forgot anything you said to me yet."

"A precious memory you must have to hold such trash! If I have ever scolded you, you may remember that—but for the rest, don't believe a word of it."

She stood on the door-step, just above him; she seemed to tower far aloft, beyond his reach; he put up his hands as if he thought to see her soaring away, and would prevent her—she took the two hands in hers, and repeated slowly, enjoying the disturbance she occasioned, as a spider may the torments of the entangled fly:

"Don't believe one word of it, poor Oliver."

"I'll give the lie to everything on earth first," he answered passionately. Then she answered as if she would soothe him.

"There! there!" and he was a captive, with his hands in hers; a willing captive too. For one moment an unutterable hope seemed to possess him; he could not speak and venture all. The charm was too quickly broken; she dropped his hands, folded her own together with a calm coolness that fired his fears. "I must go back. They will all wonder."

"Yes," he said bitterly, "it's always they! Always some one besides Oliver. Well! go on!"

He was surprised, however, when she shut the kitchen door, and, without speaking, obeyed him. She went her way lightly laughing; but he actually brushed two or three tears with a rough hand from his cheeks, as he, with a curse, went his way.

If the preacher was disposed to preach a practical sermon, he had furnished for him sufficient material. Worldly ambition was a fruitful theme. So also was charity—love. And if he had need of illustrations, they were at hand, and abundant. No need to ransack the ages.

4*

He had already stood behind the school-house desk, and preached to this people—and he remembered the faces of a few of those gathered at that time before him. He had observed, with the thoughtfulness of a man who understands that time and opportunity are never to be made light of or wasted, that on that occasion his words seemed to fall not on stony ground—that throughout his preaching he succeeded in holding the attention of his audience. Particularly he remembered the young girl who came in with the old man, introduced to him by Elder Green as father Roy. This girl, Sally Green had told him, was the school-teacher of Martindale; but within the fortnight a change must have taken place, for here, under this roof, was another whom they called the teacher.

The minister asked an explanation of Sally the next morning, when she came into the porch, where he sat reading, before breakfast.

She came out to take an observation of earth and sky, not expecting to find him there, but the discovery was not displeasing; and when he spoke she sat down on the bench opposite him; the porch was narrow, a mere covered passage to the front door of the old house, and it had the advantage of apparent seclusion, while it commanded a distinct view of the tavern, and the road, and the country round about. Just outside the narrow yard was the row of poplars and the "hitching-post," but not a shrub or bush broke the view from door or window.

Sally seated herself for a talk with the minister, not entirely at her ease, though quite conscious of the attractions in which she was arrayed—for she had dressed herself this morning with unusual care, and had this thought to depend upon, that she was the Elder's daughter, and sole heir, and quite independent—unlike this school-teacher in the house, in whose favor she was by no means prejudiced.

Mr. Collamer opened the conversation by asking after her friend, the young lady who was teaching the Martindale children on his previous preaching. The subject had somehow escaped discussion last night, when Mr. Carradine was under criticism.

Sally told of "Carradine's doings" with a deal of spirit, and contrived to cast some reflections on the position of Miss

Fuller. "How did Miss Roy like it?" he asked, apparently interested in what he had heard.

"She could not help herself," Sally answered. "He did not care what anybody liked. But he said to father he wondered the child's spine wasn't broken." She just glanced at Mr. Collamer as she gave this bit of information—his eye caught hers, and he held her.

"Was it so bad as that?" he asked.

"No, of course not," she replied quickly, as if she feared that he would suppose *she* had brought the charge. Perhaps there was more of conscious guilt than conscious innocence in the mood that yet allowed this prompt vindication. "But that is like him."

"It was very unfortunate," he said, musingly. "Very unfortunate. How uncomfortable it must make the poor girl!" He was thinking that he might introduce into his discourse some soothing word for her. Against this kindly wish grated the voice and the words of Sally Green.

"She is glad, though, to be done with teaching, I believe. I don't think she was meant for a teacher. She is not so patient as some. The children teazed her, and they know it. I've seen her right tired."

"No doubt," said he. "A teacher's life is no pastime. I have tried it. Under some circumstances, it is not to be coveted."

"But there's some that like it—there's Miss Fuller. She means to be a teacher always, so she told Miranda."

"Then they're friends. I'm glad of that."

Sally surveyed the speaker with ill-pleased surprise. His ready sympathy was strange and unintelligible to her.

"Friends?" she said. "Maybe; they are both poor and work for a living. I suppose that brings them nearer." There spoke the heiress; the purse-pride of Esther Green. Mr. Collamer smiled. He could not see as clearly as could Sally, the significance of the fact that Randy was a poor man's daughter; had never travelled beyond Brighton; dressed poorly; knew nothing about fashions. He could not understand that Sally's endeavor was to establish in his mind a distinction between friendship and acquaintance. *She* had no *friends* in Martindale! though born and bred there; and she was quite out of her proper sphere, condemned to the dullness of this farming district.

"Mr. Carradine seems to be a man of wealth," he said, not willing to drop that point quite yet.

"Oh, yes; very rich. But you wouldn't know it, except by going over his farm. A foolish way of spending all one's money. Don't you think so?"

"Why, what does one see on his farm?"

"Cattle, and sheep, and horses. He always has the best premiums at the Fairs. He sent to England for his South downs. He was the first man in this country that brought them out. I forget what it cost him; but a sight of money. His Aldernys too—he's famous for them. It's all he thinks of, cattle and sheep. He'd risk his own life, and that of every other man he could get to work for him in winter weather, on account of those flocks of his."

"Then he is kind to animals?" observed Mr. Collamer, quite cheered to learn that the man was not perfectly worthless.

"He'd turn his house into a sheep pen any time; and he's been known to do that in the worst weather. Poor Mrs. Johnson, she wasn't brought up to any such works. It's amazing curious—a man so kind and careful of animals, and so hard on men and women."

"I'm glad to find he has so much humanity in him."

Then the minister turned the conversation to Sarah's self. He was interested in hearing her school experience; he was curious to know what her present occupations were; and if she had planned for herself any course of study, or any useful pursuit in particular! What most interested her—and if her answers exposed her to the harsh criticism of an exacting intelligence, he judged her with lenience; her foolishness, and vanity, and frivolity, and petty ignorance, did not make him miserable. He could pardon it all with the readiness of one who has hardly expected anything better. He had not quite the notion of Mussulman or Chinese concerning women, because he was not born in Turkey or in China! He believed in the souls of women! but the faith had not urged on him its conclusions, though it did modify his action.

Very composedly, in her room, sat Mercy Fuller, writing a letter to Brighton, which she intended to ask the minister to take for her, if it chanced that he was to return home that way.

Very thoughtfully Miranda Roy went about her morning work, and prepared herself for the meeting, after laying out for her father the clean clothes he was to wear that blessed day. Very peacefully the old man sat in his Sunday suit full two hours before the time of assembling, reading David's Psalms.

But the heart of Miranda was not calm, and the thoughts of Sally were fluttering; and Miss Fuller wrote in her letter:

"It seems, if I may judge after five days' observation, that Martindale is much like other places. The people are human, after their kind. No doubt a respectable tragedy, in five acts, might be made out of their real experience."

"I shall preach," said Mr. Collamer, from the text, '*Are there few that be saved? What is that to thee?*' I will show them the meaning of charity."

Huldah Green was praising the Lord after her special fashion, as she hurried through her work, and dressed herself, "all of a tremble," after that needful haste, which was always so surprising, so incomprehensible, to Sally.

CHAPTER IX.

THE GATHERING.

For the first time since the day when the school-house was opened as a place of worship, Peter Carradine appeared among the people, dressed in his best clothes in modest compliance with the Sunday habit of his neighbors.

He walked down the hill towards the red school-house, leading Harry Johnson by the hand in a very well-behaved manner, edifying to behold. The little boy carried his mother's hymn-book, and manifested a becoming child-radiance on that bright Sunday morning. Now and then he would dart away from Mr. Carradine and perform an independent caper, expressive of his state of beatitude; a captured butterfly, or a flower snapped from its stem, were the trophies he carried with him even to the school-house door—but nothing so profane was allowed across that threshold—so the fly took to its wings, and the empyrean aspirations—and the flower lay wilting on the ground in the hot sun, with many other spoiled, neglected treasures, on that holy day.

Carradine wakened in the morning with a purpose of attending meeting that was clearly ascertained. At the breakfast table he announced his purpose. Mrs. Johnson dared not express her perfect satisfaction thereupon, but neither could she forbear saying:

"There's the young man that preached at the last preaching, he's to preach again. Harry saw him riding up to Elder Green's."

"Young or old," said Carradine, "it don't matter much to me; I'm going. He's not quite a fool, I hope, though, this young preacher."

"Oh! why you hardly ever heerd such a young man. So lovely looking; and speaking out so strong; you might think it was a spirit, Mr. Carradine." That was plainly a rebuke for his profanity—but it was spoken in a way that did not try his patience too far.

"Well, if he preaches Gospel, well and good. But I don't want to hear of his notions!" said the man, with an aspect rather threatening, though by no means terrible. Such a mood as this present could not excite to any manner of disturbance the woman, who understood his moods so well.

Among the few things Carradine had inherited from his mother was an old hymn-book, on whose fly-leaf was written, in a cramped hand, but legible as print, "Marcia Camp," and under that maiden name, the name of "Carradine." He was looking into it this morning.

"She was a girl when she wrote that," he said to himself, "a pretty girl—spry, and quicker to think out any business than I've seen again." And, as he meditated, the eyes of Mercy Fuller seemed to look out from the page, and he almost fancied for a moment that they were like his mother's eyes. But a clearer recollection, that seemed to stir him so much that he shuddered, banished the face of the intruder, and left alone, in the space of darker shadows, age and sickness, death and ruin.

The leather covers of this book were black with age; its leaves were yellow, soiled and tattered; he thought, as he stood there in the door of his chamber, looking over its pages in the early morning, that he would not part with it for any price.

It was before sunrise that he stood there with that book in his hand; and the hymns he read were some that he had heard Harry repeat, and some that he had heard Miss Fuller recite for the child. And it seemed now that among these hymns were some he had heard his mother sing, how long, oh, what ages ago! Yes, and turning those pages, he came to one that was folded together. He opened it almost as he might have opened a coffin lid. It was the "dead past" whose domain he entered. Could it be without trembling, if even without fear, that he read these lines, to which her finger seemed still pointing?

"Disconsolate tenant of clay,
  In solemn assurance arise,
Thy treasure of sorrow survey,
  And look through it all to the skies;

> That heavenly house is prepared
>   For all who are sufferers here,
> And wait the return of their Lord
>   And long for his day to appear.
>
> "There all the tempestuous blast
>   Of bitter affliction is o'er;
> The spirit is landed at last,
>   And sorrow and shame are no more,
> Temptation and trouble are gone,
>   The trial is all at an end—
> And there I shall cease to bemoan
>   The loss of my brother and friend."

Alas for life! in death alone she had found brightening prospect. Not any promise more of this world's blessedness! All it had ever given her was broken! Its hopes had all deceived her.

Carradine's going to church this morning was an act sanctified by this remembrance of his mother. Let curious eyes set watch on him, and faithful memory recite the bitter past; he sits there in his black coat, in his right mind, as serious a listener as the preacher's discerning eyes shall fall on. And among the people are some anxious souls who speculate upon the chances of his becoming a member. Only bring him round to that point, and the man who sent to England for his Southdowns and Arden horses would not be dependent on the town of Brighton for his preaching!

When he came to the door of the schoolhouse, Carradine and little Harry Johnson met Elder Green and his party. His most astonished mother, (much I wonder if she gave thanks that morning that the feet of Peter had been led down to the Lord's house, and whether she prayed for him!) Esther, was in her Sunday gear and Sunday countenance, and every wrinkle seemed to underscore the "Sabbath frame of mind." There was her son, on whose arm she leaned, who seemed to move in her shadow, so grimly grave he was in his stiff Sunday clothes. There was Huldah, walking with Miss Fuller, and the one was mild and the other calm, and they breathed in the morning balm and rejoiced in the Sunday brightness. Last came Sally, and alone, for the minister had preceded them by a few minutes, and already sat in his place behind the desk. Sally must have forgotten the veil she had threatened. Her little bonnet was not eked out by anything so hideous. It was the pink silk hat she bought last summer, that she might be decent to walk in the procession with Miss Stein's young ladies. The effect thereof never failed to startle the modest Elder, but grandma Green's emotions were of another character. What she had eschewed her life long in her own behalf, she advocated, heart and soul, in behalf of Sally. Why should she not be the leader of fashion in Martindale? Only the old lady proposed the question under a form varied a little from the above. Pink hat and black lace shawl—alas, poor Oliver! Had the blue coat and the brass buttons, and white waistcoat, no chance at all that day? He was doomed to sit and see her eyes fixed on that young preacher full an hour and a half.

A long time Miranda and her father had sat quiet in their places, waiting for the gathering of the neighbors and the coming of the minister.

Not lost upon him was the look of surprise that accompanied the nod of recognition when Carradine stood one side until the Elder's party should enter the school-house. Not lost on him was the friendly greeting, in which he saw no surprise, with which Mercy Fuller bade him " good morning."

Mr. Carradine sat down on the bench nearest the door, for the comfort of the breeze, not to escape observation—indeed he could not have chosen a more conspicuous position, for his seat commanded a view of the entire congregation. He seemed not to be thinking of himself in such a manner as to be awkwardly conscious of his presence among a body of people assembled for worship.

But he sat stiffly, and apparently unobserving, with Harry by his side, the little flaxen-headed, rosy-cheeked lad, whose face was round as an apple and eyes bright as two stars; what an aid and stay that morning to the strong, determined man!

When the hymn was given out he found the place, and followed the minister in his reading through every line, no easy task, for his eyes were unaccustomed to such print; through the reading of the Scripture his eyes were on the minister. He was Peter Carradine, and if he chose to sit in the school-house that hot Sunday, and listen to what a young man had to say—whose business was it, pray?

Once he looked around upon his neighbors, took a deliberate survey. But when Mr. Collamer began his sermon his attention seemed to be absorbed by the speaker.

The minister preached according to the agreement he had made with himself. He preached with power, and had his evidences in the attention, the kind and degree of attention, with which his words were received.

If it was in his power, he said before he went into the school-house, he would make those men and women feel that he was speaking to *themselves*, and not to their neighbors.

Peter Carradine, who seemed to loom up through the discourse more and more conspicuously as a tower of strength, inviting assault, was not the main point of attack, not the only character that had a searching investigation. But his method of receiving the word was altogether original. He nodded his assent—he looked the broadest encouragement on the young man, as if to say, "Go ahead, I will endorse and sustain you, my fine fellow, through it all," and at the conclusion the wonder was that, in his state of feeling, he did not rise up and thank the preacher for his sensible remarks. He might have done it privately, but for the announcement which followed the preaching.

The minister's endeavor in behalf of others was not entirely a failure. Look at what was going on in the hearts of some of our friends, while he continued speaking.

Sally Green was wondering whether it was possible that she had said more than she meant to say, when she spoke with the minister about Miranda; and she winced under the suspicion that he had seen through her words; she recalled her speech with painful distinctness and precision, and, while satisfied that she had spoken the truth merely, she had the conviction of a purpose not entirely honest, to deal with. And all through this preaching she was wrestling with an angel, to evade his blessing. The Angel of His Presence, the Voice of her Conscience, was speaking in a tone so loud, she could not deny her hearing. Yet would she resist His conviction.

Only in partial revelation she beheld the highest human good. Dimly revealed stood human love before her foolish heart. She desired it. Her desire, of course, must be after her own fashion; truer than she could interpret; deeper than she could make intelligible. It was satisfied, when it could get nothing better, with poor Savage's admiring worship.

But here, now, was a finer spirit imminent, in whose presence she was not quite her ordinary self; before whom she felt doubtful of that self; to whom she found herself speaking as she did not to others. Her charms, her fortune even, seemed depreciated in value when she estimated them, for him. She wondered what would come of his apparent interest in Randy's affairs; she compared herself with Randy. She would consent, she thought, to be converted, if by that means anything could be gained. Ignorantly, selfishly, she might long, but the longing in its essence was divine, as the infant's who cries for the moon; as the warrior's who conquers the world. Vain, curious, she bade fair to come as short of *love* as Alexander came short of dominion whose existence was unguessed by him.

So she listened with noteworthy interest to the preacher's earnest words, not unobserved of those immediately surrounding her, nor of the preacher himself. Impressed by her solemnity, Oliver's face lengthened, but his eyes were not withheld from wandering. She wore no veil, that was a comfortable sign.

Samuel Roy gave his reverent assent to every word the preacher spoke. He believed, he hoped all—and prayed through the preaching, "Let Thy word prevail!" and twice a hearty "Amen" escaped from his abstraction, in full endorsement of the speaker's words.

His daughter meditated:

"What brought Mr. Carradine here? To affront me, I reckon, and get the opinion of the people. There isn't a soul in Martindale dare say his soul's his own when it's against Peter Carradine. Are there few that be saved? I should think likely; but he seems to make it out pretty clear it's none of our business. I like Senior for one thing; he's no hypocrite. Likely Peter didn't want Miss Fuller's good opinion! Senior says right out, no, I don't want any of your meeting going. Them that makes a profession are only serving in disguise, and making on the sly what they'd lose by their religion. And, according to my opinion, he is in the right of it. I wonder if, when I keep the public with him, there'll be a chance for me. If I could get religion—he seems to make it extraordinary plain! Oh, if I could understand it all as he does! He looks as an angel just lit on the earth might look, and gospel means glad tidings, father says—he looks full of them certainly. There's Oliver Savage watching Sally as a cat does a mouse. Let me see him catch her!" And so on; disquieting her heart in vain, coming back, continually coming back, to heed what the preacher was saying—seeing in the mortal man the glorified angel, as often as she came, and sighing from her heart as she thought of the wisdom and the knowledge he had, whose possession she regarded as forever unattainable by mortals such as she.

Huldah Green bethought her of numberless kindnesses it was in her power to perform to her neighbors—and some of them came to her like illuminations—she was eager to go forth on the kindly service. How could it be that she had never till now thought of these things? With suffused eyes, and flushed face, she looked at the young man whose godly counsel had taught her of them, and blessed him from her heart.

And the Elder thought that, should it please the Lord to grant him such a son-in-law, he would depart in peace. Half the congregation would have comforted him with prophecies to that effect had it been possible for them to guess that such a thought intruded among *his* Sunday meditations!

But the Elder's mother was not altogether pleased that Mr. Collamer should make so free with mysteries, explaining 'em away till there didn't seem nothing left but was clear as daylight—nothing to hold publicans and sinners by.

The announcement alluded to, made by Mr. Collamer before the concluding prayer of this Sunday service, was to the effect that, in the beginning of next week, a camp-meeting would be opened in their neigborhood, of which he had been requested to inform the brethren.

Mr. Carradine's head lifted a little more conspicuously at this. The expression of his face entirely changed. He looked around him with scornful incredulity. Was—it—possible!

Confronting this exhibition, but not the least dismayed by it, the preacher went on to state the purpose of the proposed meeting. It had been undertaken, on mature deliberation, by those who believed that great good would result from it. He hoped his brethren would regard it in the right light—

not as a " religious pic-nic," but as a movement directed by the Spirit of God.

If, by his presence in the school-house, he had seemed to countenance any such proceedings, Mr. Carradine was bound to set himself in the right light. The immediate influence of the hour and sermon was quite lost in the displeasure which he felt, and deemed himself called upon to proclaim to the neighborhood.

He began at his own table, with Johnson and wife for an audience. But began so mildly—for his ire had by this time greatly moderated—that Mrs. Johnson undertook to argue with him. An indiscretion that distressed her spouse, who never in his life had disputed with the proprietor.

" Certain, you disremember the blessed times of Whitfield, when people came together in such crowds there was no room for 'em in any building that was made with hands."

" There! you say that!" he cried, coming out so suddenly with his emphatic speech as to startle her and frighten her husband, " It's because I remember, that I stand strong on the opposition! Bring on your Whitfield, or Wesley, any one for that matter who'll draw thousands of folks together, all for hearing what they've got to say. Am I the man to hoot at 'em? I'd be at the expense of putting up a platform and tent for such a man myself. I would indeed! with pleasure. But now, bring on your men! and look over this district. What good is such a meeting going to do?"

" It's to bring in the outsiders," began Mrs. Johnson,

" Pops," said Harry, addressing his father, curious and puzzled, " what's a outsider?"

" Sch! sch!" was Johnson's answer. Carradine overheard the two, and said:

" Uncle Carradine is one, and pops is another of what your mother means, but Harry isn't, for the Scripture reads, ' of such is the kingdom of heaven.' "

" It's them," said Mrs. Johnson, moved perhaps by Carradine's words, to give an answer slightly varied from that he had returned to Harry's question, " as 'ud never think to set foot in a school'us, or meetin'us, or barn either, for that matter, for worship. There's many will come to look on and think no disgrace to be seen standing up under trees a listening to Gospel. They look on as 'twere a frolic—but 'taint none o' that, as they may be brought to see God willing."

"The minister named it right, though, when he said you wasn't to look at it as a religious pic-nic. But you *do*. And that's what it *is*."

"There's some," she answered, "as comes to mock and stay to pray. I can't think of anything more blessed than sermons I've heerd in the woods; and prayer-meetings I've attended when I was a girl. I seemed to get nigher Heaven in them days than I've been since I came to Martindell. And a camp-meetin' was the solemnest place this side of it."

Her seriousness, and the courage which he seemed to think was requisite to this confession, induced Mr. Carradine to say:

"Ah, if folks were all like you, Mrs. Johnson!"

At which she blushed crimson, for she had looked at herself during the preaching with anything but admiring eyes.

"You're laughing at me, sir; but I know what I know. It was at camp-meetin' you set so little store by I got all the religion I've ever had. It isn't much, but, thank God! it isn't less! I was a giddy girl as e'er lived, and it was there the arrer struck me, and I was slain of the Lord."

"I thank the Lord for raising you up again, Mrs. Johnson. So does Johnson, here," said Mr. Carradine, gravely; but, though gravely, neither of his hearers felt quite sure of him.

"I've got nothing agin the camp-meetin'," said Johnson, secretly siding with his wife, though he could not contend with Mr. Carradine, as she had done.

"Up the hill you can count six meeting-house steeples; show me the one that's crowded of a Sunday. If every man is doing right as he sees it, where's the use of his being riled in order to find out the settlings of him? A clear spring of water's a prettier sight than a ditch filled to the brim," said Mr. Carradine.

"It's for outsiders," repeated Mrs. Johnson, speaking timidly, as she returned to this argument; "for the outsiders, and warming up of the professors—goodness knows, we need it. I don't see nobody too good. It's for them that *wants* to go, too. We can't all see alike, sir. It's well we can't. I won't set up for a Judge in Israel. Things 'ull take their course."

Gradually, out of consideration for each other, it appeared, Mr. Carradine and Mrs. Johnson dropped their weapons and went on with their dinner peaceably, each rejoicing still in an unaltered conviction. Mr. Carradine a little impressed by the woman's magnanimous rejection of the judgeship. Did she mean to remind him of the rights of private feeling?

All that afternoon, Sally sat in the porch, where she was seated when the minister took his leave of the family. As he came out from the "keeping-room," he took from the bureau where her father kept his religious library, (a select collection of a dozen volumes,) a little book, "Baxter's Call," and brought it to Miss Sally. Had she ever read this volume? No. She turned the leaves a little serious, a little curious, and a good deal fluttered. She had glanced ere now at the pages only to close them and throw the book aside with speed. But now he said:

"Oh, my dear young lady, if you would only believe what is written there, and take it to heart, and act on the truth, how grateful should I feel to God for the disposition I now have to urge you. Youth and beauty and wealth perish; truth only is eternal. And from this golden book you might learn rare things concerning it. If I might dare to exact a promise from you, it should be that you would study it."

"I will, if you set so much by it. But it looks very dull," said Sally, who was manifestly moved by the earnestness of his appeal and the directness of his glance.

He had already her father's assurance that, of course, his family would be on the camping-ground during the holding of the proposed meeting, and he now volunteered the wish that she might find satisfaction in the services, and he went away hoping something, as a Christian man, from the interest she seemed to manifest in regard to that appointed gathering.

A long time after his departure from the town, Sally sat in the porch, by no means finding *Baxter's Call* importunate. With wandering thoughts she yet endeavored to follow its leadings, and very solemnly she looked over the chapters Mr. Collamer had specially pointed out. But it was very,

very dull to her, if indeed she rightly understood what the writer was aiming at. By-and-by she fell into a reverie, and the book slipped from her hand to the floor. Though she snatched it up again, it was not to read in it any longer. She laid it on the bench beside her and began to think of the preacher, to recall him as he had looked and spoken in the school-house, and just now in the porch. What he had said, less than his good looks, his eloquent manner, had made the impression on Sally.

He seemed to be exercised very much also on her account she thought. During the sermon he had fascinated her, compelled her attention by the way in which, now and then, his eyes fixed full upon her. A dozen other persons, men and women, old and young, could have reported the like fact as of their own experience that day; but Sally fancied that it was peculiar to herself, and made the most of the belief, for it flattered her vanity and endorsed her own view of her power. She dreamed diligently all that afternoon, and saw, among other things, that the camp-meeting was destined to witness, or to herald, many important events. And she reflected with a satisfaction that sent a ray of pleasure to her face, that the gray bonnet she wore last winter, with modest bits of cherry-colored ribbon set in the demure trimming, was the hat that, of all others, most became her; surely it was plain enough for the head of the strictest professor? Also, she remembered that the wives of the orthodox ministers of Brighton were not by any means remarkable for their grave attire. What was there, after all, in a color or a cut, that sensible people should take offence at, or recognize as a symbol of good or evil!

Meanwhile Samuel Roy had talked the sermon over from beginning to end, and had found his daughter full of acquiescence. This brought them by degrees to speech in which Randy felt more interest, and the departure from the Sunday strain was so gradual and natural that it was even unobserved by Samuel.

"Yes," she said, answering his remark that he thought all the neighbors had been present at the meeting that day; "yes, I don't know as one was missing."

"'Cept Senior Jobson. It would be wonderfuller to see him brought in than Carradine even."

"Senior has lived in this country a' most as long as father; hasn't he, father?"

"No, child, no. Senior is a young man to some of us. I remember the first year he came in 't Martindell. I was an old settler then. But I never knowed Senior for a meeting goer yet. The tavern's a bad place for one of his make."

"There's worse men than Senior Jobson, though. Even when he's in liquor, he's more reasonable than some that's innocent of a drop. It isn't likely that he'll ever quit the tavern stand. Is't?"

"I'm led to hope incredible things for all this deestric. I never see a camp-meeting yet as wa'nt a day of the Lord. There's some that's weighing on my heart like lead. And over them I'm given to hope there'll be shoutings of Hallelujah, before this week is ended."

"But you don't think 's likely Senior will ever shut up the Spread Eagle? That's his living, father."

"He might keep a temp'rance, Randy. It's no sin for 'm t' commodate the public; and there's them that travels about wouldn't be beholden to any but a public for a lodgin', but I've lived to see what I feared to see when Senior Jobson come to me and said he'd boughten Widde Grover's hum, and was going to set up for a landlord. Says I that day, think twice about that'n, Senior. I remember it clear, says he, standing up afore me looking proud and ekil to anything, 'it's sink or swim,' said he, a looking sort o' terrible, 'it's sink or swim!' And I knowed it was. But it's been all a sinkin', Randy. Jobson hasn't a better friend than I be, though it's rare I cross his threshold. He's swum, he thinks. That's the worst of it—t' appearance he's drownded, Senior is."

"While there's life, there's hope," said Randy. "There wouldn't be danger to father if he should be kind to Senior —friends like, as once, who could wonder at it?"

"I'd put out to save him. I'd swim a rough sea. Though when he got into his gambling ways there was ugly stories about Senior. There was hard-won earnings that changed hands suddenly. But it's the worst of Senior, you can't catch him; he's ily. He dodges round and round, and it's my opinion that if e'er a man went through a gimblet hole, Senior is that man. Oh! I've had hopes of him! and there's been times when he seemed just ready to step into the kingdom of Heaven as if he couldn't help it, it come so nigh him—but afore one could thank God for 't, he was off again. No—you can't tell me anything about *him*. I don't like to say it; but I'm feared, I'm feared he's a hopeless case."

"'Twouldn't be so if he had any one to care for him," said Randy. "See how kind he is to Junior's children."

"They're to have his fortin, I'm credibly informed. Ethan Allen is to keep the tavern when they're all dead and gone. That's his plan."

"But Senior might be married himself, father, I should think."

"He's been to nigh unto that more'n once. He'd want a womern like himself—and may I never live to see such a one come into Martindell!"

"Why, father!" said Randy, and the little laugh she gave was a snare; it would set him on to illustrate his meaning: she was not mistaken.

"I've seen such a womern," said he. "I've seen 'em down to Brighton. Gadders about, free livers, nussing their bodies and letting their souls go to rot. They skeer me, them womern, with their flauntin fine ways, along with their boisterous speech."

"Why, father, you think such a woman would take Senior?"

"What's he want of a wife? To call in his customers, I say—the sort that sits guzzling and gossiping in the bar to make all agreeable."

"Oh, no," said she, "that isn't Senior Jobson's notion. I'm sure of it. If he took a wife, it wouldn't be for a sign-post, but for a woman to be kind to, who'd help him to be a better man and keep a better public. I believe that's the right kind of o' woman would be to Senior."

"Randy, mark my words. I don't know what he's thinking of in these days—getting married, like's not—but such a man won't never pick out the right kind of womern, he'll keep on as he's began. How's he going to know what's good for 'm—running aground so in all his sailing?"

A knock at the door interrupted the old man. Randy opened it, expecting to see the person whom thay had been discussing—there he stood—and then she was surprised. Her father, who had risen and followed her to the door, put out his hand. A vague conviction that Senior had been *led* to make this unwonted visit on a Sunday evening, made him offer his hand cordially, and he gave the innkeeper a hearty welcome.

"Come in! come in!" said he. "Randy, set a chair. Ye'r welcome, Mr. Jobson, and isn't this a Sunday even to do the soul o' man good?"

"It's a fair night coming over us," answered Senior, standing on the lintel, tall and bland. "You're enjoying it here so with Randy, I do' know as I'm priveleged to ask— a favor."

"Sit down; sit down, Jobson," urged Samuel, moved to feel that a day of the Lord might even be at hand, so seriously and so kindly Senior regarded him, and so fine the innkeeper looked in his best Sunday clothes.

"I would, thank ye, but Junior's wife is poorly, and she sent to ask the favor that Randy would come sit with her for an hour."

Of course a request of this nature was not to be withstood. Roy was even more urgent in hurrying her off, than Randy was in haste to go, for she believed that Senior had invented the case of necessity. But she did not express her suspicion when they had left the house and passed through the lane, where the night shadows were increasing in spite of the young moon.

Having passed the lane gate, Senior drew her arm through his, and took her hand.

"You didn't much believe about Junior's wife," said he; "but she *is* poorly, and I am going to have a little supper for her, and I want you to help us."

Randy half drew back.

"Have you told them?"

Senior strode on so resolutely, she could not but follow— and a little tighter grasp of her hand seemed to certify that he was not going to permit any wavering in her dealing with him.

"No," he answered; "whose concern is it but yours and mine? I was over to town to-day, and I found a fine lot of fresh oysters. They'll relish with poor Jane. And what's a good feast worth without good company? I never was the man to sit down in a corner, like Jack Horner, and eat my pie. What's the reason I've been waiting for my wife so long? For the time to come round, and now it's come. I'm able to support her, and I can begin to enjoy living."

"No one ever thinks that Senior Jobson hasn't come to that yet. He looks as he enjoyed life."

"What folks think isn't the rule I've lived by, Randy. Mind that. I ain't a man to stand peering into my neighbor's face, or trying to learn what rule he's going to judge *me* by. Let every man judge himself. There won't be the devil to pay so often."

"That's what I think."

"Yes," said he, "and I expect the man above will bring it out all right, about. I don't see why the expectation isn't honoring of him as much as this setting to and praying, you know how they do't; you've been brought up in the midst of it. And I'm told they're to have a camp-meeting, now, over to the hemlock woods."

"Yes," said Randy, "they are! Did you go to the preaching to-day, Senior?"

He laughed at the question. "Why, when d'ye remember to have seen that sight? I was meditating about the new building all the morning. I can't keep it out of my mind night or day. But in the afternoon I had a congregation of my own, and the preaching was brought over; and *I* preached, and damn me, but they said I had the best of it. They said I was spiled for a tavern keeper. It was in my mind once to preach! I never told that 'afore to living man or woman. It's a cross atween the worst and the best, I've made up my mind, that takes to preaching. I mean the preaching that's worth paying for. I don't disbelieve in preaching, mind ye. A good round sermon's to my mind. But I know pretty much all the fellows can say; and it's ninety-nine times out of every hundred you hear what's got no more life in it than—than saw-dust. If a man preaches to *me*, I want him to show first that he's a human being. I want him to show that, added on to what *I* know 's in natur is something else I don't know, that he's got hold of, somehow, and is just as true. That's the kind of preaching I want—and don't get."

This was the sum of the address Senior had delivered in his bar-room that afternoon, with great applause. But his vehemence was now considerably abated, and his whole manner softened, having for his audience a solitary woman, and that woman Miranda.

"It's the kind of preaching Mr. Collamer gave us this morning," said she, and there was not a word of his utterance but she would remember, so that when she spoke of Senior to her father she might encourage him to hope greatly in behalf of the innkeeper.

"*Gave us,*" thought Senior.

"You won't be going up to that camp-meeting, I hope," said he. It was to preface for the question that he had introduced this conversation.

"Oh, yes; I promised father I would."

"Next thing you'll be getting religion."

"Do you think it's likely?"

"I don't know whether it's likely or not. But you've promised yourself to me. And what I've bargained for I want, mind that Randy. Don't go and spoil yourself with them folks. They're not our kind. It's good enough for them. It helps 'em on, poor critters. They say it does, and I really think they gain by it. But you're a good, honest, free-living and free-spoken woman—and your heart, that's what you give to me!—And you're free to tell that to any one who's prying about and wanting to change it."

"You needn't fear for me, Senior," answered Randy. "I used to think different, but now I've changed my mind about it; I believe you're in the rights of it. All the praying I ever did yet hasn't varied my experience one whit, as I can see. It's good for some, but not for me. They say it's because I don't believe enough."

"Seeing's believing," answered he. "But, Randy, I don't want you to go to that meeting."

"Senior Jobson, father is getting to be an old man, and he's infirmer all the time. He said this afternoon, says he, 'it isn't likely you and me will ever have the chance to go again together to camp-meeting,' and he's set his heart on my going. Now, what'll you have me do?"

"Why go!" said Senior. "I might resk the harm, I guess," and he laughed through the mild-spoken words, for Randy's speech, when she was thoroughly roused, never failed to charm him—he felt bewitched by the danger of playing with edged tools.

"Yes" she answered, still speaking with spirit, "you

might! And if it would be a comfort to him to have me converted, I do'know but I'd be willing; and if it didn't do more for me than it does for many, you wouldn't receive no damage! nor—the Spread Eagle either!"

"It's lucky we're right here under the wings of the bird o' freedom," said Senior, with unabated good humor, though he had lost a point. "You and I might get into a snug quarrel. But I ain't the man to badger a woman. You go to the camp-meeting. I can trust the woman I want for a wife."

With these sentiments passing from his voice into her heart, Miranda followed Senior Jobson into the blacksmith's kitchen.

It was not late when the supper party broke up. When Randy came home she was surprised to find her father sitting before the fire he had kindled—neither reading nor singing, but wide awake; and, as his first words showed, he was gladder at her return than he had been troubled about her absence.

"Daughter! the Lord be praised!"

"Amen, father," answered Randy, and she sat down beside him on the hearth. "Have I been long gone?"

"It might be. But how's neighbor Jobson?"

"Comfortable. Better than she was. It's the children that weighs her down so, poor thing. I told Junior that maybe it might happen I'd have them up here off and on, by turns—it wouldn't be only a neighborly turn—and their keep wouldn't be anything to mention. I could take care of them."

Father Roy said:

"So you could, if any one. It's the Lord put that kindness in 't yer heart, Randy. I'm sure I'm agreeable, after the camp-meeting."

"Yes, that's what I was thinking—after the camp-meeting."

"Daughter, Peter Carradine dropped in just after ye left; had ye got out o' the lane? Did ye meet Peter?"

"Peter Carradine been here! what for?" exclaimed Randy, and her voice was harder than in its last speaking. "That was a leading!"

The poor old man seemed to be taken aback by these words, as if he had not expected them. Indeed, during the last half hour, in the warmth of the glowing fire and the calm of the Sunday evening, he had only thought over the pleasant points of the visit, and had almost forgotten what he desired to keep out of mind.

"He's wanting to see Randy," said he, in a conciliatory way; "he asked after you; and said 'twas only on the school-keeping question he had any difficulty with you."

"He did !"

"But he was down on business."

"Talking business of a Sunday. Why, father !"

"I know—I know," said the old man, "it ain't the right thing, Randy. But he just talked it, and I couldn't help."

"Because it was Peter Carradine. Happen it had been Senior Jobson, couldn't you have helped it ? *I* don't mind, but is't fair to be so easy with one, and so hard on the other ?"

"He wants to buy the medder land 'yond the brook—he says it's for grazing—and would accommodate him great—and certin it's far off for an old man like me to labor in."

"It's cutting up the farm so, piece by piece, will make no farm at all," said Randy, not in the least pleased by the proposition. Clear enough, her father was growing old; he needed a good adviser and a good manager. She thought of Senior and was glad. But the old man had not finished his report of the visit.

"It's a big price, though, he offers. It's fifty dollars to the acre, Randy. I never heerd the like in my time. Fifty dollars for that six acre lot! d'ye see ? It jest wipes off that mo'gage, Randy."

This announcement startled her. It was a long time before she answered; at last her steady gaze was averted from the dying firelight, she looked at her father.

"Does it suit you ?" she asked. "I don't own the farm; I didn't earn it by money down, and work at clearing, years and years. Do you want to sell it ? It's the lot that looks so pretty from the lane, with the willows 'long the border. We planted them years ago—and how fast they did grow—every one of them living to this hour."

She knew what recollections were connected with that planting. And she knew how dear that lot was to her father. No portion of his farm but he would have chosen to part with sooner.

"Why couldn't he have asked for the land long-side the road—easier to get at, and better? He knew the store you set by the lot, and if he was meaning to do a kind thing, of course he'd spoil it before he got through."

"Don't say it, daughter, don't say it. He meant it kind."

"If you wanted, though, to keep the lot, I'm free to believe 'twould all come round right yet. I don't want his favors. There's ways to get out of debt to him without his help. And if there is, wouldn't you choose to be beholden to some other man?"

"I wouldn't like to go agin Randy's wish," he acknowledged. "I told him I couldn't answer for 't; I must see my daughter. Peace is better than lands, and good will is better than money. I wouldn't like to go agin your wish. It's what I said to him. It's what I'd say to any man as came to talk of buying. She is young and I am old, and she will live the longest." So the old man put away the temptation of fifty dollars an acre, with the feeling of one who has wasted Sabbath hours and paid the penalty.

He now raked out the embers, and covered the handful of fire in the corner of the great chimney—he had kindled it there instead of in the stove that stood on the hearth; he wanted the cheerful light, but it had served him poorly; it had gone out now as utterly as the dream from which his daughter had wakened him. Randy noticed that his face had lost the really happy expression it wore when she came home. How old he looked, how gray, and grave, and feeble!

"You can think it over," said she, trying to relent somewhat; "maybe you will have a dream—maybe we shall both have—but—I don't believe it will encourage our dealing with Peter Carradine."

"Well—well—but don't be hard on him! We're all sinners, Randy. We're all sinners." He touched on this ground with a spring, as one might who felt the firm shore rock under his feet again, after having lost his ground. He had come back now to texts, and hymns, and prayers, and with these he closed the evening.

It was late in the night when Randy fell asleep. She

had so many things to think of that must be mused over in silence and in darkness But prominent among all these thoughts of the Spread Eagle, and of Senior, and of the camp-meeting, was this, that Mr. Carradine was trying to make peace, and that without his aid in devising, she had found a method of her own for paying the debt that weighed so heavily on her father's mind.

The reader is wondering if Randy's lover stood before Randy's eyes as merely the satisfaction of debt? If her brain in its calculations, by no means her heart in its aspiring, felt the influence of his life?

CHAPTER X.

IN THE WOODS.

A few days after the camp-meeting had become a fact in the woods, Mrs. Johnson prepared for her second attendance, and this time Miss Fuller was to accompany her, with Johnson and Harry.

Elder Green brought Mary up to the red farm-house in his carriage, and she sat on the front seat of that remarkable-looking vehicle with the Elder and Sally, while under the cover, on the back seat, were Esther and her daughter-in-law, Huldah.

Mr. Johnson's team was already harnessed, and the horses tied to the post in front of the lane, for these were not the hard-worked farm cattle, but the "kindest" fancy horses on the place, large and handsome, and of fine cream color.

Johnson's heavy black broadcloth coat lay on the seat he was to occupy—he intended to carry the garment on his arm after their arrival on the ground, but any further use of a coat on such a day was not to be thought of, unless the ladies should insist.

Mrs. Johnson was dressed in her black silk gown, her best dress these ten years, turned and made new last fall, and she looked as solemn as became the happy occasion. The six short curls of fine red hair, three of which adorned either temple, were all in place; the purple gauze cap-strings were tied squarely and unrumpled; she had on her new thread gloves—she was in her happiest mood. The gloves were of a lilac color, and had worn her two summers already. They cost her three and sixpence in the town. She had her hymn book wrapped in her white handkerchief.

Staid and comely Mrs. Johnson, what a day will this be to you! How will you and your sister Green enjoy this precious season in the woods!

"I want to go—I want to go—*I* want, to go—there—too!"

Little Harry was to sit beside his father. Happy and expectant little fellow, dressed also in his best—in blue cloth coat with the brass buttons, each embellished with the "spread eagle," no relation to the tavern stand of Martindale, I testify—are you not an heir of freedom, a representative man, my boy! And he has on his cloth cap, with the long "taussel," that dangles at the side; it is a blue cloth cap; long they hesitated between the blue and brown, but the brown spots and fades—and a cap is a cap, my son, and this head-piece cost two bushels of wheat. His collar is broad and white, and tied with a blue ribbon.

The ribbon was the only bit of finery and pride in which the heart of Mrs. Johnson indulged itself that day. It sometimes filled this mother's heart with trouble when she questioned of herself *whether*, in truth, she had renounced the world; yes, sometimes she even asked herself how she *could* renounce it when her boy was here to live in it as a man. Not really the worst boy in the world; and to her the most precious. And now she had her doubts, when Harry stood before her so radiant and blooming. Once after she had fairly taken her seat, and that preparation was off her husband's mind, for he never would untie those horses until everything and everybody was in its place, she disconcerted the whole party by getting up suddenly, as if she had forgotten something. But she sat down again as hastily, with a red face, much disturbed, though she said nothing.

Finally, when it seemed that Johnson's arrangements were all completed and there yet remained a moment, she turned to Mercy and said:

"Ain't the blue ribbon out of place, Miss Fuller?"

"Too gay do you mean?" asked Mercy, her eyes following the mother's anxious glance, and quickly divining her thought.

"Yes—speak quick. I can get out and change it yet."

"Do you suppose," said Mercy, "that the birds have gone into mourning because there's a religious meeting under the trees where their nests are?"

Apparently satisfied with this assurance, Mrs. Johnson smoothed her dress, folded her hands and smiled. She *might* enjoy the ribbon, and the boy who wore it, to her heart's content.

"I am sure," said Mercy, "you will be thanking God, in spite of yourself, more than for anything else, for this bluebird of yours."

"Oh, as for that, I gave him to God long ago!" said the mother, in a low voice. "I'm sure I did. It's treasure lent, Miss Fuller."

Mercy Fuller sat beside Mr. Johnson, with Mr. Carradine's new hymn book in her hand. He brought it to her at the last moment, after she was seated in the carriage, and hoped she would make herself comfortable. But he shook his head when she said he had best go with them. Mrs. Johnson urged the invitation, but he altogether declined it. Nevertheless, when he went back to the porch he was amazed to think that he had done so.

Long after he had lost sight of the wagon, and the rumble of the wheels had died away, he mused over that pleasant thought, so new to him! A young face to look kindly on him! a young voice to express such a wish as she had just expressed! It had not been for nothing.

Yet he thought this over in such an exaggerating mood that, unavoidably, he was compelled to call himself to account at last. He did it with impatience. On what, after all, was he reckoning so fast? She had merely spoken to him a few civil words; Miranda would have said as much, and more. That thought brought him to his feet, and he walked up and down the piazza. At length the sum of his meditations escaping him, he caught up his hat and went off towards his barns. But the exposure had been merely to himself—and yet to himself!

"They're no more alike, those two, than if they were made up of different flesh and blood. One is a crab-apple, the other a peach. I'm glad I've seen her. I take it for a Providence that she is living in Martindale this summer. If those children don't learn from her teaching! I could learn myself. Never too old, they say. It isn't all writ in the book that folks have to learn."

It was just ten o'clock in the morning when Johnson cracked his whip, and the horses started off on their vigorous trot. It was the hour which he had secretly proposed to himself for leaving the farm-house, and he calculated that by eleven they should reach the camping-groond.

Their road lay through a beautiful farming country, which seemed alive and active, for every cross-road was sending out its deputation, and along the main roads hundreds of carriages were passing that morning in the direction of Hickie's corners.

Of our party, Mrs. Johnson's thoughts, never communicated with perfect freedom or confidence, were to-day subject to an unusually severe supervision. She would fain restrain all wandering tendencies. Had she not her burden to bear, and to watch over? The woman was all a wife to-day, a praying, anxious wife.

Johnson, therefore, never taking kindly to meditative moods, and liable to suspect that things were not going on pleasantly if, in a company of two or more, silence exceeded speech, felt moved to talk—and the subject on which he was best prepared to speak was the condition of the lands through which they were passing, the owners thereof, etc. A train of observations to which his wife desired not to yield, from which she would fain have withdrawn her husband's mind. He was too much taken up with such things. And she hoped so much from this day's privileges in his behalf.

If he must talk about persons, though, *let* it be about ministers! Thus she led the way, and Johnson was content if she would only speak. The theme was sacred to her mind.

Thus they came near the camping-ground.

As they drove across the hills and approached Hickie's corners, a scene spread out before them of exceeding beauty, once viewed never to be forgotten.

It was a broad valley, through which ran a river, so the stream was called; a stream nearly dried at this season,— but in the spring and fall, for weeks together, its bed was full of waters. The fields, beautiful in their varied early verdure, spread up the hill-sides at either hand; here and there were parcels of forest land, and all through the meadows, as in Martindale, but on a broader scale, traces of the ancient wilderness remained.

The wheat fields, and fields of rye and corn, made Mr. Johnson smile; the market would demand all that the country could produce; he would not be afraid to have his crops compared with the finest of these. They did not pass down through this fine valley, but, turning to the left, made a descent of half the hill, as far as John Hickie's place, where Johnson was to leave his horses.

The party alighted in the lane, and while Johnson went to secure place for his horses, his wife and Mercy, leading Harry between them, went into the field through which the people passed to the camping-ground.

The field was lined with wagons and vehicles of every description; two thousand persons, it was said, had already assembled, and from the way in which they were now flocking in, the conductors confidently prophesied an attendance of from eight to ten thousand before the end of the week; everybody was rejoicing by anticipation. As it was, two thousand souls gathered in one place, for worship and instruction, seemed no light matter, and many walked about as if under the solemnity of this conviction, bearing it as a weight.

Mrs. Johnson was full of concern, as I have said. She carried Johnson on her heart that day. She said to Mercy, while they stood awaiting for him:

"It's said that precious young man, Mr. Collamer, preaches this afternoon. I'm laying up a hope by him. There's one wife'll be prayin' an' hopin'. D'ye think t'll rain afore night?"

"Rain, mother!" exclaimed her husband, coming up behind her and touching her lightly on the shoulder. "Come away." And so they went to the wood.

Dame Johnson was not startled by her husband's sudden reply to her strange question. She had been startled the moment before, however, when his appearance suddenly checked her confidences. If anything, her husband's cheerful speech increased the shadow of her face. Not because the voice was cheerful; but at an unlucky moment he had recalled an unhappy thought. Johnson was eight years younger than his wife; and this discrepancy between them had of late been growing into a disagreeable prominence.

Johnson's wife had reason to think that there was too much meaning in the "old woman" of her spouse. Since she lost her front teeth she was even less a beauty than before. She was no longer in her prime. True, she gave no evidence of this in any inability to labor; she was strong and quick as ever; she had lost no "knack" or skill. Often she was reminding herself of these facts. Alas, it was only in her heart that the assurance was lodged—vain to seek the outward evidence. No other soul could see it well as she! Perhaps it was unguessed of every mortal except herself. Tall, strong, capable woman, her life was bound up in that little youngish man, and she was going into this forest church with him, praying that the Lord would take him to himself this day, before he should give himself away forever to the devil. She was not the only soul that hurried into the place resounding with praises and prayers, with cries of beseeching, the Hosannah, and the rejoicing "Hallelujah!" crying out of human sorrow's depths, "Oh, Lord, send salvation!" "Oh Jesus, come down now!"

As they came into the enclosure, they found that the ministers were descending from the rude stand they occupied; the congregation was breaking up; morning service was concluded.

The accommodations of the place were those usually prepared on such occasions; we will walk about with Johnson and his wife, and show them to Miss Fuller.

Cabins, boarded or covered with white cloth, and called tents by that token, defined the limits of the ground, and in these we discover all the comforts deemed needful for a week's life in the woods. Abundant straw is spread over the ground, a matting for the feet, or a bed, as you may take it; beyond you will find a rag carpet, bedsteads put up, kitchen utensils hanging on the posts and rafters. Everywhere, in the rear of each cabin, a cook-stove. These stumps of trees are turned to use as candlesticks—here, by night, you shall see flaming torches casting a strange light on the magnificent old hemlocks. Night and day, the work of prayer, and song, and conference, and exhortation, is going on. The people are here for a purpose—and unanimity of purpose among two thousand persons is producing a result. It is getting to be a serious question what is to be done with this great congregation, hourly increasing. Whether other tents shall mark out another ground, and another platform be put up for preachers, and other rough board seats be placed for audiences. The enthusiastic say a dozen separate churches on the ground would not be one too many. The more cautious fear the result of attempting to draw off interest from the first point of effort.

Our friends hear these discussions as they walk about and urvey. They incline to different opinions—and the general inpression is, that wherever Mr. Collamer stations himself, there will the mass of the people be, for the young preacher, it almost seems, is the life, the soul of the meeting. Johnson, who feels strange and out of place among so many people, would be glad to get away into some quiet corner—he thinks the congregation quite too large. But if there should be a division among them, Mrs. Johnson thinks there might somewhere be a word said which Johnson might miss, to his endless hurt. He could not be in all places at one time. But, at least, he should be in the company where Mr. Collamer was, on this she had decided.

So cogitating, they went through the circuit, at one point passing by a cot-bed containing an invalid woman, bed-rid these many years, brought hither for no miracle-working, but to renew the blissful memories of some youthful season, a picture painted in celestial colors—she is getting her foretaste of Heaven. She will carry back to her lonely room what visions of seraphic faces, and voices celestial! Despise not thou her image, as she lies there among her gross surroundings; passing by with wonder, let not the exposure fill you with disgust. In all her weary years of isolation and of pain, no glory, no beauty like this, of the unanimous congregation; and the magnificent hemlocks, the pretty faces, and the stalwart frames, and the rugged, gnarled and knotted figures, bent, distorted by toil, are forming a great picture gallery she shall be able to revisit henceforth, long as she lives.

She caught a glimpse of Mercy's face as they were passing by; it was a fair face she saw, and she desired another view—so she coughed and groaned, and Mercy turned her head, and seeing that infirmity had come to the camp-meeting, she advanced to the ground whereon all stand as equals, and said:

"Sister, I am glad to see you here."

"Praise the Lord! Praise the Lord!" was the answer, loud and clear. "He maketh the dumb to speak and the lame to walk, and the poor have the Gospel preached!"

"May He make all thy bed in thy sickness," answered Mercy.

"Don't He! Don't He! Couldn't He say, 'Mary Jane, rise up an' walk,' though she's been bed-rid these years—it's twelve year, ma'm, come the fourth day of July. Don't He hear? Don't He see? And if He's willing can't I bear it?—Oh, yes! Oh yes! Glory! Glory!"

A number of people, attracted by the loud voice and the shouting, crowded around the door of the tent, close beside which stood the cot-bed, and Johnson edging off by degrees, drew the women after him.

"Oh, what fun!" exclaimed little Harry, in great glee. Past women nursing infants, washing children's faces—reading silently—gossiping around the stoves—praying in secret—the secresy of silence, Johnson looked at his boy and seemed to be in doubt as to whether a smile were quite the proper thing—a glance at his wife's face might have enlightened him—but since they came upon the ground, somehow, his wife's countenance was not the index that he desired to search. He was loth to surrender himself to her influence this day. He had, in fact, the conviction that her purpose was to "bring him in," and all the resistance he could offer was forthcoming in such peril.

The morning's sermon had produced a decided effect; powerful in some instances to cloud reason and control sense. Here and there were groups of saintly persons gathered about some sister or brother who was being raised from the depths of despair to the life and triumph of an assured hope. The contagion was fast spreading.

In the midst of one of those groups, knelt two young converts with their arms around each other; they were Sally Green and Miranda Roy. Sally had sought her friend on her return, and "found her," as when Sally left her on the ground last night, poor Randy had prophesied that she would find her, if alive "in the Lord."

Mr. Collamer rose up from the midst of this group as our friends drew nearer, and announced that the time appointed for the prayer-meeting in the Martindale tent had now arrived; and himself led the way to that enclosure.

When he saw Johnson and Mrs. Johnson, and Miss Fuller, his face lighted up with an expression of real pleasure. He shook hands with them, one by one, and taking Harry up in his arms, said that he was none too young to come to camp-meeting, and enjoy the kingdom of Heaven.

"Of course," he said, "you will all come to the Martindale tent. Come! there is room for all." And he went on, carrying Harry in his arms, who, between the pride of the moment and his natural diffidence, looked down somewhat sheepishly from his elevation.

Two or three benches were ranged side by side at one end of this tent—at the other end was a trunk, a pile of bed-quilts, and several feather pillows, for the use of such as should come within the circle.

Space was immediately made for Mr. Collamer and the party following him. The persons gathered had only waited for him—he had promised to join them, and although the services were to be conducted in a manner entirely informal, still the promise of his coming was sufficient to give the prospect of the meeting another coloring from what it would have had void of such expectation. A hymn was given out, in singing which all joined. Then Mr. Collamer requested one of the brethren to lead in prayer. It was Samuel Roy whom he selected for this office—notable for his power in the conduct of such service. For this reason the minister called upon him; it was not any man's or woman's approval of the proceedings he was conducting that he desired, it was the spiritual activity of mind and conscience in those gathered there that he aimed at—and the plain earnest speech of Samuel could conduce to that end, if any mere man's speech could do so. And not to save Miss Fuller a shock by his rudest fervor of speech, would he at this time have selected another man than Roy. He had such faith in his system. And he believed it to be merely a blandishment of the devil that this young woman could not see through her prejudices, as she had owned to him she felt incapable of doing.

All unconscious that there was in the world such a thing as criticism, happily, strongly thus unconscious, that of all persons a critic had dared to intrude into that tabernacle in the wilderness, and that this critic had appeared in the person of the young lady he had sheltered through the rain storm —the new teacher in Martindale—whose voice he had heard last Sunday in the singing, and told Randy it was a sweet, holy voice, this man began his prayer—kneeling, as did the entire company, in the thick litter of straw—began, continued and ended his supplication. Not without mighty fervor; not without frequent bursts of approval in the suppliants around him, who endorsed his petitions in their beginning and ending; he, meanwhile, increasing in fervor, till it seemed as if the frail old body in which the pleading spirit was lodged would be rent by his cries. It was strange to see his face paling, while drops of perspiration gathered on his temples and rolled down his thin cheeeks, which began to grow scarlet, crimson, while, with rolling of palms and clapping of hands, the body cheered the spirit in its upward flight.

Deadness or feebleness of feeling was impossible after this; cold observation seemed a profanation, as, one after another, women and men, they took up the strain of supplication and responded with ecstacy of shouts and crying.

When Mr. Collamer saw the quiet, serious sympathy expressed in the face of one woman, the fairest of the group, he entertained a hope for Mercy, conceived then and there.

No wonder that, with the soul's upward pressure, and the deep conviction that, among all these hundreds of people, some might be fed with living bread that day, the minister ascended the stand in a spirit that would demand all his power of him.

No wonder that his sermon exceeded anything that had been heard from the preacher's stand since the meeting opened. There was no influence wanting, all things were propitious.

Mr. Collamer's friends had long prophesied what his career would be; but he exhibited powers in this preaching of which no one had prescience. Powers great enough to enkindle every heart that heard him with a fiery glow of prophetic impulse.

He made the woods alive, **not only with his voice**, but with many voices which kept up a chorus throughout of solemn delight and approval.

For two hours he preached on the glory and love of God. All the pathos and poetry of which he was master, all the eloquence of entreaty, all argument, he seemed to exhaust; he himself never before felt his true power. And he now became aware of it in such a manner that he would ever after hold high possession of his noblest self.

The congregation was in tears when he ended—that vast concourse seemed to be moved by one lofty thought, one grand sentiment. And moved by it they were—into transports that seemed metamorphoses—into ecstasies like revelations. The dead silence which followed when he sat down, exhausted, and covered his face with his hands, was unbroken till he arose again, clasped his hands, and said something that could not have been heard half-a-dozen paces from the stand, but which bowed the heads of every man, woman and child before his seraphic presence, and before that Divinest power which he had invoked. Then did his prayer go forth for them—a prayer in its beginning fainter than the sound of the wind among the trees—fainter than the robin's chirp as it sounded from a branch, but higher it lifted, fuller swelled the sound thereof, until above wind, breath and bird-song the human voice did swell in cadences of noble music.

Then the heart of the assembly broke into sobs and sighing—and responsive Amens, and glad shouts of Hallelujah! and ever, stronger above all, arose the preacher's voice, as if it would bear aloft all the turbulence, and it did upbear until, in a dead silence, fell the royal benediction:

"The peace that passeth all understanding keep your hearts and minds in the knowledge and love of God, and of his Son, Jesus Christ. And the blessing of God Almighty the Father, the Son, and the Holy Ghost, rest upon and abide with you all."

CHAPTER XI.

MIRANDA'S CHANGING HEART.

AMONG the most rejoicing within the shadows, the sacred shadows of that grove, was the heart of Samuel Roy; for his daughter stood conspicuous among the converts who were making the wood vocal with new songs. Now were the prayers of a lifetime answered! Now was the servant ready to depart in peace, since his eyes had seen his salvation!

Trained by a loving intelligence, a loving reverent acquiescence in the Divine laws of life—I should this night have had this girl within my happy knowledge a representative of all that is noblest in woman. For her heart's instincts were generous and pure—she was courageous, she was strong, she was aspiring; she would dare follow out the truth as the truth was revealed to her. She dared to be converted at this camp-meeting; in spite of all difficulties and dissuasives, dared. She was able to think kindly of Miss Fuller. She made mention of the name of Peter Carradine with caution. She could pray for her enemies. *Almost* she could say with St. Augustine, "*How can I be angry when I remember my own experience? Let him be angry with you who knows not with what difficulty error is shunned and truth is gained. Let him be angry with you who knows not with what pain the spiritual light finds admission into the dark and diseased eye. Let him be angry with you who knows not with what tears and groans the true knowledge of God and Divine things is received into the bewildered soul!*"

In the disturbance through which she had recently passed, elements of character whose existence she had not suspected had been thrown into violent exposition. This revival, in its stormier phases, attracted Randy's vehement nature, excited as it now was; and there were present causes, as well as others more remote, that acted on her with a power she was not prepared even to fear, and much less withstand.

She went to the camp-meeting with her father, and was present during the preliminary services; and there they had remained together, day and night, from the beginning. Though unconscious of the fact, she went there a fit subject for the operation of any commanding influence, not less impressional because she had given her word to Senior, and, according to her own judgment, stood in "no danger" of the "religious fever," whose contagion he seemed to dread so much.

After the storm of passion through which she had lately passed, the serene and blessed influences of nature impressed her as they had never done before. Singing bird and waving branch, leaf-shadow, and wild flower, the wind among the hemlocks, the perfect calm when the air was still, the afternoon sunlight slanting through the straight trunks of the old trees, the hill-side at whose foot ran Silver-creek, broad and deep, where baptismal rites were celebrated, the chirping of cricket and grasshopper; to her eye and sense there was nothing in all the varied influences of this surrounding life, human and other, nothing to disgust or weary. Her lot was to labor. The phases of common life were those with which she was familiar—she was accustomed to no other. These people around her talked of the meeting as if it were a foretaste of Heaven—so they called it. Was she longing, while she listened, to understand their meaning? Had she not consented to Senior's doctrine—had she not spoken with contempt of the conversion of many of their neighbors? Could she consent to render in turn any like superficial homage to the Most High?

But she began to listen, and to pray, at last, and was pricked in her heart. And there were those surrounding her who understood the signs; a thoughtful face, a sigh, a tear, were indications to be hailed with solemn joy and deep thanksgiving, and more importunate supplication. It was Mr. Collamer's preaching that brought her to this strait. She had seen his eyes upon her—she had felt herself astonished and trembling before the searching words by which he did not seem to explore for his own enlightenment—all was known to him—but in order that she might be shown to herself, as in fact she was, without any intervening disguise of self-love. She was not the only one who had this conviction, and trembled under it. It was the power of the man so to bring truth to their hearts, thus to awaken them.

Speaking thus he had the Authority which office typifies His spiritual attitude was such that she could look up to him with the confidence of an appeal. He who knew so well what was in the heart, its needs, and the richness and vastness of the heavenly resources! Yet what was her need? Was she not strong, young, capable? The promised wife of Senior Jobson, the anticipating keeper of the Spread Eagle? He made her apprehend the fact of death, that it was the only certainty concerning this mortal state on which she could rely! He showed to her the perfect beauty, and the holiness of true natural affections! He called upon her to purify her heart and serve and honor God, by worthily serving and honoring His image—human nature. He showed her the Divine law as operating in all created life, and called on her to render reverent and joyful obedience. By it the trees of the wood came to rejoicing in perfect strength and perfect beauty—the flowers of the field were adorned in their perfection—the cattle flocked upon a thousand hills—and human love came into exercise of its best powers, and did its perfect works. The mother who most wisely loved her child, the most reverently served her Maker; the wife who had truest devotion to her husband was the most faithful servant of her Lord. He showed her how allegiance to humanity was allegiance to God; and she yielded herself to his teaching, seeing that she had up to this time scoffed in ignorance, which was not, therefore the less blasphemous Surely she should be the better child, the better wife, the better landlady, for this. Poor Senior! would that he could be persuaded to come to the meeting. But it would anger him to urge him; she had time yet, a lifetime, in which to do the work she must perform for Senior.

And so there was in all this experience something beautifully, sacredly real to Miranda. The peace she felt was past her understanding, but how ascertained it was! And then, widow Green's friendly encouragement, and the Elder's blessing, and her father's joy, and Sally's sympathy—for Sally was among the converts also, and she had already led in prayer, urged by her grandmother, who would have it known that the Elder's daughter stood on the Lord's side.

All this made Randy very happy, it made her very happy too that Oliver Savage attended the exercises so devoutly. Oliver had been a wild youth; he had caused his poor mother great trouble since her husband's death; but now he was interested, he listened so earnestly, he prayed for himself with such fervor, and he asked the brethren's prayers so humbly, he confessed his wrong-doing with such penitent expressions, and with so many tears—fairly surrendered to these influences, you can hear how Randy's voice, so strong and sweet, bears up the words—

" Salvation! oh, salvation!
The joyful sound proclaim,
Till earth's remotest nation
Has learned Messiah's name."

As the reader understands, Mr. Collamer's preaching searched the depths of hearts whose secrets were quite hidden from him. He had by no means gone far in his discoveries concerning Miranda as his words led her to suppose. But as her experience became known to him, by his own observations, aided greatly by the remarks of her friends, and at length by her own confessions, his interest in her was more and more aroused. He saw perhaps more clearly than any other person who had knowledge of Miranda, the danger in which she now stood—it must be his care to avert that danger.

And as it happened that the young people were often gathering together for reading and conversation, and prayer, he came into frequent personal communion with them, and addressed their individual condition as he deemed he could not in preaching. And he spoke with Miranda as well as with the rest. Always his speech referred to the vital concerns of life; and his utterance had a veteran gravity, a saintly solemnity.

There was danger in his experiment. A danger of which he took no thought, and of course no precaution.

But how, as he spoke, and she listened to this preacher, in public and in private, through prayer and exhortation, did every other image fall from among her imaginations! Utterly, irrevocably they fell!

How mildly she listened! How eagerly, how gladly, and with what believing! What a spirit of discipleship was this that learned of Mr. Collamer! In his presence she was conscious of no pride to support. She had no strong will to resent or direct when she yielded herself to this young man's saintly ardor. A word of directing encouragement from him, why it was sufficient to set her valorous soul to climb ing the "shining bastions" of the city whose walls are of jasper and sapphire, emerald, topaz, amethyst!

More beautiful than anything she had dreamed of concerning man or angel, was the spirit, the presence, of this man, of which she now and then obtained startling glimpses, that seemed to break through the black rifts of this world's common and unclean, as sometimes on rapt vision, the white robe and harp-sweeping hand of some spirit that shall be troubled and tempted no more. She waited for his appearing. She hung upon his words. She was content to pass through wastes to reach him—to come within their sound. And deeming that these experiences were religious all, how rich she deemed herself in them. Oh, rapturous days! Oh, sacred influences! Experiences to be remembered for their brightness through darkest years and trials! to remain forever an assurance and a token.

Yes, it was easy to forgive Mr. Carradine. Easy to pray for him! Easy to acknowledge Miss Fuller's perfections. For her—the will of God.

It was Heaven indeed that she had entered. But the Heaven that might yet be taken by violence from her. Assaults at those gates of pearl, might they not yet prevail? Alas, if its fair defences were yet to be carried! or its golden streets to be surrendered to the rabble!

No wonder that she saw the sunbeams falling through the branches, slanting to the grass, during those wondrous afternoons, with a light so new! No wonder that she seemed to hear the songs of birds as never before. That their notes enchanted her. That she watched the flutterings of leaves, the gliding of the worm : listened to the running water ; looked upon her neighbors with a gentleness so new that she confounded it with the work and grace of God. Who shall deny that such sovereign work it was!

How kindly disposed she felt towards the poor, hardworking people, her friends and neighbors; and all these strangers who had come from far and near—these thousands of persons! More than she had thought were in the world, in spite of what she had read in books and newspapers. The multitudes of children too! how gentle was the voice that spoke, how tender the gaze that turned to them! the gentle voice—the tender gaze of Randy! Immortal souls for the saving work of love—for the human happy homes! So she greeted them.

It seemed to her that she could never again speak ill of any human being. God's pity seemed to have descended on her heart. She felt a new spirit informing her natural energy, and always she was expert in labor, and was strong. She could toil from morning until night, and day after day, for years. What had she to do with weakness or infirmity? She had risen to the labor whereto she was called.

Why should she withhold her gratitude from him who had been chiefly instrumental in turning her steps from darkness to light? Why should she not pray for him? Why should she not ask that his life and health might be preserved to usefulness and honor? And when he knelt to pray, or rose to address the multitude, might not she regard his continuance in these exhausting labors, that seemed even too great for him, as the answer to her prayer? And if she could for herself, or for another, speak with the Almighty, and prevail, oh, should she ever cease to plead in his behalf, wherever he might go—whatever he might do? And she would watch him as the rising of the sun, note its noonday, see its glory and its work.

Ah, yes, true heart of woman! But now, if the blessing wherewith he is blest includes you not? If you shall indeed behold him rising as the sun, under which the violets and the thistles bloom—even poisonous plants! If you shall see this Apollo, with his "far-darting" spear, smiting to death; if you shall see icy streams unlocked by him— hoary rocks all dripping—fruits ripening, rich vines on the hill side, precious hot-house products—even the wild thorn, and he shall give to some fair moon her light, this mightily illuminating sun, will you *then* be content. and praise God for him, and pray for moon as well as for sun-shining? And beseech that no confusion be permitted in the spheres?

CHAPTER XII.

WHAT IS A COUSIN GOOD FOR? ETC.

NIGHT was coming on when Mr. Johnson reined his horses in before the farm gate. The silence of the homeward drive had been scarcely broken. Each individual brain was busy with its individual thinking, and even Johnson was now indifferent as to whether Miss Fuller thought, or did not think, his wife unsocial. The influences of the day, and of the solemn company had not been lost on him. All the way home he was thinking that, if a praying spirit could be put into him so that he should not mind the sound of his own voice, how comfortable it would make him. He was aware that he had something to repent of—but how to repent? It would please him if he could be set right, so as to lead the life of a Christian man henceforth. He had overheard his wife praying, not long ago, that he might yet become a burning and a shining light. He wished it could be done! So thinking and so wishing, he sat up stiffly in his seat, with an unusual solemnity of countenance, and spoke gently to the horses when they inclined to lag too much. He was impatient withal, for he longed to get away by himself, he wanted to be entirely alone. This work he had got to do was so difficult—the very sight of the faces of those women in the wagon only aggravated him—it seemed to be so much easier for women than for men to get religion! But if he were once alone he thought that perhaps he could come nearer to God! That was speaking after the manner of his wife.

For he must believe, what he had never doubted—though, now he came to think of it, how awful it all was! Look unto me and be ye saved, all the ends of the earth! God actually on earth once, speaking with a man's voice! looked upon by men; a human being to look at—once a child, and a boy, and a young man, at the last and utmost only thirty-three years old, younger than Johnson! This Jesus—this King Jesus! Omnipresent too—standing, wherever he might turn, standing, looking on him. Here even among them as they drove home in the wagon. "If any man will open unto me I will come in. Behold, I stand at the door and knock!" Here, then, in wife's heart, and in Miss Fuller's—and in Sonny's heart, too, for did not Mr. Carradine say that Harry was not an outsider? Of such is the kingdom of Heaven!"

He wished he might be able, just for once, to look into Mr. Carradine's heart, and discover *his* belief—for Mr. Carradine had his own thoughts on these subjects. But, at least he knew pretty well his wife's way of thinking. She was old in these things. And, then, could he not take a little courage, remembering that he had seen the teacher singing with the great congregation, looking as if she were very much in earnest—not at all above the business, even she!

> "Salvation! oh, salvation!
> The joyful sound proclaim!"

Yes, he must try to think of these things. After all, he could not rest satisfied any longer, as he had continued to satisfy himself, that Mrs. Johnson's goodness was enough for her and for him, and for a houseful of people. Mr. Collamer said it was a personal matter—you must pass through the straight gate single file. No one gets in without a passport. Perhaps he would talk with wife, when Harry was asleep. Poor woman! he knew how glad she'd be to help him—poor old girl! But to make a clean breast—to own everything!

Mercy was to spend the night at the red farm-house, as the Elder's family remained on the camping-ground.

Work had not gone altogether well with Mr. Carradine that day, and now, for at least an hour, he had been expecting and desiring to see Johnson drive up to the gate. There was some important work yet to be done before dark; at least Carradine now chose to think so, and if he had not seen Miss Fuller in the wagon, he would have failed to repress the impatient salutation on his lips.

Johnson understood the symptoms he perceived, and his devout aspirations and purposes were clean forgotten as he trotted off to the barn.

"The plague's in it," he said, as he hurried through the unharnessing; "if I was dead, I wonder if he wouldn't expect the farm to up and off. Ne'er a chore left for him, but all the orders give out to the men, so he might a slep' all day with his handkercher over his head—and night come everything's head over heels!"

In the course of another hour Mr. Carradine was in another frame of mind. He wanted to know about the meeting, and what Mercy honestly thought of it. Her report did not seem to please him; she must still have over the old adage, "Many men of many minds;" but he joined in her praise of young Collamer, and said that, if she and Mrs. Johnson could allow that there was any good in such gatherings, he must, of course, believe in them, though the meeting still went clean against his judgment.

People called him a boisterous man, he said, and Johnson swore that he was equal to any forty-horse power; but, for all that, he liked quiet as much as another man; and praying didn't seem to him more likely to be heard in Heaven for the yelling of it. He liked gentle ways, and quiet voices. And work that went on smoothly in the house, without disturbance. When Mrs. Johnson was sick, Randy stayed in the house a month and more. There were few things Randy couldn't do; but the house seemed filled with people when she was about—and he believed that it was her fault little Harry was such a crying child when he was a baby. He had thought, from what he had seen of her while there, that she was better fitted for school-teaching than any other work—but he had found out his mistake.

He checked himself when he had spoken thus far; and after walking a few times across the piazza, came and sat down again.

"Randy hasn't troubled you since you came to Martindale, has she, Miss Fuller?" he asked.

He averted his eyes from Mercy while asking this question—and did not look at her when she answered:

"No. We are good friends, I think. We shall be."

He seemed, on the whole, satisfied to hear that.

"Did you see her to-day?"

"Yes—she was in the tent."

"Noisy?"

"Oh, no—quite silent."

"You know they say she is converted. That's what they call it. And she has been praying for me down there; and getting others to do it. I'm sure if you were among them, Miss Fuller, I should be much obliged. But I wouldn't expect anything so very desirable if that young woman's prayers could be answered. But they think it marvellous she should take to praying for me, who had been her enemy —that's what they say of it. She ought to call me her friend. She ought to be obliged to me to that extent. For if ever a man told her the truth about herself, I am the one."

"Poor girl," said Mercy Fuller.

"Why do you say that?" asked he. "For I take it that every word you say means something."

"If she is what you believe her to be, Mr. Carradine, she has to endure herself. The worst kind of necessity, according to my mind."

"I'm willing you should pity her after that fashion," said he.

Little Harry was playing on the steps by himself, and singing, meanwhile, the burden of one of the songs he had heard in the woods.

"Come and say your hymn to me, boy," said Mr. Carradine.

The child came instantly, and began the recitation, and at first, when his memory failed, the teacher prompted him— but presently her attention seemed to wander, and when he came to a full stop, instead of helping him, she took him on her knee, and said:

"When I was a little girl, Harry, I had a playmate of about your size, and we lived in a farm-house near the sea."

"Near the sea?" he repeated, seeming to be in some doubt what that might mean.

"Yes—you don't know what it is to live by the sea, do you? As far as your eyes could look, when you stood on the beach, you could see the waters of the great Atlantic Ocean. Yon great grass-field made me think of it, Mr. Carradine, when I saw the wind sweep across it. You know how the rye-field looks in the wind, Harry?"

"Oh, yes; beautiful!" he answered, looking at the teacher with beaming eyes.

"I haven't seen the ocean since I was a little girl; I wasn't older than you, Harry, when the old place was all broken up, and ever since I have been drifting about, up and down, and the sea seems very large, though it certainly has its shores. I must believe that."

"You might take Martindale for an island, then," said Peter Carradine, secretly disturbed as he looked at the teacher, and seemed to perceive the meaning of her words.

"Did you like to live there, so close by the water?" asked Harry. "Did you ever see the ships? The great big ships?"

"Every day almost—with all their sails spread; how beautiful they were! We loved it dearly, my cousin and I. We never were afraid. I don't think we knew what fear was. We used to sit on the shore, there was a high shelf of rock just beyond the reach of the highest tide, and there we sat. Sometimes the great waves came rolling in, as mighty as if that hill should come moving along like a great dead wall, its edges all white and curling. It is a great many years since I have seen them—but once seen they're seen forever. Sometimes I dream I am there. And then to wake up, and find all so still around me! Except when there is a thunder-storm, there is nothing to remind me of the wonderful sea."

"You don't like it here in Martindale, then! I was afraid you wouldn't. Why should you?" said Carradine, half displeased, and yet ready to justify her.

"Oh, yes—it is beautiful here, I think, only different."

"What became of your cousin?" he asked; and there was an exacting authoritative sound in the question, sufficient to make one smile. Mrs. Johnson would not have perceived it, but Mercy Fuller did.

She was so long in replying, that he was ashamed and sorry to think that he had asked. Yet, even now, it seemed impossible for him to acknowledge that it was no concern of his. And yet he did acknowledge it.

"It's none of my business, of course," said he.

"It is natural you should ask. But I cannot tell what has become of my cousin. After his father and mother died he lived in college, and was a tutor there when he graduated, that was years ago. He was very young at that time. A remarkable lad; and always seemed to me twice as old as I, he was so grave and thoughtful. He loved the sea with a perfect passion, and books almost as well, though with a different love. I believe he will have an extraordinary career, if he lives. When he was in college no one thought he would graduate; but he laughed at every prediction, and said he meant to live because he thought it worth a man's while. But when the time came he was so feeble that he could not pass through the examination; but he would deliver his valedictory, and people listened so, that not a word of it was lost; and at the close the students carried him home on their shoulders. They were so proud of him. Everybody supposed that he must pay for his honors with his life. The students thought he would never lift his head again from the bed where they laid him. But I heard from him afterwards, that he was a tutor in the college, and a law student. You will understand that, though I hear from him so rarely, I never feel far away from him."

"It is strange you should be separated," said Mr. Carradine, not by any means delighted at what he had heard.

"It could not be otherwise," she answered; "perhaps it will not be always. We cannot tell what a day will give us. If Horatio's mother had lived, everything would have been very different. She would never have allowed him to run the career he has. I sometimes think she must have been the wisest woman in the world; for I don't think I ever met a mother like her; not one that took such loving, wise and thoughtful care of a child. And I never saw another woman so possessed of a sense of the Divine justice—nor one who understood so well that what she planted in the child should be reaped again. I have seen what she thought, and what she hoped to do, in a letter she wrote a friend—and I can look back to her actual dealings with us, especially with Horatio, and understand how really she was acting on the strength of belief. She would have made him a generous, holy man, whose aspirations would all have been heavenly and God-like, with a human demonstration. She would not have carelessly left him to grow up as he might, expecting and hoping that God's spirit would by-and-by descend upon him, and convert him out of a man of selfishness into a man of God. She would have built a temple fit for the indwelling Holy Spirit. It has seemed to me more and more the greatest calamity to all of us that she died so young. For, when I think of the children I have seen, it seems to me there's not another mother in the world alive to the knowledge of these things as she was. But I have the confidence that, whatever delusion Horatio Aptomar may pass through, he will, in the end, prove to be in some sort the realization of his mother's purpose. For, after all, a mother's work is the great work of the world."

How listened this man to this unlooked-for and strange speech, that seemed to be uttered because the moment, and by no means the auditor, drew it from her. Fancy the stolid faces, the frivolous, leering faces, the doubtful and unbelieving, the contemptuous and blaspheming questioners, that, in all courtesy, might have waited through the tedium of such utterance! Is it beyond your power to summon such an audience of familiar human faces?

Mercy was surprised when she looked at Peter Carradine; he sat bolt upright beside her—his massive countenance had in it an expression that glorified it; every feature was grand with the evidence of his heart's, his soul's full intelligence and response to her speaking. Men might not have recognized in him their neighbor; but it was not with men that he was dealing now. It was with a woman who had been moved to speak. Let her speak on! Why not? There is no danger, my young friends, that you will often be dismayed by a repetition of her discourse. Mercy seemed in her heart to be solving the Woman question; and doubtless it is, at one time or another, in one form or another, proposed to every woman in the world; but there are numerous ways opened whereby swift feet may escape with a burdened brain or heart into " Vanity Fair."

"Then you don't believe," said he, taking swift hold of the one thought she had uttered with which he could most readily deal; "you don't believe in these sudden conversions they talk about?"

"There is no end to the goodness of God. I cannot limit Him. He can forever open new ways of escape. But he did not mean that this human life should fail us; of that I am certain. Nor intend that we should look on death as a door of deliverance—nor that we should go as strangers and pilgrims through this world. But that while we remained here, we should find here our rest; our Divine satisfaction, in the beauty, the glory, the unlimited ability of doing and being. Woman has never yet fulfilled her work. Fulfilled it! she has not begun to imagine what it is; what she may do, and be, in this world. The Catholics worship a woman, and render her honors as the mother of Jesus. As the mother of a Divine man! But a mere expression of the simple truth would seem almost blasphemous in the ears of most women. Not if spoken in any moment when they were lifted into their proper life by a noble love. But the most of them are incapable of that life, and how should they be competent to any other? It is not woman, but it is women, that move the heart to hopelessness, and doubt, and all manner of unbelief. Every man has an ideal which woman was meant to make good. And so has every woman a God to be incarnated in love. Her unbelief is death—the real death of the woman. And the body of death that remains when her life has left her, can it work anything beside corruption? I speak to you as if I were meditating a speech. I have heard women speak of their rights. If they had made the men of the world what God intended they should make of them, there would have been no need of this complaining. Martyrdom is endured in silence, if nobly at all. 'He was dumb, as a lamb before her shearers so opened he not his mouth.' Through countless generations the sins of the fathers are visited upon the children."

What Mr. Carradine might have attempted by way of extenuation or of argument, we shall not discover, for, as Mercy ceased speaking, Harry's gray cat ran across the piazza with a young robin in her mouth, and they all started to their feet, as if to prevent an accomplished destruction.

"You might think a little bird could get on," said Carradine, as he came back to the piazza, "without such a misfortune."

"Now, learn a lesson from the robin, and be still," said Mercy to herself.

Carradine would, on the whole, have been better pleased had he heard nothing of the cousin Horatio Aptomar; at least if, hearing of him, he had not received an impression that seemed to justify Mercy's praise. What could such a woman think of such a man as himself for instance, with such thoughts as she had, and such recollections? Yet she had expressed them as in a not unworthy hearing; she had not seemed to fear misunderstanding, or that she would prove unintelligible. And he had understood her! With her presence his ideal had sprung into life—she answered to all she had inspired his heart to desire—not within his range of apprehension was anything more lofty or more beautiful than the mere woman who had been speaking to him, in the piazza, he chose to think, and not merely making the result of the day's meditation vocal; and the cause of that meditation, her cousin!

When he was alone he sat thinking over her words—comparing her with every other woman he had seen, with the ladies he had sometimes met at Brown's house, in Brighton, or at Mr. Martin's. Those fine ladies, of whom he had obtained flitting glances, taking himself speedily out of their way, though they were kind and gracious, feeling that their presence was no place for him. But was Mercy less a lady than those? He fancied her, in that pretty muslin dress, standing in the midst of such a company! She would not have looked out of place. She would have *felt* at home among them, as much as such an honest spirit could. For she would not look on frivolty in woman with patience. How could she, after what she had said? No; for it was not in her nature.

Perhaps, among those gaily-attired women, Peter Carradine's suit would not have been preferred in vain. And yet he never would have dreamed to desire such a possession as he might thus have gained. He was thinking of all this, and wondering if other women had such thoughts as she had acknowledged—such beliefs. She had said that they did not believe. And was it for this declaration she had made, that he now regarded her, as he had never before, and as he felt he never should regard *another* woman! But until she had expressed her convictions he had not thought that any such were possible to any human being. And before she uttered them he had begun to see what he now saw, in clearer light, in regard to himself and her. But he found that he *had* aspiration and an ideal, and that she satisfied both. So far as himself was concerned, he was convinced that it would be the consummation of a blessedness he had never so much as imagined, if he could hear her saying that she loved him; he felt drawn to seek her again and tell her that he placed his life in her hands, to do with as she would. But the sudden conviction of what the loss would be if she should show him his folly, as certainly she would, withheld him; not the thought that she could not be prepared for such a declaration—that it would, by its suddenness, surprise her beyond a possibility of seeing any right or reason in such a step.

So ended that day to him.

Johnson's day was ending scarcely less notably. He stood by his window, looking out. His wife had gone to bed, the candle was still burning, and he had said to himself, "Before I put out that light I'll speak to her;" but there he stood, and the prospect was that his speech would not be immediate. Indeed, the candle burned into its socket, and he did not perceive it. Then arose his wife and put the light out, and went up to the window, and said, in an agitated and yet resolute voice:

"Johnson, what's it mean? If you don't want to tell me, pretend there's nothing the matter. Only 'twould do you good, I'm let to think."

Then he turned and answered her, humbly enough:

"I'm trying to give myself to God. But I can't. I always thought that you was good enough for us both—but —help me, wife. The devil won't let me go along with you; or the Lord is angry; or what is it, I don't seem to see anything or know anything. I feel to believe I've lost my reason outright, and am like an idiot."

His wife, while she spoke, had dropped on her knees, and had hidden her face; when she knew that he was kneeling beside her, though she had thought to pray, she could not speak, but burst into tears.

Then he cried: "Oh, Lord Jesus, come quickly! come now! come down! come down! come this very minute! I've been a long time about it. I've put it off a great while, but I am here at last. Oh! for wife's sake, make me to be saved."

"Not for my sake, blessed Savior, but for thine own dear mercy's sake, thou lamb of God!" she said, fervently.

"Well then, oh Lord, because she asks it, hear me!"

"Nay, oh, blessed Jesus, but because thou hast promised that him that cometh to thee thou wilt in nowise cast out, for thine own precious promise's sake, hear Johnson."

"Yes! yes! oh, rend the heavens and come down!" he cried.

"Thou art here!" she responded with solemn composure—this was the wife's hour! "Are we not talking with thee! Hast thou not said that, when two or three agree, as touching anything, they shall ask thee, thou wilt hear? We are ignorant, and blind, and foolish, but thou art wise and seest all, and art rich to all fullness. So may we plead with thee! So may we ask thee! For he has something to ask thee!"

"Yes, Lord! To forgive us of our sins—make us thy true children—make us humble—make us—make us." There poor Johnson utterly broke down. He knew not what he wanted—what to ask.

"We know not how to ask what thou knowest so well to give. But, oh, give us patience for to wait on thee, and to believe that, when thou seest the time has come, thou wilt give us to see light. We have been a long while about it. We have wandered a great way from thee, and we are lost if thou wilt not come over the mountains of our transgressions, and love us freely, and forgive us all things! And thou hast promised. We will wait for thee!"

"How long, oh Lord! How long!"

"Blessed Savior, Jacob served seven years for Rachel, and seven more on the top o' that, and it was easy, for he loved her! Be not angry with us—give us patience—shall we not be able to love thee, and serve thee all our lives, only for the hope that, when we are done with earth, thou wilt receive us into heaven!"

"But, oh, the burden of sin!"

"Put it upon Him, poor Johnson! Put it upon Him. He said, my Jesus, didst thou not. 'Though your sins be as scarlet, they shall be whiter than wool!' Cast your burdens on the Lord!. Come, Johnson, make your full and free surrender—you can do no more than that. He must do the rest."

"Yes! yes! that's what I've been trying to see. Here I am, oh, Lord! do the work; do the work! I dun no' any thing; I can't do aught. I seem to have become a child for foolishness; but I shall see, if thou gives light."

"Yes!" said his wife, in solemn asseveration.

"I shall walk if I get the light."

"Thou art the way, the truth, the life!" responded she.

So as pilgrims struggling through the flood, they came up to land again. To land! Stumble not thou at it; I said not to the summit of the everlasting mountains.

"Wife," said he, "I'll never forget how you've helped me on this night."

"It is God!" said she. To him be all the glory, who had restored Johnson to her! "Who else could help you, poor Johnson?" and a deeper truth than either could perceive was in the speech of both.

When somebody said to Mr. Carradine:

"Johnson is converted," his answer was not in the least like that anticipated. He said, gravely:

"Well, sir; Mr. Johnson is a good man—so is his wife. I could always trust my property with Johnson."

And when, subsequently, after much hesitation, the farmer brought himself to say to Mr. Carradine:

"We want to bring Harry up all right, sir, and make him understand that all our blessings come from above; and so, if you have no objections, we would like to make a little remark in his hearing, when we all sit down to the table, after Mrs. Johnson has got our meals ready—" there he paused.

"Go on," said Carradine. There was quite as much compulsion as permission in the words as he spoke them.

"Would you have any objections, sir?"

"I don't understand you," said Carradine, with a brief

wave of the hand. Johnson understood the familiar sign. If he had an explanation to make, let him do it, and not waste another man's time.

"To ask a blessing," said Johnson, speaking very loud and fast.

Carradine laughed, but he checked himself in his laughter.

"I was thinking," said he, "do you take me for a scoundrel? Why, ask for your blessing. Don't you suppose I'll be glad if you get it? You ought to let your boy know you are a praying man—and that you've got a Father —above—as well as he!"

So, when Johnson, in compliance with this permission, said, one evening, as they sat about the supper table, "Oh, Lord, for this, thy bounty, make us thankful," Carradine surprised them with his prompt "Amen," and he added, "That's very neat and well done, Johnson—don't you ever omit it. You can say it in a breath. It's like sauce to the meat; I like it. We haven't brought all this out of the ground without some help, I reckon—and I don't understand how we never thought of it before. But I hope we haven't been as ungrateful as we seemed. Mind, don't you ever leave it out of the reckoning again."

CHAPTER XIII.

CORRESPONDENCE.

Miranda came home from the meeting with Sally Green, in the Elder's carriage, and she was busied for the remainder of the day in making the house seem "homelike." She occupied herself industriously until the milking was done, and the cows driven back to pasture. Her father would return with Elder Green in the morning, not before; and she must have all things ready for his comfort, so that home should seem as welcome as he was to it.

And now when her work was done, the house seemed lonely to her; so she took the hymn book, which had become in the past days so great a treasure to her, and went out to the big walnut tree, in whose shade was a bench that had stood in the porch for twenty years—but they had spared it from the house on an occasion, and ever since it had stood against the trunk of the mighty tree. Under these branches, it might be, she would find herself returning to the spirit which had seemed to be *her* spirit while they remained in the woods.

But she was really in a mood when a song of praise, or a burst of rapture, was quite impossible. She was tired and lonely, and thinking of Senior Jobson.

But surely, it could not be that He whom she had found in the wilderness would now abandon her. He would not forget her here! Sally Green had said to her, as they came home, that Mr. Collamer was going back to Brighton to-morrow. And she seemed to be surprised that Randy did not know it.

The reaction she was now experiencing was very natural —the solitude in which she found herself served merely to exaggerate the evidences.

The hymn book, she found did her now no good. While she read, her thoughts were wandering; she could command her heart through even one of those strains of thanksgiving, or bursts of praise, so frequently on her lips during the past days.

She was thinking of other things than those revealed by faith. Of persons whom her mortal eyes beheld; whom her mortal hands could touch; whose presence had made her heart beat fast with warm delight: or who had chilled it, and disturbed and wounded it, during these days of the meeting.

"I could be a better woman," thought she, "than I was asking to be be made. But, oh, what if I shall be a worse one than I was when I went up there!"

She left the bench in her disquiet, and walked along the lane to the farm-gate, and looked out upon the road. Did she look for Sally Green?

Had Senior heard of her return? Would he be coming up? She had time now to think of him. In spite of her promise, she had been converted! Could she compromise at this hour?

The old farm gate swung heavily behind her as she walked out upon the road. She took the road and walked slowly along—very slowly did she walk, and she was saying to herself: "Why should I always be going against my will?" Then she retraced the steps she had taken towards the tavern.

Why should she hasten? She was going nowhere. Not home as yet; it was so lonely down there.

By-and-by she saw, coming through the dim twilight, a figure that moved with directness, and with purpose, towards her. That was not Mr. Carradine, though he came from the direction of his house. And certainly it was not Mr. Johnson. It startled her to see that figure striding along so rapidly, with such determination, as one travels mindful of the bourne. She trembled; from head to foot was shaken. Yet this was not fear. No man than Randy more courageous. There was not a road she would have hesitated to walk, in the vicinity of Martindale, from sunrise to sunset alone. No, it was not fear, it was hope and suspense in conflict, that shook the frame, by no means weak; that stirred the spirit, by no means easily moved.

She thought, at first, she would return. She was going nowhere. She might as well return. She was tired—next day she must be stirring early—and might better be asleep this moment than wandering about, for she was tired, and that was the matter with her.

Still she kept the road, until she and Mr. Collamer could no longer doubt who it was they were about to meet. It was now nearly dark, but Miranda could see the smile on the minister's face; the smile that came for her, when he recognized her; and he thought he saw she was glad to meet him.

"I was going to stop for a moment before going to Brighton," said he. "I found I must go to-night, and I wanted to speak with you before I went away."

She joined him going down the road, and said:—"You can rest awhile, sir—and take something to eat."

"Thank you, I will," he answered; as frankly accepting as she had given the invitation.

Had she but thought to inquire of herself now, would not Miranda have found that all the influences of the wood were again around her? Could she not have opened the hymn book once more, and would not the aspiring sentiments unfolded there have so borne her soul aloft that she could again have cried:

> "Lend, lend your wings! I mount! I fly!
> Oh, grave where is thy victory?
> And where, oh Death, thy sting."

Mr. Collamer sat down in the porch of the humble farmhouse, and Randy busied herself preparing a meal for the tired man. By-and-by, before she summoned him, he went into the house and sat down by the table, where there was a candle lighted, and began to look over his note book. While he entered some items on a fresh page, he was thinking of affairs of quite a different character. And he said as he put up the book:

"You get a little time to read, don't you, Miranda? You're not always at work."

"Not always—but generally speaking busy, Mr. Collamer."

"You don't object to that, I dare say. Idleness would not agree with you, I think."

"I don't mind work as some do, maybe," said she. "I have made your tea pretty strong, sir."

"Thank you. I shall get to Brighton before midnight, on the strength of it."

"Couldn't you get any one to drive you over?" she asked.

"Oh, no—it isn't necessary. You know we must train ourselves, we ministers, to all sorts of hardships. I don't call the foot-journey one. But it is our business to be able to perform any service that may be required of us."

"I might harness the horse and take you to Brighton, easy," said Randy. "I should'nt mind it at all, but be very happy."

The kindness of the offer did not pass unnoticed of Mr. Collamer—but he must go his way on foot, he said, as he set out. He needed the exercise.

"I have heard how industrious you are," said he presently, moving away from the table, and taking Samuel Roy's old easy chair to the door, where he sat down. "You are fond of reading, I dare say, when you have a pleasant book."

"Yes, sir," and she did not make this answer because assured that it was the reply he would choose to hear. "I like it well," she said. It was true. Opportunity would have made a student of her.

"Then," said he, "I shall be able to give you some pleasure, I hope. I have some periodicals at home, which I will send you, if you will allow me. And maybe a book now and then, if I come across one that would please you. And will you read them?"

"I thank you," she answered; "I thank you, I am sure, that you should take the trouble!"

"If you will only tell me what the books are to you, what you think of them. Whether you like them—and why you like them," he stipulated.

"You will not be here," she answered, surprised.

"But I shall not be far off. Not so far off but I would hear, if you would only tell me," he replied; and as she looked towards him, in some doubt what he could mean, his face shining out from the dark shadows of the corner was like the radiant glory of a star. As far off maybe, but as real, as beautiful.

"You know where you will be stationed," said she.

"Not exactly."

"Yet it will be in this neighborhood, you are sure," she said—the tone of his answers perplexed her still more than the words.

"Oh no, not at all sure. It may be a hundred miles from here. But—I hope, that I shall never, as long as I live, be so far away that I cannot hear if there is anything in your mind, or heart, that you would say to me. You do not seem to understand me."

"No—I do not!"

"I should wish to hear from you. I should wish, I know, to speak to you. If I should write you would be certain to receive the letter. But—would you answer it?"

"No!"

This answer was so unexpected, that, for a moment, displeasure seemed to struggle with the young man's surprise. And he surely had a right to know on what ground she refused him!

"Why will you not, Miss Miranda?" he asked.

"Why then?" she answered. "Why should I write to you?"

"I said it would give me great pleasure to hear from you. To know that you are well, and how you passed your time. And if you thought well of the books you said I might send. And if, indeed, you received them in safety."

He spoke these words with a dignity, and a gravity, and a friendliness too, that invoked her honesty; overcame all her scruples of pride.

"I could not write a letter fit for you to read, Mr. Collamer," she said.

"Oh, then!" This brief exclamation was wonderfully expressive. It was for such a reason that she refused. He could manage such scruples, he believed.

"It is practice that makes perfect," said he. "I dare say you have not been accustomed to write much."

"I never wrote a letter in my life. You would be ashamed of it, if I should send you one."

"Try me, and see. How proud you are! That pride will interfere with your best spiritual growth, Miranda. You might comply with my wish, as a matter of discipline if on no other ground. Besides, if you need a teacher, am I not your friend? I assure you I will not be a hard master. Besides, do you want me to think that you do not care to know what I am doing when I go away from here? What the Lord's dealings with me are? About the people I shall make my home with, and the work that occupies me? When I am gone, shall you care no more about it than you do for all those thousands we saw in the camp-meeting? Strangers whom we may never meet again till the great day of the Lord?"

"I shall not forget you, sir," she answered. "There is no danger, sir. If I never see or hear from you again, I shall not forget you." Senior might have heard her say that without a misgiving.

"I like to hear you say so. It would go hard with me to think that I should no sooner be out of sight than out of mind. I should be gladder to think that, when you remember our camp-meeting, you would remember that I was among the brethren.

"I shall not forget it, sir. You helped me very much. I shall never forget how much."

"But then, you will not say that I may hear from you."

"Yes, sir—you shall hear."

"You will let the promise hold you?"

"I promise you," she repeated. "I never give my word for one thing, meaning another. If you want to see what a poor scholar a girl can be, you may. I never set up for a scholar. When I took the school to teach the children, I knew I could teach them to read and write, and spell—and geography and history. But I never expected that any one would think I was a scholar."

"No matter," said he. "Learning is not everything. No one would ever call you an ignorant woman. And I think that you will find, since you have given your heart to God, that there is a constraint upon you—compelling you to improve every faculty he has given you. I dare prophesy that you will find your whole being quickened. Intellectually as well spiritually, you will strive to do Him honor."

"Oh—you don't know, sir—"

"Yes, I know that it is best of all we have a lowly estimation of ourselves. Humility hurts no one. It is time I should be going."

He arose, and buttoned up his coat, and took his staff. It was now quite dark, but the full moon was rising.

"Good-bye, sir," said Randy. "And I'm sorry to say it."

"Good-bye," he answered. "And may God Almighty bless you from day to day—make you strong in every good word and work. Trust in all His blessed promises, Miranda. Let us seek to fulfil all His word, and try to live to Him, wherever we may be." Here he paused. He would do more than bless her by his priestly office. As a human friend and brother, he would yet take leave of her. "As soon as it is determined for me where I shall locate, and perhaps before, I shall send some word. I shall direct to the Martindale post-office; to your address. And you will be so kind as not to keep me long in doubt about my letter—whether you get it. You will have a long walk to take to the office. The mail comes in on Wednesdays and Saturdays. Perhaps you will find me then. It will be my fault if you do not. If you will let me speak so soon. For I do not wish to trouble you, my dear sister."

"Next Saturday?" she mused.

"Yes."

"I will go down to the postmaster's."

"You will not be sorry then, if you do not inquire for nothing."

"No—not sorry."

"Good-bye, then."

So they shook hands, and Mr. Collamer walked up the lane—passed through the great farm gate, and took the highway.

Miranda sat down on the door step and watched the rising moon. She sat there perhaps two minutes. She then arose and put away the tea things and the table—snuffed out the candle. Next she resumed her place, and she now had her hymn book in her hands.

She did not need to open it while she sang the hymn in which she seemed to hear the voice of the great congregation joining her:

"Softly now the light of day
Fades upon my sight away;
Free from care, from labor free,
Lord, I would commune with thee!
Thou, whose all pervading eye
Nought escapes, without, within,
Pardon each infirmity,
Open fault and secret sin."

The night was clear and still; such a deep quiet over hill and valley, that the sound of Randy's singing travelled farther earthward as well as heavenward, than she hoped for.

When she struck the notes of the second verse;

> "Soon, for me, the light of day,
> Shall forever pass away;
> Then, from sin and sorrow free,
> Take me, Lord, to dwell with thee,"

Senior Jobson, who had gone into his upper lot on some errand, caught the strain, and said to himself, "That's Randy;" and made it in his way to go home by the lane.

She had finished the verse, and was wondering why she had not mentioned Senior to Mr. Collamer, and wishing that she had done so, and questioning whether he would be pleased to know what she had promised the minister, when the innkeeper's voice rang out:

"Eh! I thought it must be Randy come home again. Good even."

Randy started to her feet—she was pleased, perhaps; great, certainly was her surprise.

"I was just thinking of you," she said. "I'm alone. Father isn't coming till to-morrow. Sit down, Mr. Jobson. How is Junior's wife?"

"So as to be moving. So you've been to the camp-meeting, and got home again. Anything gained a' that?" He took the seat she placed for him, and now, would it be given her in that hour what to speak? If it had not been to-night, this meeting! If it had been delayed till to-morrow! She had been so occupied with other thoughts—she had only begun to meditate on Senior's view of these things, which she had been brought to see in a new light. But here he was, and much must now be said that might easily make trouble—all depending on his way of taking it.

"I enjoyed it. You know I went up to please father."

"But, by all accounts, you stayed to suit yourself. What's become of the young loon who's stole all the girls hearts. I mean the preacher. Col—what's his name?"

"Collamer? He's gone to Brighton," answered Randy, pained to hear him spoken of with disrespect. Pained, if she but knew it, to hear him spoken of at all by Senior.

"He's been meddling with your business, I'm told. I laughed when I heard that. You couldn't help it, of course, any more'n you could catching a fever. It's a certain case with women. But, now I've got you back, I ain't alarmed. You look like my Randy," he said, turning her face toward him, and for a moment intent on studying it. "It might happen once in her life, says I, to please the old man, for his heart is set on these things. But Randy's true as steel to them she's give her word to."

"Yes—you're right there, Senior. But you ain't the man either that would be looking black and sour on a woman for taking some good thoughts into her heart, that would make her a better daughter and a better wife."

"Only for the speech o' people? They'll be calling the Spread Eagle, Saint's Rest, I expect. And you'll be having all the priests putting up with us—and you'll never dance any more. And you'll be getting up prayer-meetings in the bar—and Jobson will have to wear a white choker. The Spread Eagle might as well go to roost! You've shot him in the wing, poor bird!" There was an appeal in this lament not to be resisted.

"No—no—it won't be so," said Randy; "it isn't so at all. Of course we shall keep the tavern, and I won't interfere with you, if you won't with me! There, is that a bargain?"

"Done!" said Senior. "I thought you'd act up to yer promise. I didn't believe Randy was the girl to wheel about and change her mind, all for a set of knavish, psalm-singing, whining rogues, in a week and less."

He spoke with the exultation of a man who has won a bet —indeed, since the tidings of Randy come down to him from the meeting, he had been arguing with himself, and his conviction was that she would stand by her promise at all hazards. And such now was her purpose.

To prove to him that it was, she told him about Mr. Carradine's visit and proposal to her father. If her conscience had interposed between them, and if expediency had alone been consulted in accepting Senior's proposals, here, she showed him, was the opportunity afforded of liquidating the debt of the farm—and now was the time to show her suitor that believers must not be yoked with the ungodly!

It has not for a moment been supposed that Randy ever

lavished on her suitor the love of which her heart was capable. Neither had she for a moment been troubled by a consciousness of love withheld. The love had never been drawn out enlightened, enlivened. And her sense of honor now held her true and faithful to her promises, while her courageous spirit suffered from no self-suspicion, no fear that she should not be able to render all the service she had promised, both to God and to man. Senior had shown himself so ready to befriend her father—the reluctance her father would feel in accepting such service, only made her the more grateful for it.

He seemed to think the proposal Carradine had made for the land was one that proved his good will, beyond a doubt—and said that, after all, Peter had the heart to do the right thing, though it wasn't easy to deal with him; still it was by no means lost on Senior that Randy persisted in declining his favor, and relying only upon himself and the Spread Eagle.

So they talked together of their plans—of the building—and the wedding they should have on Christmas day, when all was completed; and Senior made all secure by saying, after he had risen to go home:

"You're in for it three hundred dollars to Carradine. Take that." He gave her a little strip of paper, printed, and written over. "That's our marriage contract," said he; "all your father's to do is, write his name on the back and go to bank and get his money, hand it over to Carradine. There now—do you see how it's settled? It's money lent, you know, and Randy's security! And here's a little note, if your father object to the money; it's all ready for him to sign; and when he reads it he'll see it's a token that I've lent him the money. But I don't want it, you can keep it with your things. Damn me, I'll trust the woman I've asked to marry me!"

Randy stood holding the papers he had thrust into her hand.

"Why you don't—you don't mean it! You ain't going to do it. Three hundred dollars! I!—I can't go security for't. I'd never sleep a wink again."

"I'll resk that," said Senior laughing. "If you can't settle it any other way, though, for your peace o' mind, let him sign the note—I guess he won't be troubled much for collecting, and I shan't take any interest. You girl! can't I trust you for that? Ain't you willing to save your old father's mind. Just depend on Senior, and let him depend on you."

"I never heard of anything like that!" said Randy, bursting into tears.

Senior was perplexed now beyond measure. If there was anything in this world that could disconcert him it was to have a crying woman on his hands. He could manage Junior's poor wife; but Randy's tears were a different thing.

"There! there!" said he, as he might have coaxed a child. "One'd think I'd done her an injury. Randy—Randy—"

"I mustn't let you do it. It's kinder than any one has ever been to you!" She had in mind the criticisms and strictures—and the judgment prophesied against Senior through many a year.

"Why, there! You're modest—haven't you been kind to me? You're the old man's daughter. If he had a son—and the son had been tolerably prospered, and had money in the bank and was going to build, wouldn't you think it odd now, if he couldn't spare a little to get the old man out of difficulty, special when he knew the security he had for't was of the best?—no chance of losing a cent? What would you think, my girl?"

"I think it's of God's leading," answered she. "I think I'll show the father he's been mistaken about his son. And that he's a prop to lean on."

"You will—you will," exclaimed Jobson, exhibiting a degree of pleasure that would have seemed incredible to his companions. Why should he care to have old Samuel Roy's opinion modified, or be covetous of the honor of propping such infirmity?"

He left her satisfied with what he had found, and Randy was persuaded in her mind that her promise to write to Mr. Collamer was a matter of no such importance that she should bring it up to-night. Mr. Jobson would never object to any means of improvement she might see fit to make use of.

CHAPTER XIV.

WHAT AN INKSTAND COST.

NEXT morning saw Miranda standing in the back door, waiting a moment till she should greet the rising sun. She had been up since day-break. There was work enough to be done—out-door and in-door service to be rendered; many a step to be taken in her father's stead; for she was experienced in farm labor, and could have conducted it with hardly less skill than her father, through one season and another.

She dressed herself in the dawn light, singing the while for company—then she looked at the cheque and the note, Senior's gifts last night, and laid them carefully away. Kneeling down, she prayed aloud for him, and for herself, and for Mr. Collamer, and for Sally Green, for Miss Fuller and Carradine, naming them all by name—then she went forth from her chamber and began her day's labor.

She did not expect her father till evening—and she worked with an energy unusual, even with her, thinking that in the afternoon she would look for her writing-book, and practice penmanship a little; for the letter she had promised weighed upon her thoughts. She had ten days, however; full ten days must pass, many more, it might be, before she should need to write to Mr. Collamer. She would make good use of the time, and she seemed to think that Senior, as well as herself, was concerned in it, that the handwriting should not entirely disgrace her.

But when work was off her hands, and she had prepared herself to sit down to her table, behold, the ink was dried in the old cork inkstand—and there was not a pen fit to make a mark—and her writing-book was missing!

Having satisfied herself of all these facts, Randy was not

the girl to sit down and regret. She immediately devised various methods by which to avert the disappointment. That on which she decided was to go to Elder Green's, and borrow of Sally what she needed. So she put on her sunbonnet and set out for the brown house on the corner.

But, arrived at the house, to her surprise she found the doors all locked, and no signs of life, except that Miss Fuller's window was open, and a pitcher of flowers stood upon the table before the window—it seemed to testify that she had been there that day.

Perhaps Miss Fuller might be at the school-house.

But this suggestion was unpleasant. There was Senior— she might go to him. But the house seemed to be full— wagons and horses were in the shed, and before the door; very likely persons going home from camp-meeting had stopped to laugh over their experiences with the jovial innkeeper.

She must go home then, for there was no neighbor near of whom she could ask the favor she desired, or who could grant it if she asked. There was the school-house, she thought again. Miss Fuller might be there. It was not pleasant to seek her on such an errand. But it seemed still worse to go home with empty hands, for she had set her heart on writing in the copy-book that afternoon.

How quiet the country was! The school-house looked as still as if its doors and windows, and the heavy blue blinds, had not been opened that day—as if no noisy children had run in and out. Perhaps such was the fact. She could not tell; she had not for the whole day heard the sound of a human voice.

So she went along the path that led to the little house; but when she tried the door it was locked. This new hindrance provoked her, as if it had surprised her. She wanted her writing-book and pen. How could she tell where the teacher kept her key, or kept herself? *Her* property was within the building, and she knew how she could recover it without asking aid of any one.

In the rear of the school-house was a window—it opened into the wood-shed, and the door that led into the shed had no lock.

By this method, then, she enters the school-house—looks

around her with some sadness and a sense of humiliation that exceeds her sense of injustice. Here and there she observes some slight changes. There are maps on the walls, and a great multiplication table—a black-board also—and some pretty prints of lovely young faces, nicely framed. It looks as if Miss Fuller kept the school!

Thus thinking, Randy opened the teacher's desk. She sees her book in one corner, a pen lying upon it; but before her hand can touch her property, the heavy lid falls with a crash. She thought she heard a sound—how her eyes ran up and down the room, searching its dark corners! No—she was alone. But she could hear her heart beat, she had had such a fright! She would rather die than be found under that roof. The first time she saw Miss Fuller she should tell her of it, but to be caught there like a thief!

Her hand was again lifting the lid, when the door was thrown open, and Mercy Fuller stood upon the threshold, towering as some awful statue of Nemesis, before Miranda's eyes. It seemed as if lightning had struck her, and paralyzed her, but only for a moment, for she exclaimed:

"Oh—oh—how under heaven did you happen to come here to find me acting like a thief?"

"I wanted a book," answered Mercy, full of shame and pity, for she believed as any other person might have done in regard to this intrusion, and the consternation of poor Randy.

"I never—never shall be able to make you believe that I came here on an honest woman's errand. I should think that the devil himself had managed the business," exclaimed Randy, and she dropped into the teacher's chair, with difficulty controlling her tears, for she felt that she had something to do besides giving way to her tragic sense of this complicated moment.

"You will make me believe whatever you choose to tell me," said Mercy, approaching nearer. "I'll take your word, of course. As I would that of any other Christian woman."

"You will!" cried Randy, starting to her feet again.—"Then I'll tell you what I mean, if I can. But it seems to me I'm killed. He said I was too proud. I wonder if pride hasn't got a death-blow now."

She clutched the desk as if to prevent herself from falling—and her face grew so pale that Mercy, alarmed, ran out to the spring, in the grove near by, and brought back a cup of water, which she would have constrained Miranda to drink; but she turned away, and said:

"I'll stand or fall on my own ground. Wait a minute. I am not a child. But I'm shamed to death. Now, stand round where I can see you full. I want to know if you believe me as I go along. Last night ma'am—I never thought I should be telling over this story with such feelings as I have. Perhaps it ought to be kept a secret. But I'd publish it on the house-tops afore I would have you, or any other woman, or child, think what by good rights you think, seeing me climb through a window to get into a house that was locked up, and wasn't none of mine. Thank the Lord! I'll keep my independence yet! Last night Mr. Collamer, he stopped in t' rest, on his way to town. I knew he wasn't coming back to Martindell, and he knew I knew it—and came to say good-bye. It was natural enough that he should wish to, after what passed up in the woods where I experienced religion." She said this as if she wanted the response which Mercy instantly gave.

"Certainly—natural enough, as you say."

"And he seemed to think—he is a kind man—that he ought to have some interest in me, knowing I was one of his converts. Though that wasn't the way he looked at it, for none of us, says he, are converted to any *man*, but to faith in the Lord Jesus."

"Yes," said Mercy, with friendly understanding.

"So, as he was going away, he asked me some things about myself. If I liked to read—and would I read some books of his if he sent them to me? Which, I am sure, was very kind of him," she said, as one who appeals for his own justification.

"Very kind," was the answer, spoken with a sympathy so full that it could not be mistaken. For Mercy admired the firmness that persisted in recounting all this, to the exposure though it might prove, of her shrinking heart.

"And then he asked me—"

This hesitation prompted Mercy to say:

"No, Miss Roy, you must not. I have no right to hear it. I have not the slightest doubt you can explain why you are here. I have no suspicion of you whatever. How could I have? Your secrets are your own."

"I'll make myself as clear as daylight to you," was the answer. "I should be ashamed ever to look into your face if I didn't explain. But I'll not be ashamed after."

"Then go on. I shall keep your secret."

Miranda went on, as if she had not heard this assurance.

"He asked me if he should write to me; would I answer his letters. He would want to know about Martindell, and all the people, and if the books came to me safely. I told him—I am glad I told him—that I should never write a letter but he would be ashamed to get from me. For I had never written a letter. But I forgot, for once I did; and I remember well what it cost me. But he encouraged me to think he would be glad to get the letter; and practice would make me perfect, as it did other people, he said. So I promised. And to-day I was thinking, while I was at work, I would come down and borrow of Sally Green, for I have lost my copy-book, and the ink was dried up, and I had no pen. I knew that Sally would not object to lending till I could get down to Brighton. But when I went down to the house I found it was locked up—and I was more disappointed than I ever was, I think. I ought to have gone home. But then I remembered the school-house—and where was the harm done, for all I could see, if I did not find my things, I could pay for any damage. So I came down here, and the next thing set up against me was the door locked. Then I was determined I wouldn't go back, and I remembered the old window. If I had broken my neck getting through, it would have served me right. And I came to your desk, Miss Fuller, for I thought I could borrow of you, and tell you in the morning—for I meant to bring it back."

"If you will take the pen and ink, and keep it, I will thank you," said Mercy. "But unless you do, I shall never excuse myself for wondering a single instant what it could mean when I opened the door and saw you. Why can you and I not be good friends? We have taken a good many steps toward it to-day, I think. Let this pen and inkstand be the evidence of our contract."

She fairly urged the cedar pen-holder, with its bright steel pen, and the little inkstand, into Miranda's hands.

"If you are not accustomed to writing," said she, "I am. Would it be any loss, or an offence, if I should give you direction now and then? I only came here for a book; if you will wait, we can go back together. I think Sally will be home by this time; she went down to Brighton this afternoon. Here is your copy-book. I kept it in the desk, it seems, without knowing it."

But, as they walked together towards Elder Green's, Miranda saw the Elder's carriage coming over the hill, and knew her father must be now at home. So she said, when they came to a point where the path struck into the highway:

"I shall never forget this day, if I live as long as Methuselah. I am going to show you that I can put down my pride. I will let you look at my copy-book, and you will know then how much I feel like writing a letter to Mr. Collamer."

"But you promised," said Mercy.

"Yes—I shall write the letter. He shall see exactly how it is."

"That's pride too," said Mercy; "not the worst kind, though."

"It is. It's pride. I wish—Miss Fuller, I wish you would pray it might be taken out of me."

"Is not that your own prayer? Do you suppose our Heavenly Father turns his face away from us, that he may not see what we desire? He hears you when he knows that you would indeed be humble, as becomes every human creature. I know that He will bless you. But I will ask it of Him. Then we must indeed be friends if we pray for each other to Him."

"Each other!" exclaimed Randy. "I for you?"

Mercy did not answer, but Randy, looking at her steadfastly, said again, not speaking this time as before:

"I will."

So ended the hunt for a medium—spirit not seeming sufficient. The letters should have a meaning surely—costing such a price, not mentioning the postage.

I have, of course, no words adequate to represent the state of Miranda's mind, either as she walked along the path that led towards home, or when, after two hours' steady talk with her father, she sat in her room alone, and made that first determinate essay with pen, ink and paper.

She wrote in the copy-book one line. No more. Her hand trembled too much, her heart beat too violently. So she wiped the pen, closed the inkstand, and put up the book sat down before the window, with her back to it, and gazed into darkness, and thought over her success in speaking for Senior, for her father had consented to talk with him next day!

Impetuous had been the action of Miranda's life; impulsive, fickle, not quite reliable, she had seemed to be. Violence had sometimes marked her conduct. Few and uncertain, thus far, had been the demonstrations of her love. But now the strong tide of feeling flowed with steady certainty in one direction. As she had never seen a woman who equalled Mercy Fuller, so she had never loved one as she now loved her. She longed to demonstrate the fact.

She went over the scene in which she had been enacting a part so extraordinary. At every point of it she could recall some word or look of grace—or of tender kindness, exceeding by so much everything she had rendered or received heretofore. Grateful, beyond any sense of gratitude of which she was ever before cognizant, she felt towards Mercy. It was a relief to know that she understood about this business of the correspondence. She felt that, somehow, she was safer. She would keep nothing from her henceforth. She meant to be a friend. To use this proffered friendship to its utmost highest use. And, as she thought, she had really some adequate sense of what that highest use might be.

Oh, it were something rare and fine to hear often such a voice?—to feel often under such a gaze! To be counselled by such serenity and wisdom.

How willing was she to come into such subjection as communion with this kind of character supposed! What aid, and help, and joy might she not anticipate from it!

CHAPTER XV.

DIVERS GIFTS, AND WAYS OF RECEIVING.

The next morning Samuel Roy was in his barn at work, and Randy in the shed churning. Sally Green appeared.

"I thought I would come up and see what there is left of you," said she. "It isn't so easy to bring yourself round to business after such a week."

"I don't know," said Randy, continuing her work, while Sally sat down on the kitchen steps, "I found so much to do when I got back, I couldn't see my way clear yesterday. It was hard to keep from shying off the treadmill."

"Plenty to do, of course—we are to have the teacher back to-day. I don't much mind that, though," said Sally. "She takes care of herself very well."

"You ought to be glad, I think. Any one that lodges her will be well paid for the pains," said Randy, to Sally's amazement. To her displeasure also; it was like Randy to take religion in this exaggerated fashion, and slay herself on the sword of duty.

"Nobody knows anything about her," she answered coldly; "she seems very well. But I don't know as it's so much of a favor. Besides we haven't any children to send to the school! It's nothing but bearing other people's burdens. We can't help that of course."

"I wish she would come and stay with me. I do indeed. I like her well," said Randy with a spirit which Sally could not help seeing was genuine; and she liked it none the better.

"Why won't you have her here to stay, then?" asked she, incredulous.

"If I could make it as pleasant for her as you can, I wouldn't stop to think twice," answered Miranda. And her friend thought, "True enough—she is converted."

"I was down to Brighton yesterday," said Sally. "I saw Mr. Collamer there—he walked down from Hickie's."

"Yes, I know it," replied Randy.

"Why, did you see him?"

"Yes—he was on his way. He did not mind the journey."

Sally's face changed. She felt her pleasure lessen greatly, in what she had to say.

"I saw him in a shop, and he had these two hymn books—and one he gave to me and the other is for you! He wrote our names inside. And he said it was in remembrance of the happy days we spent at the meeting together."

Randy left the churn, and wiped her hands, and took the hymn book Sally gave her; but she laid it on a shelf without opening it.

"Why don't you look at your name, where he wrote it," asked Sally, turning her eyes full on Miranda, more than ever doubting and suspicious.

"So I will," she answered; and she took the little book and read. "J. Collamer, to his friend Miranda Roy, in remembrance of June 1, 1840."

"Now you may read mine," said Sally—and she thrust her volume before the eyes of her friend, who, for a moment seemed unable to comprehend what was before her.

"To Sally Green, with the best wishes of her friend, Joseph Collamer." Then followed the same date, June 1st, the date of an eventful day of the camp-meeting, written with a flourish that made the page conspicuous.

The difference of phraseology, still more the difference of penmanship, had evidently produced an impression on the mind of Sally.

"He is going to write to father when he is located," said she; "and—" She did not finish the sentence.

"Shall you use your book?" she asked.

"I always used my mother's—but it hasn't all the hymns in it—not all we sang at the meeting," answered Miranda. "This one has better print, and how smooth and white the paper is!" She laid the open page against her cheek. "It has the feel of satin," said she.

"I shall never use any other book—that's what he said he hoped."

"Did he say so?"

"Yes," answered Sally—but she did not add that she had first told him that it was the only book she should now use.

"I suppose that is what he gave them to us for—use," said Randy ingeniously.

"Are you sorry to have him gone, Randy?"

"Yes."

"He will be coming back."

"But then his work will lead him to very different places from this, Sally—such a man!"

"I suppose he is going to make a great preacher. That's what they all say. You saw there wasn't a man up there to the meeting that could begin with him. How lovely he looked."

"He seemed to show me the truth clearer than anybody else—it seemed easier to think right, and to do right, when he was near to put you in the way—or clear up difficulties—show you your mistakes," said Randy, thoughtfully; and she was churning at a rate something short of imperative in its demands on the butter. "But, lovely? it was terrible to see him I thought."

"I guess we all felt the same way about that," said Sally. "Do you suppose—I wonder what kind of a woman he will marry! I think Miss Fuller would just suit him—don't you?"

"I thought you married her to Mr. Carradine the other day."

"Of course I did—people never marry where they ought to, it is said. *I* don't know anything about it. Don't you think, though, they would make a good match?"

"Who?"

"Who?—I just said. The minister and Miss Fuller. What's her name—Mercy."

"No," said Randy.

"Why not!"

"Because they don't seem to be alike. Besides they don't seem to think alike. I suppose that's what I mean by saying they're *not* alike. They are both quiet persons, and they know a great deal about the world, of course. But they would never be married."

"You know a good deal about it!" said Sally, laughing. "Of course she'll have to take Mr. the hedgehog, because I said so. According to that way of doing things, I guess *you* had better take Mr. Collamer."

Did Sally see the sudden start that answered to this proposition? Did she see the sudden flushing of the face before her? To what purpose were her eyes fixed so intently on Miranda, if not to see, to note, and to remember?

"Don't talk so," answered Randy, speaking as if she had been pained.

"I think," said Sally, indifferently, as if it was of the merest speculation that she spoke, and no one could possibly be concerned in the conclusions she arrived at, "he will want a wife who has money. He is so free—that's what father thinks—he's very free with his money. He has a little, but it can't last forever, the way he uses it. He has such liberal notions, it would be misery to him to be married to a poor woman. When he gets to be a great man, he will need it more and more. He makes so many friends wherever he goes, and if he buys hymn books for all the girls he sees—I suppose he does, don't you?"

"Very likely."

"If I thought he did, I'd never look into mine then!" said Sally, in a pet; but she laughed when Randy looked at her astonished.

"You would not?" said Randy.

"No indeed. I would have liked it better if—if he had n't said anything about you, of course."

"Would you, Sally, truly?"

"Would I? Ask yourself. Would you?"

"No, I think not. I hope not, surely. Why should I?"

"Randy, you are going to be too good, I see. That's you, no half-way about it. That's what grandma said when she prophesied about you—it's a true daughter of Samuel Roy that you have got to be. Are you going to do everything to suit everybody for the rest of your life? Suppose I asked you to send back that hymn-book to Mr. Collamer. Would you do that?" Again Sally's looks, as she regarded Randy, belied the words and tone in which she spoke. Underneath the bantering inquisitiveness was a more serious curiosity.

"No," answered Miranda.

"Oh? Why not?"

"Because I did not ask him for it. And it pleased him to send it to me. So I shall use it just as I have used my mother's. And I am glad he sent it. I shall learn some of the hymns too. And I mean to learn all those we sung up there so often in the woods."

The serious, mild manner in which this was spoken, seemed to produce its effects on Sally. She said:

"You're Randy yet! You're not going to be grandma's kind—nor your father's either, I guess. You won't be an awful perfect saint!"

"Mind that you, for your part, Sally, take your mother for an example. There's no such woman in these parts as Huldah Green. I didn't see a single face up there that looked like hers. But I expect your grandma is more of what we call a praying woman."

"I'm crazy to stay here, Randy. But there—you've got your hymn-book. I couldn't sleep half the night for thinking I must come up so early to bring it to you, and wondering what you'd say about it. What will you do all day?"

"I've work enough to keep me going on till Saturday night."

"You used to be always reading. She seems to have a lot of books on her table; if you would like to come down some time, you can look at them."

"Some time, when she is at home, I will come down," said Randy.

Miranda went on churning, thinking as she did so, "What could Sally mean?"

Sally returned home questioning as doubtfully, "What's Randy thinking of?" And it seemed as if something had come between them to make unlooked-for and unwelcome revelations.

It came to pass that Huldah Green's thoughts did revolve around the teacher during the days of her stay with them, in such a way that she often found herself, while Mercy was at school, conducting her labors with a view to securing a few minutes of uninterrupted chat with her. The duties which occupied her days must by no means be neglected—but they could be arranged with foresight, and completed perhaps in less time than they generally required. Even habit must surrender before a sufficient cause. She was drawn, and day by day became more conscious of the drawing, towards Mercy, by a subtle, irresistible influence.

One afternoon, the teacher came home from school and found the family in the midst of a consultation which seemed to have provoked a good deal of unpleasant feeling.

She was not taken into the counsel of any portion of the household; and Huldah seemed to be the only one who did not actually avoid her when the family had dispersed. So far from avoiding her, she took her knitting work and went into the large east room, the pleasant family room, and sat down there by the window, and when she saw Mercy passing the door, she called her in.

As they sat talking quietly together, Huldah suddenly laid down her knitting work, and said the very words she had hindered herself from uttering, under all provocation, since the beginning of her married life.

"When you are thinking to get married, Miss Fuller, don't marry a widower; don't marry a man a great deal older than yourself too. Those are my advice."

"I will try to recollect," Mercy replied.

"Yes, you smile—but. Well I suppose one may as well, if he has a good conscience in the matter. I ain't partial to tears myself. I was never a crying child, and I can't be a crying woman. I suppose one has to learn the trick young. But there seems to be a deal of trouble in the world, of one kind and another, Miss Fuller. People wouldn't give me credit for much experimental knowledge; but still I'm not so dead ignorant of it. And that is the way of Providence to lead us. There would be no holding of us in, with bit and bridle even, I expect, if it wasn't for our experience, which humbles us and keeps us low."

"I think a good heart, truly happy, would not be the proud heart He holds far off," said Mercy.

"You don't expect He meant us to be truly happy, any one of us."

"Why yes, indeed!"

"Are *you* a happy woman?" asked Huldah. If she had

thought a moment, she would not have asked the question. But she had asked, and Mercy answered:

"Yes, I think so. Very nearly, Mrs. Green."

"You are younger than I am. I have looked about; I have thought it over a good deal. We all have our burdens which to cast on the Lord, and find him sufficient."

"Well for us that it is so," responded Mercy, of whom obviously nothing but response was now required.

"I have been married now this thirteen years. Sally Green was seven years old when I came to this house, and the Elder gave her to me, and bid me be tender of her. I suppose, Miss Fuller, if I had nursed and brought up a house full of my own, they wouldn't have caused me the trouble that child has. Not that she's different from other children; but I was always so afeared of doing wrong by her! I wanted to do right. I felt so sorry for the little creatur whose own mother was dead and buried. And that was one great reason why I come. The Elder wanted me. And I knew if I didn't take him, then some other girl would, and maybe for his money, who wouldn't be tender of the little girl. Besides I had been a friend of her mother's. But Sally isn't like her mother. Sometimes I think it would have been better for all if I had kept outside the house. But I did it thinking it was for the best, and a leading of the Lord. Which the Elder said it clearly was."

"I have no doubt of it," said Mercy.

Huldah looked up so brightly, and seemed so thankful for the encouragement there was in this assurance, as to prove that it was well deserved. But a shadow crossed her face the moment after, as she went on.

"There has been many a time when, if she had been my own, I would have done differently by her than I did; but then somebody would have thought me cruel; and it was the child's loss, to my mind, when she got off many a time with just a correcting word, and hardly that sometimes; for it was the Elder's belief that the Holy Spirit would do all the work, when she got beyond us, for she was the child of prayer, says he. She might have been much different, it seems to me. For now that she has got religion, it's on such contrary ways the Spirit has to work, and there hasn't been a miracle performed for her yet. There's something wrong about it somewhere. I don't want to seem blasphemous, as I'm sure you'll believe, Miss Fuller; but you know a great deal, and it seems to me you'll see it clear; if she'd been trained right there wouldn't have been no occasion for any trouble about her. I don't see that it's easily done, when any one has always had his own way in everything, to come round and see the right truth about giving up 's way to God. I'm talking about Sally Green! She's my child! As good as mine, every bit and grain; but I feel to think the Lord won't lay it up against me if I chose to keep peace in the house instead of setting 'em all up against me in a body. But I've made a mistake somewhere, for it's come round, what I feared, by being too kind—just as it was going to, if I had gone the other way. Did you ever think one way was about as dangerous as another, being overly kind, as bad as overly cruel?"

"There must be reason in all things," said Mercy, feeling that she was not called on to say much. It was n't counsel but expression, vent of her own thoughts, that Huldah wanted.

"The very words I've had on my tongue's end a thousand times," said she. "You don't think I am a talking woman? It's rare that I have any words. I've worked hard, and found it was the best thing. If I'd nothing to do but sit and fold my hands, the Lord have mercy on me! And there isn't the man or woman in the town of Martindell can say I ever made the first complaint against the Elder. But there's been a mistake somewhere, and I'm free to own it; because, for one thing, I think if you see anything in Sally goes against your sense of right, she being a member, you would speak to her! You needn't tell me that you've done it. It's for her. For her mother's sake, whose eyes I've felt have been watching me these thirteen years. And if you could know how I've prayed to her to show me what she'd have me to do for Sally's sake! For a mother's heart, I thought, could show me best of all—and I never had a child of my own. Sometimes I've longed for it—but I thank God! things are so. For if they had been otherways, they might have been worse. If I'd known better what a mother's duty was, I might have performed it worse, and been like those who, after they're exalted to heaven in privileges, show they're only fit to be cast down to hell. It's all a curious business—but it would take an angel for a woman to do her duty by a widower and his children."

"I believe that," said Mercy. "And I'll help you if I can. Martindale, for all its pleasant farm lands, so pretty and quiet, seems to be very much like the rest of the world, Mrs. Green."

"I suppose," said she, "it's wisdom is the making of us all. And I don't feel to believe we are wiser than our generation, here in Martindell. I hope, Miss Fuller, that I am not a proud woman, set up with notions because the Elder is what you'd call a rich man for a farmer—" Again she hesitated, but seemed to think she had gone too far to retreat, for she continued hurriedly, though her manner became more composed and assured as she went on. "I know that the most valleyable men in the country have worked their way up—but there's a difference—and there's some that havn't got it in them to make men of theirselves. I know that, no matter how poor a man, if he was a right down noble fellow, I wouldn't object to giving Sally Green to him. But it's to be happy people are looking for when they set up for themselves—they must be good if they are to be happy, I expect. And that is the reason that, for thinking of what will come on Sally if she keeps on with Oliver Savage, the peace of my life is gone."

"And who is Oliver Savage?" asked Miss Fuller.

"He's a widow's son that lives up the road beyond Peter Carradine's. He's harvested now three years with Elder Green. He is not the man, Miss Fuller, not the man for Sally. He wouldn't do for a son to the Elder. You wouldn't think, Miss Fuller, that Sally could look at him, and think of loving him, and living all her life with him. But it's coming to that! it's coming to that! There's nothing short that I can see. Talking's no good. I dursent speak a word, for it's the thing that's hardest to get that people set their hearts on having mostly. And she would never believe that her father and I cared more for her happiness than for anything else in this life—for we are getting old, and we must leave all—and she will be left, and must stand for herself, and if she hasn't her husband to lean on, and work with, and look to, and love!"

"If she were never married at all, Mrs. Green, I don't

see that it would be the most dreadful thing in the world," said Mercy.

"Not by a great deal, Miss Fuller! But she *will* be married. It's in the nature of things. Her father is a rich man, and a good man, and she is his only daughter, and not a bad-looking girl—"

"She is very pretty."

"Yes, *we* think so. Then, if she must be married, isn't it the chief thing that she should be happy?"

"Yes—surely."

"Oliver Savage will make her miserable. He'll ruin Sally. And she'll ruin him! But they don't see it. You can't make 'em see it. You can't think how it worried me up there at the meeting. And I am not a worrying woman. But I couldn't get it out of my mind so as to enjoy religion as I have. But I tried to think what I would if Jesus was on earth, and I knew he was just as near as if we could see him—and so I asked him to help us—but, Miss Fuller, such things seem to run their course. And I've the misgiving that, after we have prayed our best, we don't get just for the asking; if Sally should take Oliver, her father never will consent to it, that would not be the Saviour's pleasure. I cannot think it would be. It seems to be too late. Sometimes I feel as if we would all go to destruction if it did happen and—. He is a carousing fellow. That's his reputation. I know he was very serious at the meeting. He was brought in at the revival, but the last time he was here he didn't look right to me, as if he was sober and diligent, serving the Lord. If he was set up—he is a dreadful vain fellow—I'm not slandering! I want you should see Oliver —if he was set up once into a fortune like, not so slaving poor as he has always been, I'm afraid to think what he would come to. He curls his hair and dresses in a white vest on Sunday—you may know him by that token. It isn't because he is too neat and nice, but because he thinks so much of himself—"

There was a supplement to this conversation, which was broken off by the entrance of the young lady in question. She came through the front door, and so into the large sitting-room of the many windows and the yellow painted floor. She seemed a good deal excited, and fluttered about several moments before she spoke, or seemed likely to alight. But when her mother put down her knitting-work, and said to Mercy that she would bring a light, Sally said:

"Mother, do you think Oliver has been asking me to go to Brighton with him for the Fourth!"

"H'm," said Mrs. Green. "Oliver?—Oliver Savage? What did you say to him, Sally?"

"I told him, if I went, that I should go with father."

"Right!" said Huldah, out of the fullness of her surprise and satisfaction.

"But I didn't tell him I should choose to stay at home before I would go with him."

"Would you, Sally? Would you now, dear?"

"Why yes, mother. What are you thinking of?"

"Thinking that I am glad you say so, Sally. I wonder that he asked you."

But Sally did not tell that she had half given her promise, not a week ago, for this very ride, and had it not been for the hymn-books she would certainly have gone. But the hymn-books had changed her mind and had set her to thinking more anxiously about Randy Roy than Oliver Savage.

When Oliver, foolish and vain, and presuming as he was, met her half an hour ago and said to her:

"I was on the look-out for you—did you see me coming?" she answered:

"Did I see you coming? No! I wasn't thinking of you."

He looked at her as much surprised as if she had not been the Elder's daughter and an only child. Then he said, speaking with far less confidence this time:

"I wanted to say something about the Fourth, you know."

"About the Fourth?" she repeated. "What Fourth?"

"There are going to be great doings at Brighton. Oration and procession, and fireworks; but it will be the best of all to see them with you, Sally. That's going to be my pleasure in it."

"Oh, I shall go with father and mother," answered she.

"What's that!" he asked, or rather demanded, as if he had a right.

This tone was new, and seemed to make its impression on the girl. She did not wish to offend Oliver—she thought just now that she felt sorry for him, and vexed at herself.

He saw that she was confused, and added boldly:

"You promised me. Don't you mind your promises better than that? Isn't any one to depend on you if you give your word?"

"Did I promise? I don't remember it."

"You gave me to believe that you would go with me. And I expected it. But if you had rather go with your father, of course—"

"You'll be down there, won't you?" she asked impatiently.

"I don't know," said he; "likely not. What would I go for? There's half-a-dozen girls would be glad enough, but I am not going to invite them."

"What's the mere getting down there? The pleasure is in walking about," said she. "Walking about with the crowd and seeing the sights! That is the Fourth for me."

"Who are you going to walk with then—your father too?"

"Father will be looking after mother and grandma, I suppose. Two women will be enough for one man to take care of, I should think. If you should happen to come along when the crowd was pretty thick and noisy, I think father would be glad enough to have you look after me."

"Oh," said Oliver, greatly relieved, and looking his gratitude with great admiring eyes; "I understand. You're on my side, Sally, if he isn't! I'm satisfied! Golly, you beat me! you beat everybody for your way of doing things."

"Who said I was on your side, or he wasn't? I don't want you to be saying around the country I don't keep my word, or I'm proud. That is what I mean," answered Sally, sharply. But he cared not what she said. He should be seen on the Fourth of July walking about Brighton, hand in hand, with Sally Green!

CHAPTER XVI.

"WHAT IS SMALL AND WHAT IS GREAT?"

The ten days that must intervene before the next Saturday were passing, one by one.

Miss Fuller's week at Elder Green's had ended, and she was now at the next house whose doors opened for her.

Sally was not sorry. Such industry as she had manifested during the past few days was wearisome to her, and she had occupied herself thus diligently only that she might avoid the presence so distasteful to her. She expressed no dissatisfaction while the guest remained, nor relief when she was gone—it was rarely that the whole mind, rarely that the true mind of the girl betrayed itself; and she was afraid of Miss Fuller.

But Huldah, the mother, was full of hope, and even satisfaction, thinking of the improvement she fancied she could see in the daughter of the house; mistaking the constraint under which she was living, for a real change of life and purpose.

In her leisure moments, day by day, Randy occupied herself with the copy-book.

With some hesitation, she showed the book to Miss Fuller when she came to thank her for the cherries sent to her by little Harry Johnson; but she had no reason to regret the criticism thus invited. Neither she nor any rightly striving mortal would ever hear aught but encouragement from Mercy Fuller's lips.

The gift of the cherries deserves to be dwelt upon for a moment as we pass, because of the circumstances attending its offering.

One morning Randy went into the lane, as she had done on other mornings during the past week, in the hope that she should see little Harry pass by. She wanted to make her peace with the lad; and the case had been a hard one if she had failed to do it backed by a tree full of luscious cherries.

To her surprise, when she came to the tree that stood nearest the gate, for one side of the lane was bordered by these trees of early fruit, she saw Harry standing close by the rail-fence, and looking up with longing eyes at the branches, which grew so low that, standing on the topmost rail, he might easily have reached them. But evidently he had committed no trespass or depredation as yet—his hands were full of clusters of "pokeberries"—there was red ink in prospect, and he seemed already to have made some rude experiments in pressing the juicy fruit, if one might judge from the palms of his hands, incarnadined.

When he saw Miranda approaching him, the little fellow's face was covered with confusion, but he stood stock still, though his impulse certainly was to run away fast as his feet could carry him. She saw at once that the conference she had somewhat dreaded remained in her conduct, according to her will, and was not disposed to make a mistake in using opportunity.

"Oh, Harry, is it you?" she said, coming quite close to him, and speaking with that frank, kindly voice, which had won her the confidence of the children before the unfortunate day with which we began her history.

He hung his head and ground his shoes through the dust of the farm road, that ran between the fields bordered by those famous trees.

"I wanted to send some cherries to Miss Fuller," said she. "I am so glad you came. I was going to look for you, for you can carry the basket to the school-house for me. Will you, Harry?"

The boy looked up, unconscious now of the tears with which his cheeks were wet, so kindly Randy spoke.

"Yes, ma'am," said he. "Goll darn it!"

"And when you come back at noon, if you stop," said she, "you shall find another basket ready for you to carry home. And tell your mother, if she wants any cherries to dry, she can have them. I've dried a bushel, and they're not half gone yet. Everybody's trees around here seemed to fail but ours."

She was now standing on the fence, plucking the ripe fruit by the handful, and Harry was gathering up the treasure into a pile for Miss Fuller's basket.

"Eat as many as you want," said she. "How do you like the new teacher, Harry?"

"First rate, I does!" he answered, with a little defiance it seemed. He thought Randy would have something to say against her; and—but would he actually support her if thus the cherry prospect should be endangered?

"I knew you would like her," said Miranda. All right as to the cherries! "She is so kind. And she knows so much to teach you. You must learn all you can while Miss Fuller stays in Martindell. I wish she could stay forever!"

Yes!—she actually meant it! The child's eyes were not to be deceived as he fixed them in undisguised surprise and questioning on Miranda. She was actually in earnest.

"*Be* you converted, Randy?" he asked, with his eyes fixed on her, apparently for this moment forgetful of the fruit.

"Oh! what makes you ask that, Harry?" she said, blushing scarlet, and seeming quite distressed.

"I heerd say so to hum. Father is. And I saw you the day when we went to camp-meeting. Oliver Savage, he said you was one of the sisters now."

"How did you like the camp-meeting, Harry?"

"Oh, I liked it. But it wasn't fun, like the Fourth of July down to Brighton last year. We're going down to see it again. Be you, Randy?"

"I guess not."

"Uncle Carradine says we ought to have a Fourth up here to Martindell. He brought me such lots o' torpedoes and fire-crackers!" Saying this, he threw a torpedo slyly against the rail fence, and was mightily pleased when he saw how startled Randy was at the explosion. Then he said:

"Wouldn't you like it now, 's well's the camp meeting?"

"Oh, it is very different. The meeting was so pleasant—I can't tell you how pleasant it was to me."

"I should think you was converted," said he, thoughtfully surveying her.

"What do you mean, Harry?"

"You tell me first, now—be you?"

"If it means to be converted to be sorry, very sorry that I got out of patience with you that day, I am!" said she, looking straight at the little fellow, who swung himself around on one foot, with a private "Goll darn it," to get rid of the embarrassment he felt, she looked at him so earnestly. "And it would make me happy if you would just say that you forgive me for it. And I shall love you always. And give you all the ripe cherries you want, as long as these trees stand." That was a climax! He looked up at the laden branches—surveyed the first fruits of forgiveness with a bright recognition.

"Kiss me," she said, "and then we shall be friends always."

God's own forgiveness, she believed, was in the kiss she felt upon her cheek. Then Harry ran off, quite convinced that Randy was converted, ready to fight in proof of it, if that were necessary. When he brought back the basket, at noon, he brought also a bottle of red ink, viz: juice of the "poke" berries, which he had pressed through his pocket handkerchief, for her. Years afterwards that bottle stood upon her shelf, a relic, prized with fond religious care.

Already Mr. Roy had given his note to Senior Jobson, and the Carradine claim was wiped off from the old man's farm. It was brought about in this manner.

The day after her father's return from the meeting, Randy took the opportunity to mention Senior Jobson's visit, and his talk about the mortgage. She dwelt upon the fact that he had seen how disagreeable it must be for the old man to feel, under the present circumstances, any indebtedness to that man—made much also, by repetition, of the fact that Senior had heard of Carradine's attempt to get possession of the fine lot across the creek, and that he regarded the offer as by no means a creditable one to Peter.

Then she showed the old man the check on the bank, and told him that, if he would have the money of Jobson, all he need to do was write his name on the back of the slip of paper, and take it to the bank; in less than twenty-four hours Peter Carradine's claim would not be in existence. The great result of a transaction so simple seemed deeply to impress old Samuel, but he went away to his work saying little—secretly disturbed by the suspicion that this might be a temptation of the adversary.

But by-and-by light seemed to dawn on his slow-reasoning mind, the business appeared in a new aspect. What if Senior's advances were the first signs of a drawing of that man towards a better life, and to the work of faith? What if, in any manner or degree, he should be responsible for the future career of Senior Jobson? Would it do for him to hold himself aloof from such a man with a Pharisaic pride?

And then he could not question that to be free from the old debt would be a pleasure to Miranda. He wanted to please the dear girl. She had not urged him, he reflected; she only told him what Senior said, and showed him the check, and remarked that it was kind of Mr. Jobson, and a true neighborly act, according to her thinking. And Randy had a reason for this which, of course, remained unguessed by her father. Who could prophesy the changes that might take place before Christmas? By that time, it might be, her influence would have made of Senior Jobson a man whom her father would rejoice to call his son. And if change did really take place nowhere except in the rebuilding of the Spread Eagle, time enough to disturb the old man's wonted ways of thinking when there should be need.

Roy had begun to regard Senior and his check with some favor, urged by the reflection noted above, when the innkeeper made his appearence, with intent to conclude the business. Jobson was a shrewd judge of character, and the necessity of coming to an understanding with Samuel Roy, did not in the least perplex him. He was certain that they should finally agree, that the old man would be influenced by one motive or another, so far as to accept the service tendered him.

He was certain, because he never disappointed himself; whatever he had the will to do, he did; and was by no means to the last degree scrupulous in employing the forces by which his pleasure was to be accomplished. Though a talker, he seldom took himself or any of his doings for a text—not even his brother entered into his secret confidence. He belonged to the class of people who are a surprise to their friends; uppermost is a bland, easy exterior—good humor—no aversion to fun and frolic at the proper seasons—a familiar manner—quite insinuating in his talk with younger men—an alluring freedom from the laws of moralists underneath, an alertness that can never be surprised; a penetration that cannot be deceived; a force of will that may be blind, but still is under check, and some sort of guidance; a strong man under the dominion of the flesh, who could yet swear by his conscience. By far a richer man than any one suspected, for he had been prudent, in spite of seeming prodigality, and his inn was a popular place of resort to the people round about.

It was really a matter of the little consequence he represented, that he should offer to loan Samuel Roy three hundred dollars—and this was the best way he could devise to resent the Carradine affront. He knew Carradine well enough to understand that nothing would touch him more nearly than poor old Samuel's mild refusal to come to his terms of reconciliation.

He said to himself, as he crossed the lot to treat with the old man, that he should wind him round his finger in less than ten minutes, and so the event proved. The feat was done so cleverly, so " neatly," he said to himself, as he retraced his steps, without taking with him anything to show the liability of Roy, that he was disposed to think it one of the best operations he had ever carried out to a successful conclusion.

But when he went back to the tavern, he asked himself why he shouldn't himself perfect the transaction—get the money from the bank for Samuel, and let the old man settle with Carradine before night? It was Jobson's way. Deliberate in planning, but working like a whirlwind when the arrangements were complete. So he saddled his horse and rode down to Brighton, procured the money, and was back again before noon. Roy was hardly surprised at this, though the kindness of the act quite overwhelmed him. Tearful and confused, and apparently oppressive to the recipient, his thanks rolled out.

He came into the house with Jobson, and told Randy what had been done.

"Then you'll sign the note, father," said Randy. She had already written his name at the foot of the note, and now brought it to him, with a book and a pen wet in ink—

he was to make his mark. He did not seem to quite understand her, but he had a way of yielding to his daughter in most matters, for he was old and feeble, and relied more than he knew upon her youth and strength. So he took the pen, and held it between his teeth while he put on his glasses.

"I'll read it for you, father," said she; and she took it up to read.

"Pooh," said Jobson, "none of that;" and he seemed about to take the note from her—but she stepped backward beyond him, and said, in a resolute voice, that made Senior think of the Spread Eagle exultant:

"We can't borrow money of any man, sir, without giving something to show for't. Who knows what'll happen?"

"Who cares?" asked he.

"I promise to pay three hundred dollars, at my convenience, to Senior Jobson, for value received," read Randy. "And here I have signed your name, father, and now you can make your mark. Right here," pointing to the place.

"Certain," said Samuel, then he looked up at Jobson, "it's all right. Who knows what a day'll bring forth?"

"Very well—sign away," said Senior. "There's no telling what six months will do for a man, Samuel. So make your mark."

It was a trembling cross that stood for the old farmer between his Christian name and the name he had inherited When he had made it he looked up at Randy, but she had turned away, and was standing by the window. Jobson only stood by him, and Jobson took the note, and said:

"There's no knowing what'll happen to a man in a day or a year, as you say, Samuel. I may die, you know—I reckon I won't leave you to be badgered by my heirs—when you get the money, pay it, if you like; and if you can't—" he tore the note into a thousand fragments—"it's between us three. If you was my old father sitting there I'd give it to you. And you *are* a father in Israel, you know. So now don't worry. I never had a chance of helping my old man—you just consider that, far as this little transaction goes, you're standing in his place."

As he spoke, Jobson had been approaching the door, and now he stepped through it into the sunlight, pulled his hat over his eyes, plunged his hands into his pockets, and went back to the tavern.

"Now, father," said Randy, making haste to supply her father with a new set of thoughts, "slick yourself up, and go pay Peter Carradine his money before he's an hour older."

The old man looked at the package of bills, which had been counted at the bank, and was labelled on the outside of the envelope, in great letters, plain for him to read, "Three hundred." But he did not stir.

"Yes," said she, with more spirit; "I'll get out your coat, and brush it; go into the shed and wash, and it can all be done up before night. Then we'll sleep easy, I'm sure; there's a man for owing a debt to, that don't want a cent of interest, and tears up the note! And very likely, money being scarce, Mr. Carradine'll be right glad to get it to-day—if he isn't, where's the difference? We're glad to pay. Senior Jobson is a better man than we took him for. We ought to be glad to find that out! He spoke as tender as I'd speak of you, of the old father he'd never been able to help."

"He did speak right tender," said the old man. "He's a kind heart, Jobson has. I never thought I'd be beholden to him, though; and I wouldn't train in his company for sights o' money; but I'm hopeful he is to be brought over. Look a' that now! and he's never bragging what he does like, it's not the first time he's remembered the old man. Any way it's cheating of the devil so much, Randy?" The old man asked the question, longing that she should answer according to his desire—and she did, and her assurance went for more than even hers would have gone for, in deciding such a question, before the camp-meeting.

It was yet quite early in the afternoon when he set out for Mr. Carradine's, with the money in his pocket, and the injunction on his mind that he was not to satisfy any curiosity as to where the money came from, or how it had been raised; for, of course, Mr. Carradine would be curious—no one thought that, at this time of year, Mr. Roy would be in possession of a sum like that.

But Mr. Carradine asked no questions—showed no curiosity; checked even his expressions of regret that the old man should be unwilling to part with the lot he had tried to bargain for. The mere fact that Samuel had taken this step, showed him that he had deeply wounded the high spirit of the humble house—that, under a galled sense of the wound, they must have bestirred themselves to be free of him. He checked even the expression of real regret he felt; and he saw that Roy was there to pay the mortgage not as one who had been persuaded against his will.

This new feeling of independence was not founded on a fact that would equalize the future relations between the two families. Carradine, kindly and generous at heart, liked not to think that it was the feeling that his neighbors did not love or trust him that strengthened the barriers between him and them—he would fain have had those barriers removed; but no expectation of such an event for a moment deceived him.

When he saw how peacefully Miss Fuller passed through the performance of her school duties; on what easy terms of good understanding with herself, and those around her, she lived, her life seemed to him lovely as an early summer day; and his, in the contrast, like a surly November. Continually the influences of that serenity and cheerfulness were telling upon him, and disquieting him. He could not rest quietly in the thought that she was here. She would soon be going. In a few months at the longest. Was he to fall back on Martindale, with its glimpses and touches of Brighton? Satisfy himself with the Johnsons, and the Greens—Samuel Roy and Randy, and the rest of the neighborhood?

He found strange consolation in the fact, often as he thought of these things, and very often he was thinking of them, that Mercy was poor, defenceless—working for a living. His riches seemed to gain a new importance, and to have a new significance, considered in connexion with her poverty. But it was not often that they were speaking together, and very rarely he mentioned her name, unless it was to little Harry, in whose studies and progress he seemed to take a new and extraordinary interest. Often he was looking over the boy's school-books, particularly the Reader, which he bought for him in Brighton; so he said and he wrote Harry's name in it; but it would be long before the child could make use of anything so advanced. Carradine's memory was remarkable. Was he secretly studying the reading-book for his own edification, when he read some story or poem from the " big boy's Reader ?" Oftener than any one suspected, he was thinking over those best thoughts of the wise poets and law-givers, and his life was being nourished by them.

CHAPTER XVII.

THE LETTER.

Mail-day, and a day of days to Randy. Longed for, yet arrived at with feelings so disturbed that it had been difficult to say whether there was most pain or pleasure in them. When the clock struck one, she was awakened; she must rise in time to watch the arrival of the stage that brought the mail to Martindale, by seven in the morning!

She must go down for that letter. Senior must know about it. And would Senior care? She thought not. It pleased her now to think how Senior trusted to her.

At last it was daybreak—at last breakfast was over; at last she heard the post-boy whistling on his way, for at the hour when he usually rode past she went out to listen.

Never did day take its time with so provoking composure as this Saturday. She had concluded to wait till twilight before she went down to the tavern, but long before that hour the week's work was ended, and she had dressed herself, and as a last resort, betaken herself to her knitting. But knitting! what if a dozen men sat round the tavern steps, as they always did, on mail-days! Was that to hinder her taking a saucer of ripe strawberries down to Junior's poor wife? How many days was it since she walked through the lane gate?

So she put on her sun-bonnet and started with the saucer of ripe berries, the choice ones of her morning's gathering in the field.

To her surprise, however, as she came near the tavern, there was not the usual gathering of gossips in waiting while Senior dispensed the items from his newspapers. A strong wind blew from the east, and the audience had followed the reader into the bar-room, so that Randy came up to the door of the blacksmith's house quite unnoticed—except by Sally Green, who stood at the back yard gate, with her bonnet on, waiting for anything, it seemed, for when Randy crossed the road and entered the blacksmith's house, she followed her in time to hear Ethan Allen say, "No; she's gone out, and so I'm tending. There's a letter for you, and a bundle of stuff; and it's paid for, too. See there."

Whether the boy's astonishment was excited by the "stuff" itself, or by Randy's surprise, as she received her mail, or by the sudden appearance of Sally Green, who came in and stood before Randy so quietly as to bring a deeper flush over the girl's face, and a good deal more of confusion into her manner, is not here to be decided.

The girls walked out of the blacksmith's house together, not quite at ease in each other's company; but Randy had said to herself that, if Sally Green was curious, she would answer her questions. And Sally was curious. She asked who sent the stuff, and Miranda answered:

"Mr. Collamer, I expect."

"Mr. Collamer! writing a letter to you! What does that mean?" exclaimed Sally, with a surprise that did not originate in pleasure, and certainly the manner of its expression communicated none.

"He spoke about it, and said he had some papers I might like to read—for he knew we didn't get the reading of many." And I cannot say that Miranda, in making this answer, was wholly regardless of the fact that Elder Green was by no means generous in the matter of loaning newspapers.

"It's queer you kept it to yourself so. You didn't tell me you looked for a letter."

"How could I know that I should get one till it came?" was the answer. Randy tried hard to master her impatience, and Sally was pleased to say:

"Let me look at the post-mark. Frankfort," she read, taking the package from Miranda. "That's the mark that was on father's letter." Then Sally began to tear the coarse brown wrapping on which the address was written so legibly and carefully, it was evident that the sender intended his gift should not go astray. Randy's impulse was to put out her hand to arrest Sally's work, but she sought to disguise that impulse by tying her bonnet strings, and Sally tore the wrapper open, through the middle of the address.

"There's a deal of reading," said Miranda, looking well pleased, as she saw the bulky magazines in their brown covers. "It will be good for father."

"Yes, for those that like—reading isn't my way. I'm glad he didn't send 'em to me. Though he knew, of course, I could buy all the books I wanted."

"It was very kind of him," said Randy, thinking of the hymn book with Sally's name written on the fly-leaf.

"He ought to have a rich wife, though," observed Sally. "A rich wife to keep him going. He isn't the man to marry any poor woman. He won't either. I don't think much of these ministers after all."

"Oh, Sally! You didn't think that up to the camp-meeting, a little time ago."

"I've changed my mind about it all. I don't believe one bit in revivals, either. It's all excitement, and leaves you worse off than you were before."

"No, you're saying of that to get me to talking," said Randy, looking with a serious, searching gaze at Sally's face. "I'll never believe it wasn't true what you said up there. How he had helped you on to lead a godly life—to make you wish for one, and choose one. And you promised him your prayers when he asked us: How could you do that, and think so at one time?"

"Pooh, what a fuss you make! You *will* be one of grandma's kind—look out!" said Sally, laughing as she gave the caution—but she did not look at Randy. "It was all excitement. We used to have such at school. It was as good as a circus, or a theatre, or anything, that camp-meeting. I'm glad I went. I'm glad it all happened—now I know all about it—and I don't think there's anything in it. There! but if you say that to father he won't believe you. Of course you wouldn't be believed."

"You don't mean what you're saying!" exclaimed Randy, the more positive, because now and then during the past days the shadow of some such thought as Sally had here boldly uttered had crossed her own mind, and terrified her. "You can't mean it! Oh, it's awful to see you looking so, as if it didn't matter whether you spoke in earnest or in fun! You *did* feel up there that he had helped you see the truth."

"No, I didn't. I was like the man in the whirlpool at Niagara Falls. I was in, and I couldn't get out. As for you, you're dead in love—that's the matter of you, Randy."

Randy's face turned scarlet—then it was deathly pale. It was with difficulty she could speak what she had thought she would say before Sally uttered these last words. The words came from her now with trembling and pain.

"I feel it in myself," said she. "I know I have gone back. I can't keep my mind bent as I did on those blessed subjects all the while, and my thoughts wander, and my heart is cold, but I know I turned to God, and I know that Jesus Christ is my Saviour. And I depend upon Him—I depend upon Him to act up to His promise. I *will believe* in it! He sees how I'm tried, and He's willing I should be tried, or I couldn't be. I expect it is always so. We must only believe the more, the darker things look. That's what they all say, Sally. And we're Peters walking on the water for a testimony. And there's Zaccheus sitting up in a tree for curiosity, he is a witness that the eyes of the Lord are in every place, beholding the evil and the good. We cannot help ourselves. But He can help us."

"I wish," said Sally, after a weighty pause, during which, according to her power, she had considered Randy's words; "I just wish I had never gone up there!"

"You do?—After all that was done for Oliver, too! And we felt it in our own hearts, and saw it with our own eyes?"

"I wish," repeated Sally, "that I had never gone. What was that you said about Oliver Savage?"

"Wasn't that meeting the saving of him? He went up for a frolic, and was gambling when the word shot into his heart."

"Nonsense!" said Sally. "There's more been said against him than them that talked will be able to answer for"—

"You know he told us himself that was what he went for—and he owned it when he spoke in the meeting."

"He might better have kept it to himself, then. He isn't half as bad as he tried to make out—not half. And there wasn't a young man on the ground to compare with him for pretty looks. What makes you turn against him so?"

"I?—Why that is strange for you to say. Ask him if he don't reckon me among his friends. When he got into the trouble about that bad money, ask him who kept him from starving three weeks, till the talk stopped, and who drove him down to Brighton after dark, and saw the last of him that anybody saw around here for five years."

"Yes, I know that, Miranda," said Sally, in a softened voice.

"He ought never to have come back, that's all I'm sorry for. But maybe that is wrong. For if he was led, and came back to be converted, he may make a good man yet for his poor old mother to depend on."

"There's Mr. Carradine!" said Sally. "Wasn't he as wild, I'd like to know, as any fellow ever was? And where is there a soberer man?—all his wild oats sowed, as anybody can see. And he gets richer and richer every year. He could buy out all his neighbors. And he's got some mortgages that might make trouble in some houses where they hold their heads high, if he chose to put them through. So, what if Oliver has been wild, that don't show anything."

"But he isn't like Mr. Carradine. There's more danger of his going back. He ought to be encouraged—but I don't think he ought to be praised. When Mr. Carradine turned about from his practices he couldn't have been got back into them, I should think. He hated himself so for what he had done, it wasn't likely he would be doing of it over."

"Yes—well, when Oliver gets to be a rich man, then it' will be time to praise him, I suppose. It's the money people set the value on, after all."

"No it isn't, Sally, it's the character."

"A beautiful character Peter Carradine has!" exclaimed Sally, with a scornful laugh. "Lovely, to be sure."

"There's something strong and noble in it. And that's what Miss Fuller was saying to me. She said that he seemed to her like a great mountain, so sure, and so strong."

Sally laughed again, not quite so scornfully.

"What did I tell you," said she, "when you called him a hedgehog?"

"I told you once I didn't call him a hedgehog. I said I should as soon think she would love a hedgehog." But as

Miranda said this, she was aware that there was, just at this moment, less confidence in her mind on that score. "She'll marry him yet. And when you see such a woman marrying such a man, you'll wonder. People always have to wonder at such things. I guess *I* will give them a chance."

Miranda checked the eager words on her tongue's end, and Sally said :

"What should you think to see me married, now ?"

"That would depend some on the man."

"Well, we were talking about Oliver Savage. What if I took him ? You say he is a kind-hearted fellow, and excellent looking, so what do you say to my taking him ?"

"I don't think that you will," said Randy, uneasily reminded at this moment of what it was that had secretly troubled her, that undefined consciousness, through all this walk and talk with Sally Green.

"If I had to choose between him and Collamer, what would you say ?"

"I don't believe you would wait to ask me my opinion."

"I'd make up my mind so quick ?"

"Yes."

"I'd take the minister ?"

"Wouldn't you, Sally Green ?"

"Randy, you are as cautious as a fox. If I make up my mind to Mr. Collamer, I shall marry him. I could do it in six months. Women manage these things to suit themselves. I don't know why I should be in a hurry to quit the old house and set up for myself. No end to troubles then. Oh, I was going back without telling you what I left the house to tell you. Did you know Miss Fuller is going to have a kind of exhibition the third of July—and all the people around are to be invited to come to the school-house. Will you go ?"

"Yes, if she asks me."

"I thought you wouldn't ! You don't seem to have laid up a thing against her. I've kept you a good while from your reading. Are you going to read those books through ?"

"Oh, maybe. But you shall have them too. Well, good-night, Sally."

"Good-night. I thought you was more in a hurry than you'd own. You'll lend the letter too, I expect !"

Miranda had not gone ten paces further up the road when she met Oliver Savage. They passed each other with a kindly word, and in less than five minutes Sally, who had turned to retrace her steps in a sombre mood, looked around to see who was coming, and saw the man who occupied, not very pleasantly, her thoughts.

CHAPTER XVIII.

THE FRIENDS AND THE LOVERS.

SAMUEL ROY has finally gone off to bed, after having turned page by page the magazines he was surprised and pleased to know Mr. Collamer had sent to Randy. He had prayed for the young minister in the evening prayer, and his daughter said Amen to every word. And now, at peace with all the world, the old man lies down to rest and to wonder. Randy has fastened the house door—it is a simple process; a thief has never crossed that threshold, and nothing could exceed the sense of security with which they lay them down to sleep. She is in her room—and there is nothing now to hinder the reading of that letter. Now, for the first time, she may fairly look at it.

She took it from her pocket, that bit of white paper, written over, sealed and stamped—such a seeming trifle—such a mighty matter. If Sally had only left unsaid those rude words about Mr. Collamer !

She observes how securely the seal secures the contents of the letter, whatever they may be. From his eye it has passed to hers; no intervening gaze. None have come between them. No wonder that she hardly breathed, and that her hands trembled. For "no human soul can approach another human soul and it is a light thing." Not idly or wantonly mayst thou cross the sacred limits—to every desecration there is penalty attached. What he has written, what thou shalt read, Miranda, it is all done under the scrutiny of God; God, and God alone, is in your secret. Does that knowledge give it additional sacredness and power? If so, well.

Thus she unfolded the letter, and read.

And what did she read? To what purpose should one

copy here a dozen sentences or more, decorated somewhat with the heart's broidery, simple flowers, and chaste, every one. The words that electrify one soul fall coldly on another. It is the mind and heart that discover their meaning. Vain to repeat the vowels and consonants. People will idly chatter the secrets which should have died with the dead. And the greedy ear and the gabbling tongue, think you *they* shall ever reach the sacred mysteries which these words pretend to discover? The secrets of love can never *be* revealed. The loving alone know them. No rehearsal can give them to the unloving soul.

Yet, when I write that sacred word, I know that I shall draw an audience of consecrated souls around me. I know that hands cannot fashion the mystic characters of that divinest name, but there will be a hushed and reverent attention, an eager, craving audience, a heeding as prompt as the bowed heads of worshippers at the elevation of the Host.

There will be tender smiles of sympathizing intelligence, and, at the worst, sad heeding, when I say that Miranda opened the letter with tremulous eagerness, and looked at the fine and regular tracery of the pen on the white paper. Over that page he had lingered, thinking of her—thinking thoughts he should transcribe! what he should say to her of herself—what he should tell her of him. Must Senior Jobson be taken into the confidence? Easy, generous Senior? What was it Sally said about her being dead in love? It was a hateful thought, that hurt her. It made her blush even in the presence of these words Mr. Collamer had written.

There was nothing trivial, cold, indifferent in those three pages. They were warm with friendly inquiries, and hopes, and suggestions; thoughts hopeful, courageous, religious. His place, he said, was already appointed for him. He was going to a large town, and should have a large congregation. He deemed that this was well for him. He was afraid that, if he had the opportunity, he should be less zealous in labor than his calling demanded. But here he should find duties that could not be neglected—it was a missionary station he would occupy—the people were poor; his heart and hands would be full, and he should indeed faint in the prospect but for the hopes that were set before him, and the sacred promise that they should all be fulfilled. He asked her to remember him in her prayers. That she would never let a day go by that she did not ask for his enlightenment and strengthening. He should not forget her. It was his great privilege to remember her when he came into the holiest audience. There was no good thing that could bless a woman's life that he did not desire in her behalf. But, above all, that she might be guided from above. And at the end he wrote himself her faithful friend. And begged that she would not keep him waiting long for tidings of herself.

She had said to him that she could not write a letter that he would not be ashamed to receive. He told her that she could not write one he would not be proud to read, for he knew her heart and her head—what both were capable of thinking and of feeling—and a little freedom in the use of her pen was all that she required. A few lines from her, he begged her to believe, would stand for more with him than the best composition of any other woman he knew. Was she indifferent to that assurance?

And the best thing she could tell him was that she was in health, as her soul prospered. That the Divine and human life were well, together. No other news from her could be so welcome to him.

Let every prize be proven. Doubtless 'tis good to discover veins of precious metal in the heart of a rock—it widens your way through life; will it plant your feet in Heaven? Or, oh! ye heart-sweeping poets, is the gain of gains hid in this world's praise? or, in the ribbon you gained for the blood you gave, brave soldiers, whose proud business was to give life for the Italy which should be made free from Alps to Adriatic? Or, simple woman, poring over a letter, have you a better evidence?

She brings out her copy-book, and opens its last written page, and compares the writing therein with this of the minister's letter. She needs all the assurances he has given her to make these lines and pages look not their worst. But she will write to him, because she has promised. She will do her very best. She will tell him of those things he speaks of; and what he desires to know of herself. If she tells all that concerns her, it will still be little. There has little happened since he went away. Nothing happens in Martindale. So it seems to her! But it was not news he asked for in the letter. No, he had not named a name but hers.

She wishes that Sally was here to read the letter with her. She wishes that Mr. Collamer were here, that she might speak to him about Sally; for Randy feels troubled. Did Oliver Savage join her? Of course he must have fallen in with her on the way home. Her heart sinks under the weight of a foreboding. If there were anything in the letter that would serve her friend to know—if he had mentioned her, or spoken kind words of her, Miranda thinks she would go down to Elder Green's in the morning on purpose to tell Sally and give her the letter.

But *is* she sorry that he made no mention of Sally? Why did her eyes first scan the pages, and then turn back with quiet satisfaction to begin at the beginning? Why had she felt disturbed to know that Elder Green had heard from Mr. Collamer? Why was she so conscious that she and Sally were not dealing quite fairly and openly by each other these last ten days? What meaning had she heard in Sally's words? What token had she seen in Sally's face when she had spoken so familiarly of him, and of his need of a rich wife? —as though she were hesitating in her mind whether or not the man should be more to her than a friend? Were they both drawn towards him in a way that estranged them from each other? Could she find, to her satisfaction, constant proof that these two had no fitness for each other? Did she feel in the least tempted to encourage the suit of Oliver Savage? If she must answer any of these questions with a "yes," where, among her thoughts, stood Senior Jobson?

In her strong hand, under her pillow, lies this little letter—a lever to move the world. Miranda falls asleep, knowing she has a new friend on earth; she does not say a friend of friends. Yes; he is just and true; in any strait she could call to him, and he would be her helper. He is fulfilling all her ideal; he is coming day by day into her consciousness—a king of men. She has no capability of reverence, no impulse to homage or adoration, that cannot culminate in him. Beyond that she is incapable, and it must rest with him whether from that point they shall ascend to heaven, or descend to the blackness of darkness.

But a solemn dream oppresses Randy when she sleeps. All night she walks among ruins. Up and down crumbling staircases, through deserted rooms, whose walls and roof are broken, whose floors are unsafe. And where she walks dancing feet have been, and laughing human voices—and eyes softened by love; and hands have crossed in friendship and have clasped in hate. Lights have flashed that promised to illuminate all coming darkness, so proudly they glowed, and they have burned out! There has been music that left nothing to be desired, and harp and viol are broken, and the singer's voice and the musician's hand are alike to be known no more.

Over the walls the ivy creeps; the owl looks down and seems to reason sadly. Is this the old tavern? Is this the Spread Eagle?

Come, oh builders, and restore the ruin! Plant the staircase and relay the floors! Give to the house a roof once more, and purity to the walls! and loving voices and kind eyes, and willing steps to the dark solitude. For still the world shall stand, amid the ruin of neglect; though you cannot atone for the past, oh! can you not hope for the future?

In wakefulness, perplexity, unrest, Sarah Green is watching through the night. Not indeed *dreaming* of a ruin, which haply the morning shall rebuke. She prayed that she might not be led into temptation when she came into her room, but since she arose from her knees, has she not ceased that playful strife with the tempter. For there is no earnest rallying around her conscience in the endeavor to save her soul alive.

Her heart is full of disappointment and of passion. Her self-willed spirit, in its rebound from opposition, is set with a tiger's courage and purpose. She would not grieve past all consolation to know, in the morning, that Randy would never waken to the light again. Well, then, had she loved Mr. Collamer? She denied it when, alone here in her chamber, she surprised herself by that question. Wherefore, then, so take to heart the fact that he had sent those books, above all that letter, to her friend? She pursued not this train of investigation, but her thoughts turned, as if with a fatal *finally*, to Oliver Savage.

But half-shuddering she thought of him. Still she held herself to the thought. She had never felt so kindly towards him as to-night. When he took her hand and they walked along together, his voice had never before so pleasant a sound. And when they passed by Mr. Carradine, and hands speedily unclasped, and each walked alone, though side by side—hands clasped again, as by an involuntary impulse, the moment he was beyond sight, how thought she of this? With a pity for poor Oliver? For then she must recall how he began to speak to her of himself, and his complaint because every body seemed to be against him. He almost despaired, he said, of ever getting on in the world. Other men had friends to help them. He would go to sea, he thought. There was nothing for him on land.

What did he mean, she asked? And Sarah tried, as she now remembered, to speak with indifference; but she felt sorry for poor Oliver, and wanted to help him. If all men stood against him!—her pride seemed to be roused—she would like to show all men that Oliver Savage was not to be used that way in this world! She could make of him a man to be envied. She had half a mind to try! What if she defied all counsel and judgment! Others did not understand him; they could not see him as she did. He did not speak to others as he spoke to her.

When she asked him what he meant, he had answered that she knew very well. And when she assured him that she did not know, he said:

"If I had you, Sally, I wouldn't mind the speech of people, nor any other thing."

"I don't see," she had answered, "what great difference the having of me would make, Oliver."

Then he said—she recalled each word, and its tone; how strange that any word of his should move her so that it should seem, while he was speaking, that if he felt thus towards her, no matter what all the world thought!

"Because I love you so that you would satisfy me, and nothing else in this world would. I thought up there in the woods that, now I had got religion, I should be happy. But I've been miserable ever since. It seems to me it's you I ought to get, instead of religion, to make me religious. And it's come to the pass that, if I've got to give up the thought of you, I'm giving up everything else. There's nothing else I want. There's nothing else that has the power to keep me out of harm's way."

Sarah Green trembled to hear these words, they were

spoken with such passionate power, and she yielded herself to believe that she believed them. To imagine that she thought herself responsible, even as he pronounced her to be, for the future of the lad.

Besides, he said he loved her. That word had a sound as if spoken by the voice of the charmer. When she came to the fact that it was only Oliver who said it!—but for a moment it was the word, and the sound, that arrested the woman.

They had not gone immediately home. They wandered far out of their way, down under the willows, along the margin of the deep, swift-flowing creek.

"I do not want to hear you say such things," she had replied. "It is of no use. No use at all. It can never be."

"Yes," said he, with confidence, "it is. You feel just as I do."

This tone, so unusual, so unexpected, astonished Sarah Green. Before she could answer, he continued:

"If any one should tell me that you liked another man better than me, I'd not believe it—not a word. And if I went away because I'm a poor man, and you're a rich girl, too proud to marry me, I should know all the while that you was thinking of me—and if you married another man, you would not love him half as well."

Did she resent this speech? Did she succumb to it? She said:

"Is it my fault that I am the daughter of Elder Green, and that he is what you call a rich man?"

"No—but it's an almighty little circumstance that you are going to let come between us, to ruin both of us. It isn't the richer or poorer that has anything to do with this. Can't you see it, Sally? As if it was your money that I loved!"

"I can't think," said Sally; "while you speak so, it seems to me it must be true—but I know all the while it isn't. Everybody says it isn't."

"Yes; it is true!" he repeated. "I knew that you must see it at last. All that ever made you think it isn't true, is because you have been trained up so that you take other folks' opinions of me for your own. But they're not your own. They never were, and never will be. I love you with all my life—and you love me as well. There isn't anything so beautiful to me in all the world as Sally Green."

"If it is so—" she began, then she hesitated.

"If it is so," he said, taking up the words hastily; "if it is so, who's a right to say a word against it?"

"Nobody!" said she.

"Then it's settled."

This climax of his argument startled her.

"No it isn't. It isn't. What have you been talking about? You seem to think you have only to show your pretty face, and a woman will be sure to like it!"

"Now, Sally Green! Did I see you for the first time yesterday, or last week? or have I loved you all my life—all my life? And I won't say yet it's a pretty fool I've made of myself. For I know how it will all end."

"But you know, too, how it must come about. Oh, you are cruel—it's wicked of you. If they take you home to live, it will be because I am their only child. But what right have I to disappoint them? That's *all*, Oliver."

"What right has any one to come between you and the man you love?"

"Let me be sure first that I love him, anyway," said she, continually revolting against the show of confidence he made in his assertions—and yet they were having an increasing weight—and he could see that they had.

He did not now answer—and she added presently:

"As you say it's I that have to live with the man—father isn't going to marry you, nor grandma, nor—Huldah. But don't talk about it any more."

"There's nothing else to talk about."

"Hundreds of things!" she said, trying to speak gaily; but as he continued silent, she added, "wait till the Fourth—we can talk about it then, when we are all at the celebration."

"That is your way—wait, wait. But if you know your mind, Sally—"

"That's it; I don't"

"It's only because you like to be cruel, and are curious to know what I'll say next. I'll say nothing. I'll go blow my brains out. Blast me if I don't. I keep a pistol loaded."

"It seems to me," she said, "you might talk a little different. You'll live as long as you can draw a breath. Talk reason."

"What is the use of talking at all?"

"None, to be sure."

"Then, if that's the way you feel, we'll just say 'farewell forever.'"

Oliver took to weeping.

Then she must console him. But she made no haste in this. Still, before he could break out into the inevitable reproaches, she said:

"Be still, then. I suppose that I must give you my word. Take it. I'll marry you. And I don't care if it is on the Fourth." It was but a leap, and she had reached this point!

Then he sprang to his feet, threw his arms round poor Sally, and kissed her into a conviction that all this was wise and well. That she had saved his life. That at bottom he was a noble fellow. That she loved him. That she was not perverse, and ignorant of the first motion of true and royal love. That all this that had passed was not the mere madness of passion. That jealousy, envy, pride, self-will, and nothing nobler, nothing mightier, made the power of the passion.

Could she think of all this in her silent chamber, through the wakeful night, with composure, with satisfaction? But she was not vascillating in her mind. At first she thought it was all folly, at least to have promised Oliver. She was surprised at that promise—what, to fulfil it in a week! But something rose within her to stop this vascillation. Why not first, as well as last? It had been a long time now, as Oliver said, that this might be the end. Loved him—he called it. Had she loved him? How well he seemed to know her. Yes, it must be so. Yes, it was so.

Of course her father and grandma would not like it. But they would take Oliver home He could live here, in this house. Room enough—that was not the objection. And why should she not be married? Then her father, after all, if he were not so obstinate, might be glad of the son he would have. He had said many times that Oliver was an excellent hand at work; and, moreover, among such good people, he would doubtless become the man they blamed him for not being! She could find it in her heart to pity the life he led on that miserable farm with his people. They would not miss him. And then—if he *was* poor! She was rich enough for two; she would be glad to share her all with him. And if her father would not be reconciled, he could give her her portion, and they might then go live where they pleased ; out in the world, far away from stupid Martindale.

But, my young friend, you see it was the last thought she had that there could be anything like duty in consulting with these home friends—that she had no apparent suspicion that, of all persons in the world, they *might* be the best and most loving !

And, my old friend, you are moralizing on life's failure, threatened here. You are saying, all this, and worse, comes of teaching a child, from the cradle, that his will and his pleasure, by no means his parents', is to control his life. You see a sin in such training, and you say, " The wages of sin is death."

Good people, in general, let us go to sleep, for it is heartbreaking to think of these things.

Would you have Sarah Green become the hindrance and disturbance of a good man's life ? The defeat of his career, the disappointment of his heart ? Let her alone ; there are enough to take that work upon them.

Would you have Oliver Savage degrading the excellence of any purer woman ? The scourge to drive her on to heaven or to hell ? Nay, rather leave me this one man, and experiment among your neighbors.

CHAPTER XIX.

THE DECLARATION READ.

By two o'clock on the afternoon of the third day of July, the school-house was well filled with the children and their parents, who had come in to attend the examination. The morning review had passed off with such success as to bring out in full force all the neighborhood as witnesses of the second part.

Sarah Green went down for Miranda in the morning, and found her making all haste with the housework—and she was spared that solicitation she had supposed she must make before Randy would be persuaded to attend the "public." For Miranda had promised Miss Fuller she would come, and the teacher had asked it as a personal favor.

So there were Sarah and Miranda sitting side by side all day. And in the afternoon Oliver Savage came; and Mr. Carradine was in constant attendance, and the entire Green family, and the Johnsons, and the Jobsons, except Senior, and all those other people of whom we know nothing, not their names even, who took an interest in the teacher, and towards whom, every one, Miss Fuller held so friendly a relation. It was noticeable that, though on Sundays very few of the men wore their coats at the meeting, those now gathered in the school-room were in full dress. There was a smell of dill and caraway, and an odor of sweet clover, mild and permeating, that met whoever entered by that lowly door; and there was an order and quiet, a neatness and decency, through the mass of persons, as well as proceedings, that seemed to many a person to emanate from the teacher.

It was what Mr. Carradine thought, namely, that every pleasant influence of the place was directly inspired by her.

She had on a white dress to-day, it might be for the benefit of Sally, who pretended a mortal aversion to the "old blue." How pure! the very embodiment of purity, and the illustration of goodness, she looked, to Peter Carradine! Then what an attitude was that maintained by her towards these children! so full of friendly condescension! so full of tender interest!

They all felt that they must do their best, in justice to her. Without having inspired in them any hateful spirit of emulation, she seemed to have so influenced them that they took pleasure and pride in showing what she had done in their behalf. They were proud of their teacher. But, they were very human children, too. Do not suppose that she had trodden upon roses while she led them, and had felt no thorns. This school was very much like others—a rabble of young folk; only she had been successful to a degree that astonished beholders in controlling them. And that was all.

In going through the exercises—in the elocution, and the reading, and the singing, and arithmetic, they had done themselves and Miss Fuller great credit—and now the two hours of examination were ended.

Miss Fuller signified it by rising in her place and saying:

"The exercises are now concluded, my friends. Next Monday the school will open again. I hope the children will all come punctually, so that we may go on with our studies without any useless delay. I thank you for all your attention."

She turned away from the table, as if expecting that they would now depart.

But through the last half hour Peter Carradine had been nervously waiting for this very moment, and now arose, and exclaimed in a voice that arrested every soul:

"Friends!"

He saw that all eyes were on him; there was no retreat. He must go on; and he had no wish to do otherwise; this was his time of pride.

"Friends!" he repeated, and he established his footing more securely, and looking around him, proceeded with deliberation. "I am sure you must all be pleased with this exhibition. I see you are. And I think we have all good reason to feel satisfied. Miss Fuller has done us a great honor by teaching the children of Martindale this summer. I don't think she would be afraid to have us ask the children what they think of her! So I propose, for the children's sake, that Miss Fuller have the thanks of the people of Martindale for her kind attention to our little folks. If she was a gentleman teacher she would expect it of us. But, seeing she is a lady teacher, she don't expect it, I suppose— yet that's no good reason why we shouldn't give her what's her due. Those in favor of it please say ' Aye !' "

Again he looked around, and a broad smile covered his massive face when the response rolled up from young and old.

"There it is, ma'am," said he, with a not ungraceful hand-waive, as if offering her a gift. Then, immediately, he continued—he would not risk his opportunity—" I was going to ask a favor of the teacher," said he, and this time his eyes fell to the floor, and when he lifted them it was on Miss Fuller his gaze fixed. "To-morrow, ma'am, is the Fourth of July. For one reason and another, we, up here in Martindale, always feel that we must go from home to have our celebration. We are either too poor or too stingy, or else we don't really care for the day. So it seemed to me, as long as we were all going to be here together, old friends and neighbors so, we might ask Miss Fuller to read the Declaration of Independence for us, if she would be so kind. I brought it along with me—and see here, friends! haven't we got our revolutionary relic here, too? Here's neighbor Gibbs. Can't we have our Fourth of July in Martindale ? It's only taking time by the forelock—and that's what our fathers did in the war! Can't we shout, up here, ' Long live the Fourth of July !' on our own account, as well as go off to say it with the people of Brighton ?"

As he closed his speech, Mr. Carradine advanced to the table, and laid the book before the teacher. She bowed, but looked around her to see if Mr. Carradine's wish met a response ; for a moment there was dead stillness in the school-room, and several persons felt as if they should fly, according to subsequent confession, they were so excited, and so amazed too.

Then up rose Elder Green, driven as at the spear point by the looks and motions of his wife, with many breaks, he said :

"It gives me—great pleasure—Miss Fuller, to second Mr. Carradine's request. I feel to say that he has expressed an unanimous desire of the friends here present. The exercises have done you great credit, certin."

"Oh, make an end, Elder!" said his mother, by a telegraphic sign. But he seemed to take no heed, went on dragging the words out one after another, investigating each apparently from its root to its extremities, as he pulled it up.

"The town of Martindell ought, certin, to have the day commemorated. And if the children hear the Declaration read by—by their instructor, to-day—they, and the friends assembled, will not be likely to forget the—'the day we celebrate.'"

So saying, he bowed all around and sat down.

Then, in the midst of the applause that followed, in leading which Oliver Savage was boisterously conspicuous, Miss Fuller advanced yet nearer to the table, took up the book, and looking over the assembly, she seemed to see a pleased expectance, an endorsement of this wish on every face.

"It gives me pleasure," she said, " to think I can confer a pleasure, my friends. I thank you for allowing me to serve you." Then she opened the book, sat down, and read from first to last that noble Declaration. Read it all—powerfully — movingly — to the astonishment of every auditor; who felt quite sure, maybe because it was *their* celebration, that never had it been so read by man or woman. This decision will have a hundred repetitions to-morrow. Martindale will be a critic.

"Now's *your* time, uncle," said Carradine to neighbor Gibbs, when Mercy had closed with that famous, solemn pledge, " Our lives, our fortunes, and our sacred honor." The old man, who had sat as if on the point of springing to his feet any time the last ten minutes, in spite of his age and infirmity, did not wait for urging.

He got up, sustaining himself by his staff—steadied himself, old, shrunken, white-haired, wrinkled mummy of a man, veteran of '76, and said, (who that heard him would forget the change from his usual mumbling tone to anything so direct, and clear, and manly):

"I can't make so much noise of hurraying, my dear, as I could onct," he said, when the vehement cheering that greeted his rising had subsided; "but I thank'ee. Goody gracious! I never heerd the like o' that afore. I'll ne'er hear its like again. It seems to make a boy o' me. Now I've got some tokens of old time up to my housen. If you'll come over you shall take your pick. I've been offered sums for 'em; but I want you should have your pick." So saying, he wheeled about, as if at an order in his prime, and said:

"Come, Peter, you promised to get me back safe, lad. I'm old—I'm past threescore and ten."

So, though the assembly had risen, every one stood back, and let Mr. Carradine lead out old neighbor Gibbs; and many were the kindly words addressed to both men by the bystanders. Never was Peter Carradine seen to such advantage as on this afternoon.

"A pretty fine hedgehog, after all," said Sally to Miranda, but just then Carradine held out his hand to Randy and shook it heartily, and said aloud, (he meant every one should hear):

"I thank you for coming. I wouldn't have expected it of another girl but you."

"He might better kept his opinions to himself at *this* time o' day," said Sally Green. Randy frowned at her, and repenting the frown, smiled—somebody said there were tears in her eyes. And Oliver Savage laughed.

But Randy said aloud, so all around her heard:

"Do you suppose I'm not glad there's such a teacher come to Martindale as Miss Fuller. I've expressed my mind about it often enough." And she went to speak with the teacher.

At which Sally looked vexed, and turned on young Savage with a "What are you laughing at?" that silenced him.

The rest of Martindale were thinking with considerable self-gratulation that they had for once celebrated the Fourth at home, without any drinking, and without any expense. But this fact only incited them, for the most part, still more urgently to go down to Brighton next day, and spend what had thus been saved, both of money and time, according to the good old Jefferson counsel.

CHAPTER XX.

FOURTH OF JULY IN PROSPECT.

That should have been a pleasant night in Martindale, when everywhere the busy preparations went on for due celebration of to-morrow. It was rare that lights were seen burning so late in the farm-houses round about. When all to-morrow's house work that it was possible to anticipate was done, busy fingers were still flying—unfinished frills and flounces must be gathered and sewed; nothing must be left till morning. Sufficient for that day was the work thereof.

In Sarah Green's closet hung the white muslin, freshly starched and ironed; the blue ribbons in her drawer were ready to put on. She had no work to do. She might go early to bed, as her mother counselled; advice on which she meant herself to act, with the rest of the house. But Sally did not feel the need of sleep—and the stillness of the old house oppressed her when she sat, she alone wakeful, in her room, till midnight.

She could but think it might be the last night she could spend in that room. If, as she did not in the least fear, *if* after to-morrow her father should forbid her to come into his house, was she prepared to renounce it forever? She asked herself the question, knowing that a very different future was in store for her. They should return to this old farm-house—and it might be to this very chamber. And she was satisfied with Oliver for her portion.

But, somewhat disturbed, she had been in the school-room and since, thinking of Miss Fuller. The secret of her life, its beauty and its strength, was full of mystery, and of enticing mystery to Sarah, when she had come within its influence, and subsequently when the examination at the school, and the reading of the Declaration, furnished themes for home-talk. That was a very different kind of life from the one she was now leading, and had been leading during the past days—so tranquil, calm and pure—so lovely and so good.

But it is not to be supposed that Sally could not make excuses for herself, that she could not say that such a life as Miss Fuller's was not the life for her. That she could not find some merit in the act she contemplated for to-morrow's celebration ; that she could not see in the conduct of her parents, justification of her own acts.

Why should not persons, when they gave themselves away, consult their own hearts in the act, and not the wisdom of another ? Of course she was the person most concerned ; it was to a very narrow argument, and a very narrow view of that narrowness, that she confined herself.

But how restless the girl was ! There seemed to be nothing on which she could fix her thoughts for two moments with anything like repose or satisfaction. She could not even fix her eyes on anything in the room without compunction. Nothing had happened since she came home from the school-house that would seem in itself worthy of record ; and yet there was not a half hour that had passed since then on which she dared trust her thoughts to dwell. The conversation with grandma, Esther Green, when they went out together in the garden and gathered the first ripe red currants for tea, when grandma told again the stories of old celebrations of the Fourth, stories which Sarah had heard so many times ! It seemed to Sarah, while her grandma held the basket into which she poured the currants, that her hand trembled more than usual ; and how old she looked as the afternoon sun fell broadly on her face, throwing every wrinkle, and the white hair, and the blue eyes, into such relief ! And when they walked into the house together the old woman said—never would Sarah forget her voice, or the words of its speech :

"Well—well—time is short—but eternity is long ! How dreadful for them who will have to repent their sins through all eternity ! To be preyed on by the worm that never dies !"

And it occurred to Sarah, when she helped old Esther up

the steps, what if this were for the last time! Possibly any great shock, any wounding of her pride, or disappointment of her wishes, might startle her out of existence. Stern, harsh woman that she was, who would care to throw a shadow on the aged countenance, when the blue eyes were taking their last look of life? Was it likely that, in the silence of the house, and the solitude of her chamber, Sarah would care to dwell long on such thoughts as these?

Then, when she was plaiting the frill to be pinned in the neck of her dress, and her mother was ironing her father's black silk neckerchief, and her own cap strings and bonnet ribbons, and Esther's white silk handkerchief, and they might talk together in the large airy kitchen, so orderly and clean, Huldah had said:

"Seems to me the girls don't now-a-days look out for Independence as we used to do. It was the greatest day of summer to us! But 'twas rare that it came up to what we expected of it. And that is the way of everything I find since then."

"I suppose you used to go in processions with your young men; and you won't own it, mother, but that was what made it so very fine to you! You don't expect I could be mighty gay, just thinking of riding over to Brighton with you and father, and grandma, behind the old grays—those raw-boned farm-horses?"

"Worth a thousand dollars the span, and the best pacers in the country," said Huldah.

"Yes, but mother, you can't expect it should seem so very gay to me. I wish I could make it, but I can't. I wish—" here she had spoken after a little pause, with exceeding energy; "oh, I wish, mother, you would just leave me at home. And I'll have a long quiet day here by myself."

Huldah looked up from her work—she was more troubled by this wish than she betrayed; not only because Sally expressed it with so much vehemence; she had felt that there was something she did not understand about Sally for the last week, as if the girl had some purpose in her mind that no one knew, and which her mother should know.

"Your father would have the day spoiled for him outright," said she. To argue on her own ground, or in her own behalf, would have been folly. She did not deem the Elder quite so impotent.

"No, but you could persuade him. You can make him see that black is white, mother, if you wish to do it. Come!"

"But why should I do it? He would feel just as disappointed, though I did persuade him to it. The Fourth don't come but once a year. And when such days do come, the way I always used to look at 'em was, that then was my time to do what my parents wanted me to do, for when the day came round again they might be dead and gone!"

So Sarah had abandoned that point. Fate would have its way! It was not her fault if they insisted on her going to Brighton. There was duty towards others to be done, as well as to her parents—she had promised Oliver. And who would dare say that the result, if she should disappoint him, was of no consequence?

Then she ventured to say to Huldah:

"If I could go now, as you have half-a-dozen times, with some young fellow in a carriage, driving a fast horse, that would be different! And I had such an invitation, but I knew you would not hear to it, and so I said no."

"That was to Oliver. I thank you for that, Sally, and so does your father."

"He was at the school-house this afternoon. Did you see him, mother?"

"Yes."

"You did not speak to him."

"But I was off 't the other side of the room. Of course I would speak to him if he was near."

"He is a member now. If there is any good in that, the other members ought to show it, I should think."

"So should I," said Huldah. "I spoke to your father, and he would have invited him to tea, but he takes an ell for every inch, Oliver does."

"Then I suppose he knows it's a right he has; for he's no fool."

"There's no one hopes of better things for Oliver than I do," said poor Huldah. "I'm always hoping for him."

"I believe it," replied Sally. "I believe that, if you saw he was likely to go to destruction, you would put out your hand as quick and as far as any other one to save him."

"I think I would. He is a clever lad. He might tell you I have showed myself his true friend in some serious times."

"He never has forgotten anything of it all. He calls you his second mother, sometimes," said Sally, who had reserved this argument for an emergency. It had its weight.

"I'm sure," said Huldah, "I'd warn him as quick as I would an own son; and, as you say, I'd go as far to save him as any other person."

"You wouldn't stop to think whether others would go as far; you'd look at your own heart and let that take you; so I've heard you saying, mother, many's the time."

Huldah could not deny this. Perhaps she had no wish to do so, but she was disturbed by the feeling that her words were carried farther than she meant to have them go; and were used in other ways than she intended. So she said:

"It's difficult dealing with a young man like him. He is the kind that takes the ell when you give him an inch. Nobody would have a right to help him at his own expense. I mean, you couldn't, Sally! He don't sense things as a young man ought. He's reckless, and don't think of anybody as he does of himself. No right down good man could dress himself as he does, and think so much of his fine looks, with his hair puckered in that way, like a girl's, and that blue vest and white neck tie. He looks like a different person when he has on his working rig. But when he has on his finery he is feared of the rain as if he was made of sugar. Besides the money throwd away on such things, and he can't afford."

Then her father had come into the kitchen and called for a candle and said:

"Here's a letter from Mr. Collamer, to read—out of sight ain't out o' mind with him." And when the candle was lighted and brought to him by Sally, she stood holding it till he should read the letter.

It was full of pleasantness. The minister told of his situation, his charge and his church ; added some items in respect to the society at large, its prosperity and prospects ; inquired after the neighbors, but particularly after Elder Green's own household, especially after his daughter. Was she in good health ? And, if she should find it too much trouble to reply, would he make her his scribe ? And he sent his love, a Christian brother's love, to Esther Green and Huldah.

Poor Calvin Green! he thought much of Mr. Collamer ; and he fixed his eyes on Sally as if his thoughts were engaged in a novel and curious speculation. He was thinking, in fact, that, if he had no son-in-law to succeed him on the farm—some day, when he and his mother, and his wife, were asleep in the graveyard—it might be well if his money should make life easy to some hard-working servant of the Lord, in holy orders. And never had he looked at Sally with quite such longing hope as now, when he sat with Mr. Collamer's letter in his pocket, watching the girl as she helped her mother through the remaining preparations for the Fourth. Fair was she in his eyes. If he had spent on her education twice as much, he would have deemed the investment about the best he had ever made.

Of all these things must Sally think. But impatient of these thoughts, she went to bed, determined she would think no more ; but the sleep to which she would fain resign herself was long in coming.

CHAPTER XXI.

THE FOURTH IN FACT.

We begin the day with Mr. Collamer. He sat in his study, in the basement of his church; on the table before him lay the letters which a little lad had just brought him from the office. What time he gives to his books, or to writing, the minister spends in this quiet room; but he lodges with the family now occupying the parsonage, for he cannot see why he, a single man, should burden himself with household cares; so, with consent of the people, he rented the house, his appointed home for the year.

Among the papers brought to him is a well-folded letter, bearing an address as legible as print, which he opens, first of all. He smiles as he glances at the quaint characters—but his eyes fill with tears—tears which do not drive away the smile.

"It has cost her something," said he; and he turned the page to see the length of the letter; it might have been treble the length, and yet not have filled the sheet. She had taken him at his word, he found; had told him of Martindale, of the neighbors, of the crops, of the services held in the school-house since he left. And he read every word down to the signing of her name, without one evidence of indifference, or impatience, or proud failure of appreciation of these humble items. There was one paragraph that gave value to the rest; he read it more than once, he read it many times; and seemed to discern in its wording something to be prized.

"Now I have written to you, Sir, my heart fails me to send it. But something bids me, kindly. And when I try to find the meaning of it, it seems to pass me, and come again and go till I am dizzied trying to follow. Then, when

I stop thinking, it seems to me that I need ask for no other excuse, since you wished for the letter. I said you would be ashamed of it! But I seem to see, Sir, since you answered me, that there is nothing to excuse such a feeling, if the heart be right. And I mean right when I think of your business in this world, and pray to God to bless your coming in and your going out, your preaching and praying, your going from house to house, your baptizing of infants, and your comforting the sick; and the sad mourners, and your standing by the open graves when the last work is done for the poor body that can be done for it in this world."

And to this she had signed her name in full, his " friend and servant in the Lord, Miranda Roy."

He said, as he slowly folded the letter:

" I've seen prettier women. I've heard sweeter voices than hers; and them it might be easier to help on through life; but I never saw a woman yet I thought was to be trusted as she is—gentler, milder, maybe—but it's like leaning on truth, or the likest thing to God's truth, to rely on her. Steady and kind, firm and tender; good things in a woman."

He beheld her this, and thought upon her so. And through all the noise and clatter of the day, though a score of interests claimed him, and varied work was done, a presence of woman seemed to go with the young minister. " Steady and kind, firm and tender." It might almost seem that, unconsciously, he was trying to establish a correspondence between his life and that of Miranda. Was it possible that he should do so without some abatement of his own peculiar power? Was it possible that he should do so, and come thus into fuller possession of his highest power? That he should come thus to his fullest life?

CHAPTER XXII.

THE FACT CONTINUED.

Miss Fuller was to go to Brighton with Mrs. Johnson, Johnson driving the bays. But Carradine seemed not quite persuaded whether to go down on foot or on horseback, or to drive in his buggy, or whether he should go at all to the celebration.

He knew that Mercy would not return to-night; that she would spend the remainder of the week at Commissioner Brown's house, with her friend, Commissioner Brown's daughter.

He was very much disturbed in view of this prospect. Mrs. Johnson had told him what her purpose was, and he had said to himself repeatedly that it was not his business; still he could not make it so. He felt, in opposition to this assertion, that it was his business; his alone; no other person's truly; his alone. Man full of gains, he seemed to have somehow lost his soul.

Of course it was absurd. It was perfectly silly for a person of his years and standing to harass his mind on so slight an occasion. Let her go to Brighton; and let him stay or follow, of what moment was this?

But when he saw her black satchel lying on the table in the hall, with a woollen shawl beside it, a veil, and a parasol, and a fan, the heart of the dealer in lands and grain, cattle and bank stock, was yet more sensibly moved. He went into his room, and dressed himself for Brighton.

When he came forth again he saw Miss Fuller in the yard, admiring probably Mrs. Johnson's poppies, for they grew just along the fence near the gate, where she was standing —poppies, purple, and pink, and red, and white, double and fringed. Perhaps she was training the morning-glories, which grew so fast, and put forth their vigorous creepers in every wayward direction. He always admired that morning-glory walk : year after year, since the first year they came to the farm, he had seen Mrs. Johnson careful, in season and out, for the morning-glories; and it seemed she had succeeded in exciting some interest in their behalf in the mind of Mercy Fuller. Indeed he, had heard the teacher say that she remembered a porch where a shade of morning-glories grew; as rich a purple as ever was fashioned into an emperor's robe, and a white as pure as the daintiest day-lily.

And he, Mr. Carradine, had felt as grateful to know that she cared for these homely flowers, as if some special endorsement had thereby been set on Martindale, and Mrs. Johnson, and the farm-house on the hill.

She was going to Brighton. She had lived in the world before she came to Martindale. Yet he thought that it was not safe to let her go! He thought she had been growing prettier every day since she came into the country! He had marked the changes with pleasure! Secretly had marked them—yet was sure that all must observe them—would not have liked it had any failed to observe! And still, he could wish her plain as Randy! There was no danger in sending Miranda to Brighton. You perceive he was entirely a paradox at present.

But he went down to the fence—and when he saw that she really was twining the morning-glories around their several supports, with a careful touch and gentle, he said :

"They will be in bloom, perhaps, by the time you get back, Miss Fuller."

"Oh, no; not for two weeks yet, I should think. See how very small the buds are. You know they are there better than you can see them."

"Yes, to be sure," said he. And he thought—*it was because the time seemed so long to me the summer might be over for all I knew.* And somehow he expressed this feeling.

"How long shall you be gone ?"

"Four days."

"I was reckoning it as if it was longer than that."

"Only four days," she repeated. But it was not displeasing to think that the time should seem long to him.

She could not recollect that ever any one, except mere school girls, in love with every new face, had ever said to her that the time would seem long of her absence. And this, it seemed to her, regret that she was going, was in Mr. Carradine's words.

He did not leave her to doubt concerning that.

"You might be in Martindale that length of time without my seeing you, but I should know you were here. It's different, you're going away."

"But only four days," she said, looking up, and speaking very kindly. She seemed almost laughing at him. And yet he could endure that without anger, so kindly was her voice.

"No matter if it wasn't but for one day," said he; "how can I tell what will happen?"

"But you know," said she, "nothing ever happened in so short a time as that!"

"Something happened," said he, seriously, "in a great deal less time. I was thinking of when I first saw you down at the Commissioner's. It did not take us long to come to an understanding then," said he, "for we both knew what we wanted. I must have a teacher, and you wanted a situation. Pity everything cannot be managed as easily." Then he said something about the crops, half complaining. Whereat Miss Fuller, surprised, asked him if, by all accounts, this was not the most promising season farmers had known for years.

"Yes," he said, "a rich harvest, of course. Every man's barns will be full—but what of it?"

"A good deal, I should think," she replied, manifestly amused, yet doubtful about his mood.

"Does man live by bread alone?"

"But at least there will be no talk of ruin this year."

"Why not?"

"Are farmers really never satisfied? I thought that was a slander."

"I have never known an out-and-out failure any season. I never feared one either. Grumbling gets to be a habit, and, of course, where so much depends on things you can't control, as the winds, and clouds, frosts and blight, and insects, a farmer's life must be pretty anxious. But does man live by bread alone ? I see it may be the most disastrous year to me I've ever known."

" You must have looked for a great deal."

" It's clear, Miss Fuller, I never looked for as much—it took me of a sudden—the great expectation—but I cannot give it up—I can't endure to give up this, I don't know as you could call it a hope—though why not ? It's as hard as to understand a woman. And that's what I've been trying to do."

" To understand a woman, Mr. Carradine ! Who could believe that ?"

" Miss Fuller, when I was a young man, I never ransacked the woods for flowers to present to a young lady. I didn't take to learning hymns, so that when she read or sang 'em I could follow in my mind, without a book, and think them over when I was going about my business. I did not know what a singer David was till I learned it from a woman. I want you to know what I have been doing and thinking, ever since I drove over to Brown's and engaged you. As you understand what I meant, when I was dubious about the harvest, there's only one kind voice can make all it will bring worth anything to me. And you must say the word, Miss Fuller."

But when he had done speaking, it seemed to Peter Carradine that she would never say it. Then and there he convicted himself of madness, and of folly ; of utter presumption. It was by an effort that he prevented himself from going off before he should hear the words he expected to hear when she should speak—a clear refusal, no matter how she might disguise it.

" What shall I say, Mr. Carradine ?"

He looked at her, astonished. She was plainly troubled —her voice and her look showed that she was. Did she really not understand him ? At least she was willing to speak to him again ! Imperious, proud man—yet where was his imperiousness, his pride ? It was even as he had said, suddenly all possessions were jeopardized ; suddenly their value needed to be pronounced upon, decided, by a voice, not of stock-jobber, nor speculator, nor controller of the market; but of a woman, young and frail to look at, to whom, however, somehow he had attached all his notions of steadfastness, and power, and eternity. It was not bone and sinew, it was not flesh and blood, it was not house and lands, it was not crowded barns, but a subtle spiritual power, independent of all these material things, before which his soul surrendered. And "go" or "stay"—the word she spoke must have his free obedience.

So he said, with a voice new to him, that never before had conveyed thought of his to mortal ear, a voice in which no pride was, except that of love, and no authority, save that of love, a pleading voice, that was noble in its bravery:

"There is but one thing that I have hoped for since I saw you—that is yourself, Miss Fuller. Not for Martindale—though great would be the gain—but for me! Not for the good you can do this people, though I understand it; but for my heart's life—that is what I mean—that is why I ask you. And it seems to me, ma'am, as if the Almighty had persuaded me to do it."

It was the good gift he had more than once asked, this man, at work in his fields and woodland, before sunrise or at nightfall, or in the hot noonday when resting under some shady tree—asked, knowing that there was a Power presiding over spirits, as well as over seasons, watchful of human hearts as well as of sparrows:

"Give me this life to make mine better, richer, purer!"

But he had the magnanimity to add also:

"Not if any wrong shall thus be done to her! Hear me not, if to hear be to interfere with some better portion she may have."

And now, as before God, he had asked her, and would know the answer of Providence.

Instead of replying, after a moment, Miss Fuller stepped out of the morning-glory walk to the path leading to the house; she looked toward it anxiously, as if the distance between her and it were interminable, and she was more agitated than Carradine had supposed that she could be. After she had taken a step or two, she seemed suddenly aware that he was not coming with her; then she turned and stood still, looking at him. But he also seemed to be spell-bound, as if he could not move. Or else, was it his pride? Not pride. He had given his destiny into her hands. She must do as she would. He could say no more.

"Will you come?" said she. It was her smile he followed, not the words she spoke. For having gone thus far in hope he would go no farther, except on some good assurance.

"I did not know you thought of this," said she, speaking kindly, evidently troubled.

"Think of it with me."

"I dare not. I cannot."

Carradine had said to himself that, if ever he should speak of this to Mercy, (and this morning he had thought that, before she left Martindale in the fall, perhaps by that time he should be able!) he would do no more than state the wish he had; she should act according to her pleasure; he did not want a wife whom he should need to persuade against her will! But now he said:

"Why do you not dare? If you could love a man, you would dare. I know—for I—it is only love that could give courage here. But my love for you must have made me blind, for how could I be so mad as to think you—could love me."

Peter Carradine! thus disloyal to himself!

She did not answer, but seemed plunged so deep in thought as not rightly to comprehend what he was saying.

"But," said he again, for any speech was better than such silence as this, "I never loved any woman before. And that you have made me love you, and carried me where I never supposed I should go; it seems to me it is not possible for one to love another so without—as if you must know what you have done to me! As if I must be something to you!"

"It is true," said she; "it is not possible, Mr. Carradine."

The words came from her faster than she was wont to speak, but with such distinctness that he lost not a single tone. Each word became henceforth a sacred possession. Unexpected as her answer was, it affected him no less strangely than a cool dismissal of his suit had done. Pale from his deep emotion, the strong man turned his face full upon her, as it seemed, in solemn wonder.

"Then you are mine," said he; but this was not an assertion, it was a question, rather.

And even in asking it he seemed to have received his answer. Looking at her, his hope was dashed with the conviction not to be withstood longer, of an inevitable defeat. No mood of his could change her view of this business. Otherwise than gently would she not deal with him. And yet, what were the rudest blow, the most savage thwarting, to the steadfast kindness of the look, the manner that denied him? Thus far he might come, no further, in approaches to her life. Here must his proud will be stayed.

There was something in her aspect that produced more than the mere pain of disappointment in Carradine. Something that excited him as a difficulty that must be met—an opposition that must be controlled. After all, he would not submit to her decree! He would enter the lists against her, if he must, and conquer, as it were an adversary!

A blast from Johnson's shell summoned them to breakfast. Mercy heard it, and it quickened her answer.

"Your reliable and responsible ally, Mr. Carradine, in any good and necessary work; but, don't think there's any other way for us."

She had begun to walk with rapid steps towards the house; he kept pace beside her, not speaking again till they came to the door, when he said in a changed voice, and more natural,

"Yes, there is, Miss Fuller, and I shall try to prove it to you."

It was not, he deemed, after all, one of those affairs in regard to which proof is irrelevant.

After breakfast, Mr. Carradine said to Johnson that he had concluded to drive to Brighton, and he would take Miss Fuller in the democrat, with her leave; she would thus get to town much earlier, and so escape the dust and confusion of the road when it should be crowded with carriages and people.

Miss Fuller, after a moment of rather surprised reflection, consented to be driven thus, and Johnson went to harness the sorrel. Rather thoughtfully he went about that business, for the arrangement made a change in the domestic programme which he liked not to communicate to Mrs. Johnson. He foresaw the talk and prophecies that would be repeated on the road to Brighton. He should be called upon again to defend Miss Fuller.

CHAPTER XXIII.

BY THE WAY.

Instead of preparing for Brighton, Miranda went down to Elder Green's early in the morning, to charge Sally with commissions. She supposed it was her father's rheumatism that kept her at home. Was it this indeed? Was this the sole and independent cause?

When Senior happened in, a day or two after the letter from Mr. Collamer, Randy showed him the magazines he had sent her, and told him how it had happened, and offered to lend them to him, would he like to read? And while he looked over the pages carelessly, to please her rather himself, for he was no reader, he said, she had in mind the letter, and it was less easy to make mention of that. At first she had thought that, of course, he must know that a letter had come to her through the office, and, for it was the first she had ever received, he would probably be curious about it; and he had a right to know. But when she spoke of these periodicals, and brought them to him, he had apparently no knowledge of them, asked no questions that betrayed an expectation that she had something to reveal. Perhaps, then, he knew nothing of the letter. Nevertheless, she said:

"He wrote to me too, Mr. Collamer did; he is settled in his church, and wrote about it. I'll get the letter if you'd like to see it."

"Why no," said Jobson, "I don't care about it."

"It was only to tell of a new place, and how he liked it, and the people. And he asked about Martindell. So I had promised I'd let him know, and I answered his letter."

"All right," said Jobson; and he said it so heartily that, if he had proposed then and there to take Randy to Brighton on "Independence Day," she would not have thought of an objection.

But when that day came round, her father seemed to stand between her and the celebration in an insurmountable way. And thus when Ethan Allen came at nightfall on the Third, to say that Randy could go with his mother, they were all going in the easy wagon, and her father seemed inclined to have her go, she answered that she would not leave him. And when Senior came up in the morning and offered to take her down to see the procession, promising that she would not be gone half the day from home, she was still more firmly fixed in her filial resolution.

The fact was merely this. Randy was in a condition of mind which no manner of show could interest. External things had no longer an independent charm for her. They might have hereafter, but not as once; and she was passing through a stage wherein it seemed to her that they could never have again. I doubt, even, if she would have much rejoiced had the Indian doctor worked one of his marvellous cures on her father that day; had loosened joints, and sinews, induced in the old man's mind the spirit of '76, and set his eyes toward Brighton. Her father was not quite easy in his mind about her decision. His indebtedness to Jobson was felt by him in ways quite new, unknown to him in relation to Carradine, while the mortgage was in existence. The thing he feared had come upon him. He was in direct communication with the ungodly. In debt to a publican, and a wine-bibber. His only consolation, when he had leisure to survey the business—and he had ample leisure after its transaction—was derived from the suggestions of hope, that was grounded in faith, and bore fruit in charity. Possibly—indeed how not—this was a leading of the Lord, to secure Senior's conversion. But he must be careful—wary—let the Lord work by him—but it must *be* the Lord's work. So he would have consented even that Randy should ride over to Brighton; but her determination to remain at home was immoveably fixed, it seemed that he might not interfere therewith. For interference also might be no less than an attempt to frustrate the Divine will!

Randy found Sally in her bed-room, dressing for the holiday. Her white muslin dress was spread out on the counterpane; on the pillows lay her black lace mitts, her fan, and fine hem-stitched linen handkerchief. Sally stood before the glass, arranging her hair, with serious face—for this was a serious occupation.

"Why," she said, when Miranda came into the room in her everyday dress, with her gingham sun-bonnet in her hand, "what time are you going to town?"

Randy explained.

"Go!" urged Sally. "Go! you have left your father alone before now."

"I don't mean to do it again, though—for pleasuring, I mean. You don't know how feeble he has grown this summer, Sally."

"I don't see it. He looks to me just as he has since I was four years old."

"I'd see it quicker than any one. I hope it's my fears that see it—I hope it isn't true."

"Of course it's your own getting up. And Fourth of July don't come but once a year," said Sally, who had set her heart on dissuading Miranda from this little sacrifice to filial love. "Can't you get enough of Martindale all the year round?"

"Oh, it won't seem dull; besides you'll see enough for two, Sally. You always see more than I do. You're quicker, and you're brighter every way."

"I can't see for two," said Sally, in a vexed tone, and she took down her hair and began to dress it over again. But she did it so quietly, without any impatience of gesture or touch, that it seemed not her ill success that troubled her. "I can't see for one, even! You're going to stay home to please your father—I'm going to Brighton to please mine! Huldah, (yes, I mean mother, you needn't look that way, because I call her Huldah,) she insists it wouldn't be any Fourth to father at all if I didn't go. So I'm going. And I hate it. I hate the fuss and the noise. Mind that! there's different ways for us to be of service. It's likely I can't oblige one without offending another. I can't see for you, and you can't see for me. I can't see things as father does. I wish I was in Jericho! How do you like my dress?"

"It's a pretty dress," said Randy, who had been standing at the foot of the bed admiring the pretty embroidered trimming of the loose sleeves and the waist.

"I never wore it but once—and I'll never wear it again. But to-day it is so warm, and I'm tired of everything else."

"I like a white dress, but it don't agree with me; though I never tried it, to be sure. There's two things I was going to ask you to do for me in Brighton," said Randy, helping Sally to put on her dress.

"I shall—I—what is it?" asked Sally, blushing scarlet—she had nearly declined the service, thinking that this was no day for doing errands; she had one great and absorbing service to perform; it was enough.

"I want you tell me all you do and see, for one thing—" she hesitated. Sally said:

"I told you I couldn't see for you, but I'll try. We shan't do anything but walk about, and roast ourselves, and sit in the church, like owls, listening to the oration. That was a pretty performance in the school-house yesterday, wasn't it? Getting a woman to read the Declaration of Independence! What would they do if we acted on it for ourselves, we women? What's the other thing you want?"

"I want two copy-books, and half-a-dozen sheets of white letter paper—ruled, you know. And some good pens. Here's the money." She laid half a dollar on the table, wrapped in a bit of paper.

"Two copy-books, a dozen sheets—"

"No, half-a-dozen."

"White and ruled—pens. I'll remember. Keep your money. I'll make you a Fourth of July present."

"I laid the fifty cents aside for it—so take the money; I had rather you would. I saved it on purpose."

"That's nothing; keep it for next time. But who's to have the letters? Collamer? I'll give you this white dress to be married in. Own up."

"Maybe for no letters at all," answered Randy, looking out of the window; then she said in a changed voice.: "you mustn't talk so about Mr. Collamer and me. It makes me feel ashamed. It isn't right on any of us. He doesn't care for me any more than he does for that looking-glass; and as for me, I'd be a fool to think of such a thing. I've got others to think of. I wish you wouldn't talk so; it made me sick to think of it when you said I was dead in love with him."

"Well, well; no matter how you take things. You needn't marry him; I won't make you. But I think it is written." Sally's eyes were fixed on Randy as she spoke; she smiled, but her look was abstracted and sad. "You think I'm cross. I'm not. But my head aches. If I should get my neck broken to-day—or be blown up by the cannon, so that I could never speak to you again, you may know I haven't laid up anything against you."

"Sally! Sally! come, come. Your father is waiting!" called Huldah from the first landing on the stairs. Sally seemed to hear with a dismay that her unreadiness did not account for. For she was never ready at the appointed moment, and usually it was a matter of very slight concernment that she should keep others waiting. For a moment she stood motionless; then she said:

"Help me—here are the big pins. Fasten on the ribbons so they will stay in their places. If there's anything I hate it's falling to pieces all day, after you're dressed. Town folks to stare and laugh. That's one thing I hate to go to Brighton for, town folks are so impertinent. They spend all they have on their backs; and they've got the notion that a hut in town is better than a palace in the country! (not to be wondered at either.) There—that will do. You're handy. How I tremble. No—it's the blue shawl I'm going to wear. The net one. Will it do? I won't forget your paper and the rest. There—thank the Lord! I'm ready."

So she took one last look in the glass, and saw that she was Sally Green, and hurried down the stairs. Randy followed.

Elder Green, his mother and his wife, were already in the carriage; and the doors and the windows of the house were fastened, except that through which the girls now passed.

"Lock the door and bring the key," cried the Elder, but Sally walked on, leaving Randy to perform that service. When she gave him the key he complimented her.

"That's you for a safe hand. Here's my girl! Nobody ever expects anything of her, for all her bringing up." But as he leaned forward to his daughter, and helped her to the seat beside him, it was a smile of genuine pride that met her gaze. He knew to a certainty that not a girl in Brighton could compare with Sally. But she stung him after her own style.

"If you don't expect anything, father, I'll try to not disappoint you."

He smiled again; it is said that there is a certain degree of pleasure communicated by every kind of pain. A little short of knowledge—fire and ice are one, in the sensations they occasion.

Thus they set out, smiling and bowing at Randy, who went home with the half dollar in her palm, finding it difficult to deem her friend unkind, ungenerous.

"There!" exclaimed Sally, when the horses were trotting through their first quarter of a mile.

Her father looked up, startled, as though about to rein in the steeds, but she said "Nothing!" and laughed at his fright.

"You haven't forgot your ribbons," said Esther, the grandmother, "that is certain."

"Here's a pin, Sally. You had best fasten the handkercher to your waist. You'll lose it, maybe, getting out and in," said her mother.

"Is it the hem-stitched one?" asked the Elder.

"Oh, I'll take care. Yes; it's the hem-stitch," she answered, not very patiently. They were all too attentive, too thoughtful of her. "Father, let me drive."

"No, no," cried Esther, "not on Independence day—I won't be drove to destruction. What is the creetur thinking of—with every team in the country on the road! Elder, I'm too old to be throwed. At my time of life to be bedrid!"

"Grandma, I'm not driving," said Sally, harshly rebuking the old body's fears.

"But, you foolish creetur, don't I know you couldn't ask for the moon, but your father would set to thinking if he couldn't get a line long enough to draw her in?"

"There's many a thing I might ask for long enough before I'd get it," answered Sally. "You are so suspicious."

"I couldn't have brought up a boy so and lived in the house with him," said the Elder, and he never would have said this, for he did not exactly think it, had not his daughter's mood made him a little uncomfortable. He was sensitive to all her moods and changes, and to-day he stood for peace; he would fain ensue it. He thought the acknowledgment would make Sally more quiet and kind.

"What would you have done with a boy?" asked Huldah; she asked because she thought that the Elder had something on his mind he would like to express.

"Made a man of him!" he answered, so promptly as to prove that she was right in her suspicion. "Men understand they can't have their own way always—they have to give up. But girls—it's coaxing they must have. It's never do this, and she doeth it. Girls are girls, and boys are boys."

"And a long, easy rein is bad for one as 'tother," said Esther Green.

A remark that was lost on Sally, for she was thinking again of that which had caused the sudden start and exclamation five minutes ago. How that it had been her purpose and intention to pray for direction, when she had dressed herself, before she left her chamber. For guidance, that day! But Miranda had come and hindered her—and here she was, to go her own ways—to take counsel of herself, and to keep secret her counsel; limiting the Almighty. And this was Independence Day.

As they approached the town, the inmates of this, and, I suppose, of every other carriage coming in from north, south, east, and west, gradually were drawn out to forget themselves, and the familiar life they had left behind them, in view of the strangeness of scene and of face in this broad field of conjecture and observation.

Brighton was alive with dust and noise, with policemen, military companies, bands of musicians, fire-crackers, and spectators. At sunrise the roar and the rush began; and it had waxed in volume and in swiftness ever since. Everybody understood that this was to be the greatest celebration Brighton had attempted in years, and everybody came to see if this was true.

Elder Green got rid of his horses as soon as possible, and on the crowded steps of the inn where his grays were always sure of the best treatment, Sarah saw Oliver Savage standing.

The whole family recognized him at once, and Elder Green, who was in some perplexity as to what he should do with his women while he went to see to his horses, relieved at the sight of a familiar face, beckoned to Oliver, who at once made his way through the crowd, and stood, all respect and deference, by the Elder's carriage door.

Would Oliver just stay with the Elder's folks ten minutes ?

The young man hardly answered in words, but opening the carriage door, helped the ladies to alight, and Sarah last. Happy they were to be conducted by such skill as his through the crowd into the back room of the little inn, at whose window he stationed himself, that he might accost the Elder when he should go up the lane, and let him know where the women had found shelter.

CHAPTER XXIV.

THE FACT CONCLUDED.

The Elder's mother might now adjust her shawl and bonnet, and the Elder's wife her cap strings;—as for Sally, she sat down silent on the hard old threadbare sofa, having taken a mere glance at herself in the glass. A disdainful glance it seemed, as if it were not of the slightest consequence what figure she made; and this feeling had perversely stirred, because she caught the admiring glance of Oliver at the moment that she turned her eyes toward the glass.

"Don't you want to look at yourself! Are you all right?" asked her grandmother, whose earthly pride was centred in Sally Green's good looks.

"Not through that lace and 'sparagrass," answered Sally.

"Well, you're all right," said the old lady, who seemed to be on the point of appealing to Oliver Savage if it were not so. Such purpose, if such she had, was frustrated, and herself startled, by Oliver's voice shouting to the Elder, who had passed by him unobserved—so he leaped through the window, and ran after him; and, it seemed hardly a moment after, appeared at the door of the room, following the Elder.

"Come," said that good man. "Are you all ready, my girls?" then he laughed, for the spirit of the day had already inspired him.

They came, one after another, to the door, and, for the first time, the Elder seemed to be at a loss. Then he said, with generous trust, "Mother, you take my right arm. Wife, you take my left. Oliver, bring on Sally."

This arrangement, fulfilling, as it did, the expectation of the young people, seemed to impress them. Oliver's eye shone triumphant. Sally looked more grave; but she seemed to see something of moment in this prophecy fulfilled, as if it were even a providence!

Huldah appeared disposed to revise the arrangement. To say that she would walk with Sally, and not trouble Oliver; or that she would walk with Oliver, and leave the Elder to look after his mother, he would find the steps of one as much as he could direct; but a glance around the company made her restrain these words. She could not be for ever interfering, disconcerting and displeasing everybody. And so they walked down the street according to the Elder's injunction; careful, at first, that no other foot passengers should break up their party—the younger following closely in the footsteps of the Elder But as soon as they were fairly mixed in with the crowd, Oliver drew from his pocket a little package, and gave it to Sally, without speaking.

"What's that?" said she.

"The bride's gloves," he answered. "And I have the ring in my pocket. A pretty gold ring to put on the finger of my wife."

"A good many days from now," said she.

"Oh! you haven't changed your mind. When I saw you in the carriage, with the white dress on, I knew what I knew before, that Sally Green could never break her promise. And if you were dressed a hundred times for it, you couldn't look so pretty."

"But you look like a bridegroom, don't you, Oliver?" she asked, curtly, surveying him from head to foot, with a glance so swift and sharp it scathed him.

"Not if you are ashamed of me," said he, firing up. "On no account. I made myself decent, I thought. I said to myself, she will expect that."

"So you have," said she, relenting a little. "Give me the gloves. We won't quarrel here in the street."

"I went down," he said, speaking with delight. "I found the minister—and he don't know you nor me; so there won't be no difficulty. He said he should have his hands full to-day, and the earlier we come the better."

Then said Sally, as if once for all—in a determined voice, yet it was a woman's voice—"Now hear me, Oliver. I said I would marry you to-day. And I mean to stand by my promise. But when we find father and mother again, not a word! Things shall be as they are till autumn. I've been thinking it over on the way down here. You're not to speak a word till I make the sign—but go on as you have. Only better, I hope. And try and make father like you."

But he swore that she was too hard, and she shouldn't make all the bargain.

Then she answered, "Very well. Let's hurry on and overtake them. And here are your gloves. Keep them till I ask for them—but if you find another girl you can talk over to believe in you—such a fool as I am—"

"Now, Sally, hush. Have your way. Here is the minister's house. They are hurrying on to get down to the Square. If we are quick about it, we shall join them in ten minutes."

It was at last the possibility of such expedition that seemed to decide the question! A gentleman in threadbare black suit just then opened the door, and while she, in her mind, was still hesitating, Oliver said:

"Here we are, sir!" and they stood in the passage, and Oliver had closed the door behind them in an instant. The minister seemed to understand the circumstances. He led them at once into a little room that looked like an office, where sat a young person writing in a book. On the entrance of the party, he took out from the drawer of the table a narrow strip of paper, on which various devices were engraved, and drawing an inkstand towards him, dipped the pen lying thereon in the ink, and wrote with a flourish at the left corner of the paper,—it was a marriage certificate he had thus signed. When he had done this, he looked for the first time with deliberation at the young persons before whom stood the minister. He saw what did not seem to greatly interest him—a respectable looking young fellow, and a pretty, well dressed girl.

When the minister addressed the man he arose, and stood through the ceremony—it was not three minutes long. Then, for they had none of their time to lose, the bride and bridegroom signed their names to the certificate, and Sally took off her white gloves—Oliver put the ring upon her finger—she drew on her black mits again, and they left the house. Hardly a word except those needful in the progress of the ceremony had broken the silence of the room. Within how still! Without, in the thronged street, what laughter, and fun, and noise, and strife!

They had been within that house's door just seven minutes, as the town clock in the tower opposite informed them when they emerged into the street, and joined in the throng that was passing towards the Square.

"Now," said Sally, "I've done it! don't forget your promises. We shall have a good day to-day."

Oliver drew her arm within his without speaking, and they hurried on. Then she lifted up her left hand and looked at the ring.

"If you didn't know what this meant, should you notice it?" asked she.

"Should *I*?"

"Would anybody, do you think?"

"We shall see," he answered. He rather thought that "anybody" would; but he chose to let things take their own course now. He was, for his part, satisfied with what had been done. How proud he felt as he walked arm in arm with Sally. It were worth while to scan that poor trivial human pride of his—so cheap and so common; the pride that sets up one man, and sets another to creeping and cringing through the world—that world which would make better natures than ours blush, if they could by any means comprehend its vacuity and folly. He was thinking, as he walked with Sally down the street, that now he was Elder Green's son-in-law,—and a rich man. He would like to see any man attempt to put *him* down! He was not in the least the same person that he was an hour ago! He would be one of the rich men of Martindale at last!—should have his horses, and his carriage, and there would be different living in the old brown farm-house when he and Sally took the place of Elder Green! The poor wretch was congratulating himself on the fine clothes he would have, the feasting, the ease, the authority, and had no higher thought of the part he had taken this day, and of his part in life henceforth, than thousands just like him have. Anything that could have dignified the transaction recorded was far removed from it.

They were longer than they had hoped in regaining their party, and both were struck, and both laughed when they came in sight of Elder and Huldah Green, and the Elder's mother, their faces looked so anxious and so troubled. Old Esther was was quite pale with the excitement of her walk, and this crowning disturbance.

But the young people took it easily when, with one voice they were interrogated,

" Where *have* you been ?"

Sally explained how they had got separated, it was easily done—and then they had seen a blind man with bagpipes, led by a boy who imitated the singing of birds, and they stopped to listen ; all which was true, and found credence, for Esther said that she was of a mind herself to stop, only the Elder wouldn't hear to anything until they got down to the Square. He wanted to see the procession form, and then he promised they would go and hunt up all the sights.

So they all stood together now on the steps of the Court House, and watched the preparations, and Oliver won a thankful smile for himself by getting a chair for Esther ; a fact which excited as much notice and surprise as if he were a magician, and had made it to order. He might be an utterly worthless fellow, selfish, foolish, vain, but that did not hinder his making himself very agreeable at such a time. He was observing, and his eyes never rested for a second— there was little that escaped them, and he made spectacles of himself for Esther ; and ears of himself for the Elder, who was anxious to know every order that issued through the Marshal's trumpet.

When the procession began to move, the crowds along the sidewalk also set in motion, and the Elder's family, attended by Oliver, followed with the rest, in that wandering which did not really terminate until they were all fairly stowed away in their carriages, and the horses' heads turned homeward.

Oliver grew bold in the latter part of the day to ask the Elder if he might drive Sally home by moonlight, after the fireworks—a request the father had not to deny, for it met with Sally's instant refusal. And to hear her speaking out so promptly set all their hearts at ease, for after the service he had really rendered them was over, they had all of them misgivings whether such a day might not have been bought at a dear rate, if it seemed to encourage Oliver's pretensions in his own mind, or in Sally's.

Her prompt refusal to remain set all their hearts at rest, and they went home agreeing that never was such a Fourth.

But when Oliver helped Sally into the carriage he did not see the ring on the fourth finger of her left hand, and it was enough to trouble him for the remainder of the evening. Though he said to himself, of course she must have worn it, only it was hidden by the black lace mit.

How many minds, I wonder, of all who celebrate "Independence," remained, from morning until night, untroubled by personal concerns, and the affairs of their neighbors?

Mrs. Johnson said to her husband, on the way to town in the morning: "It may look fair to her, but who would ever a thought *she* would have need of a warning!"

"I don't see it so," said Johnson. "She was going to Brighton, and so was he, of course. I never knew him to lose a Fourth. I knew he would have out Sorrel, just as well before he said it as I did after. And of course he would like to have a pretty young woman alongside. Who wouldn't?"

Mrs. Johnson looked as though she considered her husband's obtuseness contemptible, but she said nothing of the sort. She tried to be as patient and forbearing, now that they stood on a Christian equality, as she had been in days when she prayed as for life for his conversion. "He is fond of her," said she. "And it may look fair to her. But till we got used to Mr. Carradine's ways he was a dreadful hand to deal with. And he is not after her kind."

"He is not the same man he was, though, when we first came to Martindell," Johnson allowed. "And I think it's you that did it."

"I want to see the end of it," said she, not indifferent to his appreciating praise, though she had habitually regarded it as her right—especially at times when it had been withheld.

"But you wouldn't want what you expect to come true?" said Johnson, forbearing to look at his wife even when she did not answer. Then he continued:

"I don't think it will. He is an impossible man to drive—but you know that them that understands know how easy 'tis to lead him. That's what she will do."

"But she must be a deep one! How should she know the way?"

"Because they was meant for each other," answered Johnson.

"Oh, you! how can you tell that?" returned his wife, in spite of herself constantly betraying her vexation.

"Wife! what's the matter?"

"Mind the horses. Do you suppose that she really cares one pea straw for—him?"

"Yes'm."

"The last woman! He might as well be tackled to a wax doll."

"Why don't she take an interest in the stock, as womankind don't often, not in general. When she made them pictures of Ajax, as she calls 'em, and the big horse, and drawed them flocks o' sheep for Harry, could she done it if she didn't see their purty pints? That's what he likes. He likes to hear her praise 'em, better than cattle dealers, or them that comes for trade. I know *him*. As if for all the world she was brung up among 'em."

"No better for a farmer's wife than a wax doll," replied she.

"He don't want a wife for a hard-working woman—don't ye see it? I've seen him fixing his eyes to her white slim hands, as if they was a lily. Didn't he say once he didn't want a wife for a drudge when somebody was recommended?"

"The first man of that way of thinking, then," returned Mrs. Johnson. But she seemed at once to repent the words, for she dropped the extraordinary and most hateful subject, and allowed herself to be taken up by the sights and sounds among which they were passing. And Johnson, assured by repeated words and looks that she was herself again, began to look about him with a brightened face, and to breathe more easily.

As Oliver Savage fancied, and yet could not believe, Sarah had not on the ring when she rode home. She had taken it off and pinned it inside her belt, determined that as yet no suspicions of what she had done should be excited in any person's mind. This was the reason of the act as acknowledged to herself. But it was not really the reason. Had she, without suspicion, loved the man, she had the measure, and that quality of self-will, that would have led her to make no concealment of the marriage. No fear of consequences would have constrained her to secrecy.

Perhaps she feared still less the scrutiny to which she might be subject at home, than that of Miranda. Nothing ever escaped Randy's eyes—it seemed to Sally that her secret would betray itself to her when they should meet. But before she could carry up the package of paper, etc., she must go home. She must take off this dress, no longer white and pure. This bridal dress, which she meant to wear no more. Then she must help about preparing supper—they were all so tired. Perhaps it would be too late to go to-night in search of Randy.

"We shall have rain before we get home," said her father. From the darkling sky he looked at the girl by his side; how could she be screened and defended? That was the question that disturbed him. Wasn't there room for Sally behind there?

But she laughed, and her lightest laugh thrilled him always.

"Then we shall get all the Brighton dust washed off before we come to Martindell—that's good—drive slower, father, please." Her satisfaction when the rain came driving down upon them was not shared by the rest of the party—and when they came to the shelter of the shed, her laughter was incomprehensible, as she pointed to her dripping and ruined bonnet-strings, and looked down on her torn, tumbled, soiled white dress.

But when she ran into the house, and then up to her chamber, and threw off this holiday gear, she could nowhere find her wedding ring.

CHAPTER XXV.

MR. CARRADINE CONSULTS WITH MRS. JOHNSON.

Mr. Carradine came back from Brighton alone in his democrat, for Miss Fuller was to remain with her friends until Monday morning.

He had driven her down as rapidly as he promised; there was not much such driving, even that day, on the road to Brighton; and there was no recurrence to the morning topic. The success of the celebration in Martindale, the delight of the old "relict" in the school exercises, the prospects of the Brighton turn out, the state and quality of the crops on the farm lands they passed, such matters sufficed for the moments of the drive. Mr. Carradine had really cause to congratulate himself on the dignity with which he had deported himself. He did no such thing.

One might have supposed that of all days in the year duties urged upon him most imperatively that day, from the haste with which, declining the Commissioner's proffered hospitalities, he drove from his door and through the town; but not towards Martindale.

In the vicinity of Brighton were many handsome residences of "gentlemen-farmers," as they were called, and these were in the mind of Carradine. He had acquaintance with the proprietors of several of these places, and his purpose was the same to-day that it was a month ago; if any change had taken place in it, is was merely the change by which a plan remotely possible, became immediately imperative.

He slackened the reins when Sorrel had brought him to the southern borders of the town, and drove more quietly through the suburbs of Brighton, for he was hesitating as to which road he should take; on his choice depended the style of mansion he should visit. His hesitation seemed to be decided by the troops of country people thronging into town. He took the quietest road, and went to enquire concerning Hooper's stock.

As he drove along the carriage road through the handsome grounds, his eyes seemed to have acquired some new nerve and power. All the way he was enquiring diligently what it was that made this place so charming to the eyes of Miss Fuller. For, he now remembered, and the recollection startled him, as in it were the most wonderful coincidence, if indeed he might not call it providential, he remembered how Mercy had spoken, with eloquent gratitude even, of the charming effect produced by the tasteful arrangement and decoration of the grounds about the Hooper mansion, and asked him if he had ever seen them.

He *had* seen them—yes—but surely never as now. Never *had* he seen more grass and flowers, more trees and gravel walks, under an atmosphere so glorifying as glowed over slope and dwelling on this sultry July day. And one might fearlessly have certified to the man's admiration, who watched him on that drive. His breeding had not taught him to conceal even his surprise, and much more, his pleasure. On the spot he yielded generous tribute to the day, the hour, and place. But Miss Fuller was responsible for that. Where she had praised, he might safely stand up in his waggon, and closely survey the scene through which he passed at Sorrel's slowest pace.

At the end of his drive Carradine could have given a correct estimate of the number of ornamental trees he should require, the quantity of gravel, and the time it would take Johnson, with assistance, to transform "the slope" into a lawn like this.

For Mr. Carradine had a well arranged design in view, else would he never have driven here to make this observation.

As he approached the house, a workman busy in the grounds came forward, hat in hand, with the information that the master and his family had left home in the morning, not "for the Fourth"—they had gone on a journey.

A brief conference with himself was all Mr. Carradine required. The event, untoward though it seemed, need not deter his proposed investigation of the stock, nor, what was more directly to the purpose, an interview with the head gardener, nor indeed, as it proved, with the head housemaid.

In consequence of all the enlightenment he received, Mr. Carradine drove back to Brighton, and home to Martindale, with a "ground plan" in his mind, and a book on *Landscape Gardening* in his pocket, and a bargain well considered among his calculations, that should yet be made with a high authority among the Brighton architects.

From this time forth his mind was occupied with one thought; his brain teemed with plans for the future which that thought devised. He calculated, and provided, for every contingency. Prominent among his plans for the future was the removal of the Johnson family from his own house to another farm, on which stood a building, respectable and commodious, capable at least of being made so. In a time that surely was to come he would wish to be no longer under even such observation, and exposed to such criticisms as possibly he might have at the hands of those friends who had gone with him through the hurry and worry, the toil and rest, of the past ten years.

Though he might never marry, why should a man hoard his money, hide it in banks and in mortgages, and live like a beggar? At the moment when he drove away from Mr. Hooper's "pleasure," he recognized a new claim on him, as a man of wealth. It was his *business* to beautify the earth; at least so much of it as that nook he occupied, when the eyes of other people, such eyes as Mercy Fuller's, could thereby be refreshed.

Many were the improvements to be made in the old red farm house on the hill before he would again ask a woman to become its mistress. But the house itself should stand. He would no more have thought of removing that "landmark" than he could have brought himself to remove the ruins of his father's house from the face of the earth.

More than once this solid, unpretending man, this grave, taciturn farmer from Martindale, this dealer in stock, went over to Brighton and walked through the gay furniture ware-rooms, making himself a judge of fancy woods, of damask and brocatel; and if he crossed the threshold of any house in town, no man was more observing—the carpet on which he trod became a known thing to his eye and his touch; the use of useful and of ornamental things was solved to his apprehension and appreciation; his sense of comfort daily was enlarged, made to take cognizance of the ideas of others,—how broad and fair, enriched with what splendor did the ideal Home arise! The Home of Peter Carradine.

Any decent order, any mere abundance, was good enough for him, he constantly assured himself; and as constantly allowed that since he had more money than he knew well how to use, he had a special call to embellish and adorn the nook of ground which God had given him. Was not Adam set in the garden to keep, and to DRESS it!

But in fact Mr. Carradine was thinking constantly and solely in all he did and purposed of Mercy's taste and pleasure: and constantly did he endeavor to conform *himself* to her, adopting ways that harmonized with hers. It made no apparent difference in his secret calculations even, that he had been unable to achieve her consent. He did not shut himself up and out, to old habits of barbarism. Carradine was loving, once and forever, a spirit and a fervor that was not himself; and in many ways did he endeavor to conform to it. It was a moving spectacle. Where such sights are distinctly seen, above our mists and bewilderments, far away from our dull oversights and sad misapprehensions, it must have been a beautiful spectacle. To become conscious of imperfection and deficiency, humbly and reverently a disciple, is always a fair sight—and this they saw who from their heights looked down in tender sympathy on Peter Carradine, and wished him well, and haply furthered him, if not his endeavor.

The farm house must unquestionably be changed—and in many respects. It must be painted throughout—and two coats at the least. Whitewashers, and plasterers, and paper hangers, must prove their skill on the loose dingy walls, and the discolored ceilings. He would consult with the men. And with Mrs. Johnson also!

With Mrs. Johnson at once! And he never thought to wonder whether Miss Fuller had betrayed him, and his failure to her.

Nor did he wait for any "more convenient season," for any special moment, when all things should make the way to such speech easy. Carradine had not been so gently dealt with as to have become a student of the ways and means of a cautious self-love. It came out as if he had asked any question about field-work.

"Mrs. Johnson, let me see how long is it we have lived in the old rookery together?"

"Ten years, Mr. Carradine. Ten years lacking one month. Coming September, we're up to the day when Johnson and I first stood out there and heard you bothering about the crockery that was broken on the corduroy."

"Yes, yes—and you looked like a couple of drownded rats, and very homesick, when you saw the crockery. You never thought it was made up to you—and I know you couldn't, in reason, if I gave you a crockery store out of Brighton. I know when a bit of the old comes on the table—the dish for the honey—you keep that by itself yet."

"I never gin it into another's hands for a washing—it was give to me before I ever see Johnson."

"Ten years!" mused Carradine. "I thought it wouldn't be that long when we were getting through the first twelve-month. But we understand each other better now. I hope we shall always live within sight of each other, It speaks well for us all, that we could live peaceably under one roof so long."

"That's what we're often saying, sir, Johnson and me," she answered, drawing a long breath, and to herself observing, "There's something curious hanging to the tail of this here."

"And there's that boy of yours! I couldn't think more of the chap if he belonged to me. I had Harry in my arms before he was two days old. I shall look out for Harry. I'm Harry's uncle, you know. That makes me brother to you! Do you like the relation, Mrs. Johnson?"

Mrs. Johnson could have smiled with her whole heart, if it must not needs be she should smile with but half a one. There was something coming yet! Mercy Fuller flashed before her thought. It was for that her face flushed, and not by any means because of Mr. Carradine's kind pleasantry.

"There's nary one out the house, sir, stands a chance with Uncle Carradine with Harry," she answered.

And now there was a pause—the silence was that which

novelists compare with the profound stillness that precedes the storm's revelations on a summer's day. Then, in a lower voice that was quite natural, spoke Carradine,

"I've been thinking of fitting up the Bronson farm-house, Mrs. Johnson. I was round there this morning, looking at it. It seems a pity such a good house should go to ruin, all for want of tenants; and that's what you've said to me more than once. And not half the work you have up here in this big barn of a place."

"As to that," said Mrs. Johnson, with a pang of quickening intelligence, "I don't know who could say I ever complained of the red farm housen! Work is work, wherever you find it. And I'm none of your grumblers, Mr. Carradine, whatever else I be."

"Bless you! don't I know it? But I want to do the best by you—that's all. You'll be your own masters and mistresses down there, and feel more at home, I'm sure.— Besides, it will be handier there for Jobson. Vastly. I always thought this house stood in an out of the way, ridiculous situation, except for star-gazers. I don't mean to have the heft of the farm work done up here much longer. That's one reason why I think it will be best to get you and Johnson, and the chap, to living down there in the fall. I can make a nice little place of it, and it shall be all done to your mind."

"That's *one* reason—what's the other, Mr. Carradine? I expect it isn't *us* you're thinking on, altogether."

There was nothing more to fear now; the cloud was rent, the bolt had fallen; she had a right to know the worst. That her voice expressed—and that he recognized.

"The other," said he, looking at her as if ashamed of his embarrassment, so confident that she would be pleased, or should be pleased by the announcement—"the other is that I am going to make the old place all over again, and it won't look any longer so much like a rookery. You *ought* to be glad of it. I know you well enough to see that you *would* approve of the changes if you were once fairly outside."

"Are you going to be married, Mr. Carradine?"

This was a question. Before he answered, Carradine looked through the soul of the woman who asked it—then his face softened, the displeasure with which it had quickened passed quite out of sight—and he said,

"What woman in the world would have me, do you think?"

Quick was the answer—"There's plenty, I guess, that's got business enough on hand of setting their caps for you." But before the words had fairly escaped her, the penitent soul of the woman fell low before the thought of Mercy Fuller.

"Would you give your consent, then, Mrs. Johnson? I'm sure you would be glad if so much was to be made of Carradine after all."

"Pleased, sir! Then 't 'll happen! I knew it. No! I'm not pleased one bit nor grain. What's any woman going to do to make more of you, but a bill of expense?"

"Well—well, I thank you for your good opinion. If ever I take a wife, and I don't see that it's likely, you must think I've got a prize, for I shall have one, Mrs. Johnson. We've thought alike so long, you know, we must keep it up to the end."

"Prize! there ain't no prizes! They say it's a lottery, marriage is! But if I thought Miss Fuller was a blank, and warned you of it, sir, you couldn't be made to see it. Nobody ever was, who got his mind set that way."

"Miss Fuller!" said Mr. Carradine—"what made you think of her?"

"Who else is there to think of?"

"Why, one needn't go as far as Brighton, need he, to find a good wife? Ain't the girls of Martindell good enough, any one of them, for Peter Carradine? Now I put it to you, Mrs. Johnson."

"May be," she answered. Then looking at him as if puzzled and impatient with this strange talk, "I know well what you think. There's one woman, not reared in Martindell, goodness knows where she did come from, but *she's* good enough. I've nothing to say agen her, but it took a stranger to come here and work a miracle, as one might say, a'most."

"You're mistaken, though," said Carradine quietly, amused by Mrs. Johnson's unusual spirit, and the vexation she cared not in the least to conceal.

"Now there's Randy," he began—but he got no further. That was the word too many in connection with the foregone.

"Randy! Yes, and a first best of a girl. But all you could do for her was to pick a quarrel. How 'll I forgive myself when it was my own boy set you on to that?"

"I think much of Randy, Mrs. Johnson. And you're in a fog—that's all. We're friends at heart this moment, I believe. I respect Randy. You must believe that. She's a good woman—a fine girl, Randy is."

"Thank you, sir, for that! You never said a truer thing," said Mrs. Johnson with spirit, and she looked for the instant as pleased, as if she had received a personal compliment. He took advantage of that moment.

"Come," he said, "I'm going down to look at the farm-house so that I can give my orders when I go to town. I want your advice." And he started off. She could not do otherwise than follow. She knew that there was no reversal to be expected of his decision. He had said that marriage was *not* his intention—or, as good as said it. And though she did not quite believe it, the assurance half reconciled her, strange to say.

Accordingly they walked down together to the Bronson farm house.

And Mr. Carradine, leading the way through that habitation, which Mrs. Johnson knew he had intended, in the spring, to turn into a store-house when the fall should come, pointed out to her the changes he would have the carpenters make in it, and explained the effect to be produced by paint and furniture, to all which she gave her consent, and seemed while he was speaking, almost pleased.

He was glad thus to construe the expression of her face and the words she spoke, for he would not have been easy in his mind if he had thought the contemplated changes would really long disturb that pains-taking, honest woman.

But she had in the end disguised her real feelings. The source of many a future hour's homesickness was hidden under her consenting smile. The big housen, which she had often complained of, never looked so pleasant to her as when they returned to it from visiting the Bronson cottage. Henceforth the old red farm house was to stand in place of the village home she had pined for these many years. To its doors and windows she would fasten her flags of distress; the banners of memory, covered over with significant devices. There her Harry was born—there her husband was converted—there the baby died. There she had toiled—and all her rest was there! What misunderstandings—what reconciliations under that old roof! The farm house on the hill was become a sarcophagus—and there was entombed her glory!

CHAPTER XXVI.

THE PROGRESS OF AFFAIRS.

Miss FULLER came back to Martindale on Sunday afternoon; and on Monday morning resumed her school teaching. Full of calm serenity she went about her work—things external took their usual course. Except that Mr. Carradine began his improvements, making preparations for the work he intended to prosecute vigorously when the season's hurry should be over. Sometimes he might have been found in an hour of rest reading books that Mercy talked about. Sometimes he might have been found in quiet conversation with her, but to their talk any third person might have listened without apology. Mrs. Johnson was at a sore loss.

When the improvements were at length begun in the old house, and became legitimate subjects of neighborhood speculation, in that a modern residence was manifestly to be made of the ancient dwelling, Mr. Carradine vouchsafed this gracious answer, that he had concluded if he *must* grow old, he would not at the same time grow rusty; he had done as much as any other man towards improving the stock of the surrounding country; he had imported more than any other man within a dozen miles, had hazarded and lost more; and having done this duty, he was now going to do his pleasure, while he held it to be a duty also, and he advised his neighbors to follow his example, and not live in worse houses than they gave their cattle.

He got through these explanations with a better grace, and more readily than he anticipated—for the comments and speculations of his neighbors had in prospect made Carradine sometimes nervous. It seemed to him as if one and all must see through his notions. And yet he was not, he hoped, attempting to make of his house a decoy. Surely Miss Fuller was not a woman to be won by any such device!

Miranda, in these days, was not neglecting penmanship. Now and then a letter came from the minister, bearing her address; it always had an answer. But never letter came or went that was unobserved by Senior Jobson. Once he read half through one of these epistles from the minister, for Randy placed it open in his hands, but it did not interest or amuse him; he saw nothing in it except a decent chirogaphy —as to suspicion or jealousy, he would as soon have thought of any other nonsense. Not he! the girl he trusted and asked to be his wife was, as Cæsar's wife should have been, above suspicion. "Not at all, or all in all," she was to be believed in, and he, a man ostensibly without faith, credited to the full, wholly relied on Miranda. To the full, I say— that is, according to the necessity admitted, the desirableness acknowledged.

The fact that he desired to marry her, recognized her efficience, admired the vision of the future landlady of the renewed Spread Eagle, did not necessitate on his part a love that should transform him to the entire retrieval of his character, taste and being. His regard for Randy was the finest sentiment, and the best developed, of which his state was cognizant, but so far as it was developed it was not an omnipotent sentiment, capable of his entire transformation.

But as these letters came and went, how were they read, how written by Miranda? As by one who sees an opportunity of improvement, and ambitiously avails herself thereof? She was, in truth, a severe student in this matter, and the letters were such a rescript as had authority with him to whom they came.

They were religious themes that chiefly occupied them; it was under this form that the highest life of Miranda escaped her and came within another's cognizance. Sometimes she would repeat to Senior what she had written on some point, but he did not often see it in her light, and passed carelessly, if not rudely, over some matter vital to her, and sure to be recognized as such by the deep-thinking man to whom she had more directly addressed the meditation, or confession, whichever it might be.

This was the truth concerning her; that since the camp-meeting Randy's life had grown in a direction unforeseen by her, or by any mortal man or woman of that town of Martindale ; through avenues unnoticed before, the tide of her life was pouring, in its richness and its strength ; a pure and sparkling tide, whose banks seemed firm and high ; no danger now of the wasteful morass, the dismal slough! All was open, clear and pure !

And Sally's accusation, which had caused her much pain indeed, had done no damage surely—possibly much service. One does not fall in love if he is on his guard against surprise, from without or within—does he, oh gentle reader ? Randy might trust herself to read and to write those letters. Growing every day in wisdom, and in goodness, as her father testified, and as Jobson could not help seeing, and as her own heart might have told her, she could not also, at the same time, have suffered from an increasing blindness that could hinder her from seeing the way she went, whither she was going. What must be the end ? Certain it is that conjecture as to what the end of all this friendly intercourse might be, did not trouble her. So she would have said and deemed had the question been suggested. But there were other matters that did greatly trouble Randy. At times there was that in the manner of Sally Green that she could not understand, and it greatly disturbed her. It surprised her into doubts, and questionings, connected with past experiences—the days of camp-meeting—the gift of the hymn-book—the letters Elder Green sometimes received from Mr. Collamer, and the Elder's acknowledgment to Samuel Roy, that, if the minister wanted *his* daughter, he would say *Amen* to it, and *God bless her*.

Since that morning when Randy helped Sally to dress for the celebration of the Fourth at Brighton, it had seemed to her as if something hindered their approach to each other. They met but rarely, and on those occasions Sally's mind seemed to be pre-occupied, even gravely absorbed.

Besides, a mania for household industry seemed to have seized upon her. She occupied herself zealously with matters of domestic economy, in a manner perfectly astonishing to those familiar with her lifelong habits. There were times when, in view of this change, which was accompanied by an unusual docility, blessed Huldah Green regretted that she had unburdened her thoughts in regard to Sally in Miss Fuller's hearing.

Sally and Oliver did not often meet in these days. The ring she missed on her return from the holiday was not to be found, though she had searched the carriage, and the shed, and the lane. Oliver, disturbed by its continued invisibility, asked some plain questions, which were answered with something like evasion. She had told him that he must look for no change in his circumstances until autumn, and, of course, expected that he would abide by that decision; meanwhile it was not her purpose to excite suspicion, or to disturb any person's peace of mind merely for the sake of decorating her fourth finger! In the fall he would see that she had done wisely. While she spoke thus, or while they remained together, it was not difficult for Sally to convince him—but he would not stay convinced. Returning to the squalor and discontent of his own home, or to the daily toil by which he lived, he was ready to give credence to any bar-room gossip concerning Sally's doings or intentions, or the Elder's purposes and ambition concerning her—or he allowed some unfortunate word of hers to rankle in his memory, till it was sore and exasperating. Until she should acknowledge him, he felt by no means sure of his great prize, in spite of marriage ring and marriage certificate.

Moreover, Oliver had legitimate cause for much mental disturbance. He was encumbering himself with debts. He had the faculty of borrowing money, and of spending it again in ways that might seem to a sober-minded person incredible. The surprising part of it was that he himself never seemed to know what he had done with his capital—so it was also that often, when at Brighton, he was making such purchases on credit as nobody but lunatics or imbeciles ever dreamed of doing. Running in debt for finery and folly, being clearly an imbecile or insane style of business. Alas, poor Oliver! must he not make his wife some bridal gifts? and those showy, precious ornaments, he knew she would admire them! he should be able to pay for them soon. One way and another, it was all easy enough. And so he put his neck into a halter.

I wonder, thinking of it, if it had best be written? Will any one credit that he could believe a man might buy favor of his wife by a gift of gold and stones? (at the worst fair imitations.) Will any one credit the story that this young man took immoderate satisfaction in the person he arrayed, even at the cost of some distracting wonder as to how his tailor's bill was to be satisfied? Could Sally's expression of pleasure outlast her rebuke of his extravagance? Could the condition of his mother and his sisters alleviate his delight as he remembered a look of admiration, or some kind word of Sally's? But then he was a man of large expectations.

Sally's anxieties about Oliver turned in various directions. She had not entire confidence in his discretion—and more and more she dreaded the confession of the marriage. A morbid fear was gaining ground, and she now regretted that she had not at once shown her father the certificate. Since she became more helpful and obedient in the house, her relations to the family seemed to have changed entirely; she felt herself drawn toward her own people, and less and less toward Oliver. She shrank from seeing him, from conversing with him; and these signs, so ominous, were hailed with joy by her parents.

Indeed, it seemed so clear to them, that apprehensions on this ground were idle now, that Elder Green had no hesitation, as the summer harvest approached, to engage Oliver among his hands; and Oliver accordingly came down to labor in the fields, and break bread, and sleep under the roof that sheltered the daughter of the house.

The afternoon on which he came he found Sally alone in the kitchen; her father and mother had gone to town; and Esther Green was taking her usual nap. When he came to the door and saw Sarah within, he tossed the bundle of clothes he had swung over his shoulder into a corner, and said:

"Here's something I've been trying to make out. See if you know what it is. It sounds to me like a love letter. I'd like you to write me one!" And he gave her a folded bit of paper.

She took it, but without looking at it, said:

"I will, if you'll promise to go far enough to pay for the postage and trouble."

"How far may that be?" he asked, in doubt as to her meaning.

"There," said she, handing him a newspaper which she

had been reading. It had fallen on the floor while she sat meditating what she read.

"Read that letter from Australia. It is a good way from here, I should think. And it might cost a great deal to get there—but if you cared to go and make your fortune, every one does that goes, I think I could raise the money. I would try."

"Will you go too?"

"No, but I'll wait here for you till you get back again!"

A single expressive sound escaped his lips. And he looked at Sally as if he were wondering whether she could be in earnest. She smiled. She had expected no better success—and yet, oh that oceans rolled between them! Thus she vacillated; vexed like the waves—tossing to and fro—seeking rest and finding none. And matters were not improved for either as they now sat in silence, reading what each had given the other. For the Australian letter, if it reported great gains, rehearsed likewise great hardships, pains and dangers; and danger and toil were not among the things Oliver Savage coveted.

The written paper Sally held in her hand she recognized at once as the work of Miranda. Small, fine characters, as if copied from some quaint old manuscript, legible as print, and this was written:

"Yes, it does please me to write to you, Sir. Sometimes I think, so uncertain is our life, it may be I shall see your face no more. As I write to you, it seems that you could not be farther away. Not if you had gone out of this world; only then I must remember that between us and the dead no letters can pass. They cannot tell us so that we shall not be mistaken, of what they are now thinking, or what they now do; neither can they say what now they most long for. But all this can pass between us. There seems to me something like eternity in my feeling towards you, and in my speaking to you. As if it had gone on forever, and would go on forever. Ever since I said to you on the camping-ground 'I am lost; I despair!' and you took me by the hand and said, 'Be saved! Hope all things! I bring you word from my God, this he desires you to do;' I seem to feel assured that he *did* send you to speak to me. And so long as you speak I listen as to one He has sent. Then you will ask me if you should ever, for any reason, because of much work, or of weariness, or from any other cause, cease to speak to me in this way, would I feel that the great God has withdrawn from me?—Means to bless me and guide me no more?—To cleanse my sins and give me understanding no longer?—I must say, Sir, no. Earthly friends may fail, but He cannot. And I think I should not feel, under any circumstances, that you had really failed me. It seems to me I should know that nothing could really hurt our friendship; that though, all our lives, it should seem to be dead, we should find in the next life that it too was alive again."

He had said he would like her to write him a letter, taking that for a model! She was painfully conscious, as she looked at him, of the utter lack of the ability which feeling confers to write such a letter to Oliver. Yet, let any person try to show her that she does not love him! or to prove his unworthiness!

"Did you make it out?" said he, dropping the newspaper.

"Pretty well. It is Randy's writing. To Mr. Collamer, I suppose. She writes to him."

"Don't it sound like a love letter?"

"No. It's about friendship. Friendship and love are two things."

He seemed to think he did not need she should explain that to him.

"Your father says I must be here, off and on, three weeks."

"If you should go to the gold diggings, it would be harder work for a little while," said she, "but no work at all, for all your lifetime, after that."

"I don't expect to be living *this* kind of a dog's life a long while yet," he answered. "You musn't expect it. I'm your true and lawful husband."

"Don't speak that word again under this roof, till I give you leave!" said she, hurriedly, in manifest alarm.

If he had spoken as if he was by no means decided that he would not assert his rights, she assumed a tone not less threatening—and the contest between them was begun with a spirit that promised no speedy surrender on either hand.

"I don't know about that. I don't know about that! When a man marries a woman, it's expected, if she gives her free consent, that she will be known as his wife, and not be ashamed of what she's done. But there's no way to please you."

"Yes, there is," she said—she would conciliate him. "I have my reasons. I don't want father to be troubled about anything through harvest."

"Troubled!"

"Yes! you know you are not the son he would be like to pray for. You can do as you please, but I'm tired of trying to keep you to your word. What with looking out to know if you are sober, or not in your right mind, and likely to tell all, you wear the life out of me. And if you want to speak out, all I say now is, speak! Tell about our marriage!"

"By thunder, there's our father and mother coming now. If you dare me, I will!"

"Dare you! Well then, do it! Then you'll hear me saying to father that I know I was a fool, and was overpersuaded—but I'll have a divorce—and I can get it! You needn't think he would spare any money to set me free from you. He can prove that I was crazy, I am sure, in any court!'

So saying, Sally walked into the next room, and left Oliver sitting in the kitchen, studying the newspaper, which he had spread out on the kitchen table. Oliver, it may be guessed, said nothing about Sally's sudden exit, when Huldah Green came in and found her kitchen thus occupied.

"Here's Oliver!" she exclaimed. "Alone! Why, couldn't you find any one in the house?"

Here Sally came in, and though it assured the mother's heart when she saw the indifference with which the pair met and regarded each other, still she thought the girl, after all, rather hard on the poor fellow, and made up by kindness for the pain he might have felt at Sally's manner.

She had indeed, for a time silenced Oliver. As she could well see. But even this assurance was not comfortable, satisfying. She felt no certainty that, at all times, under all circumstances, until she should choose, she would compel him to silence. He was rash, fiery. He might by a word expose all, if his pride felt any damage, if for an instant he seemed to be ranked with other laborers by the men themselves, or their master, or their master's wife and daughter.

He was not long in discovering that she was by no means so entirely at ease in her mind, so prepared for any event, as she would have him suppose. He took advantage of the fact whenever she chanced to be with him and the other laborers in her mother's absence. There was a strange freedom in his words and looks, which she did not resent, and which made the workingmen regard him with surprise, for they all held the Elder's daughter in great esteem. Sometimes they cautioned him to keep more quiet and behave with more respect, but the silly fellow was not to be warned; and always boastful, it was not likely that he would drop the practice here.

So they acted on each other, till the bold self-willed girl was a captive to her fears. They beset her wherever she went. She was in perpetual alarm. She and Oliver seemed to live but to torment each other! Oh, if the certificate could be destroyed as the ring was lost! Oh, if a fact could ever cease to be one!

One day her father came into the kitchen, where they all sat at nightfall. Esther Green, and Huldah, and Oliver. He went up to his daughter with a ring on the tip of his finger.

"There," said he, "you like such things; there's a plain gold ring for you—I found it in the shed—you may keep it for the owner."

"Let me see," said Huldah Green; and, having examined it, she passed it to her mother; so it made the circuit, and came back to Sally, who tried it first on one finger, and then on another, but it only fitted the fourth finger of her left hand.

"Don't wear it on that finger," said her mother, "that's for the marriage ring."

"Then I shall have to put it around my neck," said Sally. But she drew it from her finger and let it lie on her palm.

"Perhaps it belongs to Oliver," she said, and she handed it to him.

He was burning with wrath, but he took the ring, and laughed at his own clumsy attempt to pass it over his little finger.

"It must be yours," he said, and gave it back to Sally. She held it again on her palm.

"That's the wife's finger," said Huldah Green again; and she showed her own gold ring—and lifted the old hand of Esther and showed on it a similar adornment.

"Almost worn out," said Esther. "I expected it would have worn through before this; it was a fine gold ring, and your father paid a pretty sum for it, Elder. He paid as he went along, and the balance he had left when he had bought the ring and paid the minister, wasn't over and above a pretty small start. But we were prudent. We wasted nought. It's the fine gold that wears well. But we must all wear out. The ring is getting thin, Huldah."

Sally now took the ring up from her palm, and put it upon her finger, and said she must ask the neighbors' girls if any one of them had met with a loss. She thought she knew the finger it belonged to.

CHAPTER XXVII.

A FINANCIAL CRISIS.

OLIVER watched his opportunity, and when he found Sally alone, said, gloomily:
"So you lost the ring?"
"Yes. No good luck in that," she answered, with a sort of doubtful defiance. Let him not take her to task! It was far from his purpose—farther than it was from his desire.
"But father found it—your father did; and you put it on before them all!"
"Yes, and I mean to wear it, Oliver," said Sally, for she thought that, perhaps after all, it was an omen for good that her father had found the ring. And, besides, there was something in his voice and face that moved her. It was a long time since she had spoken words that had so kind a sound to Oliver, and he advanced at once upon them:
"Come, walk over to Roy's, and see what Randy's doing."
"I'll walk with you," she said, "but not up there."
Accordingly they went down the road toward Brighton, and Oliver held the hand that wore the ring, and said how strange it was that she could make him so happy, or so wretched by a word. That if, any morning he went out into the fields, and could think of any pleasant thing that she had spoken—or even a pleasant look, though she said nothing to him, it satisfied him for all day. Sometimes he thought if she could once see how it was, she would never let him go without making a sign that would cost her nothing, and yet be worth so much to him.
Sally replied. She called him foolish, silly; said that, as long as he knew she was his wife, why did not that con-

tent him? But, nevertheless, it pleased her to see that he was in earnest, that he felt all this. To know that he did depend upon her precisely as he said. Incapable as they both seemed to be of any nobleness of action, the very name and words and signs of love could yet control them.

As she spoke, Oliver recognized in her countenance and manner the signs by which he first had dared to hope that he might win the Elder's daughter—and he was now so audacious as even to imagine that possibly, before this walk was ended, he might persuade her to go home with him to a confession. He had his special reasons for wishing that the acknowledgment and reconciliation might be made at once.

As they walked along the road, a person approached from the opposite direction, driving at a rapid pace, which was slackened as he drew near. From a distance he had suspected that the errand on which he came might take him no farther than the wood on whose edge they lingered.

The man was a constable from Brighton, with an order for the arrest of Oliver Savage; and he was no stranger to either Sally or Oliver. He had often dined and supped at Elder Green's, as he went to and fro in his errands about the county, and he knew the Elder's pretty daughter. And now, when he saw this pair together, it puzzled him to decide how he should manage the business. A moment's reflection, and he had thus decided the matter—"Oliver is a vain, foolish scamp. If there's anything going on between them two, the sooner it's ended the better." So he jumped from his buggy, laid his hand on Oliver's shoulder, and showed him a warrant for his arrest.

Oliver took it, glanced at it, crumpled it in his hand, and seemed undecided whether he should fight or run away: But he might as well have attempted one thing as the other, under the band that was upon him, the iron hand of the law, so well represented by the constable's strong grasp.

"What's this?" asked Sally, the first to speak.

"Only a little business I want to see Oliver about down at Brighton, Miss," said the man.

"What is it, Oliver?" she demanded, turning to him.

The constable stood back a step, and surveyed the two.

"It's nothing," said he. "I won't go. There—I won't."

"Oh, none of that, my lark. The easier you go, I should

say, the better for you. And the quicker too. Come now, get in."

"Wait a minute!" exclaimed Sally, very pale, and very frightened. "I don't understand it—and I must, or how can I do anything?"

"It isn't anything," said Oliver, struggling between his shame and the hope that she would really rescue him.

"You are going to be taken off by the constable," said she, "that's not for nothing. If he won't speak, you can tell me, Mr. Rowl. What's it for?"

"I don't know," said he; "I don't know but I might, if the young man is willing."

"I've a right to know," she assured him.

"Oh, that alters the case," replied he, looking from the boy to the girl; "he's been borrying the dust down there on false pretences, that's all; them he got it of think it's time to look after their money. He hasn't done the fair thing—and then he took to being uppish about it—so they wouldn't stand it. That's the business, for short."

"Who did he borrow of?"

"Don't tell her," exclaimed Oliver. "It's nobody's business."

"Well," said she; before she spoke this word she had put forth her hand, as if to arrest the constable—she struggled hard to speak, and to speak seemed for a moment impossible. Now she added, "I don't want to know. How much is the money?"

"Fifty dollars, ma'am."

"Must he go to Brighton?"

"Why, if I could get my money—"

"He is working for my father, and all the hands are needed—" She made this statement, but saw in a moment that it was not going to avail; and also that the constable suspected that there might be a weightier cause for her anxiety.

"Can't you pay the money?" she asked Oliver.

"Why—no—not to-night. No! I haven't got it by me, and that's true. I'd be glad to send it, but I haven't got it handy."

"Have you got it anywhere?"

Some sense of the figure he was making before Mr. Rowl seemed to present itself to Oliver; he looked at Sally as if about to question her right thus to interrogate him, but concluded to reply frankly,

"No, not that much. I haven't! I've only five dollars in hand."

"If the money is sent you before to-morrow night, will that do?" said Sarah to Mr. Rowl.

"He ought to go with me," answered Rowl, doubtfully.

"But will it do? Can you let him off, though he don't deserve it?"

"Before to-morrow night; sure?"

"Yes, sure."

"I might, if you're anxious;" again the constable seemed endeavoring to satisfy himself what the relation between these two might be, but he could not understand it—so foolish and so abashed, in spite of his show of defiance, seemed Oliver—so imperious, and angry, and resolute the Elder's daughter. It seemed to be out of no tenderness or regard for him that she was thus interfering between the law and Oliver.

"You shall have the money to-morrow," she said.

"Well, Oliver," said the constable, releasing the young man from his grasp now, for the first time, "I'm glad you've got so kind a friend. I hope you'll try to deserve it." Then he turned to Sally. "I'll keep your secret, ma'am. If you're willing to pay fifty dollars for him, that's your look out, not mine, understand."

And he turned from the pair, got into his buggy, and drove away. He had no sooner left them than Sally turned towards Oliver,

"Walk on," said she.

But he would have remained to excuse himself; to explain; to devise some plan; at least to hear what she would say. She would say nothing, but repeated:

"Walk on. Hurry. I want to be left alone. I've seen enough of you!" She said it with a spirit which he did not care to question. So he went on obediently.

Then she sat down by the roadside, in the shadow of the wood, and thought she should conclude on what was best to be done. But the first moments of thinking wrought a powerful change in her; the strength she had seemed to possess quite failed her, she hid her face and gave way to a passionate flood of tears.

When Oliver had left her, he did not turn back again. Indeed, the further he went the less disposed he felt to return. He feared to hear what Sally might say when she should begin to speak. And she had promised to settle that claim with the constable; so he was secure, for anything she undertook he knew would be performed. Much trouble the recollection of that debt had occasioned him; but now it was all right; and he seemed to be born to good luck! After to-morrow he could praise her for what she had done, and he was not afraid. Only for the present he was glad to walk on according to her bidding.

It seemed as if that flood of tears to which the poor girl yielded were exhaustless. But if Oliver had retraced his steps in ten minutes he would have appreciated the truth of the sage observation, "It isn't the lightning we are afraid of—but it's the thunder that does it!" And he would in like manner have acknowledged.

He would have seen Sally sitting erect entangling herself among devices—prompt to act with necessity; avoiding a too close observation of what was past help. There was but one way by which the promise she had given could be fulfilled. She knew that her father had money in bank wherewith to pay the workmen. She would not ask him for the sum she needed—she could better own that she had taken it, when he should discover his loss. She had ten dollars of her own—Oliver had five. When she had paid the constable, she would let her father know that she had saved Oliver and the general body of Christians from disgrace; and if he took it well, perhaps she might then acknowledge still farther!

This, then, was the plan in which finally she rested; then, for it was getting dark, she arose and followed Oliver.

But she saw no more of him that night. And as in these days every member of the family was up before daybreak, so by candle-light they were ready to retire. When she went in she found that Huldah was the only one astir, and their talk was brief. Ten minutes after Sally entered the house the only sound to be heard therein was the singing of the cricket on the kitchen hearth.

CHAPTER XXVIII.

THE DESPERATE REMEDY.

Elder Green was the most careful of men in keeping his accounts. During all his years of farming and house-management, he had made record of every item of expense; he had his gains and losses marshalled on the pages of these books in such order that, at any moment he could tell precisely "where he stood."

Perhaps the practice had helped to render him a trifle more worldly-wise and prudent than he might else have been; perhaps it had oftentimes impeded his generous impulses, and, as year by year went on, helped to the formation of that disposition which the neighbors sometimes said was "tight as the bark of a tree."

For the past five or six years, Sally had been her father's book-keeper; and she could compute interest and foot up columns, as readily and neatly, he affirmed, as any man in Brighton. Perhaps he was mistaken in this, but he was very proud of her skill and quickness, and not without cause.

It would be easy, therefore, easier for her than for any other person, to supply herself at any time when the money box was full—as was the case at present—though she was aware that the abstraction would be known at once—for though he trusted his accounts to her keeping, they were all daily under his supervision.

Sally saw Oliver before breakfast—he had gone to the farm to harness the horses, and she followed him with a basket, to hunt for eggs in the hidden nest. To call him to breakfast also, as her mother advised, when she returned from the egg-hunt.

"I am going to send the money to town this morning," said she; "let me have the five."

But the "five" was as remote as the fifty. He had made a mistake, he said; he forgot, but he had given the money, all he had, to his mother, when he came away from home. For a moment she seemed angry, and like to demonstrate the hot emotion, but it was not demonstrated; she merely said, in a tone that sent a chill over him:

"I expected as much. I'm very glad you gave it to your mother."

She had been thinking all night of the divorce she had chanced to threaten, and was not disposed to think more kindly of him now that she stood before him. Not that the coarse gray blouse and the faded blue cotton pantaloons abated so much from his fascinating power. She had not been won to marry him by any exaggerated opinion of his noble qualities, still, that he was lacking in them all, even to her apprehension, did not help the matter any.

He went on harnessing the horses, thinking of Australia; but when he drove them from the barn, and looked over the beautiful farm-land, and made some rough estimate of the value of this year's crops, he took another and less desperate view of the case.

It was yet quite early in the morning when Sally went up to old Samuel Roy's.

As she walked through the lane, she heard Miranda singing. Contrary to her mood as the effort might seem, she broke out into the familiar strain, and so came singing to the kitchen door.

Miranda sat in the middle of the room, with bushels of peas around her, which she was shelling in order to dry. For a moment Sally seemed to be dismayed, but the favor she came to ask must be granted, no matter what stood in the way. So she said, answering Randy's salutation, speaking in a dictatorial way, not new or strange, and so modified as to be less offensive than usual:

"I am going to take your place there—you must go to town for me."

"Ten bushels," was the answer. "What's the matter at Brighton?"

"Nothing's the matter at Brighton. But something's the matter at Martindale, or I wouldn't be up here giving my orders."

"How pale you look. Are you sick, Sally—what's happened?"

"Nonsense. Don't ask any questions. I've a secret, and I'm going to keep it. Understand? Is the horse in the stable?"

"Yes. I heard father say"——

"Randy, go harness him."

"You scare me," said Randy, getting up and walking out from among the heaps of podded peas. And she came and took Sally's hand, and said, "It's burning hot."

"I haven't slept much. I don't feel very well. Does that satisfy you? Let that be the end of it. I shall be well enough when I hear the horse clattering down the lane, and know you are actually on your way to Brighton with your mouth shut."

"I'll go," said Randy. "Peas or no peas I'll do your bidding. You wouldn't ask it for the sake of fooling."

Then Sally threw her bonnet on the table, and set to work in Miranda's place.

"Get ready quick," said she, "for there's no time to waste. Though it isn't a matter of life and death to be sure—only an affair of my own—a piece of business. So don't worry, my dear, good angel."

Randy saw that action, not words, was wanted of her; in the first place she went to the stable and harnessed the horse, then, returning, dressed herself. Half an hour, and she was ready.

Then she came to Sally Green.

"Now, what more?" she asked. "Give your orders. I'll trust you that you won't sent me on a fool's errand."

Sally took a little roll from her bosom. It was sealed, and had the address, "Mr. Rowl, constable, Archer street, Brighton."

"All you have to do," said she, "is to go and find him. You know Mr. Rowl?"

"Yes, I know him. Give him this?"

"And if he isn't there you might wait a little, maybe,

till he came. Because—because—I shall be anxious, very anxious, to know if he gets it. I'll tell you—I saw him yesterday, and I promised he should have it—it is something that belongs to him. It's money—it's fifty dollars—I told him I'd send to-day. But I couldn't go myself—all the horses—I couldn't send anybody either. Nobody but you, Randy!"

"Oh, well," said she, "if it's all right, Sally, it's a pity if I couldn't serve you a good turn. If I find him shortly, you'll have me back again before noon. But I shall have time about the peas too; you needn't mind."

"I shall stay," said Sally. "Once in a while I can do as I choose, and I choose to stay. You needn't stop at the house. If you see anybody, though, you may say I'm helping you. For, of course, there'll be a wondering what's become of me. It's a plague that one can't breathe without asking leave of somebody. How far is it to Jericho, I wonder?"

"They're so tender of you, Sally. If they didn't love you so, they wouldn't be so careful," answered Randy, with a gentler voice than usual.

Will any woman look into the heart of Sally as she sits there in the silent little kitchen, surrounded by the tokens of Roy's life and Randy's; there, where the spirit of minister Collamer was doubtless not long ago invoked?

Now that this business is thus far accomplished, she can breathe. But to a better purpose, one would think, she might conclude the whole matter by ceasing to breathe forever. So darkly has she involved herself! So impossible seems to be the uttermost extrication!

Ah! no wonder, she thinks, she has been anxious and expecting—full of unhappy presentiment; not daring to trust the man whom she has dared to marry! It was to save him, she said, but how incompetent did she feel for the work! If he was yet to be saved, it was not by a woman. And yet, did she pity him. If her father but knew all! Or if she had any fortune of her own which she might this day command—yes, she would go with Oliver to the ends of the earth—to Australia—to Greenland—to death!

And yet would she? Yes, she seriously concluded; for if she had him alone, away from old companions, she and he together, he might be kept from harm. She pitied him.

She dared not think now of divorce. She was sure that he loved her. And a woman who is loved can forgive so much! Alas, poor girl, that she must argue thus at random, and prove all her conclusions to be so inconsequential!

Samuel Roy came in before noon, as moment by moment she had expected he would do, and he was greatly surprised to hear what Sally had to tell him by way of accounting for Miranda's absence and her presence in the house. Then the old man sat down to help her, though he had come in to rest. And she inquired after his rheumatism, and he told her the location and duration of his aches and pains, and made his resignation beautiful, as it came up in contrast with his ugly trouble.

Instead of arresting the sad train of her thoughts, his presence and conversation seemed designed only to furnish it with new and more potent illustration. As he held Miranda's virtues up to view, bitter, self-reproaching, unimpaired by self-justification, was the secret response, which her constant affirmation to his ceaseless talk did not hinder in the least.

CHAPTER XXIX.

THE COURAGE OF—LOVE.

Probably Elder Green could never in his life know a surprise of a domestic character so great as that which met him in the little room he called his office, across whose threshold few persons besides the women of his family ever passed.

It was a grim, sad-looking place. The floor was painted a dull gray, likewise the window-frame and door—and the walls were very white, for Huldah whitewashed twice a year, through all frequented parts of her house; experience having taught her that no one could be hired to serve her as she served herself. At one end of the room stood the high red desk—by its side a table. Here Sally sat, when at work with her father, casting up accounts; over the red table hung a portrait of Elder Green, which looked as if he might have painted it himself, with suggestions from his mother. On Sally's table lay a Bible, and the true character of that sacred volume was about as clearly evident to Sally as the true character of the represented Man was to the Elder.

He and Sally had come into the office shortly after her return home from Roy's, and they were now to look over the accounts, which had been neglected for the past two or three days. They had been at work thus perhaps half an hour, when the Elder opened the secret drawer of his desk and took out a pocket-book, whose contents he proceeded to count over.

At the moment he did so, his daughter seemed seized by some uncontrollable emotion. She suddenly laid the blotter across the ledger—closed it, and seemed about to rise from her place; then she re-opened the book and said to herself, "Be still!" and clasped her hands to control the trembling that seemed uncontrollable. She would command this moment if she died in the struggle. It was with such resolution that she came into the office; with such purpose she now remained there. And her father counted his money. Long he was about it. Twice he fingered every bill—he could not believe what seemed so perfectly clear that of the bills he put away last night some were now missing.

"Strange," said he; "very strange," he said again. Sally looked up; her eyes met his; how steady her gaze instantly became, almost fixed, one might deem it. She did not ask him, as she meant to do, what the trouble was. While attempting to command her voice, he said, in a mysterious undertone:

"Sally—here's something wrong!"

"Wrong! What father?"

"Money gone—forty dollars."

"Forty dollars. Are you sure?"

"I put it in here last night. Two hundred and forty. Here's my two hundred—but where's the forty?"

"Let me count it, father?"

So he gave her the package, and she counted the bills over, one by one. Then she gave the bundle back to him.

"How much, Sally?"

"Two hundred."

"Then—I've been robbed!"

"Robbed, father! It couldn't be." The girl's heart seemed to die within her as she spoke; she knew the symptoms she now witnessed in her father. He had been robbed—robbery was a crime—"be just, and fear not," he was saying to himself, and he would make his own application of that famous motto.

For a few minutes the ticking of the clock in the next room sounded with awful distinctness in this. Then said he:

"I can't see how—but it must be. I never lost a dollar through carelessness in my life. I put that money up—it's gone. Nobody but you, Sally, know where I kept my pocket-book. You and your mother, of course. I wonder where your mother is."

THE COURAGE OF—LOVE. 261

He seemed about to go for her, but Sally started up and laid her hand on him.

"Don't call her. I'm your child, not hers! Don't go, father. I know about the money. I expected to tell you. But it's the first time I ever borrowed of you without your leave."

"Borrowed! You!"

"Yes—you can take it out of my portion! I had to have the money. I thought perhaps you would not believe that unless I could tell you the whole, and I couldn't tell the whole. So I took the money. And I paid it out again! I haven't got a dollar of it left. And you must give me so much the less than you meant to do, sometime. That's all, father."

"Where's your mother?" exclaimed the Elder, as much frightened as amazed; he seemed to think that possibly the earth was about to open, or Heaven about to fall—he could not have been much more astonished in either case.

"I am enough for this!" said she. "We don't need mother. It's enough for me to bear, and you. She couldn't help you or me. She knows nothing about it. And that's all. I've spent the money; if you was a poorer man, maybe I'd not feel so much, for it's the rich men who lose their money and care most. I see that."

Then said Elder Green:

"Hush, daughter. Hush, Sally. I never missed a shilling before that you couldn't account for in a different way from this. Don't speak so to your father. You never gave me reason yet to think my girl was going on in by and forbidden paths. I believe in you, Sally. You've owned to it, when you might have denied as easy, if that had been your mind—and likely I never would have known. I'll trust you! I never had a secret from your mother yet—as good and kind to you as ever mother was. Call her yours! And if you say here to me, your father, with your hand on that Bible, that all you've done has been clear and upright, nothing to be ashamed for, only somehow it can't be known—I'll trust my own daughter, who has grown up in my sight—and has never gone out of my heart, and never will."

She said, but without laying her hand upon the Bible:

"You may trust me, father."

"It is enough," returned the Elder; and he tied up the

pocket-book, and laid it in its place, feeling sad and yet heroical; and trusting his daughter! Afraid, indeed, to doubt her, and, did he but know it, shrinking from the knowledge which he knew not but he might have had, had he persisted in demanding it.

For Sally, she turned away from the old red desk and went quickly from the room, and out under the apple trees, breathing as if this mortal element had some destroying power in it.

Her main thought was not of self-gratulation that she had so well managed this sad business; nor of pleasure, that her father had such confidence in her that he was willing to pass lightly an offence against all his notions of economy and prudence.

Oliver's curiosity, meanwhile, was consuming him. From the field on the upland, where he was at work, he had seen Sally going to Samuel Roy's; had seen Randy, mounted on horseback, riding down the road. Three hours later, he saw her return. And he saw when Sally come back to her father's house. He conjectured many things—his chief doubt was as to what would pass between himself and Sally when they met again. He would be glad to defer the meeting if he might. Taking extra steps to secure this point, approaching the house through the great orchard, under those old wide-branching trees, he met her.

And now would not poor love—love that is so constant under provocation, so faithful through unworthiness, so brave and generous in danger—would not love, the holy and the strong, take this case and manage it?

When he came in sight of her, Oliver's first purpose was to retreat, but he saw it was too late. He saw also how pale she was, and that nothing could be farther from her face than smiles, and he said:

"I have made you trouble, Sally. I wish I was dead."

To which she did not reply—she was either too much excited, too troubled, or too angry—which? he wondered.

"I don't know but being married may be mighty fine for some; but for me—"

"You would have it!" she answered now, quickly enough. Nothing could rouse her so soon as recrimination.

"No; this isn't what I'd have. Not by any means; it isn't what I expected, either. I expected something different. If a man marries a woman he don't do it expecting to be treated as a knave from that time on. If you married me, Sally, I should like to know what you did it for?"

"I can't tell. Because I was a fool. Marry in haste to repent at leisure. That was it, I suppose."

"No; you owned that you loved me. And I loved you, or I never would have asked you. But love isn't proof against everything. I'll be off, maybe, before you expect, and let you tear up the certificate, as you threw away the ring."

"Hush!" said she. Where was her pride and anger? She trembled before the prospect he had so suddenly thrown open to her view. He saw what he had gained, and now, would he hold that vantage ground?

"Hush!" she repeated, and she showed him that on the marriage finger was the wedding ring. "I wear that, Oliver," said she, "because I am your wife."

"Then if you are my wife, treat me as if I was your husband." There was really something like dignity and authority in this demand; and the heart of Sally revived as if under the influence of some heavenly breathing.

"Let us go down to the other end of the orchard. There I can tell you what I have done for you to-day, ungrateful man!"

So he followed her—but a few steps only she walked in advance; then she came back and took his arm, and never thought or cared if any watchful eyes should see that she walked thus beside him.

"Randy has served me like a friend to-day," said she. "I went up and asked her to go to Brighton, and carry something from me to Rowl, and she went, without any questions."

"Then you sent the money! Where did you get it?"

"I took it Oliver—for your sake—from my father's pocket-book."

"Does he know it?"

"Yes, he knows it!"

"But how? Did he give it to you when you asked him? That couldn't be exactly."

"Why not? But I didn't try him. I knew I could make all right. He trusts me so! I had ten dollars of my own. When he told me he had lost forty dollars, I let him know that I took it—that I had paid it away."

"What did the old man say then?" asked Oliver, laughing.

"He said that, if I would assure him it was all right and honorable, he would not ask any more. Say now that I do not love you! Say now that I don't treat you as a wife should do! I could have let you go with the constable!"

"Yes, but you are too proud for that," said he. "My good name is yours."

"So it is—so it is. And if there's anything that could break the heart of Elder Green—Oliver, I was to be the saving of you, you said! Then you must love me better than you love anything else. It's love they say is the savior. But you mustn't give me any more such days as this. I couldn't pass through many such for the best man on earth."

Of course he promised, and was really very grateful to Sally. And she said:

"If I couldn't trust you, and love you, what would become of me? But as you said just now, love isn't proof against everything. Some day you will have all things in your hands. I suppose I might have married a rich man —but I chose you instead. But if ever your face should change to me, or I should come to see that, in spite of your good looks and all that we have said, we should be mistaken—"

He put an end to the misgiving, at least of her speech, by a kiss—and the great argument seemed to have arrived at its conclusion.

CHAPTER XXX.

THE NEW HOME.

Miranda went on an errand for her father one afternoon, to the red farm house—a red farm house no longer. Henceforth it must be called the Hill Farm; for, among all hill farms round about, it had now pre-eminence.

Mrs. Johnson was at work, and meditating, as she looked about her.

"So! this has got to be one of the big housens of the country. No more the old place, than he's the old man. With the white paint and green blinds and green piaz to the outside, who would ever know it? I'm glad it's done too, seeing as it must be, for whatever it is it ain't hum no more. If 't been Randy he'd in his head there'd been no such doings. No such doings! We should all a' stayed together. And there'd been two sides to the housen, and Randy would 'a been a helper! It ought 'o been Randy, o' good rights. I'm moved to think my Harry—but there's a providence above us. And it's a stranger dropped out o' the clouds as you might say, for nobody knows her belongings."

For Mrs. Johnson was still "led to believe," and held fast by the believing, that Miss Fuller was in the secret, and at the bottom of all this new work that was so hard to contemplate—this work that cost so much in money, so much more in heart-ache. Nobody need tell her that Mr. Carradine really approved all this doing; the vengeance of life-long habit was to come yet, and he did stand in fear of it. Nobody need tell her.

Thus was she meditating with the most dismal satisfaction when Miranda came to the house for the first time since the old school trouble with Mr. Carradine.

"Come in," said Mrs. Johnson, confused as a simple-minded, honest-hearted woman might be on the sudden appearing of one who had been so intimately wrought up in her secret thinking. "You're quite a stranger. Sit ye down. I'm glad to see you, I'm sure, Randy Roy. It's a sight good for sore eyes."

"You're so fine here I don't know's I dare," replied Randy, looking round her in surprise.

"Try it. There's nothing like getting used to a thing," said Mrs. Johnson, sighing—and she brought a chair for her guest.

"There's no great need of my getting used to any thing in Carradine's house," said Randy. She took the chair, however—she was Mrs. Johnson's guest. "I should never know the old place."

"No more you wouldn't! Do you like it, Randy? Does it seem right to you now, such fixings?"

"I don't know. It's right splendid. But how did't ever happen?"

"Dear knows. But he's got his reason to hand like an answer out of the catechism. I said to him plain he was going to get married. He denies it, and that he wouldn't. Though he don't do it positive like. Yet if he was going to be married he wouldn't keep it from me!"

"Of course not. And there's nobody like Miss Fuller he'd do all this for, Mrs. Johnson," said Randy, speaking openly as one may with one's friend.

"I thought so myself," was the answer, cold, yet as it almost seemed, indignant.

"I wish it might happen," Randy added in a heat of generosity.

"You do! for sure." Mrs. Johnson's pleasure was not on the increase, and in fact she had now her doubts of Randy's sincerity.

"Yes, it's the place for Miss Fuller, and a good place, big and large."

"And she's a good girl enough, but, Randy, you've lost the wit I gin you credit for," said Mrs. Johnson, not now so vexed as amazed—"she's no more like Peter Carradine, that girl!"

"In a good many ways," answered Randy, with the certainty of one who has well considered the point, "in a good many ways they are as like as two peas."

Mrs. Johnson was amazed.

"Not that they act or speak alike. I don't mean that. But see if they ever quarrel." A fine glow was on Miranda's face as she spoke thus, conscious may be of no little magnanimity.

"May be," said Mrs. Johnson. "But it isn't them that quarrel that gets along the worst. I know what you're thinking of—but if you're considering that he's a bad opinion of *you*, I can tell you what he said in my hearing—to *me*, understand, with nobody by, and that not a dreadful long while back."

"No matter," said Miranda, with a start and a blush. "We're through with our difficulties, and we won't have another misunderstanding long as we live."

"It is a matter—and I'll tell you," persisted her friend, who saw Randy's blush with a quickening suspicion at which she caught with desperate hopefulness, "He said, I think much of Randy; that's what he said—and I respect her—she's a fine girl—she's a good woman. And as for me, I'll never forget that it was my Harry made that trouble atwixt you, and who knows what would 'a happened but for that!"

The question was asked with another sigh that came not easily from Mrs. Johnson, for she was not a sighing woman.

"Yes," said Randy, not blushing now, but laughing, quite as much for the relief of Mrs. Johnson's burdened spirit, as from any excess of merriment on her own part—"and what'll you think now, when I tell you on the top of what you tell me, that he's made father a present of a couple as fine young bullocks as you'll find in his drove. And that's what I come up for, with father's obligations—so now, Mrs. Johnson!"

"Say it's you, and I'll never open my mouth agen, whatever happens, to complain. Say it's you, Randy, and—"

"And be a liar. Now you wouldn't have that. Any way, you might show me the house—for we're good friends all around, and mean to keep so,to the end o' the chapter—

though it's against nature, and truth, and common sense, that Peter Carradine would fix a house up in this style for Randy Roy. What would I do in such a place now!"

"What'll anybody do with all these gimcracks then?" asked Mrs. Johnson. "There's the question. But I'll show you the place. He sent your pa the bullocks, did he? Well, I'll gin over guessing if he wasn't thinking of Randy as much as anything for that."

"Like enough it was a peace-offering," said Randy. "If it was for anything else, you'd allow he must have a poor opinion of me. Don't you go to thinking anything so foolish."

"Come on, if you'll see the housen. It can't do no harm. And I want you to see how we're turned upside down. And who'd ever a thought Peter Carradine would a set up for a show housen? With a fancy gardener to lay out a pleasure —of the slope, and medder land. And making believe the while it was for hisself, as if he cared the value of a rush for it—"

So it was that Mrs. Johnson showed Randy about the house from garret to cellar.

The parlor door was locked—but she brought the key, and threw the splendors of that grand apartment open to inspection—all the marvel of the white and gilt wall paper, the handsome carpet, the colored window shades, the various ornaments, engravings, books and vases—what not?

"That room cost a thousand dollars, if it cost a cent," said Mrs. Johnson. "I haven't got anything to say. It's none o' mine. But I wouldn't want a housen that was too good to use. It's a kind of increasing as increases cares—and that's agen Scripture clear."

Then the china closet was inspected, and every other closet. The house was stocked as a gentleman's house should be. Mr. Carradine had hesitated at no expense. He wanted his house should compare well with the establishments of other gentlemen. This was one of the great years of his life, and he intended the celebration should become a man of his place and ability.

At the end of her exhibition Mrs. Johnson plucked up the courage to say,

"When we're moved and settled, you'll find your way over the hill, I hope, once in a while."

"Moved! over the hill! who? where? what is that?" said Randy, betraying more amazement and doubt than she would have done had she known with what lingering hope Mrs. Johnson clung to the notion that after all, improbable though it seemed, Randy was the woman on whom Mr. Carradine's eyes were fastened, and whom he meant to charm into possession of all this Hill-farm splendor.

"Don't you know, though? Why, we're going to leave, to be sure, Johnson and me. We're going over t' the other housen to live. That's what we're going to do!"

"The other house?"

"That's what I mean. The Bronson house, you know—it ain't so very far off."

"Not far at all. Going to live in the Bronson house—you and your family? It's a nice place too. I always liked the Bronson farm house, it had a home look always."

This was spoken out of pure charity. Miranda was as surprised as she could easily be made by this intelligence which Mrs. Johnson had conveyed with such painfully obvious difficulty. Perhaps the good woman detected too much sympathy in Randy's voice, and she meant not to be *put* into the position of one who required condolence, for she said quickly,

"You'd never expect this old housen to be turned inside out so. It beats all the witch work ever I heard of when I was a girl down east."

"But it's beautiful to see. I declare I feel quite set up by it."

"That's like her—if you ever said that thing to him now! It's somebody's talk i' that fashion has set him on to such doings I verily believe. This here kitching now, I declare if it's as hum like as the farm yard is. It's curius, some little jobs I've been trying *my* best to get done up here this ten year, oh yes! any time! but any time is no time, and they would never a been done, *never*, only now there can't be done enough. Everything comes so easy, understand. He's free enough of his money let him get stirred up once. I spoke out my mind about the Bronson place, and he had things done up to the handle. Anything you say, Mrs. Johnson. Just name what you want. . . You must go down, for it do look right neat, Randy, and as much like hum as this'n does, but for the old turns and corners I'm used to this ten year."

She shook her head, and Randy said,

"There's a comfort in it all though I'm beholden to say. You've a witness to stand by you all along. If religion is n't for wet weather, Mrs. Johnson, we don't need it so much when it's dry."

"That's the word I needed! Thank you for it, Randy. It's a poor profession that's only good to sail by in clear sailing weather."

"And you've put yours to proof too many times. I always thought if any one had found out the worth of a belief, it was sister Johnson."

"Yes, Randy—you're right, you're right. Do you see anything of her though, nowadays?" For sister Johnson saw that Randy would soon be gone, and there were words yet to be said.

"Do you mean Miss Fuller? Oh, yes. I saw her when I was coming up this way just now. She was walking with a gentleman I never see before."

"She hasn't been up here sence the first man crossed the doorstep to go to work on the housen. Yes, once she came, and she seemed flurried for a moment when she heerd the goings on. I told her Mr. Carradine expected she would take her week here just the same—he bid me tell her so—he knew I could make her comfortable as anybody in the valley; I'm repeating his own words about it. But she has'nt taken heed to that; and she won't, mind you."

"You mustn't judge Miss Fuller—she isn't like the rest of us, Mrs. Johnson."

"No, that so. I've nothing to say agen Miss Fuller. She's a Christian young womern, I judge, and she behaves herself discreet. She's as civil to Johnson as e'er she was to Mr. Carradine, and I'll say that for her. She caught him. He can't help himself a'more than a bird in a bramble—but she's done it without any of your arts."

"My arts, Mrs. Johnson!" exclaimed Randy.

"*Yours!* for sure who ever 'cused Randy Roy of arts! I mean the girls that would 'a ogled him out of his money, if he'd e'er gin 'em a chance. It's my mind, though, when all's said and done, she'll take him (if you don't). I should think she must be curus with all these odd doings—and seeing the loads of things that have been carted up from Brighton city. There's one little room I haven't showed you yet, and dasen't. He don't like to have anyone running in there. It's a room with a big winder and has a trellish for the sweetbrier fixed up to it. We moved it to that place the first even of her stay here, you mind. He never forgot a thing yet. There's just that one winder. It's a wonderful little spot. Some pictures in bright frames all gilt round, and a stand for books or something—and a round table with a fine green cloth to the top of it, and a big easy chair that cost thirty-five dollars! And another chair, a willer one, that looks as light and delicet! He made me sit down on it, when I told him it wouldn't hold a body, but was made for a play house like as not. And that's somebody's room for private, I reckon. There never was a man thought o' more things. What do *you* think, Randy?"

"I think I shall be right sorry if he don't carry the day."

"I'd be willinger for her than for any one but you. 'Twould kill me outright so be it was the Elder's daughter. But I'd be easy enough so be it was Randy. And glad to move out of *her* way, for the matter of that."

"No, you wouldn't, Mrs. Johnson. You're a woman of sense. He and I would make quick work of each other. We should destroy each other—break each other's hearts. I saw Miss Fuller walking with a gentleman, I told you, and you'd say, if you saw the pretty sight, they were made for each other—but I'd be willing to bet she'd set fifty times more value on a man of Peter Carradine's kind."

"May be," said Mrs. Johnson, so absorbed by the thoughts that already possessed her she seemed incapable of curiosity, even in reference to the stranger, of whom Randy was making this repeated mention. She could not even wonder at Randy's quiet conviction in reference to all this matter.

But how was it that Miranda held herself so calmly confident?

She had merely seen Miss Fuller when now and then she came unsuspecting into the presence of Mr. Carradine. Had merely heard her now and then refer to the man—speak his name, or repeat some wish of his; or had been present while her father told the teacher of the rich farmer's kind treatment of the poor rheumatic, by whom he meant himself. Gestures so slight, looks so fleeting, voice so changeful, oh, ye betrayers! Should not Miranda be skilled in the interpretation? Was not Senior Jobson in the land of the living? Shall we not regard Champollion as almost pre-Adamite?

Randy believed what she said. Also, she understood her oracle, which all prophets do not.

CHAPTER XXXI.

THE COUSIN.

But who was this that walked in Martindale with Miss Fuller, and made a spectacle so pleasing to the mere vision, according to Randy's report.

No other than Horatio Aptomar, who, while attending court at Brighton, had learned, by seeming accident, of the nearness of his cousin, and accordingly had sought her out, having the leisure, first of all, for that enterprise. Moreover, he remembered that he had loved Mercy once; between that time and now a gulf lay, but not so wide that he could not discern the flowers that grew upon the banks; they nodded yet at him. And he saw the print of feet, made by children who had wandered hand in hand through many a happy year, under a loving care that was broad as the heavens, and seemed as indestructible; but as a scroll had it been rolled away.

Aptomar was a lawyer who had risen, and was rising, with rapid steps in his profession. He had great abilities—and, he had little patience.

He knew as well as you and all hard-working, earnest people, that for a man to swing himself into any permanence of power on the mere strength and agility that comes of occasional effort is just as impossible as for a clown to perform the Blondin feats over Niagara river.

He was a person of really extraordinary powers—of powers wonderfully varied. And his acquaintance with himself, was defined with a clearness and exactness altogether remarkable. The early expectation of his cousin Mercy was by no means exaggerated. He was one of the few who justify the promise of a precocious childhood in the work of after years.

A man of elegant bearing and address, without the least pretense to beauty of countenance, he exerted a subtle fascination, which, unsuspected, was usually beyond resistance. It was impossible to remain unquickened in his presence; he acted as a rare stimulant always on those with whom he came in contact, suggesting thought, and bringing one invariably to a new appreciation of—himself. Nothing exceed his suavity of manner—it was the flattery which certain minds can tolerate without fear of losing dignity.

There was nothing mean and servile in this deference, but his perfect grace was after all of a serpentine character; that of a man who has trained himself to glide through narrow and winding paths, and make his way where a straightforward purpose might find it impossible to move. He had an ambition that exceeded his apprehensions or his fears, and might become diabolical. Qualities which his mother would have trained into glorious fruitfulness and strength had been suffered to dwindle, and the energy of his ambition fostered other aims than could have had her blessing. All the influences of school and college life had encouraged that ambition; the spirit which SHE would have chastened into harmony with the other powers that influenced him was allowed full and fatal precedence. It could master conscience—therefore it controlled the man. And clearly, therefore, he was beyond himself, and wholly in the power of the world. Whatever influence he should find most fascinating, would also prove most potent; to that he would surrender. Do they, such rudderless powers, beyond computation, sail the seas?

In his profession he had won great renown for a man of his years. Over a jury his influence was extraordinary. Who could suspect, that saw him in the daily walks of life, the fierce, insatiable spirit hidden in the grace of a most becoming modesty? That in secret hours he was laboring unwearied for ends that to the ignorant would always seem results of a fortunate turn, or of a moment's stroke?

It was a notable day in his history when he drove from Brighton to Martindale, and found his cousin in the little schoolhouse from which she had just dismissed her school.

In no respect could such a meeting as this be other than

a surprise. Children had parted to meet man and woman—and what the world had done for them, what they for themselves had done, was more intelligible to either than perhaps it could be to any other person in the world. For they read the present aided by the past.

Knowing eyes discern the little dark-winged sparrows in the flocks of birds that circle under the sombre sky of the early autumn morning, around the scene of the great conflagration. What radiant bits of dazzling life as they fly on glowing wings, as if out of fairy land! What shining floods of music must issue from those golden-throated ones! But "common day" shall give us only the common song from the tiny dark-winged sparrows. The glory shall fade with the dying flame; the sun himself cannot restore it; the sun that deals in verities.

To a moment of doubting observation on the part of either, succeeded quick recognition. Then they hailed each other by name—and the silence of years was forgiven, if not forgotten. The time was too short—too much was to be told to allow any long or special dwelling on that silence. Both had been dealing earnestly with the affairs of their individual life, and with notable result. They stood in the present, more of the present aware than of the past. Present labor and aim excluded more than acknowledgment of a remembered past; of happy and fearless childhood by the ocean side; and they made haste to be done with a dreary orphanage.

So the present they explained to each other—in ways that brought the character of each into relief. Nothing did they lack to-day, of hope, or of courage.

Mercy's story was a brief one, simply told, after her own fashion, unenlivened by a single flourish of rhetoric, yet by no means a dull tale, since one could so kindle at it as did the cousin walking by her side; for Mercy had led the way from the schoolroom quickly after their meeting, as if apprehensive of his criticism of her official quarters. What kind of criticism it would be she foresaw distinctly. She wished not to hear it. His comment was,

"You don't suppose that I shall leave you in the woods here, where I've found you, Mercy?" and he turned to look at the schoolhouse; all the comment she had anticipated, and endeavored to avoid, condensed in that single glance.

"Why not, cousin?" she asked, with a surprise in her voice which he understood as distinctly as she had interpreted that look; "why not?" His face colored violently at the question, as if he heard in it unlimited reproaching for the forgetfulness of years.

She had spoken pleasantly enough, but the question stung him; and pleasantly though she continued, a fresh thorn was in every word.

"I came here for strength, for I needed more than I had—and you must know what rest I would find among these pleasant farm lands and these friendly people. Come with me, and I will introduce you to some of them."

"No, not to-day. I'm thinking of what you're thinking, Mercy—you were out of health and these people have given you more than I did."

"Why, how could you give me what they gave?" laughed Mercy, but with embarrassment, for she saw that she had wounded him—his pride probably; she knew well that pride—it was a pride to remember. "You didn't own Martindale, and it took the whole of this country town, every field of it, every man, woman and child of it, to perfect my cure."

"But you might have died here, Mercy, and I had been no wiser for it. That's my fault, Mercy. I've sinned a good deal, but this, it seems to me, is my worst sinning."

"But I have not suffered; so don't blame yourself. If you think it was wrong, I forgive you," she added, still playfully.

"You must prove that."

"I shall. I'll prove it from this moment. You'll understand by the peace of mind you'll have when you go back to your office."

"I think the cure is beginning, for I don't half believe what you say—you weren't the worn-out creature you pretend when you came here. But I'll forgive you for saying that, if you will remember what we were once to each other. In those old times I hadn't a thought but I wanted to share with you. Mercy, I feel the old need fresh as ever."

"Then I stand responsible for that, cousin."

"You do! you will! You are a good girl, Mercy. You're what I've wanted all along, I tell you, but I had to see you to find it out. When shall I come for you?" He hurried on to prevent the question that was gathering in her eyes, and on her lips. "There are beautiful lodgings for you in Girard street, the best landlady in the world, and a vicinity unequalled for entertainment. You may have art galleries and public libraries the day long, and the opera every night in the week, if it please you. Fix on the first day of October, and I shall have your rooms furnished and will come for for you, so that you shall enter on possession at that time. We are opposite the park, too—it is a beautiful situation. You shall have my German friend for your professor, and"— he was waxing in warmth and earnestness with every word he spoke, and the earnestness flashed from him, eyes, face, and limbs even, entering into the expression of enthusiasm and resolve which any passer-by must have perceived.

There was a passer-by whose perceptions were not dull— he bowed to Mercy, but his eyes were on her cousin, the stranger who was speaking to her with so much animation.

"Who's that?" asked Aptomar, arrested, it seemed, as one by some sudden barrier in the ardor of the chase.

"Mr. Carradine. A neighbor."

"*That* kind of man here? The first of October, then, it shall be. Shall it, Mercy? Isn't this precisely what my mother would wish? Let me please her! I have not been as sure of her approbation in a long while as I am now. You don't know how rich I am. At all events, I'm not poor. And if you insist on supporting yourself, can't get over your old whim of independence, you shall have all the work you want—of an agreeable kind, too, I promise. There's enough to be done, as you'll find when you get where the civilized world lives. Of all things Mercy Fuller a country schoolma'am!"

He stopped short, and looked at Mercy till she blushed. A change in her calm countenance that seemed to recall him, for he said in a tone more decisive, less expostulating, "The first of October. I won't say before that time, unless you will promise to go with me to the mountains, in September. I have been invited to join a party of tourists then, and we could steal for ourselves a day or two for the sea. I want to get a fisherman to take us out, as old Tom used—it would give us back to the old life sooner than anything else. Say September, Mercy."

"You're too kind, cousin," began Mercy.

Aptomar did not like her tone of voice, and he hindered what she would say.

"Kind! I want you—that's the amount of it. I'm selfish. They say men always are. Be you generous according to your sex! I need my old playmate—I need my cousin, as I find her. My old cousin! You would bring back my mother with you. Oh, how can you know what a life I lead! And I can't get out of it. Come and help make it more justifiable to easy-going people who have no ambitions, and don't know any better than to be as happy as the days are long."

There was something so urgent in his voice, something so potent in the memory of his mother, his mother, who in the old time said so often that she was always easy about her Horatio if Mercy were but with him in his play, and in his rovings, Mercy might with reason defer a decision, since the one she came to instantly could but give him pain, and must look like resentment because of past neglect, or like indifference to a fellow creature's need, that fellow-creature being, of all others, the companion and friend of the happiest days her memory could recall—days when his mother's house was the one that opened to receive a forlorn orphan, and his mother's voice was the voice to call her child.

"You must let me think of it," she said; "I can write to you about it. You know I am not famous for my quick decisions—I was always slow. You used to complain of that."

"And would now, if past experience had taught me that anything could be gained by it. You were never to be entreated or badgered into yielding. I remember you of old. But mother always said that of the two you were after all most prompt! That when you had decided a thing you had no need to reconsider. Yes, I remember—you would live two lives to my one, she said. For I should lose just half my time. But I have run fast so far, Mercy. There's no one else to tell you, so I may—for you know nothing about me, though you look as though you thought you knew it all. There are men of twice my age who would be glad of half the business that crowds into my office. I must have some weight in a Court room, or it wouldn't be so. I didn't get the business by fooling my time away, I can tell you. But still I am not a slave in my office—though I know if a man will not work neither shall he eat."

Aptomar had before now spoken words of not half the weight of these, with vastly more of pride. Dealing with these bald truths he let them go for what they were worth, and having stated, need not dwell upon them.

"I can see," said Mercy, and she plainly could; "for that very reason I am slower to decide than if you were a poor man yet, and struggling with difficulties."

"Yes—that is you. And you cannot understand that I need you ten times more now than if I were a poor man, quite obscure. For then I should suffice to myself—would not involve you in my misfortunes; nor set you to watchfulness and possible disappointment. Because I have gained what I have—I need you to stand by me."

"There or here, cousin Horatio—it matters not where—by you, as when we were children, and your mother was mine."

"As cousin—as wife, then, Mercy! For since we separated if I have not thought constantly of you, I have thought of no other woman. Come, join your force with mine. Not as one might do it at a distance through friendly, cousinly love—but in a nearness that is like nothing but itself—in marriage, Mercy!"

"Cousin Horatio!"

"We used to talk of that. It ought not to surprise you. There, you think I am over-hasty! I shall never woo a woman longer than I have wooed you. Recollect how long ago it began. And I tell you again I have never thought of any other wife. Mercy, would not this have pleased our mother? You look away. Let me see your face at least, Mercy, whatever is in it for me."

This appeal, for it was an appeal, powerful as an eloquent tongue, conscious how rarely it could be withstood, could make it, had its answer even before Mercy said,

"Our love was for childhood—but remember it was love not to be appealed to in evidence on this day. We should have a better constancy to hope by than we have realized."

"I am not thirty yet. Mercy cannot know how I have worked, giving myself only to work in order to stand where I do this day," he answered proudly. "I repent that loss of years more than you can regret it. Will not that suffice? What I have earned is at your feet. If you would go with me to-night and find in my home yours, the world would be better served by me than it has been. Can you not trust me? Must I still explain? You were more magnanimous as a child. Perhaps—I'll ask the question outright, has any man won more than I have?"

Mercy hesitated—but she answered, "No." Dazzled by his presence, thrilled by his voice, how should she remember Peter Carradine?

"Then," he said, "you understand me. We at least are cousins." There he dropped the point and began to speak of other things.

Exhibiting of a mere necessity so varied and so rich a culture, as he spoke, in all his speaking, as to delight and surprise Mercy; as fairly to set her on the question whether it were not a fact that rust was the Martindale portion.

His conversation stimulated her beyond any she had ever listened to. An hour wonderful to her in every future review, passed by and was gone. Like an arrow Aptomar had flashed into Martindale—and the mark aimed at had certainly been gained. He had assuredly seen his cousin—and was held fast in the vision. But would he free himself from it, and go his way to forget? Charmed again by a siren voice sweeter than Mercy's, and a touch that could thrill him yet more marvellously. Love truer and purer than he could ever know again was surely entreating him—his own love for another, not himself.

It was his nature to hope, and to expect the realizations of his hopes—so he went from Martindale not fearful—daring to trust Mercy to such influences as should surround her there. He would constrain her to know what it was to live, week by week, on the Martindale Post Office.

CHAPTER XXXII.

FOR NATURE, OR AGAINST?

MR. CARRADINE was not so easy in his mind, not so occupied with his improvements, as to have no interest in ascertaining somewhat in regard to this vision of youth and of pride by whom Miss Fuller was attended along the peaceful roads of Martindale.

The spectacle had electrified *him*, it was not the mere ordinary progress of a mere ordinary pair he had observed and continued to observe—we will not say watched.

He did not in an excess of curiosity present himself to Mercy for the acknowledged purpose of getting the mystery solved; but, meeting her by chance, at it were, on the roadside as she came from school, he told her of the difficulty which had arisen between himself and the " professed gardener" he had procured from Brighton, in regard to the meadow land that stretched out beyond the slope.

Perhaps Miss Fuller would be good enough to settle the point. Mr. Carradine would be only too glad to leave it with any sensible person. Smith's determination was, to divert the brook from its old channel in order to leave the meadows free; a purpose so opposed to Carradine's designs and desires that to mention it threw him into a heat. Seeing how much he really was vexed, Mercy offered to go with him to the ground in order to ascertain by inspection a clear view of his meaning, and Smith's plan, against which he had so steadily set himself.

Mercy's readiness to help him out of his perplexity dissipated that angry will, to the merest indecision; and now a word from her would decide the matter, and whether for or against, to his satisfaction. For, did not Miss Fuller understand about all these things?

But the point was still ungained—the great question unsatisfied, with which Mr. Carradine had strolled out to meet Miss Fuller. Until, of herself, without suggestion on his part, he was thereafter ever proud to think, Mercy said,

"You passed my cousin yesterday, Mr. Carradine. I told you about Horatio. He dropped out of the clouds, I still continue to think."

"Your cousin," responded Mr. Carradine, with a mere well-behaved interest. "I was thinking you would be like to find each other out again. You were saying some great things about him, if I recollect? Are you good at fortune telling? I know you must be."

"Better than I thought."

"Then you are pleased—" Carradine looked as if he were almost pleased himself. "But what did he think of your being here? He's not like the Martindell men. Didn't he wonder at it?"

"Yes," said Mercy frankly—meeting his glance with one as open and honest; yet it seemed almost that her eyes reflected the trouble of his.

"You told him it wouldn't be a thing to wonder at long, I expect. Such a deestrict wouldn't be like to keep you in it long."

"That wasn't the thing I said, sir," answered Mercy, pausing as they gained the summit of the hill, turning at that elevation to gaze on the landscape always lovely to her eyes. A pace or two beyond in full relief stood Peter Carradine. Something noble, strong, even granite-like, she seemed to see in that human structure as he stood there moved by what thoughts, what hope and jealousy, she dared not fully guess. Not void of heroism she saw that life of forty years. In its way had it sought for light, and on its darkness light had fallen. He had struggled, groped, gone astray—but, as she looked at him, he stood erect, and blind were the eyes that could not see, in spite of all that was apparent, something *familiar* to the eyes of God alone; something dear to God.

Aptomar had pleaded that he had need of her. Had this man a need that was more intelligible? One that touched her more nearly? Suddenly these two men, complete in unlikeness, were arrayed against each other in her secret thought. And her heart was hurried before them both as a witness and a judge.

A question urged itself to Mr. Carradine's lips when Mercy made that answer; but he restrained himself; he would urge no right to know what thing it was she had said. What right had he? And yet he may have felt a right's existence. But at least he would not attempt to make that clear to her.

"Well," she said, resuming the walk, "let us see about the vexed question, Mr. Carradine. For the meadow at least will always stay in Martindale. And I should be sorry, for one, if the brook were forced out of its old channel for the sake of any effect. It is hard to go against nature."

"Why then," said he, stopping short again, "if you're of that mind, if you go for nature, you've settled the question, Miss Fuller. I won't have a spade stuck into the sod. Not one. I hated the notion, I can't tell you how I hated it, but these dogs are arbitrary as the devil, I tell you. They laugh at your notions, your ignorance, they call it most likely, as if all they were on earth for was to make money out of honest folks by their new-fangled foolishness; it won't get a better name out of me. I'll have that meadow land left as it is, and as it always has been since I drained it. I didn't mind about the slope. But that brook! I can remember when it was a feat to jump across it from one stone to another—and there's where we used to skate when it overflowed and froze in winter time. There were low bushes growing down there once that bore a kind of berry—" his voice faltered. "I've never found a better in the woods—and I tried to keep 'em alive from that old stock, but it died out. I've seen my mother gathering water cress down there . . . it was a long while ago, Miss Fuller, but I can see that sight yet . . . Maybe you're tired, and won't care about going on to see it, after all, Miss Fuller." For her footsteps seemed to falter.

"I care," she said, and continued walking with him. Presently she added, "I heard you speak about Mr. Hooper's grounds, sir; you liked the way they were laid out. Your land lies differently, but I should think at quite as good advantage."

"Yes!"—he was well pleased. "I've said that often enough, but you'd think land in Martindell was another thing from land in Brighton to hear that fellow talk. We've quarrelled ever since he came here—it would disgust you! and I sent him off about his business once. But I had to get him back again, for Johnson and I were clowns at such work as we had got ourselves into."

This fact, sore in experience, had its first mitigation when Mr. Carradine had confessed it to Mercy. He smiled when he spoke, with less embarrassment and less displeasure than he had felt until now in view of the troubles he had endured in keeping his contract with the landscape gardener from Brighton.

"I'll stop his talk though, about Hooper," he added. "I've nothing against Hooper, understand—but he's a man, I take it after all, in spite of his wonderful grounds."

It was Mercy's turn to smile now—and she smiled in such good earnest that Carradine broke into a laugh; so merry he had not been since he engaged in that serious perplexing work of "improvements," which had occupied so much of his thought since the fourth day of July.

Then he told her, as if certain of her interest, speaking with a freedom that might have surprised himself, of the repairs in the old farm house; how it had seemed to him neither right nor decent for a man to neglect his house as he would not neglect his barns. He remembered, he told her, what *she* herself had said about those fine houses in the neighborhood of Brighton; so, though he had done no more than was barely needful in repairing and amending, he hoped she would feel grateful to him for doing of it, even as he felt to her for suggesting the same—for this she had done certainly, though perhaps she knew it not, by her praise of other places—praise that set his own home in so shabby a contrast. He thanked her—because but for her words he might have gone on to the end without knowing anything of the pleasure a man has in making a home that has a pleasant look to outsiders.

They came now to the farm gate; but Mr. Carradine had barely opened it when Johnson came hurrying up the road, looking much disturbed, and speaking out the disturbance with the peremptoriness of real alarm.

"There's something wrong down there, sir, in the big lot.

I don't like the looks of 't. Can't you come down right away?"

"To be sure. What's i' the wind now, Johnson?" But the master had taken no alarm from the man's fright. Perhaps he felt safe on all sides, Mercy so near.

"Them black heifers is wheezing as if they had got the lung cough onto them. And their eyes running like as I never see cattle's eyes afore. If you'll come there!"

"Are they restive, and making trouble in the herd, too?"

"No, they stand stuck, as if they'd grow to the ground afore night. There's something bad about it, sir!"

Johnson wheeled about and began to walk down the hill towards the lot—he wouldn't stand there to be questioned, when his master's place was among the cattle, and not on the lawn, as Smith called it, a questioning of him. If one could believe it of Johnson, he seemed to be muttering all the way to the lot.

"Will you look at the plan of the grounds, and make what you can out of it? Perhaps Smith is around—he'll explain. And I'd like your opinion when I've pacified Johnson; he seems to be riled a little," said Mr. Carradine.

Without waiting for Mercy's answer, he closed the gate behind her—the handsome new gate which had its ornamental arch and its handsome posts of wrought iron, painted black, and shining so that you could see them from afar.

And he went down to the lot.

"There's something got hold of 'em," said Johnson, who was waiting for him by the bars of the fine ten acre lot where the cattle roved amid the richest pasturage; "it's like to prove a plague to us, sir, if it don't to them. You stand still here a minute and see if you couldn't p'int 'em out yourself, sir."

Carradine's eyes, quick and far-seeing, roved over the field—rapid was the observation, and soon over. "Come on, Johnson," said he, "we've got a work before us. Bring on the long whips; we must clear the sheep pen and get these creatures out of the way; they're dead, and they'll taint the whole drove, if we don't put an end to it."

"Do you understand the case, sir?" Johnson was amazed. "Why, we never see the like."

"Yes, like enough. They're as wheezy as if they were in the last stages of asthma. I know that symptom. Come!

get your whips. There's no time to lose here. But where's
Ajax? Johnson! first of all, lead Ajax over to the barn—
he's worth a thousand of this cursed foreign breed. There's
Roy's heifers! Thunder and lightning! if they should get
it scattering among the old man's stock!.... we've got one
day's work before us."

Mercy did not find Smith on the grounds; she certainly
made no search for him; she was still walking silently
about, observing all the changes that had been made in the
hitherto neglected grounds, and had even gone to the borders of the brook in the meadow, without having yet sought
Mrs. Johnson.

It was Mr. Johnson who at last escorted her to the house
door and his wife's presence. He came running across the
lots on his way to the house, and when their paths struck
she joined him to inquire into his fears in regard to the cattle.

Mr. Carradine understood it, he said—it was the cattle
disease he had read about, and the quickest way to stop its
spreading was to destroy the infected ones forthwith. He
accordingly was on his way to bring Mr. Carradine's rifle—
there were seven bullocks in the sheepfold waiting to be
shot, and nobody knew how many more would be down with
the plague to-morrow.

Was Ajax among them, Mercy asked. And Johnson need
not have wondered at the question, for he knew that Mercy
had given that fine name to the lordly creature, and every
one understood what a favorite he was with his owner.

No, he told her, Ajax was safe for all they could see yet.
They had put him into the barn, and if there was such a
thing as keeping disease out by doors and bolts, there was
nothing to fear for Ajax.

The news of this misfortune in the fields impressed Mrs.
Johnson. Her mood was that of lamentations, and she readily fell in with any facts of trouble.

"It's what's been i' the wind all summer," she said to
Mercy, when Johnson had taken the rifle and gone back to
Mr. Carradine. "I heard him say not long ago, if ever he
found any such plague among his stock he wouldn't tamper

with it a minute. He'd made quick work of it. It's been on my mind there was trouble a brewing for Mr. Carradine. Like enough he'll be turned into stun afore the week's out, with this trouble coming onto the top of the words he has had with Smith, who torments the life out o' him with the pleasure. You'd be right vexed, Miss Fuller, for a man used to giving his orders having a creature round asking his wishes all so respectful, and then setting out to oppose them, by and large, never giving up an inch hisself till he's got down the buttonwoods and wa'nuts—setting a man at his time of life, for Mr. Carradine isn't overly young! to waiting for such green trash, ornamental trees, they call 'em, to grow up, as if they'd fill the places of what they've chopped down so wanton, when they'd done their best! . . . . I could cry my eyes out when I look t' the old corner where the robin built her nest this ten year, the same old robin, I do believe, and see that great ugly hole, though to be sure it gives you more sky to look at, and all the comfort there's in living after all is to be able to read a title clear to mansions up there."

Mrs. Johnson wiped her eyes, having with rare vehemence thus expressed herself, and invited Mercy in to look at the improvements, " as they called 'em,"—thus she always qualified her use of the term—it would give Mr. Carradine a pleasure to know that Miss Fuller had gone over the housen. He would be sure to ask about it.

But before she arose to follow Mrs. Johnson, Mercy said, with her eyes on the spot where the buttonwood trees had stood,

" Mrs. Johnson, I could cry, too—Smith never could do anything to make up for the loss of those splendid trees! What a shame it is. What *did* Mr. Carradine say ?"

" He said—'twas wicked, but I couldn't wonder at it, he said the idiot wasn't worth a curse, or he'd get it. He was in a rage, Miss Fuller. You wouldn't a liked to see it. Oh, I tell you it isn't very pleasant getting a pleasure laid out in a old place where every thing is sort o' sacred. It comes hard ; it do "

Even as Miranda had done before her, Mercy followed her guide about from garret to cellar of the old new mansion.

And it was not an idle work, this of close observation, that was carried on there. Not idle, nor fruitless. It moved her to see the abounding evidences of gentle thought that had been taken of needs that surely Mr. Carradine himself had never felt—of tastes that for himself had never been fostered. It moved her to hear from Mrs. Johnson, how, in the first days after the changes were completed, he he had gone over the housen again and again, "deranging things with his own hands," and "notifying all," with a satisfaction wonderful to see of them that knowed how little store he had ever set by what some might even call the mere comforts of life.

Mercy praised every thing—but her words were few. She explained the use of much that had passed the comprehension of simple Mrs. Johnson. There were two apartments across whose threshold she did not pass; the parlor, and that room whose key Mrs. Johnson dared not bring for Miranda's inspection, but which she opened without comment for Miss Fuller; for she had an instinctive conviction that of all rooms in the house he would choose that she should see this.

From looking into that room Mercy turned away without a word. She seemed to have looked too far into the heart of the man who had brought all these things together, certainly not for any want of his; as certainly not for satisfaction of any pride of his. No, no; all this had been done to show her that he could afford a state equal to that of other men, whose fine farms and fine dwellings gave them their local honor.

Mrs. Johnson tried hard to conceal how depressed she was in spirit when she and Miss Fuller sat down to rest in the long porch; she tried hard to bring herself to speak of the contemplated moving, but not with success. Here, after all, was the root of offence, the stumbling block,—not in Randy, for she had been able to speak, and to confess, in Randy's hearing. Perhaps the influence that seemed always to flow out of Mercy's mere presence did now but increase her trouble—a sense of her own injustice, of her own selfishness, may not a little have plagued her. It was certainly with the impetuosity of a somewhat desperate state of mind that she at last arose and proposed that they should walk down to the lot, and see what was really going on there.

She secretly hoped that Mercy would decline this invitation, while for her own part she was absolutely determined on going; she would not have it on her mind or hands to entertain the young lady for another moment.

But Mercy was as ready for the walk as Mrs. Johnson. And, as they went into the lane, they were met by old Samuel Roy. He was in haste, and in trouble. Was Mr. Johnson anywhere about? Was Mr. Carradine? There was something wrong about those heifers. He'd had his eye on them for this two days; they seemed to be struck of something—a cough like—and from being as frisky as young lambs, they stood about as if they were under some enchantment. During the last half-dozen hours old Samuel had repeated this description many times to Randy, and he was acting on her counsel now when he came up to consult with the generous giver of that precious gift of cattle.

Mrs. Johnson looked at Mercy before she answered him.

"I'm afraid," said she, kindly, "I'm afraid there's trouble in store for all the neighbors. Whatever it is, Mr. Carradine's herd is as bad as your'n, Samuel, and we're just going down to see what's been doing. If you're minded, come along. They say there's only one cure for 'm, when they get in this plight."

"What's that, Miss Johnson?" asked Samuel, and his voice, that was full of quavers always, seemed now to have in it a deeper tremble.

"A rifle shot. And no time to be lost about it. They can't be cured, Mr. Carradine says, and it's like rot to get into a herd."

Old Samuel did now tremble; his cattle were not many, and they were his pride—his riches, I had almost said. But he had really *no* riches: he was a poor man: and in times of panic, and of crisis, not only the great stock-jobber, note-shaver and general speculator has a right to alarm.

When Carradine saw the old man coming down the road with the women, he came out to meet the party, and his first words told how his thoughts ran.

"Sam'l, old boy, I've played you a poor turn this time, I'm afraid. What are the heifers doing?"

"They're in a trance, sir, with the water running from their eyes, and—"

"Wheezing like possessed?"

"Yes sir, just so."

"I shall have to knock it out o' them, then. Go home

and put those heifers by themselves, if you have to tie them to your door. Don't let them come nigh the others; it's in their breath, may be, Lord knows where it is! but if I save a quarter of *my* stock I shall think I'm well off. Don't lose any time. I'll be over. I've been worrying about you. Yes, I have. Keep a sharp look out on the others. Johnson will be around in an hour, if I don't come. Go on."

The order was not to be argued. The old man turned, obedient as a child. Mrs. Johnson's eyes followed him tearfully—seeing that, Mr. Carradine said cheerfully,

"Don't fret, mother, Sam'l won't lose by me. I'll sell the Hill farm itself first."

In spite of his disturbance, his anxiety, and his purpose to drive over to Jackson's Corners before nightfall, in order to ascertain what he knew in regard to this distemper, Mr. Carradine had time and thought to recall the errand on which Mercy had come to his house with him. But he did not ask her criticism on whatever she had seen, until she was sitting by his side in the democrat, and he was driving Sorrel on the road to Calvin Green's, the Elder's house at present being her place of sojourn.

He inquired of her then whether he should quarrel with Smith any more, or let the mule have his way! Perhaps she had changed her mind about the brook.

No—Mercy had not changed her mind. Smith must be held in check, peremptorily; and not forgiven in a day for cutting down that clump of fine button trees that threw their shadows so far on a hot summer day.

She spoke only from the natural tendencies of her heart, and perhaps Carradine took the words for no more. Yet he thanked her with gratitude for the grace of her speech—in secret thanked her as he could not in words.

And could it fail to be with Mercy a question, as they drove along the very road where she had but now walked with her cousin, whether indeed this Martindale life was the waste he would represent? Pleasant it was, and fair; and interests many and varied were here; but at the last a waste? and the passing life a rusting out? Surely, there were degrees of culture never to be reached here, easily enough within her scope elsewhere. There was a station impossible to make even apparent here, for here it was not; but vacant elsewhere; waiting for her, it might be. To be filled, if with efficience, with no mean result; if with contentment, with what a measure of joy! She seemed to hear the city's din rolling in upon this stillness. A bright array came between her and the fair green fields where crops waved, and men labored, and cattle were infected. She saw herself summoned to a life of intellectual activity, to social triumphs, to wealth, as it is in towns. Her cousin was in his youth, in the acknowledged need of youth; in the pride of success and of endeavor, and in the need that is felt in such winning, and such struggle. Between him and Peter Carradine were many years, and more than time could account for, immeasurably more; there rolled the gulf of diverse natures, aspirations, and pursuits.

She heard the cow bells, and the sheep bells tinkling through the gathering shadows of the quiet evening; the lowing of the herd, the bleating of the fold. Now and then the rumble of a teamster's wagon broke upon the stillness; the burden of the day was over, its toil was all ended. No gas burned here till morning. Here were no festive sounds —no opera tides of people and of song. No such illusions spread over Martindale. Was Martindale too dull then, too dead for? Held it no illusion, no life which towered above the peaceful plains of the quiet valley like some old Grecian hero?

In her room she read from Homer's book, of Hector and of Achilles; read long after sleep had fallen on every soul within the town, except on Peter Carradine. Was it Ajax kept him wakeful? Or the slaughtered cattle, or the misfortune of his gift to Samuel Roy, for it seemed that even his good must be spoken evil of.

•

CHAPTER XXXIII

DEATH IN LIFE.

Mr. Collamer came up to Martindale one Sunday afternoon. It was the first day of September. The little congregation that met in the morning for worship was informed by Elder Green that the minister had taken pains to make needful arrangements, and would in consequence be able to preach to them in the afternoon. Accordingly a goodly company of Mr. Collamer's friends and "converts" gathered together, a little after noon, prepared to wait with patience the coming of the preacher. He came at two o'clock.

At five the house was vacant, and he had "fit audience though few," in a solitary woman—the woman was Miranda.

By no chance. It could not have happened by chance that after the congregation had dispersed, and Randy had walked far on the road home, she struck into a path that led her back across the woodland to the school-house door.

No—this meeting was devised—it was deliberate, and sacred must it not be, as became their hearts? As became the day, and hour, and place? The place, where but now listening men had trembled, and wept, before the power and pathos of his eloquence, who should now discourse but for one solitary soul, bringing to her a special evangel!

It pleased the minister to see Miranda looking well and happy. He could readily account for the changes he saw had taken place in her since their last meeting. Religious experience had enriched and elevated her nature. This noble aspect of womanhood, its frankness, its freedom, charmed him. Its strength seemed to reassure him—he both believed and hoped more for human nature since her emergence into this state of being.

To anything that she should say he could not listen with indifference. And it was so, that they talked first of Miss Fuller, to whom Mr. Collamer had brought messages, and a package from her cousin; for it chanced, he said, that their lot was cast in the same town, and Mr. Aptomar had sought him out on his cousin's " recommend."

And because she was talking with him, and that he seemed interested in Miss Fuller's fortunes, Randy dwelt on her own predictions concerning Mr. Carradine—whereat the minister smiled. Not unobserved of Randy, who, supposing the smile was a token of doubt, produced her proof straightway, becoming from that moment more firmly persuaded in her mind in regard to the issue of events.

"It was just for Miss Fuller's sake," she owned, "that I felt the readier to make peace with Mr. Carradine. And I've wanted every one to know I was at peace with him. He's tried to be kind to us. He missed of it in the end, but we never doubted what his motive was. He couldn't tell when he sent over those fine young heifers that we was to lose the whole of our stock by it. And he showed he meant the present for a true one, in the ways he took to make the loss good to father. He lost five hundred head of cattle himself. I believe in Peter Carradine, Mr. Collamer; but, when I think of Miss Fuller, I can't help it, I feel scared. I feel as if I ought to warn her; but then I know she can see clearer and farther into things than I ever could. I don't believe, sir, that one of us born and brought up in Martindell on these farms here. ever took half the pleasure she has in the quiet pretty country. Everything has charmed her —from the least."

" Do you really think so, Miranda ?" broke in the minister, as if he had some special and serious cause, for knowing the truth.

" She loves the whole of it. She loves even me !" answered Miranda with full belief.

"It that so great a wonder ? . . . I am so sorry to hear that your father has met with such a loss; it went hard with him, I know. But how did he take it ? patiently ?"

"The cattle you mean. He could only take it one away. Did you ever hear him really complain? No sir! nobody ever did. But it seems now a long while since it happened. I think he has almost forgotten it. Losses never plagued him much. There was only us two—and he leans on me. And he may, dear father!"

"Good daughter, that you are, it's like bearing on a strong staff. I know he feels sure of it. Keep your brave heart, Miranda, it is worth more than gold that cannot be counted for abundance."

"But I was saying," said Randy quickly turning from this theme, "she sees everything different from what we do, that's the reason she could appreciate Mr. Carradine better, I suppose. Some people say it's his wealth she'll take him for. She is not that kind of woman. She'll marry him for love if for anything."

Mr. Collamer answered that. He spoke out in a hurried and excited way.

"God *be* praised, he gives the loving to each other. He is the loving Father."

"And though, when I was at the camp-meeting, I thought surely I never could go back to the school again—and maybe I never shall—yet the thing that might have hindered me then would not now. There's nothing seems to me so foolish as such pride as I had then. We don't live so long, Mr. Collamer, that we can afford to waste time in anger and contention."

Then he asked her about the Elder's daughter; and Miranda's face looked grave when she answered. It seemed to her—she couldn't understand, but she felt it even clearer than she saw it—that Sally had changed toward her, and not only towards her. She was not happy, Randy thought. Her mind was troubled—she seemed discontented. Martindell was a dull place to her; though she was born and brought up there, it never seemed to be the place for her. Sally liked society and excitement. She was out of place on a farm among plain people. She said, sometimes, she wished she had not gone from home to school in town—that, as long she must live in this out-of-the-way place, she might better not have known that there was any other way of living. Miranda wished that Mr. Collamer could talk with her; he might show her how far wrong she was.

He promised that he would do so—but much he doubted his ability to make Sally see anything she had not the heart to see. Only experience of life could show her what life was. For the Elder's sake, and for the sake of the Elder's wife, and for the young lady's sake, he prayed it might not be a bitter experience that must bring her into the paths of peace. Then he would have drawn Miranda to speak to him of herself. Had she nothing to tell him of her daily life, more than could be written? He had thought, from expressions he found in her letters here and there, that possibly it might be needful for him to come again to Martindale some day, and in her behalf; that he might give her to some happy man. But then, thinking over all the names and faces he knew in Martindale, he could not decide the question—but she could tell—and would she?

Half playfully it seemed, and yet with a deep seriousness, he asked these questions. Any one but the gravest interest could not have been awakened by the emotion with which he saw these questions were heard.

Nor unnoticed was the sudden surprise—the hesitation—the painful irresolution—and the finally fixed purpose that seemed to be clutched, rather than quietly arrived at; grasped with energy that made her, for a brief space, speechless. She looked at her questioner as startled, as wildly as the dead man raised to life might have looked to his life-speaking Master.

"It may be," she said. "It may be," she repeated. "Mr. Jobson may not object to it. If he knows it is my wish, he will not. I can trust his secret with you—but no other person knows it. You see what he is doing to the tavern—by-and-by, in the winter perhaps, I shall be living there."

She did not look at him to observe what he might be thinking—his reception of the intelligence she had communicated; she was curious to know.

"I think you will choose seriously and wisely," he said at length, "knowing it is for life. Husband and wife must be for eternity, if in no other way, in this, in the influence they exert on one another. I shall wish to see Mr. Jobson, now that I know he is the man you love."

She received these words in silence—were these congratulations? Was this sufficient?. This she had of life, sufficient to the heart this day so longing, and so faint—yet so honest and so resolute?

If the silence in the school-house was broken again that day, he, it seemed, must break it. Yet it was not easy for him to speak; the air seemed close and heavy to him—it almost stifled Randy.

"I suppose," he said, "that I came here to-day to preach, and to see Miss Fuller. But it seems that the business that concerns *me* most, remains yet to be done. I want to ask advice of you, Miranda, as I would of a sister. You have confided your heart's secret to me as a sister might. Stand still in that relation to me, dearest friend."

"I will," said she.

Nevertheless, he hesitated now—hesitated even after he began to speak.

"I am afraid you will think that I should be able to satisfy my own mind without anybody's help. Still, I have never seen a woman but you whom I would be willing to have know me as I know myself. It seems to me when I see you, Miranda, or even when I think of you, as if my vanity must remove itself out of sight. It would hinder your seeing me as I am. And it could not but offend you."

"Your vanity, Mr. Collamer!"

"Yes, don't flatter me; you can afford to be plain with me. You are the one woman who will speak the truth to me. You don't know how I rely on you. But don't praise me. I get enough of that. I want plain truth from you; severe truth, if you find that you must speak it."

Alas, what was this he required of her! He was calling her to heavenly heights—she was ascending after him! And yet he looked as if he deemed she were to descend to him from above! How calm she seemed; but the life within her, the hidden life, was rising as a giant in its strength.

"I am a young man yet," said he, "and you might think I could find my work—my great work—sufficient to occupy my heart, as well as my hands. But there are times when the best friends in my congregation seem to me so far off that nothing can bring us together. It is my fault, I think. Not because I would have it so, but because it cannot be helped—I stand isolated, wanting the link that would connect me more closely with my people. There is a break in the chain, and a woman must supply it. Then I should be rightly efficient and obviously capable. Do you see this as I see it?"

"Yes I think it must be so."

She agreed with him so entirely in this, that he found it easier to speak the next words.

"Something very singular has happened; will you look at this and tell me what you see?"

He held in his hand a little chamois-leather case, from which he now drew a miniature likeness of a lady, so beautiful that, when Miranda's eyes fell upon it, it was the beauty of the image that startled her; that it should be in his possession, that he should submit it to her criticism, was another matter to be thought of secondly.

He was anxious to *see* what she would think, and when he saw how softly an expression stole over her features—and that she brushed a tear from her eyes—when he saw her so much moved, so silent, he did not need to wait for her words —he said:

"It has been my unspeakable privilege to lead that lady to the Savior's feet. When I tell you that a new song is in her mouth, it means even more than the great deal we mean, saying it of others. I wish that you could sing. Her voice is like a well-tuned instrument—and the Lord's song on her lips is indeed a matter of rejoicing. But she is a child of wealth, brought up in fashion—"

"You love her, sir," said Randy, suddenly approaching the point which, as he neared it, seemed yet a great way off.

"Yes."

"And she loves you."

"She gave me this little likeness of herself—yes, Miranda, she loves me."

"Yet you ask my advice, Mr. Collamer?"

"Yes, my sister. And I exhort you by the sacredness of friendship, counsel me."

Exhorted by the solemnity and earnestness of his look and manner, still more than by thought of friendship he invoked, she said:

"If God has put it into your two hearts, now can I speak? Listen to Him."

He seemed to perceive, when she had made this answer, that this was the counsel he should have anticipated; that she could not really venture to give other advice. Then he said:

"I will write to you about it—I thought I could speak

more freely, or I would have written before. You do not know, I think, Miranda, though I have told you very often, what pleasure your letters have given me."

There was no disguising the fact that both the minister and Randy gained with a feeling of relief, the open air of common topics; having precipitately retired from the confessional.

"I have often thought of you when I knew you must be speaking to me by your pen. I was very curious to know how you wrote those letters, and at what hours, and whether they satisfied you—for they were remarkable, I think. Won't you tell me anything more about them?"

She did not seem to be surprised by the question, but answered with apparent indifference, which he had been blind if he had failed to see was feigned and impotent:

"I wrote them at odd hours—as I could find the time. Sometimes when other people were asleep—sometimes early in the morning, by daybreak. How did I write them? I tried to do my best. I gave you my best thoughts and feelings; but they were all true, and not got up for the occasion."

"I believe that. And there were many things I wanted to talk over, for it seems to me you have hit at the heart of some truths that I did not possess before. You don't know what hard thinking your letters have compelled me to give to some subjects that had escaped my attention. But it will not do to get on that train to-night. I see I have missed the early cars. It does not matter though; I could afford that since it has given me a chance to talk with you." He arose while he spoke thus. "But now if I get to town before dark, I must say good-bye to you. And I shall write to you again—I may?"

"If it will give you any pleasure;" she answered, rising also—perceiving an abruptness in his leave-taking, which mere haste could not accounnt for.

"Good-bye then, dear sister," he said. "May your life as a Christian and as a woman be complete! Rounded to the fullest human joy. May you never be able to say that your work is done. God keep you, and the man of your choice! lead you in the paths of his choosing—save you with his almighty salvation. Pray for me. Ask that I may have direction from on high. That God will guide me. I need not ask you!—my sister will not fail me in this sacred work."

"No—never. Good-bye, Mr. Collamer. God bless you." The words came from her as from him, without faltering, and they went out from the school-house thus blessing one another.

The sun had set. How peaceful was the scene that spread before their eyes! how softly fell the shadows along the meadow lands. How the the swallows flew about! There were hundreds of them fluttering and flying, full of song! Masses of white clouds, dazzling mountainous, thundrous, floated under the majestic expanse.

You might have deemed this Martindale the veritable Happy Valley.

To Mr. Collamer it was wondrous fair—and as he walked toward Elder Green's, for the Elder had driven the minister's horse to his stable, his mind dwelt on this beauty, and and on the girl from whom he had just now parted.

The sun had set—would it ever rise again? Did ever the night shadow fall over our earth and no mortal eye behold it, and see a fitness in the sable shrouding? fitness attested by the sorrowing heart that sat in sackcloth, saying, will the sun ever rise again? Forgive, ye happy ones! Glory ye in the brightness! Let no one cheat you of the vision! Hear ye the singing of the birds, the cricket's constant chirping. It is the veritable sun that shines—and ye can see the splendor of the rose! Fair children! loving hearts! be blessed to life! And sing the songs of faith, your joy transforms to knowledge! only, with the patience of angels, be ye patient with the sighing ye may hear—the suffering you may see. And give of your joy in Heaven to the heaviness that groans about you.

For Miranda—while she went her solitary way, what was she saying? He had left her. At first a sense of relief too full, too keen, to be mistaken, had made her walk along the path that led up to the road, with rapid steps—but this sense of relief—that burst upward as a fountain unsealed, passed—the rock that had been rolled away was hurled to its place again, and the fountain was broken.

At last she left the the path and entered a wood on the edge of the hill. What meant this sudden dread of companionship? She sat upon the grass among the darkening shadows.

"Weary, weary life! God take me out of it! Let me lie under the sod in the old burying ground. For why should I live any longer!" and the image of Senior Jobson did not rise up to rebuke her.

"What have I to do, seeing what I see? what have I to do! My right to everything is gone. There is nothing but Heaven—and Heaven will not open because I cry at the door." Neither did the image of her father rise up to rebuke her. "Did I want his praise. What is it to me that he says I write letters that he likes? We are friends. I am his sister. I am glad I told him about Mr. Jobson. I have no brother, and no sister. I shall have both by him—he promised, He promised to marry us. And then I shall be settled in the tavern—and all will be easy. I will do my duty. I can do everything for Senior that he expects—only —all he thinks of—only—"

Then, as you have seen a leaf caught by the wind, and tossed up, and driven through the air, poor leaf that must surely flutter to the earth again, Randy was caught up, suddenly and without remedy, and whirled through emotions, and light and darkness, till she fell again to pray, "God of Heaven! so near, yet so far off! if my voice can be heard—if thou carest! can'st thou care for anything like me! . . . .

"I thank thee! I thank thee that I did not understand! I bless thee that he's gone. Don't let me even see his face again—or hear his voice. See, oh Saviour, on my knees I creep back from the abyss. I did not say the words that would have made me false to Senior. I did not say what might have made trouble for some other woman. Oh, perhaps she is not able to bear sorrow as I am, or to feel what I feel, or to wake up, as I've waked up! Don't ever let her know such sorrow! Put all this on me. I am able to bear it! And because I say to thee I can and will, and promise here to bear it, and to be true to Jobson, thou who dost sorrow in our sorrow, thou hast said it! keep every other woman this day, every other woman in the world, near to such grief, safely, safely from it! Sorrow is in this world, and thou art grieved at it. But I can endure. Forgive me. I loved him, not knowing what I did. I did not understand it. Oh, forgive me, dear Lord. I will to be strong. I will to endure. I say it in the faith that thou wilt hear and help me. Oh roll away the stone from other hearts that shuts them up like bodies in a tomb. I will lie still till the last trump, if only thou wilt have pity on some other woman suffering like me, and bring her out of sorrow into peace, where she may dare to feel the life of love!"

She ended her praying in a sudden burst of tears. Nor you nor I can know how many hearts in that same hour, standing free of the burden that had crushed and blinded them, lifted their voices in ransomed joy, saying—

"God, I thank thee, who, beyond my hope, oh, beyond all deserving, hast, by thine own hand led me to this hour!"

CHAPTER XXXIV.

"FOR BETTER, FOR WORSE."

There was one day a wedding in one of the houses of Martindale, and a goodly portion of the neighborhood came together, witnesses of the ceremony, and partakers of the feast.

Widow Savage and her daughters, Helen, and Ann Maria, were among the guests, and the sisters of Oliver were quite the prettiest of the company, though no one seemed to think so. Perhaps it was indignant observation of the fact, and that they sat crushed into a corner in spite of their new dresses, that made Sally Green conspicuously kind to them when they walked with others out into the grove, shy, and hanging back, apparently forgotten by their brother.

Recently Oliver had invited Sally to go home with him some day and visit his family—and now, when the feast was over, and the company dispersing, she bethought of her promise, and looked around for widow Savage. But she was nowhere to be seen. For a little longer, therefore, Sally made herself useful in her peculiar way—then she quietly walked off; and anticipating that her father's house, by this time, swarmed with company, she determined that she would go alone in search of Oliver's mother. Probably she had gone homeward—and if so, she could easy overtake her, for the farm was two miles distant.

It lay on the north side of a cross road—and the way was new to Sally; the way besides was rough, and her feet ill-shod.

But having set out in it, she, of course, would not turn back.

She had ample time to think, as she went her way, wherefore was she going; and what should be the nature of this interview. The mood in which she set out on her walk was such as disposed her to regard with favor whatever revelation might be made in this poor house. As she approached the house, the very isolation of its situation, its lowliness, had a sort of charm for her wayward heart. Here, it might be, she should at length find refuge! The sooner she sought it here the better, perhaps. She was almost persuaded that it would be best to acknowledge this day to widow Savage, the relation in which she stood to her son. That perhaps it would be wise, now that she was coming to the house, to ask for a home in it. Her father—sooner or later, he must know what she had done. An unwise thing —it might be—but how to be made the best of! and if Oliver only had a chance once in the world!

With such suggestions revolving in her mind, she arrived at the cottage, undecided as to what should be said and done when she had crossed the threshold and stood among the family.

Now it had happened to Oliver, that as day by day he passed Mr. Carradine's place, while the improvements were going on there, the rage for improvement had seized him. Day by day his old house grew more more shabby to his eyes. He thought of Sally, and his pride took fright. So when the white-washers and paper-hangers had embellished the red farm house, and the cottage to which the Johnsons' were to remove, Oliver determined that they should perform their magic under his mother's roof.

And as the business of these decorators was to take a job wherever they could find one, and a man's money was as good as his neighbor's, the white-washers, paper-hangers, painters, brought their tools down to the Savage farm, and transformed the place into its present pretty aspect— whereat Sally stood amazed. For it looked like a very bower of beauty, when compared with her expectation. Why Love seemed to have settled himself there, and he peeped on the girl, and he saluted her, as she stood on the steps looking into the house and around her, with smiles full of promises.

This, then, was poor Oliver's house! She thought of him tenderly, and with self-reproach. Had he done all this for her? Poor fellow! how had he contrived to manage it?

She would like her father to see! her father who regarded every dollar put upon the house in the way of decoration, or of convenience, as so much money thrown away. She would like him to come up and see this white cottage so pure and sweet, and pretty. She thought she should then need to use less argument in favor of the external decoration of the old brown farm-house that stood sentinelled by poplars.

There were a great many things that Sally could have said to Mrs. Savage—but alas! She found the house quite deserted, and though she walked about it, and within, and sat down, and stood up, and lingered, no one came, and there was no sign given her that anybody ever meant to come.

And, on the whole, glad that the visit had ended precisely thus, Sally, who did never, in spite of waywardness, altogether knew her own mind and wishes, left the house, and took the road home, and arrived at her father's house without having met a solitary creature.

For the past hour her father had been anxiously looking out for her return; at the sound of a footstep he was at his office door; twice to his wife, and once to his mother, he had said—

"I thought it was Sally. When Sally comes I want her," and at last when she came, he saw her pass the office window, and opened the door that was so rarely opened, and said—

"Come in. I want you."

He had, hours ago, taken off his dress coat, and was now in his everyday garments, but not in his everyday guise; an extraordinary perplexity was manifest in his every look and gesture. When the wedding was over he came away with a mere look at the feast prepared, a mere word with the bride and bridegroom. And since then he had been waiting for Sally.

He had his papers on the desk before him, loosely spread about. Business, then! That assurance was a great relief to her; for when she saw his face and heard his voice she trembled, and said to herself, "He knows all." But now she said:

"Some work to be done?" with the cheerful alacrity of

one who is suddenly relieved of a great fear and trouble—enabled so to see the mere nothingness of mere labor.

"Bad work," said he, sitting down on his high stool and taking up a scrap of paper, on which some words were written. "There—that's Savage's writing, isn't it? One of the painters who has been working for him said it was."

"Then why do you ask me, father?" asked Sally, looking a very natural surprise—but she glanced at the paper, though her first purpose had seemed to be to return it without so much as a glance.

"Because, in such business, one can't be too sure. Have you seen Oliver, to-day?"

"He was at the wedding, father."

"Have you seen him since?"

"No."

"No?"

"I did not go away until nearly every one had left, I think. I took a long walk. I was alone. I have not seen him. Why! did you think I had seen him, father?"

"I—I am afraid, Sally, that Oliver—he is a dangerous young man to have around! I began to think we had wronged him; that he was better than he seemed—"

"He is!" said Sally.

"No, he's worse. He's worse, my daughter; ten hundred times! Here he's been forging my notes—two of 'em —a hundred dollars each."

Sally gasped for breath. Her father thought: "It's severe, but this will cure her. I could afford to to pay two hundred dollars to have poor Sally cured. I won't be hard on Oliver."

"I thought," said he, "I could talk with you easier than your mother. For what is one to do? If I don't pay the money, you know what comes next."

"What comes next?" groaned Sally

"Prison!"

"Prison, father?"

"Yes; that's the penalty. And the proof is clear as day Here's his writing—there's himself. I've waited here all the afternoon to talk with you about it. For I said to myself, Sally is always my adviser in business. I won't act on my own opinion."

"If you did, father, what would you do?"

"Put him where there wouldn't be danger of his doing the like of this again. For it would be the kindest thing that I could do. He's a man not safe to be at large—you can't trust the fellow out of sight. If it wasn't for his mother being a widow, and his being in the fellowship of the church—"

"Yes—yes, father, since he is a widow's son, and a professor, what now do you mean to do?"

"That's what you must help me to decide about," said he. "Look on all sides of it, daughter. Two can judge the matter better than one."

She sat in silence, and he did not urge her answer. He gave her time to think. He guessed that, not without a struggle, she would come to a decision. He believed she had some tender feeling for Oliver. He would be patient with her; he would be gentle. He feared that his words had fallen on her as a dreadful blow; in spite of love, he, her father, had delivered it, and he had seen it fall—and it had crushed her! But, now that she knew Oliver, as she could not have known him before, now she would understand her father's heart! She would surely appreciate that kindness which had chosen her, and none other of the house, not wife, not mother, but child, to confide in—to counsel with.

CHAPTER XXXV.

"TILL DEATH US DO PART."

When he saw Sarah struggling against the feeling which raged within her, he thought he understood it; and he saw that it would prostrate her; he therefore stepped to his office door and locked it. Upon that hour there must be no intrusion. Then he walked off in to a corner, and sat down, and wiped his eyes—and through the silence of the room was only heard the sound of Sally's sobbing breath, the signs of the grief with which she wrestled. The sight grew terrible to him, he turned away his face into the dark corner and prayed, thinking of Jacob who wrestled with the angel, hoping that it might prove in the end that an angel now wrestled with and conquered his daughter!

But she!—Oh, pride, and shame, and wrath, what angel force was hid in your terrific mutiny?

What should she do? Whither turn? Was this the hour for confession? This a moment to own that she had wrought out in secret her own purpose; and the man for whom she had sacrificed the wishes, and the hopes of every soul that loved her, was it he that stood thus covered with disgrace, and fronting ruin thus!

Her pride rebelled against confession.

Then plead for him? This, indeed, she might do, and perhaps with success. This she would do—must do. But what should follow after? Why delay confession any longer? She could go with him to the ends of the earth—or to his mother's house! But with him? In that hour every fond feeling she had ever felt for him was under an arrest. She would confess. Then—

So, at length she controlled herself sufficiently to speak.

"Put him where there wouldn't be danger of his doing the like of this again. For it would be the kindest thing that I could do. He's a man not safe to be at large—you can't trust the fellow out of sight. If it wasn't for his mother being a widow, and his being in the fellowship of the church—"

"Yes—yes, father, since he is a widow's son, and a professor, what now do you mean to do?"

"That's what you must help me to decide about," said he. "Look on all sides of it, daughter. Two can judge the matter better than one."

She sat in silence, and he did not urge her answer. He gave her time to think. He guessed that, not without a struggle, she would come to a decision. He believed she had some tender feeling for Oliver. He would be patient with her; he would be gentle. He feared that his words had fallen on her as a dreadful blow; in spite of love, he, her father, had delivered it, and he had seen it fall—and it had crushed her! But, now that she knew Oliver, as she could not have known him before, now she would understand her father's heart! She would surely appreciate that kindness which had chosen her, and none other of the house, not wife, not mother, but child, to confide in—to counsel with.

CHAPTER XXXV.

"TILL DEATH US DO PART."

When he saw Sarah struggling against the feeling which raged within her, he thought he understood it; and he saw that it would prostrate her; he therefore stepped to his office door and locked it. Upon that hour there must be no intrusion. Then he walked off in to a corner, and sat down, and wiped his eyes—and through the silence of the room was only heard the sound of Sally's sobbing breath, the signs of the grief with which she wrestled. The sight grew terrible to him, he turned away his face into the dark corner and prayed, thinking of Jacob who wrestled with the angel, hoping that it might prove in the end that an angel now wrestled with and conquered his daughter!

But she!—Oh, pride, and shame, and wrath, what angel force was hid in your terrific mutiny?

What should she do? Whither turn? Was this the hour for confession? This a moment to own that she had wrought out in secret her own purpose; and the man for whom she had sacrificed the wishes, and the hopes of every soul that loved her, was it he that stood thus covered with disgrace, and fronting ruin thus!

Her pride rebelled against confession.

Then plead for him? This, indeed, she might do, and perhaps with success. This she would do—must do. But what should follow after? Why delay confession any longer? She could go with him to the ends of the earth—or to his mother's house! But with him? In that hour every fond feeling she had ever felt for him was under an arrest. She would confess. Then—

So, at length she controlled herself sufficiently to speak.

She looked around her—saw her father, where he sat in the dark corner of the room. He heard her move, and he sprung to his feet—he drew near to his child.

"Father, find him—bring him in here. We will end the matter."

"But how shall we end it?" said he, lingering, determined first to come to an explanation with her. For he saw that there was something that must be explained.

"You mean to forgive him. Bring him in here. Show him what he has done, and that he is discovered—"

"And that will make an end of 't?"

"Of all this—yes."

"I'll go with you in it," said he. "If anything can save him this will. But what do you suppose will become of him?"

"What do you suppose will become of any of us, father?"

"To be sure," said he. "You're right. It's the mercy of God we're all looking for."

"And for forgiveness as we forgive."

"True. But there's justice that must be done sometimes. It wouldn't do—"

Elder Green was looking from the window as he spoke—he stopped sport, unlocked the door, and called out:

"Oliver, come in here."

If there was anything unusual in the Elder's voice, it was not a harsh tone, but a gentler than seemed natural.

Oliver obeyed. But, when he saw Sally in the office, seemed to be taken aback. She did not look at him, and her face was averted. What had already taken place in the room was as far beyond his conjecture as beyond his appreciation.

But he was not entirely at ease—he was hopeful—he was always hopeful; still—

"Oliver," said Elder Green, "there's something wrong here. You have been playing me false."

"What's that, sir?" There was still hope as well as apprehension in the young man's mind. Possibly Sally had confessed the marriage—he had some reason for believing that she had. It was now autumn, and she had promised that, when the fall harvest was over, all should be revealed; and he had been on good behavior now these many weeks; and she had been kind to him whenever it chanced that they could have a word or two together. So, in spite of apprehension, he was hopeful.

"What's that, sir?" he asked.

"For two hundred dollars; that's what you threw away your good Christian name for! To say nothing of risking a prison."

Oliver's face whitened to a deathly whiteness. A prison! —a Christian name! Then all was discovered. Not the marriage? He looked at Sally; he could not command a word.

"You know what I refer to. Unless I pay those notes there's no way for you but one—it's a State's prison offence. You've ventured on, young man, a dreadful, terrible way! But I have been thinking over what a trouble it would be to your poor mother, and your little sisters, and though you might be saved from worse temptations, for the way of transgression is so dreadful easy if but once you set your feet therein, I have concluded to pay the money, sir, and let you off—but on one condition."

When Elder Green had arrived at this point he paused. Breathless silence through the little room. Sally never moved. Oliver thought, she knows what's to come next; but he did not lift his eyes; she did not move by so much as a hand's breadth from her place.

"I'm thinking," said Elder Green, "you will not care about staying in this neighborhood after what has happened. And perhaps you're not able to get off without help—" he paused, but Oliver gave no sign of intending to answer this point, "and I think it would be better for your mother and your sisters just to have you gone. I'll help you off. I'll do anything you need in that way. Go—go where you can make a good reputation for yourself—where you won't feel that every man and woman who looks at you is suspecting of you. Go and earn a good man's name, Oliver. You're young yet."

"And now," thought Elder Green, "I have ended the business for these young people forever."

He walked up and down the room with his hands clasped behind him, and amid all the agitations of the moment this satisfied him, that his darling was now safe.

A strange sort of courage, rather a bold resolve to stand upon his rights here in this house, from this moment, pos-

forgive me. Then—if you will have it—I'll choose between you and him."

"Well, get up. But don't come near me. Sit down there. Now speak. You'll choose between me and him? That's what you've done already. You've chosen. You must bide by it—bide by it, Sally! Marriage is God's ordinance—it isn't the law that could set you free, if that was your choice. You're that man's wife, afore God, if it's true what you tell me. You've told me, both of you, things far enough from truth. I wish this might be a falsehood, I wish, for once, you wasn't true, true, Sally. But you're his wife—if you can keep him to his contract—"

"It isn't true, it can't be," she cried. "He said I could save him, and I thought I loved him. But I can't save him, and he's killed all the love I ever had for him!"

"God have mercy on you!" cried poor Elder Green, utterly bewildered. "There ought to be a woman—I'll go call in your mother."

But Sally stopped him by a word.

"Wait!" And he sat down again, hopeless, and yet expecting, and repeated her word, "Wait?"

She seemed to take it, as it came from him, and did delay what she had to speak. All the while her face was turned toward him, not once toward Oliver, she seemed to be aware of his presence alone. Now she said:

"You may send me off, father—but I'll never go with him—it's been a rough road to me since the Fourth. If I believed in him at all then, or loved him at all, it's over now—and it would be a sin to leave you for him. For I love you. And him I hate—I hate!"

"You did it—you did it—you left me for him," said the Elder. "There's a thing that's done and can't be helped—never! Oh, my girl!"

But she had gained a point, gained some degree of self-control, and she advanced upon it with a confidence new even to her; a confidence which could not fail of its influence on those who witnessed it. Calmly she tried to speak—and to those who heard her, the voice had a calm sound.

"If I went with him—or if he stayed here with you—I know how it would be; dreadful for him and for me—worse for us than for you, father. So I say to you, Oliver, go, if you are wise. Don't lose a day Take anything for your portion, sooner than such a wife as I should make you. I warn you—there's nothing in you draws me to you—there's everything in me should make you fly to the ends of the earth sooner than stay with me. I'm not what I was. I'm not what I was when you saw me down there at the schoolhouse, this morning. If I was, I couldn't say such things—there wouldn't be any truth. I did love you—truly I did—but—don't ask me if I do that now."

While she was speaking, the strong voice with which she spoke, as much as the words she uttered, had caused the Elder's soul to revive within him. What she had said about the terrible things that might happen if she went with Oliver appalled him. Poor young thing—daughter so tenderly cared for—daughter in whom his pride was all centered, whom, above all things, he loved—what terrible future was she gazing at with those dear eyes? He stood forward with a parent's instinct, and a man's generosity, to rescue an imperilled woman—forgetful of what he had just now said of the inexpungable authority of the matrimonial vow.

"Do you hear?" he said. "Do you hear, Oliver?"

"She is my wife," answered the young man, planting one foot firmly before the other, as if he would assert that on that ground he based his claims, and did need no other. She is of age. She married me of her free will."

They all reflected on those words. Then said the Elder—all that a man hath will he give for his life, and she was the life of him:

"If Sally means what she has said, and I think no man could doubt it, I could take the case into the courts and get a divorce, and let you pay the costs; or you might stand trial for forgery, be convicted, sentenced to State's prison, and your marriage would not hold good a day longer, unless she chose to consider it binding. But you are a young man, Oliver—and I was a friend to your father, and I'll not be hard on you—you, who are so cruel to yourself! You shall go off! I'll help you to get away. I'll give you money to go with. I'll give you enough to support you till you can find employment somewhere. You can go to Australia! But it's on this condition I set you free, that you never come back again! Go, and make your fortune, if the recollection of what you have done will prevent your enjoying it

—there are your mother and sisters; work for them. It isn't too late yet. You're young."

No manner of wrath or sullenness would avail him; no attempt to defeat the purpose of Elder Green, who had evidently now taken the business in hand with the determination to carry out his purpose to the end, would avail him. The only thing he could do was to make the best bargain possible to make. Yet he muttered it was hard a man shouldn't have his liberty to do what he chose with himself, and go or stay, as he pleased. Whereto Elder Green answered:

"No more of that. You have earned a prison, and it's yours of right. Don't talk about liberty—I'm not taking it from you, but giving it to you. Remember that all your days. Remember that your father's friend, when you'd cheated and robbed him, *gave* you your liberty, and a chance to prove that there was more good in you than you ever showed to him or to any one. Five hundred dollars for your passage, two hundred besides, and your word that this is the last we shall ever see of you in Martindell."

Then he whimpered—said something grievous about his mother and his sisters. But again he was reminded of the walls he had put between them, the grates and the bars; and bidden to take his choice once more.

All this while Sally sat motionless and dumb, and Oliver dared not appeal to her. He began to cry outright, but Elder Green said:

"Sally, go and pack my trunk—the hair trunk that has a lock. Put in three shirts, and my socks and handkerchers. Oliver, I'll go with you to secure your passage. Sit down at that table and write good-bye to your mother. Tell her you have got a chance to go to Australia, and you spare her the pain of a parting.

The Elder followed Sally from the room, and locked the door behind him, leaving Oliver seated, where he sat in dumb silence for the next half-hour.

CHAPTER XXXVI.

OLD THINGS BECOMING NEW.

MISS FULLER sits in her room in the widow Prebble's home. It has been her home during the past fortnight. She saw from its windows at sunset that the frost had touched the maples, that the fields were brown and bare, that the orchards spoke of winter firesides, and the long evenings coming. She had met Miranda in her homeward walk, and Miranda's face was grave with a gravity so unusual to her, she had felt a friendly right, and had sought to know what care or trouble it might be, that disturbed her.

But Miranda had shrunk away from the friendly touch, and folded her arms as if to hide the wound in her heart. And she did hide it. She spoke with too much sincere gratitude of Mr. Carradine's endeavors to make good her father's loss, too gratefully of the result in the kindly simple nature of the gentle-hearted old man, to leave a doubt in the mind of Mercy that the suspicion of others had poisoned Randy's mind; *she* at least had no belief that the Carradine gift of heifers was the gift of malice, and the work of deviltry.

They had talked of many things—their talk could be but friendly—yet Miranda seemed far from Mercy that night—without holding herself at a distance by cold word, or graceless act, she was out of Mercy's reach. Only because in an isolation, beyond all human reach.

Mercy offered her books to read, a review that had just come to her—no. She refused the newspaper too, until she recollected that to hear of the world's doings might amuse her father; then she revoked her refusal, and said she would return the sheet next morning.

So she had gone home; but Mercy, who had seen her go, found that she did not out of her thoughts depart.

It pleased her to recall what Miranda had said about Mr. Carradine. Mercy dwelt on the fact so clear, that in mentioning him Randy had spoken with increasing freedom, as one oppressed with secret thoughts should speak of events that interested, and yet did in no wise concern her, escaping so the tyranny of a hidden grief. All was right, and fair, and clear, in the Ray and Carradine business.

It eased the heart of Mercy, it eased her mind, shall I rather say, to recall this manifest fact.

Mr. Collamer who brought her the books, and a message from Horatio, had spoken to her of Miranda. Had begged her, with that earnestness which was his peculiar, his fascinating power, to befriend Miranda; for, said he, she is no ordinary country girl. "I do not," he said, "place the value some may on culture, excessive culture. There are degrees of refinement undesirable, to my mind. But she is incapable of them. A better culture, however, would set her in a new light, and I covet that light for her. Even here in Martindale," he said, "you see what she has become. And there are influences here that would work for her wonderfully, if she could be once brought fairly within their control."

And Mercy had answered,

"Miranda and I are good friends, of long standing. She will grow and develop a long while yet. One must not be in haste where such as she are concerned; natures like hers cannot bear a forced growth well. Give her time, Mr. Collamer. She will do more for herself than any one can do for her. She belongs to the class who can accomplish their ends without the aid of tools; invent the tools that are needful."

"Yes," said he, "I believe it; but she suffers keenly many things that she will never complain of. It was that I thought of. Kindnesses and gentleness she will feel in the last depths of her. Give her those, Miss Fuller."

Mercy smiled, as if almost on obtruding counsel, till she saw what a serious interest the minister had in his request; then she gravely replied,

"I will see to it that she finds me always ready to serve her till she gets beyond my competence."

Mercy recalled this conversation, and remembered that Randy had refused to talk about the minister's visit, when on the day after his preaching they met in Roy's poor kitchen, and old Samuel was eloquent on the subject of that most eloquent exhortation which had made the school-room walls, and the town of Martindale to ring again. Was a tragedy going on, without earthly witnesses, in the soul of the girl whose visions had so far transcended her life-long experience?

But some things beside has Miss Fuller to think of, sitting in her chamber in the house of the widow Prebble.

She has lying before her, on the table, in her hands, the letters of youth, of ardent ambitious youth, of proud and loving youth; youth that is proud of its love, of its ambition, and yet has the grace to sue somewhat in the strain of humility. Aptomar is skilled in many languages. He calls his cousin from Martindale. Calls her often by direct appeal; oftener by dwelling on powers and places, on thoughts and speculations, on opportunities, on duties, which haply shall prove more alluring.

Not in vain does he write these things to her. Night by night, in her dreams, she is with him. But it is always as a child. They are together in the field that of old was so often flooded by the salt waves of the sea; they gather shells there, and build houses of the glittering white sand. They know the haunts of ocean birds; they find the nests of caves; they gather sea-weed from the rocks, a guardian angel always keeping watch over them, over the boy she calls her son, and the girl she calls, as tenderly, her daughter.

But out of these dreams, morning after morning, Mercy comes, to *live* in Martindale—to remember that here dwells Peter Carradine, a man who has never seen the ocean, it may be; who has certainly never played upon its sands. A man who has grown up in the midst of these valley fields—who at last has built a fancy house, which his neighbors call Carradine's Folly.

How will it all be here when she has gone? She holds three letters in her hand—and holding *them* she needs must ask the question—perfumed white pages, fairly written, dainty to look at, inspiring to read—to touch even—what other question than this—*how will it all be here when she has gone?* A few were disturbed when she came. Will any be disturbed that she goes? Yes! There has been a transformation in a soul, even as in a farm house, and what if that soul as well as that house were to stand forever a monument? Her monument. But monuments are for the dead. She never could be dead to Peter Carradine. How know she this?

Because she knew, dimly as yet, that he could never be dead to her. Knew it in spite of world-calls, and dear letters—knew it in spite of fame and Girard street—knew it in the face of every brave promise of the future. Knew it in defiance of midnight dreams of childhood. Knew it unconfessed, unconfessing.

So, though one might complain, Martindale is getting tedious, Mercy felt it not—she saw the maples crimson, but did not shudder as if anticipating the blasts that should crowd those splendors into insignificant corners of rail fences, and into all the humiliation of death; she saw the apple trees laden with the fast perfecting fruit, and heard how the nuts were falling in the woods; but the fields that are growing brown, and the woods that will soon be bare, are dear to the eyes of Mercy, with a dearness which perhaps they shall not appropriate as theirs of right. No, something not of them has given the power to them that they shall charm her eyes, and make dim the glories of the pavement, and the temptations through which they lead.

But how, without the night that followed this still evening in the private chamber the teacher occupies in the house of the widow Prebble, Miss Fuller would ever have come to full knowledge of these facts, it would be difficult, and does surely not behove me to say.

It was after midnight—she had not yet folded her letters, nor closed her book, but sat by her table reading—and all Martindale slept.

Slept? What were they doing in the house there on the hill? Mr. Carradine, it would seem, had chosen a strange hour for such an illumination.

It seemed to Mercy when she looked up from her book, as if by the waving of some great banner of fire athwart the heavens, that she had actually seen some such supernatural sight—but a moment told her that merely the Hill farm house was in flames!

And beholding that disastrous spectacle Miss Fuller did

what any one beside the reader might not have expected—ran out over rough roads, and rough fields, through the dark, and the rain, to—to what?

She did not know till she stood on the lawn breathless and pale, before the astonished eyes of Carradine. He was apparently alone there. But at another end of the building stood the man who beside himself had been the sole occupant of the house that night.

"Where is Mrs. Johnson? Where is little Harry? You are doing nothing!"

"No, Miss Fuller, the fire is doing it for me."

"Saving nothing! Is there no engine to be had?"

Mercy looked around her, was there no one to help? What was Martindale doing—asleep at such a moment!

"No," he said quietly. "I was going to get one, but I put it off. We worked the pumps till I saw nothing could be done. There was no use of doing as much as we did. And I'll not have the house mangled and spoiled; it shall all go together. I'd as soon tear a bird from limb to limb as raise a finger to save a bit of furniture here and there. You saw it. They called it my Folly. Well, let it go."

"But where is Mrs. Johnson?" repeated Mercy. "Where is Harry? It is not possible—"

"Didn't you know they had moved to the Bronson farm house? They've been gone this two days. I was keeping bachelor's hall up here. If I'd got the house insured yet, you'd hear it said I'd fired the Folly, I'd be bound. But if a man shoots his cattle, that's no proof that he fires his house, is it, Miss Fuller?"

"You could bear it better, the fright and the loss," said Mercy, passing over the rude speech that told of his rough mood.

"Yes, the Lord be praised for that I'd Mrs. Johnson out of the house! See, Miss Fuller, it has got to the little room. Did she show you in there that day?"

"Yes."

"The sweet briar was just back of the broad window; it would have made a pretty shade. Did you like the look of the little room?"

"It was a lovely spot. See how everything seems to stand out in that light. You might have saved everything from that sacred room, Mr. Carradine."

" But the room itself. That's gone! Other folks can get the like in the warerooms, but they can't get those particular four walls to stand together again, Miss Fuller. No, nor I can't do it. . . . . Why did you call it sacred?"

" Was it not to you?"

He looked at her as he answered—in the light of his blazing home he saw every feature of her face, every motion of her body, as she also of his; on her hair lay the drops of fallen rain, and the rain was falling still, but neither she nor he gave heed to it; but on his head as on hers it lay, for he too stood with bare head.

" Yes," he said, "it was sacred; for I'll say it out, since you're here, and this, may be, the end of it. Those two chairs were never empty. I never sat down in that room. Yet I seemed to see myself at home there—there, more than anywhere. I never saw myself alone in there, Miss Fuller; it was always together, you and I: excuse the boldness of it; it will be easier, since it's being burnt out of me, as you see. Out of me, like the burning out of what was best, and worth saving."

Visions of professors of dead and living tongues, of marvellous Court-room triumphs, of Girard street, and the world, why roll ye together as a scroll, as the flames roll up this Folly, leaving the heavens clear for a more beautiful Descart?

" No," she answered, " not burnt out of you, see me there with you always. Keep the memory—keep it as you keep your mother's image; in the same place. I will not crowd her out, only take me into the same sacred place."

" Yes," he said incredulous, and yet gently he spoke, " I must always walk among tombs, like the man in the Scripture. But if I may, God bless you! I *will* always see and keep you at least there," and he pointed to the flaming sacred chamber with a look of exultation.

" Always, everywhere," she answered steadily, and still those flames lit up her face, and the face was turned towards him, and in it he saw nothing but constancy, and confidence, and love.

Is this then a bonfire kindled on the Hill? Sleep on, martindale; fall gently, September rain. There's a silent chamber in the widow Prebble's house shall hold a happy woman's heart ere day breaks, and the people know how judgments wait upon Carradine !

CHAPTER XXXVII.

A NEW NICK IN THE CIRCLE.

Mr. Jobson's building operations excited a degree of interest in the neighborhood of which folks habituated to the magic-like rising of hotels in city squares can form not the faintest conception.

These operations were attended also by varied prognostications, of a favorable character and otherwise; Jobson's friends made a parade, perhaps, of these evidences of prosperity; deeming that prosperity was a token sufficient to stop the mouths of moralists and critics; sufficient to cover a multitude of sins. The Spread Eagle's patrons plumed themselves on the changes going on—even the bar-room's enemies seemed to be coming round. Old Samuel Roy, for instance—hadn't Jobson shown him over the premises, and explained to him his plans? And didn't Sammel seem well pleased? Didn't he say outright that he was proud to see such a buildin' going up in Martindell?—though some that heard him could remember how he had prayed for the young men of Martindell, that they might be kept out of that sink of iniquity—that den of pollution; though Senior himself could recollect his warnings in years gone by; his prophecies of judgment to come; his entreaties for a temp'rance; his accusations of spreading snares and traps for the feet of the unwary!

Poor old Roy! he had fallen on evil times in his old age. He had lost his freedom of speech, and not his light of conscience. He had made a friend in the tents of the ungodly —his feet were in slippery places! He was sinking in the mire! It did not help him when he thought it was because of his pride, and for Randy's sake that he had thrown off his burden of obligation to Mr. Carradine, and assumed this of debt to Senior Jobson. Especially since the reconciliation between Randy and Carradine had taken place, he had time, as well as reason, to regret what he had done.

If Miranda had shared his feeling of constraint and obligation, and she had shared it to the uttermost, and felt it in ways he could not know, that time was passing.

On the day of Mr. Collamer's last preaching she had had a revelation that "changed the face of all things." She saw what she had not seen—she knew what she had not known. We have seen already that she did not love this man; and that love in the case was impossible. We have seen, moreover, that love in connection with the agreement to marriage was never a question. It had seemed to her, under the circumstances, expedient—and supposing that she could have gone through life with her heart sleeping, as it had slept, she would have done her duty in the tavern, sustained by her religion, as thousands of women do their work, endure, enjoy—for I suppose the word has a shadow of meaning in the connection—and die. To how many of these, born to such fortunes—*born* to them, aye! the light that could have made a Paradise of earth, never rises, never shines, never sends even up to the horizon a hint of its existence.

But full-orbed it had risen on Miranda, and looking by its light, "seeing all things new," beholding Senior Jobson as he stood revealed by its purity, she drew herself back, shuddering, as if from the edge of an abyss—and debt and obligation, even pity, even friendship, even such manner of respect as she yet held for him, could no more control her action than her heart.

That she loved the minister with an unwise, vain love, (if love can be unwise and vain, as it is if it must be granted that love is loss except when it attains to appropriation,) that their paths through life were different—had nothing to do with the conclusions to which she now came. I said that by the light of her recognizing love the world was changed. Her sympathies, as they revealed themselves, her powers, her desires, rose from the plane of life she had occupied, to a loftier, that would not permit a conscious degradation. She might have married Jobson without sin once, but not now. Without revulsion of heart, without antipathy of will, without shame, once, but not now. The struggle through which she passed in the days following the wedding, was one that must end in her victory over any such impulse to self-abnegation as might; and doubtless would have controlled her, had she not known that the minister's affections were bestowed upon another woman so unlike herself as to settle the point of his love for her forever.

She understood that he was her friend, her brother. But, likewise, she understood that Jobson never could be any more. She said this to herself—she made the fact clear to her mind, and then waited for the moment when Senior should have all explained. Remembering his oft-repeated words, that he could trust his girl—trust her even to camp-meetings—trust her even through conversion—trust her promises, her silences—it was a pain to her to think that possibly he was trusting her for love too, even for more than he had ever asked. If he loved her, the word had never yet escaped him in her hearing! But, he had made nothing of his money when it could do her service; he had remembered her in ways that perfect selfishness is not wont to remember others. She could not entirely persuade herself that he would give her up without more regret than merely such as was natural under the circumstances, the regret a man might feel in being disappointed of a housekeeper who promised to be also a sprightly companion—but—it could not be otherwise—whatever view he might take, whatever the result might be. First of all, God had given her to herself, and herself He would require at her hands.

So it was that when Miss Fuller, taking Randy into her confidence, proposed that she should fill the place ere long to be made vacant in the Martindell schoolhouse, she forgot all the protestations she had made, dwelt not long on her unfitness for the office, but looked, first and last, on the opening as a providential straightening of paths.. She could endure what would be said. Of course this step would give offence—as if the honor of Martindell had been betrayed by the mean-spirited surrender—but she would patiently endure it. Better this than safety under the Eagle's Wings! Miss Fuller was her friend! What strength in that one thought! Even Miss Fuller, the promised wife of Carradine. And surely she had nowhere concealed that peace had long ago been declared between Carradine and herself.

One man only had a right to know the meaning of this movement, and absorbed though he was in his building, so that he seemed to have a thought for nothing else, when he heard from Ethan Allen that Randy was going to be the teacher again, he left the tavern and walked straight to Samuel Roy's.

Ten minutes before his arrival, Miss Fuller and Randy had sat talking in the room where Randy now alone mused over the words that had been said—the wise and kindly words—mused over the grace and dignity with which they were uttered by Mercy. They had talked of love and of duty.

And Miranda was not recalling quietly, unmoved, the speech of Mercy; what she herself had spoken had come from her with too much vehemence, had betrayed too much of what a woman cannot reveal without misgiving and bitter regret. She was calling herself a fool with undoubting earnestness, when Mr. Jobson presented himself before the open door.

At first it seemed to her that nothing worse could have happened than his arrival precisely at this time, for at once it flashed upon her that he must have heard of her purpose in regard to the school, and she had promised herself that, when the occasion, this occasion, should present itself, he should know all. Not for a moment since she formed her resolution had she wavered. There were reasons, good and sufficient, why he should still be ignorant of her purpose—the only one we need to state is that the opportunity for such explanation had not until this moment presented itself, and it seemed impossible for her to make such opportunities during the past days, crowded as they were with work for him.

Senior entered the kitchen at once, direct, as usual when he met with no impediments, and the kitchen door stood open. He had had not come on a ceremonious visit; and he made no ceremony in asking, as he threw himself into the nearest chair, and wiped his face with his red silk handkerchief, for he had walked up the hill with rapid strides, and was heated by his haste as well as by his indignation.

Indignation? Yes; he was thoroughly indignant that, after what had passed, Miranda should be thinking of the school again—actually under engagement to teach—he made no ceremony, I say, asking:

"What's this, Randy? Ethan Allen tells me you're schoolma'am again, or going to be. What's it mean?"

This was the question she had expected to hear, and yet had she failed to see that he must ask it in this manner, angrily—doubting—unwilling to believe! Her heart beat fast—in spite of her face betrayed her agitation, as she answered:

"I ought t' 've let you know."

"I should think so," he interrupted.

"I would have. I tried to see you, but you were so busy. I was in hopes you would have come up here—and if you had I was going to tell you."

"Are you going to do it?" he interrupted again. "It can't be!"

"Yes, I have thought better of it. There isn't anybody else, and I'll do better than I did before. I can, I know."

"What's that to do with it?" he asked, amazed. "You've made your engagement with me, haven't you? What's Martindell to do with that? And the Martindell brats? Are you going to give the school up when I get my house done, or may be you're thinking to move the school'us down there?"

"No, I'm not thinking of that, Senior. But it's better for me to be a school-teacher than a wife, or to live in the tavern. And that's what I was going to tell you. Can't you see how it's worn on me, thinking I must disappoint you, for I know it must be so. What we've talked about can't ever be."

"Then you're willing to sit there and tell me that!" said he, rousing himself from the stupefaction of astonishment; breaking the silence which for full five minutes after she made this announcement, remained unbroken.

"No," she answered, "I'm not willing! It's the hardest thing I ever did!" She hid her face in her hands for a moment, she had lost her self-control; she would not have him see, yet she would have him know, that she could not say this to him unmoved.

"Then what the devil's to pay?" he exclaimed, springing from his chair, and approaching her.

She too arose, but she retreated before him. When he saw that, he stood still and waited. For a moment he had thought that some person had come between them; her father, perhaps. In that case he knew what to do; but if it was herself!

"It's because I know I'm not the wife for you," said she, "and because the tavern's no place for me, but would be the worst place in the world. As it has been for Junior's poor wife."

"It's your damned religion's done it. Made a canting hypocrite of you, like all the rest! Senior Jobson is a fool. He thought Randy was safe! He believed in Randy!"

"Oh, Senior, won't you believe in her yet? I never deceived you. I did mean it. I did promise truly—till it seemed as my eyes were opened, like Paul's, and I couldn't but hear the voice that said, keeping my vows to you was breaking them to God! Senior, oh do believe me—do trust Randy yet!"

She would have approached him while she spoke, but now he retreated, and seeing that he did so, she in turn, stood still.

"Trust you!" he said. "I've done that, I'll own. I've done that once in my life, believed in a woman." He stopped short and laughed, but there was no merriment in that. She saw to what distrust his trust had given way; to what bitterness his kindly feeling toward her had succumbed. She had never imagined that his features could be wrought into such an expression as they now had; it frightened her to look upon his face, which had lost every trace of kindness, and bore witness alone to his evil passions. Seldom indeed had they obtained such dominion over him.

"Trust her! what for? Because she has lied to me? Because she had rather creep and cringe to them that'll set their foot on her, rather than stand on her own feet by the side of a man who's too proud to be a knave and a hypocrite. You've made your mind up. I don't ask you to unmake it. But, by thunder! I hate to think it's Randy's doings."

"You won't hear me. You won't, you can't—"

"You're right!" said he, breaking in upon what she purposed to say. "*I'm* what I was. *I'm* what you promised to. But you—you ain't the girl I thought for: no, no."

"It's true, that is!" she said quickly. "I'm not the girl you thought, not the girl you wanted. And that's the reason. I saw it, and I wanted you to see it, and now you do, thank God! you won't be wanting me any more."

Instead of replying to this, Senior turned away from Randy, and walked out of the house.

He strode up the lane, with his head erect, but when he passed through the gate, before he took to the high road, he paused a moment and looked around him, as if he had suspected that, somewhere, some one stood observing him; but, under heaven, there was no one.

He whistled a strain or two as he went back to the tavern; arrived there, he busied himself among the workmen: nothing had taken place apparently; he gossipped at nightfall in his bar-room with the usual spirit; and yet, did he know that a deeper shadow than that of night had fallen around him?

If only he had not attributed it all to the wrong cause—to religion, to a deceiving spirit! That thought tormented Randy. It prevented all self-gratulation she might otherwise have felt. What if, in saving her mere self, she had imperilled him anew! And, after all, was there really any danger that she would ever, through the pressure of hard work and the care of many children, and the incitement and temptation of example, sink into the degraded state of Junior's wife?

Just now, so little seemed the danger of such a consummation that, instead of shuddering in view of it, she accused herself of inventing the excuse, and writhed to think that Senior was justified in calling her a hypocrite.

He had not asked for love—she had not promised any. It was an honorable contract merely, that she had inconsistently withdrawn from.

Ah, but—marry him!

CHAPTER XXXVIII.

SALLY'S LIBERATION.

ELDER GREEN had returned to Martindale after a week's absence. The journey he undertook was not altogether a mystery in his own house. Huldah, his wife, knew that Oliver Savage had got into trouble, and that the Elder had determined to help him out of it; Esther, his mother, understood as much as this; and apparently no one knew any more.

But Mrs. Green the younger had her suspicions. Sally's variable mood, the whole summer long, had not been unnoticed by her; it seemed to her that something was going wrong in that excited and altogether unusual state of mind of which the proofs were constant.

After the Elder's departure, a dead calm seemed to hold the life of the girl. The relief she felt in the absence of Oliver, and in the fact that now her father knew all, and that she was free again, free from the apprehensions that had constantly tormented her, free from the weight of a secret of such a nature, from the dread of its untimely revelation; saved from the shame that had threatened her from unlucky discovery of Oliver's guilt—from his conviction to a prison; gratitude to her father for the swift method he had taken for her deliverance, this relief did not manifest itself in any form of rejoicing at first. She was petulant and gloomy, and her mother's perplexed efforts to conciliate and console her were at last suspended, with something like an indignant indifference.

Then Sally fell into a morbid state of being, and fostered her selfishness and her pride until she was really very near to being what, on another score, she verily believed herself to be, the most miserable of mortals.

When her father came home she was shocked at the first glance she obtained of him, when he stepped from the stage that brought him to Martindale—he looked so jaded and so feeble; full ten years older than when he went away. But he would not acknowledge that he had suffered any loss of any kind; and he made it very evident to inquiring minds that his state was by no means one that justified anxiety; even to his wife or to his mother he would not admit it, and his daughter was either afraid, or else too proud, to acknowledge that she saw any change in him.

She asked him no question in regard to Oliver, and he vouchsafed no information

So they lived.

And the suffering of sorrow endured by the parent and the child, were not to be compared. Her folly and deception had cut him to the heart; but he said to himself, how often he said it, " It was an error of the heart rather than of the head, poor Sally !" Yet, after all excuse was made for her, (and through his wakeful nights and thoughtful days, his heart was forming many an excuse for Sally,) there remained the sharp pain of this unchanging fact, she had wilfully deceived him; when he trusted her, and she saw the nature of the trust, even then she had made use of opportunity, and had chosen a base fellow whom to love !

With what pain he looked back over the past, and saw the years through which she had been growing up in beauty in his sight; how she had been fostered, cared for ! With what love and indulgence ! Never thwarted—trusted as though she had been the pure angel she looked in his eyes ! Perhaps there had been a mistake in all this ! Perhaps he had too often spared the rod ! It might be, indeed, that they had spoiled the child !

Then he remembered, " Whatsoever a man soweth, that shall he also reap," and his manner changed toward Sally. As one who had been wronged, and whom it was perhaps too late to right, but to whom at least pitying love and tender care were more than ever due ! And he remembered that Christ forgave even the ungrateful, even the unthankful, even the unrepenting.

But she took it as her right, and never was softened to say, " I am no more worthy to be called thy child."

She had been deceived. *Her* life had been ruined. Oh, is there any end to the heart's selfish sophistry?

Thus gradually her manners changed toward all around her. Her vanity became her most conspicuous power. It was in reality the spirit of defiance that took possession of her—that kept all who knew her at a distance; that wholly changed the aspect of her life. Yet she could not live alone. She had no other resource than society. The Carradine demonstrations gave her an idea. Her activity in certain directions became fearful to beholders; and though her father demurred and expostulated, he did rarely in the end oppose any of Sally's wishes. So the way of life was gradually undergoing changes in the old brown farm house, as already in the old red on the hill. Paint and whitewash, paperhangers, etc., were here in demand. And the new furniture, that elsewhere than in the shut-up drawing-room, obtruded on the eyes of Esther Green, set her to praying away, if haply she might, the evil spirit of worldliness which had crept into the house, with a setting up of notions for which Peter Carradine was responsible!

I shrink from the task of portraying the life on which Sally Green had entered—the unspeakable littleness of the vanity and envy, which, through the daylight, devised for themselves ways, means, and execution. I know that precisely such qualities, when urged into action in larger spheres, get for themselves some admiration, and command some respect. But I can invite none for Sally. She was idle, and unhappy; she had been trained up to worthlessness, and was fulfilling her mission with a consistency of purpose that almost commands admiration.

But, as time passed on, must she not begin to see the past under some illusion? And must she necessarily exaggerate the wickedness and worthlessness of Oliver? Or rather, being such a woman, why not see his faults with greater lenience, and find forgiveness easier than condemnation? Who could tell where, or how, he was expiating the faults of his youth? She had not asked her father what had become of him; her father had vouchsafed no information. They had not exchanged a word on the subject.

This silence was all the worse for her; it left imagination larger sweeps and wilder liberty.

One day she walked deliberately up to the house of widow Savage, with the purpose to discover whether anything had yet been heard of Oliver. She had seen nothing of the woman since the day after her son's farewell note was sent to her, at which time Sally had left to her mother the work of consolation and encouragement, and the transfer of the Elder's assurance that it was best for him to go; indeed the only good thing that remained for him.

"Perhaps," said Sally, going up the road and looking back now and then, under apprehension that her errand would be guessed and her progress watched, (and saying to herself with every such suggestion, I am of age, I have my rights!) "perhaps I can console the old woman, or may be they've heard some news."

Arrived at the house, she found the family in a commotion—widow Savage crying over a picture in a daguerreotype frame; the two girls sharing her excitement, which in their case took a more hopeful and rejoicing form.

Oliver had sent his picture to his mother on the day the vessel sailed for Australia; there it was! He had likewise written her a letter—brief, not quite intelligible, but apparently in good spirits, and under the constraint of excellent expectations! He was going to Australia, he said, to make a fortune for all of them. When they saw him in Martindale again, he should be able to live without work, and all they would have to do in those days would be to let him know their wishes! How long he should be away, he could not tell, but not many years he thought. Elder Green had been very kind to him. He had introduced him to the captain, and there was a nice lot of young fellows going out to seek their fortune in the same vessel. Elder Green had paid his passage, and he was well provided for when he should land. They went away in such haste, before he had time to say good-bye to any one—but if they had not gone that very hour they would have missed the vessel; he could not have secured his passage a day later. But he had time afterwards to get this picture taken, which he hoped all his dear friends would think like him, and that when they looked at it, they would forgive all his youthful follies. He went away from shore with no hard thoughts of any one. He forgave everybody, as he hoped to be forgiven, and he prayed that he might prove to be a son that widow Savage would be proud of yet; and he asked her to try and not remember against him all the little things that had come between them—and, through all the letter, he called her his own dear mother, whose face would be before him wherever he might go, all the years while they were parted from each other, and he should need no picture to remind him of her and the girls!

And this was what had set the mother to crying over the pretty picture, and the girls to hoping, after the fashion of loving age and loving youth.

When Sally Green, so fair and fine, stepped across the threshold and joined the family party, the mother's sobbing was a little hushed, and she told, with the girls' help, what had happened, and showed the miniature.

"Look at it! look at it!" and they put it into her hands with a unanimous impulse.

So she took the picture, eagerly. Looked at it, trembling.

"Oliver Savage!"

The widow looked at her, wiping her eyes. She could see as well as another—better than those two girls of hers, who asked:

"Isn't it like him, though?"

And she said to herself, "She loves my son. And that's the reason that Elder Green has sent him off! And that's what the poor lad meant when he used to say such odd things nobody could make out."

"It is as good as seeing him," said Sally, after long and silent gazing at the picture. "There isn't a man left in Martindale with such a face as Oliver's. How handsome!"

"And here's a lock of his hair, do you see? Girls, here it is—just see that curl, Miss Sally."

That too she took in her hands—a long, black, waving lock, and she said,

"It looks as if he had cut it from his forehead."

"Give me the picture here—he might have cut off a dozen locks like that, and never a' been missed."

"I wish he had cut two!" said Sally Green.

"Sit down," urged the old woman. "Here, we've never

offered you a seat!" and they all started, instantaneously convicted of that rank offence.

"Thinking of him, no wonder," said Sally, taking the first chair that offered; and she gave the lock of hair back to Oliver's mother.

"It's your father has been 's kind to help him, so you ought'o have it," said the widow Savage; thereupon she, to her girls' amazement, parted the lock, and one-half she gave to Sally. "He's to write when he gets settled—write another letter, and then the girls must write to him, he says. They'll tell him, then, we gave you half of the lock of hair, and that will please the poor boy," she said.

"No," replied Sally, hastily, "better not! Where would be the use, you know?" and she blushed under the eyes that turned upon her, and her heart was pained to hear the mother say, in an humble, apologizing voice,

"It was only to give him a little pleasure, poor boy, away out there, so fur."

"But before you write—that may be long yet, you know —perhaps I'll have some message to send." She said this to soothe the mother—she said it to please herself!

For when she went off with those treasured threads of the parted lock of hair, she put them in her bosom, and reflected:

"Whose is it, if not mine? Who has a better right? And he is mine! and I wish that I were with him! Poor Oliver! What right has any one to come between man and wife? as father said. What right has any one to take a promise given out of fear? It wouldn't stand in law! I wish father could just see that letter. He would see how good at heart the poor boy is. Poor lock of hair!" and she took it out and kissed it. "But if I told him of the letter, then he would suspect that I was thinking of him—and I know what he thinks of Oliver; if he ever gets an opinion of a man he doesn't change it, right or wrong. Poor Oliver! I wasn't kind to him, to forgive him—I know he means me. He sends his forgiveness to me! When they write the letter, I can send a word—I can say—they will never understand it—tell him I am sure that if any body prospers in Australia he will; for there's nothing standing between him and his fortune but himself! But if he thinks it is all over between us—or is angry—but then he talked of forgiveness, and of coming back, and I am sure that he could never love any body after me, for I know how I feel to him! But father need never be troubled by it. He will not be alive when Oliver comes back. What am I saying? But, in the course of nature, it will be a long while yet before Oliver will be able to come. But if I had my own fortune in my own hands—" and so she kissed the lock of hair again, and went home, and read for her father the newspaper he was waiting to have read.

Poor Elder Green! Any one that looked at him, any one except his own and only daughter, would have had no question in the thought as to whether he was passing, with rapid steps that none could hinder, in the path that stretches beyond human sight.

And if, from this time henceforth, that daughter waits upon his wishes with a gentler care than ever before; and is patient with the childish old woman, whose religious severity has passed, as she has lost her stern hold on life, into an exacting mood, that seems far enough from religious; if he sees in all the evidences which gladden his heart tokens of his daughter's repentance, and of her recognition of his justice, and that all is peace between them, and if he blesses God daily in secret for this merciful dispensation of his providence, no erring parent in the world will be quick to say that, since he was trusting in a delusion, and rejoicing in it, it should have been removed!—that he should have died in the full consciousness that the results of his training of that child were not to be set aside for any anguish of his heart!

He saw the evidences of her true repentance. Saw them in her serious face—in the industrious habits she seemed trying to form—in the spirit of helpfulness she manifested towards the different members of the family.

Yes, there was no mistake, he saw these things; they had a meaning. They meant this: The relentings of a selfish soul that had lived for its own pleasure to the pain of others. The doubting of a perversity that rarely had doubted its own wisdom—never its right—to the end that seemed good in its sight. The superstition of one who has been trained up to external decencies, and in all religious observances, and has never mistaken the form for the spirit of godliness, and the ways of life for life itself.

She could take some blame to herself. She had not read her Bible as faithfully as she should have done. She had prayed less than was right. Henceforth she would live a Christian. And so, having performed these duties to her father and to God—if Oliver *should* ever come back to Martindale, she would take it as a sign that those whom God had joined together, (had not a minister performed the ceremony?) man should not part. She would go with him.

And, meantime, if she could by any word send comfort to him in his exile, on what ground could she withhold it? Perhaps she had already greatly failed in her duty to Oliver. Perhaps she might have hindered him from the folly whose discovery had broken up their relations! She knew that, if she had stood by him to the end, her father would have forgiven both! But it was all so dreadful, and in her shame and frenzy she had really felt as if her love had turned to hate—but now!

Yes, it was she who was to blame, of all concerned. Poor Oliver was only the victim! And why pray to God for forgiveness, while there was one on earth whose forgiveness was so necessary to her peace?

You see how it was. Apparently a hopeless case. Who would have believed it! There were people who admired the Elder's daughter. She was sprightly, pretty; she dressed herself with exceeding good taste; she sat a horse well; she could drive a span; she was the pride of Esther Green; she had been the Elder's joy; in spite of herself, the Elder's wife stood sometimes in awe of her; she had had so many advantages, and she exhibited the results of the same sometimes with such a flourish.

Who would have believed it! And I confess I am almost ashamed to write of things so exceptional among domestic experiences. For probably there never was another young damsel in the world like Sally Green! Young women, like young men, sometimes make conspicuous wrecks of themselves; but probably never before, nor since the days of Elder Green, did a secret grief consume the life of a father's heart; did a character far from imbecile do the wanton work of an irresponsible agent.

Spoiled child, they called poor Sally. Oh, heart of Heaven! oh, wounded, Father heart!

She would test the will of Heaven! Would Heaven return her Oliver!

CHAPTER XXXIX.

THE WEDDING-DAY, AND PLACE.

WHILE Mr. Carradine was occupied with all his Hill-farm improvements, actual and projected, planning and procuring plans for the new house that should stand on the eminence for so much more than the old, consulting in Brighton city, and out of it, with the wise in such matters, conciliating Mrs. Johnson in curious ways that no other man could possibly have devised, occupying the place in the Bronson cottage which she had instantly made ready for him the day after that fire which was spoken of by the neighborhood as a disaster, but by Carradine's self after another manner—while he did so, and lived thus, Miss Fuller was quietly conducting her school, preparing, by every method, the way for Miranda, and preparing likewise, during leisure hours, for the change to which Time was rapidly conducting herself.

Writing letters also to Cousin Aptomar; getting finally one from him which made her smile through her tears; she might have laid that letter in his mother's hands. After this letter came, Mercy went her ways with a more assured tranquility, and every day laid at her feet some new assurance that, if she chose to receive it so, was ample justification of the choice she had made. Justification did she need! Often she went down to Brighton to spend the Sunday with her friends; and Commissioner Brown on each successive visit greeted her with a more beaming face, until his triumph, as a prophet, became too great to bear in secret with his daughter.

Busy were those Saturday afternoons in Brighton which the busy week had doled to her. And yet not mighty were the works to which Mercy on such occasions gave herself. No manner of temptation was great enough to suggest to Mercy that any debts she might contract were innocent, since she would so soon be married, and Carradine was rich! Perhaps such a resource had never been suggested to her by the devil of a corrupt society. Poor she was—and she came to her bridegroom arrayed in such garb as she had earned by her own labor.

She had no misgivings in preparing to take the step which should decide her future. After the letter came in which Aptomar ceased from reproach, and pleading, and uttered only kindly thoughts, and generous wishes, taking upon him to bless her as his mother would have done, to every future deed and endeavor, she was happier than perhaps he ever hoped to make her. Happy everywhere; in her school and in solitude; planning the future life; talking of him with Mrs. Johnson; and about all that he personified to Miranda. Yes; her day had come; and with all reverence we may say of it, as of all such days, it was a day of the Lord. When He might smile from His heavens, on a work that was very good; when He might cease to repent Him that He had made man.

In October, at the end of the term, Mercy went down to Brighton to remain there till the time appointed for the wedding.

The ceremony, as it had long been arranged, was to be performed at the house of Commissioner Brown. But one evening, Mr. Carradine, speaking with her on this business of the wedding, **told** Mercy of the disappointment of his neighbors, that they were none of them to witness the ceremony, since it was to be performed in Brighton, and in private there.

And yet, what could he do about it? He had told them that, if he could manage it, nothing would please *him* better than to have all Martindell for a witness to his wedding; there wasn't a man, woman or child, but might consider himself and herself invited. Still, what could he *do?* The arrangements that were made could not be unmade.

It was evident that though he repeated all this perplexity to Mercy, he did not anticipate from her any alleviating suggestion. Yet! oh, wonderful woman! here she was, prompt to enter into the "difficulty"—to remove the perplexity; to satisfy the town of Martindell.

"It might be done at the schoolhouse," said she.

He was a little dull, it seemed.

"How's that?" he asked.

"We might drive over to Martindale in the morning. And Mr. Brown could take the minister in his carriage, with Mrs. Brown and the girls; then all the neighbors could come at the hour appointed; and the children; all the school children, you know."

Carradine seemed for the moment lost in admiration of the skill and the kindness that had devised so readily. Mercy Fuller must have been made for him, indeed, to deliver him thus out of all perplexities. He never yet fairly stated to her any trouble whatsoever, but she could suggest a remedy.

"But are you sure *you* would like it?" he asked, for he remembered how she had said that a private wedding would be according to her notion of what should be. How well they had agreed about that. But now—how well they were agreeing about a very different arrangement!

"Oh, yes," Mercy answered.

"But," he was incredulous, the more he thought of it, "will you really like to see the old schoolhouse full on such an occasion? For they will all come."

"Why not? if they are all our friends, and come to wish us well. We shall feel almost as if we had family relations round us to wish us happiness, and prophesy smooth things for us."

He blessed her in his heart when he replied,

"Then it shall be in the schoolhouse. And I will set Mrs. Johnson to cooking a wedding feast, and they shall have tables in the grove. We'll show them what a wedding should be, Mercy, and while they feast we will go down to Brighton and take the cars at the same hour we had set. Shall it be so, Mercy?"

"Yes."

"It'll do Martindell good," said he. And then, after a pause, and some hesitating effort, "I'm doubting about the sea. If you would like it better, we might leave that now. You talked about your cousin once, and I remember how he and you lived on the beach somewhere, and you said he was wishing you would go there with him some day, you know, so, if, as is likely, you'd prefer getting back to the old times by an old road like, with one that walked it with you for company when you were younger, you and I'll put off the sea till after you've had that journey with Aptomar. That was the thing I had on my mind chiefly to say when I came down to Brighton; so think it over, and tell me the next time what you will do about it."

Mercy looked at him in wonder when he began to speak, but as Carradine made his meaning more and more intelligible, the change in her face told how this expression of his confidence and tender thoughtfulness, moved her.

"No," she said, "you have never been there. I shall be your guide. I shall love to think of eternity standing there with you. For I shall be strong as having its assurance with me, attested by you."

So Carradine drove back to Martindale, and by the next morning the neighbors were all talking of the wedding that was to be celebrated in the—schoolhouse! next Wednesday morning.

And Mrs. Johnson, though at first alarmed, taken all aback, dumbfounded, as she declared, by the part she was expected to take in the preparations, soon came to regard the service she must render in quite another light; and she addressed herself to the task of getting up a wedding feast for Mr. Carradine, as to the one great work of her life. The hero of this festival had the tact to make her see that on her operations would fall the glory of the day. A man like himself, he said, never married but once. Only one woman could have been made for him; besides, Martindale would not endure the shock of more than one such surprise as he had given the town. So Mrs. Johnson must be up and doing. She must take counsel with the knowing ones of Brighton city, as he for his part had not been above doing; nothing must be omitted at that banquet that money and painstaking could procure. She must go to the confectioner's, and buy the ornamental cakes, the frozen pyramids, the various gimcracks and devices of the table to set it off—no matter what the cost—let her talk with Miss Brown, the Commissioner's daughter, and find out what folks did when they did their very best on such occasions. For Martindale should be won, the very heart of it, by a feast which, if prepared in honor of one woman, they, at least, should see and share.

But the cider, and the wines, namely, the gooseberry, the currant, and the frost-grape, and the raspberry-vinegar, she must take from her own store, for no other vintage could supply any thing to equal Mrs. Johnson's.

And Huldah Green said to Miranda Roy:

"Randy, you oughter get up something for this weddin'. You and Sally. You oughter trim the school'us, and have the childern walk in a procession, with flowers in their hands, and their shoulder-knots of blue ribbin. The Elder will give the ribbin. He wouldn't stand at any little thing that would give them a pleasure. I saw such a sight once when I was a girl. And it would be pretty for Miss Fuller. As neat for her as for any one that ever I heard of. If they was all dressed in white! You find Sally Green, Mirandy, and get her over there to help you trim the school'us. She's a help, if you can get her to it. She knows how it oughter be done. Try, now."

But Randy did not need such urgent solicitation; she had consented to the decoration the instant Huldah mentioned it.

—And thus by Wednesday morning, the finest October morning ever seen, the wreaths were tied and hung, the festoons swung between the windows, tied with white "ribbins," and with blue; boughs were in all the corners, and over the teacher's desk was spread a white cloth that fell to the floor on all sides, and upon this cloth were sewed, in various devices of heartshape, diamond, crowns, and stars, sprigs of evergreen.

And the children were in uniform, that end being secured by much washing of hands and faces, by patient hair combing, and by the anticipations of childhood, as well as by the blue shoulder-knots and the white dresses of the girls. And there they stood marshaled before the schoolhouse, ready to march in when the bride should arrive.

The schoolhouse was filled with Carradine's neighbors, Carradine's friends, they must be hailed for this day. Had they not come, attired in their best, to witness his wedding, to partake of his feast? So there they all were, well packed, to wait half an hour before the time appointed should be told. For every one had said, when the clock strikes, Carradine will be here. He was never known yet to keep a body waiting when he had made an appointment.

Mrs. Johnson and Huldah Green, meanwhile, were superintending the tables in the grove, which literally were laden with good cheer. Report had gone abroad concerning the decorations provided for those tables, and the unlimited supplies from the shops in Brighton city, and the kitchens of Mrs. Johnson. Curiosity to see them was hardly outdone by curiosity to see the bride of Peter Carradine, as she came over the hills from Brighton, and the hands of milliners. There was many a young girl waiting the cut of some new garment, till she should see with her own eyes the fashion of Miss Fuller's bridal gear.

And while the people in the schoolhouse and about the door waited patient, or arrived in haste and heat, Mrs. Johnson and Huldah Green superintended still, those tables in the grove.

And Mrs. Johnson said, " This day must the great Martindale hatchet be buried out of sight, and shame to him who digs it up agin!" She had a task before her. It had been a relief, in view of Mr. Carradine's marriage, that she had a work to do that should keep her busy, mind and body, up to the hour of the ceremony. A sore thing it was still for Mrs. Johnson that he must go the common way, and gin himself up to some woman to be led about, though to be sure Miss Fuller might be trusted to that leading, if any woman could. Johnson had reasoned with his wife; she had reasoned with herself; she knew the merits of this business as well as another—but for once she had a right to be selfish, and to lament, and to feel that she was waiting on the burying of the man—for try your best to see it, there isn't so much difference atween a wedding and a funeral! Though Miss Fuller! any one that could see Mr. Carradine from morning till night must be set to wondering if one could be much happier if he was safe in heaven.

Now that her work was done, though her care was not yet ended, she had much to do, to maintain the smile which she had determined should stand victorious against her grief and fears this day. Often her lip was quivering. Often she started up and bustled about, as if her life depended on her doing, and she said to herself, "Well, for sure if I don't choke to death ere night, of keeping down these feelings! Oh, if it was over!"

But it seemed to her that it would never fairly begin.

How well Miranda looked this day! All Martindale gazed on her with smiles of approbation. *She* belonged to them! It had once been thought that Randy might marry Mr. Carradine. Perhaps Randy had herself sometimes dreamed of it, for once she had thought of marriage as her neighbors were still thinking of it, as a mortal device, not as a Divine Institution. Old Samuel Roy in past days had a vision of the kind. But she did not look, in truth, as if any grief or disappointment weighed on her heart this morning. Her face was more serene, her aspect more happy, than any one had seen it in a time; and so naturally she wore this composure, that people forgot their own comments on her gravity in the days that were not so long gone by. No face had now a softer smile, no voice a gentler tone, no heart a kindlier wish—nor could a soul of them all have been as successful in preserving order among the impatient children as was she, who moved in their midst with a grace unlike Miss Fuller's, it is true, but a grace that was to be discerned.

Once Randy took Sally's hand in hers, and looked at her, in a strange questioning way, that made Sally uncomfortable; but nobody thought that she anticipated the arrival of the wedding party with a degree of interest that was unknown to them all.

Mr. Carradine drove from Brighton his bay horses, and a beautiful new carriage, whose top was thrown back—and it made a spectacle. Everybody on the look-out saw the pair as they passed through the country.

A man was in waiting to take charge of the horses, when he threw down the reins, and alighted from his carriage, *not* as though that vehicle were his old farm waggon. Then he helped Miss Fuller. And they all saw, as if with one vision, that she was dressed in white, (because the bridegroom wished it,) and that she left her shawl and bonnet in the carriage, and that she looked a little pale—but, that she smiled when she saw the children, and seemed to be from that moment assured, as if conscious that she walked among her friends.

They came up to the porch together, and waited in the shade, two minutes perhaps, while Mr. Carradine was giving some directions in reference to the horses. What a silence of expectation fell on every soul there, large and little —how the eyes of the company ran from the Brighton minister sitting quiet on the platform behind the teacher's table, to the group in the doorway, the gay children, who came marching in now, heralding the Bride!

The ceremony was a brief one, but it was followed by an address that was a surprise, not only for the matter and the manner of it, which were eloquent, but also on account of the reception it met; for Mr. Carradine, reversing the order of congratulations, shook hands with the minister, and thanked him for his kindness, with a freedom that was charming to behold; then he saluted his bride, and led the way into the grove—and all the people followed, with congratulations in their hearts, which they offered in their turn, and every expression was full of good will. And presently the Lady of the feast was seeking out the timid, and Mr. Carradine stood, the model of satisfaction, observing her conduct, and the way that everybody praised and admired his wife. She was the school teacher last week, and everybody *then* admired her—but by what sort of magic has that bud bloomed into this flower, that people should now, of one accord, it seemed so, hail her, by every show of deference, and every look of admiration, the Lady of Martindale?

And what a feast was that! Children of Martindale, will its brightness ever fade out of your recollection? What a time to date by when you shall be old—for never again shall you see anything, no matter what future splendors wait upon you, to compare with the dazzle, and the glitter, and the delightsomeness of Mrs. Johnson's feast. Everybody must taste everything; the meats and the sauces, the ices and the cakes; the preserves and the conserves; the dainties, foreign and domestic—the elaborate mottoes, the dainty maccaroons; the kisses, the marmalades, the strange fruits nobody can name—THE BRIDE'S LOAF! And in a wrappage of white paper, tied with a white satin ribbon, of which there seems to be no end, every soul must have a slice of the bride's loaf to carry home and dream over.

Memorable day! What dreams must wait upon it!

Mr. Carradine at length drove off from the scene of the feasting in triumph with his bride. Everybody wished them joy. To the sea shore, to the mountain land. Among mists and shadows—under the great branches of the gigantic trees that were flourishing ere yet the Mayflower's keel grated the New World's strand; or clinging in the rough ascent of heights that would seem to overlook the world; or sailing along rivers, between smooth banks and sunny fields —between hills and famed mountains; or, whirling over lofty bridges through the narrow gorges, across broad plains of sunshine; crowded along crowded city streets, in crowded omnibuses: wherever they went on that long great journey of hundreds of miles, night and day beside her, he had consciousness, blessed and supreme, that she was with him; spirit as well as body was near. As let down from Heaven the great Vision descended, he could not misconstrue it. Mercy did love and did trust Carradine. Comfortable hope. Assurance of peace. Let them journey on.

Meanwhile there in the grove came at last an end of feasting. People began to disperse; old folk strolled away homeward in couples, and in larger companies, thinking of old times, and talking of these strange new scenes in Martindale. The children ran and played, and soiled their clothes, and did the deeds of recklessness which prepared for a tearful bedtime. Blue shoulder knots lost something of their splendor—and in the grove, and by the roadside, lay many a fading flower, since the Bride the flowers were plucked to honor had come and gone, and the wedding was all over.

And Mrs. Johnson came back, flurried and heated, with eyes looking very red, from the concealment she had sought the instant she had shaken Mercy's hand in parting. She came back to her wonted diligence, and faithful supervision of affairs. Huldah Green and Randy "stood by her" to the last bit of packing—and so were the tables and the grove well cleared, and the wagons went groaning up the hill; and, all things being considered, the damage the glass and the crockery had, was not sufficient to mention.

So the wedding ended; and Mrs. Johnson, sighing out her last waking thought to faithful Johnson, said, " It might 'a been worse."

CHAPTER XL.

HOME.

At last they came back again to Martindale. And life seems to go on as usual there. Carradine misses nothing of the old house. How many times has Mrs. Johnson secretly predicted that he would, when all this fuss was over, and he came to be settled in a place that wasn't the old place at all, and he saw all these new-fangled things he had been persuaded into buying, all these instead of the old! He was not the man who would be like to feel at home with such trash! The very last man in the world. She had seen enough to know, long before the time came that he was married! Was ever a man so restless? He had as good as allowed that there wasn't a room in the house he felt as if he could sit in.

Come up now, Mrs. Johnson, let us take an observation.

What makes a man feel at home in the house? Is it a lot of old rubbish? Old furniture—old bare walls—smoke stain, and sand brush? Old red paint, peeling off the clapboards? An old arm chair in the piazza corner? A dark little bed-room, very meanly furnished? A few old familiar objects? Then Peter Carradine verily is done for. Pray let us write *finis*, and go our several ways.

Is it a face that is always kind? Is it a voice that is always friendly? Is it a graciousness that never stoops to frown, that constantly acknowledges the rights of others to their tastes and pleasure? That is cordial, not obtrusive? That is quick to discern the charitable impulse—the good purpose in defeat—slow to condemn? Hopeful?

Is it to leave him absolutely master of his rightful position—the large liberty to go and come, trusting for her part religiously in the virtue and the sovereign power of her love—knowing, as if she read it out of Holy Writ, for her own heart has told her, that, if she shall ever cease to hold the love and trust which she has won, the fault, as the loss, is hers?

It is indeed Peter Carradine, and not at all Mrs. Johnson, whom Mercy's love is to affect, so that all changes and all places shall seem well if she but dwells among them, giving daily benediction to his life.

Good woman, do you see Carradine sitting after sunset in the great arm-chair he has wheeled from the little room which has been changed into this library for Mercy?

Do you see them sitting there together, man and wife, and side by side? She has been reading to him; but now the reading is over. It is so quiet one might fall asleep were not life so imminent!

"Ajax is getting to be a perfect giant," says Peter, speaking of the famous animal he bought in the spring, to whom Mercy had given his fine name. "You must go down and see him storm about the lot. He's a beautiful creature, a whirlwind with hoofs and horns. Oh, here—that reminds me, I have a letter from your cousin, for you, Mercy."

"*My* cousin? That's not fair. If you don't claim him, Peter!"

"Our fine cousin, Aptomar! There it is. Nobody but a lawyer could manage to write such a hand as that. I wonder the letter ever got as far as Martindale on its own showing."

"'Tis a curious hand," she mused, looking at it curiously. "We must see what he says to us."

"The writing looks like him," said Carradine, "not easy to read. Deep—showy."

"I wish he were married to the woman who was made for him. Do you suppose he will ever find her?"

"How would any one have answered for me in the spring?"

"He wants to come and visit us next August. We have a long while to make up our mind whether we shall let him come, Peter."

"So," he answered slowly. "It would be pleasant to have him here; if he could take it easy! Johnson had one of those city fellows up once on a visit, and I say you never saw a body so nearly dead and done for as the poor fellow was when he went away—Mrs. Johnson, too, for that matter. But Aptomar isn't of his kind. He would expect us to turn the country upside down, or inside out for him. I'm glad he isn't coming this winter. Suppose a man may say that to his wife, and not be taken for a crusty old curmudgeon. But we are doing well enough, are we, Mercy? Is it too quiet? Is it lonely up here for you?"

" Lonely!"

Do you see, my good woman, how he smiles at that? He is not deceived by her answer. He knows it is very truth. He knows that, when he comes home from any superintendence of his farm-work, no matter where he finds her, or how occupied, he shall see a satisfied and happy wife. And how should it be said that, to such a man, the conviction that he is the author of the happy fortunes of such a woman was insufficient to secure his deep content?

Then, oh marvellous! it is *not* in walls and furniture, not even in the accustomed and the familiar, that the secret of the home-joy lies! It is *not* in being near the usual forms, within sound of the familiar speech. Nay, among kinsfolk there be aliens! and around the homestead hearthstone, foreigners! albeit none who drew not their first breath under that very roof.

Carradine took a just pride in the beauty he had been able to put upon and within this Bronson house. He saw his wife so come into possession of these things, and so make use of them, bringing out their fitness so as to prove herself verily mistress of all, the china in her hands, the carpet under her feet, the piano under her touch, the pictures, few and fair, on which her eyes rested, all things of this house came under her superintendence, or within her use, what a fitness, what a right! And he was hers through all, and she was his!

See how they understood and lived for each other.

On that day of the Aptomar letter they walked over the hill to visit lordly Ajax in his lot. And they passed the old Carradine ruin.

On their way back, as if by mutual agreement, though no word had been spoken, they walked into the field. It was late in the autumn, and a low mournful-sounding wind was coming over the hill from the woodland, bare of leaves. A bird was hopping round the place, and some wild flowers, which the frost could not kill, were shining through the leaves of the Virginia creeper, that threw its red and splendid drapery over and around a mound of stones.

Thus spoke Carradine:

"It was just such a night that I walked here twenty years ago, and looked at the old house, and thought I would come here to live. I had rented the lot and the house—it was here I began to work. I thought, when I looked the place over, that if I got some one to help me for a day or two, I could put the place into some sort of shape, and live in it. It was years since I had stood under that roof. I can't describe to you what feelings I had when I opened the old door and looked in. I felt sick and desolate, as I had never seemed to myself before. It made me shudder when I stood there with my hand on the lock, as if I had seen the whole family sitting round that black, cold fire-place. Every one of their faces! And they did not look inviting, as if they'd have me come in. So I thought. I had put such a distance between me and them! But I tried to shake off that feeling. It seemed to be something to be shook off. I walked through the little rooms, thought over what could be done, and made up my mind I'd live there, and what I would do. I remember how high the wind rose before I got through my calculations, so that when I tried to shut the door it flew open, and it seemed I should never get it shut. But I did, finally, and fastened it with a string, for I couldn't bear to think it might blow open, and the storm beat in. For it had been a home once, and I hoped it might be again." He paused here for a moment—then he went on, sure of the listener, who stood attending with much quiet sympathy, such unfeigned interest, to his words,

"But the next day, when I came up, it was early in the morning, before I went to work, the door stood wide open, the chimney had blown down, and the roof was broken in. I was in despair. I could not set to work to repair the damage myself, and had nothing to pay another man for doing it. I was already in debt. So it had to go to ruin. And I think now it was better for me that the storm took it when it did. It might not a' been well to live in the way I was intending to live. I can see it was best for me to go among people who had different habits and ideas from mine.

It helped to get me out of some desperate hard ways. I used to encourage the belief that I could see my mother's smile on me whenever I felt that I was doing the right thing—and I can't tell you how many times I have heard her saying, 'Be of good cheer.' And the voice seemed to be that of a happy person, who sees through troubles and beyond them, and knows that all will come out right in the end, it always made me glad. I could not help taking it for a token that where she now lived there was no sort of trouble. That she was happy."

Oh, town of Martindale, how do you stand convicted! Here was he, counted for years your worst man, confessing to a woman, with tremulous voice, the thoughts and the affections that ruled him in years when your sympathy was cold, your words of good cheer few, and your suspicions cruel.

Who among you could confess to such aspirations as in those very years were lifting him, *by the memory of his mother*, a thought strong to salvation!—A memory apparently so inefficient, on which nevertheless his whole being might be lifted out of the depths of sin into the Heaven of love!

What lives are these we harshly judge, and promptly sentence! If, through blank wastes of years, we can look back and see a childhood guided by a tender hand through whatsoever human ill, a childhood wherein was planted the good seed of eternal life, let us have reverence to be still, and faith to believe that the eternal life shall yet come to blooming, though clouds and darkness seem to shroud the erring, to separate him from any *reasonable* human hope!

"Woman, behold thy son."

"We might have these ruins cleared away," said Mercy, at length, "and some evergreens from the glen would make a pretty spot of it—with a summer-house built just where the house stood. Some of Mrs. Johnson's morning-glories running over the lattice work." She stopped, and seemed to muse over the vision of loveliness that rose up, flower-crowned, from this unsightly heap.

Carradine walked quite round the ruin before he answered her.

"It shall be done," but he did not add his thought: "Who but Mercy would have thought of such a thing? What a woman! She sees everything."

"And we'll plant the trees so as not to hide the fine prospect when we come here to overlook our fortunes."

"I'll have the stuff cleared away to-morrow," said Carradine. "We can lay these flat stones for a walk."

"And the hearthstone shall be the door-step. We will not forget the past—you and I. It shall teach us."

He was thinking while she said this that he would like to have engraved on that door-step that it was Mercy Fuller, wife of Peter Carradine, who desired that this honor should be done to the memory of Joshua and Marcia Carradine. He was hoping that, from on high, his mother's eyes might look down on his joy. Thinking that he was a saved man, and a made man. And he smiled on Mercy.

Take that smile, dear Mercy, entertain it as an angel; keep its memory forever. She does not need such bidding.

CHAPTER XLI.

RANDY UNDER THE SPREAD EAGLE'S WINGS.

In the spring that followed the long hard winter, died old Samuel Roy. Rheumatism dropped its chains in the last days, and he went out of sight with a smile on his pale face, free from pain, and free from all misgivings. The birds that ushered in the bright young year, sang round the house such songs as it seems to me had a glorified echo as he advanced, a young, gentle and reverent spirit, among the budding splendors of his New Year with the Immortals. Peace to thee, blameless Samuel! Thou shalt never repent thy prayers, nor take shame to thyself for thy faith! Thou shalt be no more distracted by the markets nor by mortgages! Neither shalt thou feel any more the weight of debts that have no record! Never more shalt thou be cramped and straightened! With integrity hast thou passed through the tight places of thy journey! thy hard hands are undefiled, and thy trusting spirit is unwrinkled of doubt! I see thee sitting in a pleasanter shade than that which borders the fine lot so dear to thee. It is not the shade of willow trees—the branches are not drooping, and no dry season can affect the flowings of the river on whose banks thou standest, free from pain.

During the latter months of winter his rheumatism had a development that rendered him quite helpless. Miranda was obliged then to give up her school. He needed all her care. Night and day he needed her—her tender love, as well as her strong, gentle nursing.

From the day of her talk with Mr. Jobson when she tried to make him see what a mistake they both had made, she was a wonder to herself. On the farm and in the school-house, she worked with an energy which surprised no one but herself, for she had a reputation for industry and efficiency. She saved her father all the pain from which no mere occupation could deliver her. Of what had passed between her and Senior, he knew nothing. He had suspected nothing—and why trouble him?

As for Jobson, she believed she saw how he would take this disappointment—and she did see it quite clearly. He had kept his secret from the first; he would keep it to the last. If he took to himself any consolation, it would be this, that he had never been taken in by any of this "religious humbug," that he had withheld his assent from doctrines which could only make of men smooth hypocrites and respectable villains. He had hoped that, in Randy's case, religion would not get the upper hand of her—but it had, it seemed. Well.

He would never refer to the business she believed, again. If she changed her mind again she must let him know, for he would never inquire! He would not have been greatly surprised had Randy changed her mind. When the *Spread Eagle* stood up in all its glory—painted, and furnished with the new furniture he felt that Randy's common sense had not quite forsaken her—she must repent—and there were ways by which she could easily manifest repentance, though she did not humiliate herself so far as to make a confession of her folly. And he would not exact that of her.

So when he and Randy met there was no change in his demeanor; he inquired after her father, as he had always done—if it chanced that help was needed, and he could render it, he did so. Christian people were in the habit of making a virtue of forgiveness and prating much about it—he would show her that a man could be a man without the help of cant.

When she said to him, one day, meeting him by chance:

"Senior, you haven't got anything to show for the money you lent father, but we haven't forgot it. You shall have it again, interest and all; and if you will make out a note and let me sign it, I will thank you—so that if anything should happen to you or me, and our farm is sold, you or your family will be sure to get what's owing."

He answered:

"That business is to stand just as I put it. I reckon you

ain't spiled entirely from what you were. There's something left of Randy yet. And what's left I'll trust to. Religion hasn't spiled ye altogether." And, so speaking, he immediately broke up the conference.

It was not the least of thoughts that troubled Randy, this conviction that, by her, Senior had come to cherish less reverence for things that day by day were influencing her life more and more. There may be some who will understand the sort of desperation with which she prayed for him, and how, if any daring deed could have taken the kingdom of heaven by violence for him, possession would at once have been bestowed upon the innkeeper.

Well, in one sense, for her was the filial care and anxiety that occupied her during the winter months. What a life!— Strong and unyielding in the shows of cheerfulness making light of labors, singing the old man's favorite hymns with him, reading from his sacred books to him, to which little stock Mercy Carradine had contributed some precious treasures; thus the time passed away.

When I think how different it might have been with Samuel, when I remember the clouds and darkness amid which more conspicuous lives have set; how pride, and lust, and fashion, have tottered from their thrones and perished in their palaces, unanointed of love, disenchanted and appalled before the reality they have contrived to disguise but never could destroy—I cannot forget that, here, in this hovel, by the wayside, it was only the promise of Almighty God that was fulfilled.

When I think how different it might have been with Samuel, if, in place of woman's patience and constancy, her faith and courage, the form these virtues have when they issue from a woman's heart—when I think of how it was, and how it might have been, in that humble farmhouse, had even the child's grief found the evidence a nature like hers might well have given it, I can but conclude that, if ever mortal might expect "reward" on the score of mere duty done, then Miranda Roy might well look " beyond the clouds and beyond the tomb," and trust that she was walking in the way that is life, and that leads to it.

Many evidences of sympathy and friendship came down, through the winter from the great house to the small, with much enlivenment. But better than all things to the old man, than easy chair from Peter Carradine, or delicacies from his wife, or the general kindness of the neighborhood, was the constant presence and untiring care of Randy. Whoever came to sit for half an hour in the house must hear Samuel's praises of his daughter. Whoever prayed with him, and Elder Green did often, must hear the eloquence that praised her to the Lord, and thanked Him for her, as the choice work of His hands. If angels were commissioned to make the last path he should tread an easy one, they ministered by Randy. How could they work the work of love more securely than thus by a woman, by a child?

Thus did he go, singing simple songs of faith and joy—he well might enter Heaven singing.

Now and then a letter came to Randy from Mr. Collamer. Now and then he snatched a half hour from the rush of time, and shut himself away from " duty," to read some words of hers, which had never any other than the fullest, deepest meaning to his heart. Do I mean that he read through them sighs and tears, and weariness, and longing? Did he envy Senior Jobson? Did he fear for Miranda under the wings of the Spread Eagle?

Good friends, if from any mortal source he drew refreshment for his life and fresh courage for work, it was from this girl. He used to speak much of her to his acquaintances, but he had ceased from that. He used to think of her as of one whom he could help. He thought of her thus no longer. He, on a time, did regard her as in many things inferior—needing culture—needing education. He had ceased to so regard her. Doubtless culture and education might yet greatly avail her; but he did not thus regard her. Not because his own vanity or ease could be affected by her lacking, as what could it be to him, or how affect him? Nay, gradually she had passed into clear identification with his ideal woman, without which no man lives. But his actual daily life, and self, had other ambitions than encompassed her. He was caught in strong toils, and laboring under hallucinations that can effectually blind a man to the truth he has once in his life perceived, that his ideal is, and was therefore intended to be, the fulfilment of his actual. A sane man can really not *imagine* an impossibility. He can imagine nothing that cannot somewhere be wrought out or discovered.

The will of Heaven was as clearly manifest in and for these two persons as ever it was manifested to mortal man and woman—and one of them dimly perceived it and was true to her perception.

But Mr. Collamer was thinking of the great good he might accomplish with such a fortune and such a life in the right and holy service, as this of Miss Grey. And saying to himself, always with a personal application, no matter what form he gave to the saying:

"We are probationers; we are not our own. Our great work in this life is to live not to ourselves, but to our fellow men, and thus to God. Fortune, reputation, position, wife and children, all are His, and to be used for Him."

A goodly number of men and women argue in that way, and sanctify their ambitons thus. So is love crucified. But is he kept in any sepulchre by any seal or guard? Oh, does he not have his inevitable resurrection and ascend out of sight, into his proper Heavens, yea, beyond sight and touch of those who have profaned him and his name? But he shall come again, and the poor earthlings shall see their clouds rolled up as a scroll! Then shall the book be opened. And Love, the judge, is the avenger!

Have you seen none of these judgment days? And do you teach your children expedience or law? Sow on! but blush not for your harvest! His rain falls on the just and on the unjust; and His sun ripens the harvest, be it grapes and corn, be it thorns and thistles.

Sometimes Mr. Collamer would repeat the charitable deeds and other good works of Miss Grey for Miranda's edification. In reply she could grow eloquent thereon, so eloquent indeed that he deemed his gratitude was due for her praises, and expressing it, he seemed to see that this woman of Martindale occupied a position from which her blessing might descend upon him, "for without contradiction, the less is blest of the better!"

But he might have read a better gospel story, a more heavenly tale, in Randy's report of the last days of her father's life. And when she wrote to him that all was over, and that Mr. Carradine, according to his agreement, made before her father's death, had taken the farm off her hands, paying for it at the same high rate he had once offered for the further lot beyond the brook, and that some heavy debts which had troubled her long were now paid, and that though far from rich, she was not poor ; moreover, that she would now tell him what she had desired to tell him a long time, that Mr. Jobson had finished his building, but that she should never go into the Spread Eagle as its mistress, because she dared not think it was the will of God—and that Senior had treated *her* kindly, only it had seemed as if the disappointment had set him against the Truth, which was now all in all to her—would he not pray with her that God would enlighten that poor man's darkness, and show him the only beauty that was to be desired ; moreover, that since she had left her old home she was living at the blacksmith's, taking charge of Junior's house and children, and looking after the servants who worked for Senior Jobson, and that this was altogether unexpected to her ; but it had been asked of her the very day after the funeral, so that, instead of staying with Mrs. Carradine until all things concerning her could be arranged, she was now superintending her neighbor's house and children, and exerting herself to alleviate the cares of poor Junior's wife. When she wrote all this to Mr. Collamer, and he read the same, his heart was moved to its foundations, and he said distinctly to himself:

"I ought to say, before all others if a man only had a right to heed inclinations, to see in his desires the will of God! I ought to say to her, my heart is open to you. Come in! let me be what you shall live for in place of your dead father! Let me care for you as you cared for him. It is not right that you should spend your youth in waiting on the weakness that has, and should have no claim upon you. Thank God, you have done with the Jobson delusion!"

But, instead, he wrote, not on impulse, a well-considered and a beautiful letter, truly. Full of divinest consolations. Yes, so she received those words.

Put aside his own Revelation for another, and said : "To depart is far better." Soothed her with the testimony to the good life departed. Prayed that they might have the needed grace to follow on.

So it had really come to pass that she was living under the Spread Eagle's wings.

Yielding, against her will, to the solicitation of poor Junior, she came to take care of the miserable crew—the wretched wife and helpless children. Not a word in opposition to, or in favor of this movement, had escaped Senior Jobson. He knew that she did not come voluntarily; and if he expected anything in his own behalf from the change in her residence, the expectation was so deeply hidden that no one could have guessed it.

When Randy paid her father's debt to him—it was a few days after she had come to take care of the blacksmith's wife—he exhibited more feeling than he had allowed himself to manifest even to himself in secret. But he took the money and put it in his pocket-book when she said that, of course he would not refuse to do what her father had desired of him, first of all. When she thanked him for the kindness he had shown her father and herself, he made as though it were a matter so trivial it was almost an insult to dwell upon it; but he could not hinder the speech to which she would give utterance unless he turned away and left her. And that he did not do. For this word of hers arrested any such impulse he may have felt.

"You ought to let me feel as if you were friendly to me, Senior. I wouldn't be here under your roof if it wasn't because I want, more than anything, to make you all comfortable. That is the reason I came. And it will keep me here as long as I can be of service to poor Junior and his children. I believe that it is going to be a house of death, and if it will be a comfort to her, as it was to my father, to lean on me while she goes through the dark valley, I am sure it will be easy for me to bear it all. We must all come to it in our turn; how could I hope for any hand to make my own way easy in this world—and it is the hand of God will do it for me, and no other, I expect—if I could harden myself against weakness and pain, and the helpless little children? It isn't to be expected you could know anything about sickness and death—what I've undertook to do isn't easy, Senior; but if I could see that you was feeling kindly toward me, I would find it wasn't harder than I could get along with."

The words, spoken with something less than her usual directness, with many pauses even, were not once interrupted by a word or sign from Jobson. But when she had manifestly come to an end, he said:

"There isn't anything for you to be complaining of. I don't mean to wrong you—you're free to come and go. I told Junior you wouldn't come—but it seems you have.

That's your business, and not mine. It's a kinder act, I'll say, than I expected of you. But the devil isn't as black as he's painted—and may be your getting religion hasn't taken all the goodness out of you yet. Being more of you, may be, than of most, it would take longer."

Some people rejoice in self-sacrifices with a joy not at all heroical. There's a subtlety in the selfishness of their satisfaction by which it eludes condemnation, and usually gets to itself praise—praise that even the most discerning would be slow to express in a dubious manner.

Such rejoicing as Miranda had in the work that now occupied her was not after this kind. To come down from the tender embrace of Mercy Carradine's fine sympathy, from the serenity and order of that mansion to which, after the funeral, she had gone with Peter's wife, to this coarse manner of life, and this exacting service of sickness and of childhood, was a change that could have had little satisfaction in it.

Mrs. Carradine said, when she observed Randy's hesitation, that, in justice to herself, she should at least rest a few days in quiet. That she was not physically equal to the care of Jobson's family. Yes—yes—Junior knew it, but—

The need of her, Randy believed was really not so desperate as Junior seemed to think. Diligent search would not fail to discover some person as competent, and more practicable than herself, just now. She did need rest—repose—and, above all things, the daily fostering of such tender love as Mrs. Carradine had it in her heart to give; such as, during the past winter, had found a frequent evidence.

But there are persons in this world, ordained counsellors and comforters, whose need to receive is always lost sight of by reason of their more conspicuous power to bestow. Their strength, it would seem, does never fail; their stout heart does never faint with longing; they are machines warranted to work well, and run on, and keep time eternally. No one thinks to look searchingly into their eyes to see if, haply a tear may not lurk there; neither does any listen to discern among their voice's tones some one that falters.

Yet this was not Miranda's case—thanks alone to Mercy Carradine. If two women can love each other well—with intelligent admiration, with conviction that something is to be imparted, something to be derived, valuable, by no means to be slighted by either—Mercy and Miranda must be taken in evidence.

And when Mercy said to Miranda:

"You must come and stay with us awhile—Peter wishes it as much as I. We shall do each other good. I can give you some of my strength—and I need some of yours," Miranda's heart opened as a night-blooming flower, under an influence sweet and strange.

But while she hesitated over the Jobson petition, it suddenly occurred to her that the religion she professed enjoined the bearing of one another's burdens—and that she had no right to withhold from Senior Jobson any service that could in any degree illustrate the wonder working power of her faith. He at least would understand why she came to live in Junior's family, why she assumed irksome cares and distracting responsibilities—that it was for charity's sake, and for the love of Christ.

So she had gone down to the tavern and taken her place there.

It was a presence to be felt. A presence that assured and controlled; that tranquillized and pacified; that brought order into the midst of confusion. A presence that established peace and hope. Miranda would never fall back, dismayed, from anything she undertook with resolution. When she consented to this labor of pity, she did it in a spirit too noble to oppress Junior, or any one concerned, with a sense of obligation. Quiet, kindly and strong, she had eyes and ears for all the need around her, and within the weary frame sat the uncomplaining spirit, peaceful and believing. Glad, rejoicing, shall I say? Peaceful and believing! Peaceful because believing. Believing not for this life; and the heart that has resigned its expectance of personal blessedness for time, and looks with longing to the life beyond the grave, judge ye of its gladness!

There was room among these children for the exercise of tenderness and sympathy—in her path some simple flowers bloomed—she might pluck them at her will; and she was not ungrateful. Admire the woman's courage. Be pleased to praise her goodness.

But she could not help herself, you say; she only made the best of circumstances! As if saint or angel, or sublimest seraphin, ever could do more!

Because she did not choose selfishly, did not turn (to nurse her secret sorrows) from the calls of pain and feebleness, and childhood—stooped to a low estate with a Christlike abnegation, said to God, " Do as thou wilt, I choose to serve thee, and I ask no wages, only according to thy promise, show me what thou choosest I should do ;" because of all this, will you admire and praise this bravest heart in Martindale ?

Senior Jobson quietly looked on, and seemed to take a kind of comfort in assuring himself that the devil was not as black as he was painted ; for in this way he personified Randy's religious faith. No one need point out to him the changes for the better in the house—for in reality the tavern and the blacksmith's shop were one, and that Junior's wife was a victim to the poison of the bar-room as well as the hard work of the establishment, nobody in Martindale needed to be told. He could see, as well as Junior, the changes—how evident it now was that a woman who could control and manage, was at the head of affairs! Chidren neat and orderly ; house quiet and well-kept ; food abundant and palateable ; system and skill producing their conspicuous results. Miranda's praise was in everybody's mouth.

It set him to thinking. The exhibition, in spite of the comfort of it, was secretly a source of great discomfort to Senior. Miranda—no, she was not covetous—he knew better—it was not for wages that she was working thus. She said it was her duty that made demands and gave her satisfactions.

Try as he might, Senior could not persuade himself that he understood her. So he launched out on a sea of possibilities with a cautious daring, that seemed in no danger of stranding on a perhaps.

CHAPTER XLII.

WALKING AMONG THE TOMBS.

Now and then the doors of Elder Green's house opened to receive guests, young and old, who came on various pretexts, but really on matrimonial errands. Young men, caught by the good looks of the the Elder's daughter, or her fine dress; and older men who had regard for the heiress. One by one, they all dropped out of sight, and the neighborhood shook its head, and talked of the crooked stick with which she might be compelled to content herself at last. But Sally laughed, and said that bees would not swarm except where there was a chance of making honey; and, for her part, she preferred to amuse herself, rather than to bind life to one dull round, with one dull man.

Elder Green could never be persuaded to talk much with these lovers on the subject that most interested them. He seemed wonderfully indifferent—took it for granted that Sally must know her own mind better than he could know it for her—and never gave encouragement to any anxious suitor. But how many times he sighed in secret, thinking of the waste, the wreck, she had made of her life! And, though she had given her word in reference to Oliver, and he had told her he should rely on that, and had never referred to the subject again, oftentimes fears tormented him, and long did his fears keep him alive after all hopes of his recovery was over, for he said to himself, how could he die and leave her to the mercy of her own choice and the future?

At one time he thought seriously of taking Mr. Carradine into his confidence. Assured that, while he lived, Oliver would be certain never to return, he dared trust to no future time. Fear only, he believed, would keep Oliver from Martindale. But if ever, in spite of what had past—if ever, in spite of all her words and assurances, Sally had her fortune in her own hands to dispose of, who could stand security for her even a single day? And if—if, indeed, her fate was irrevokably bound up with that of Oliver Savage, what could hinder the consummation of that fate when he was gone? She would go to him if he might not come to her.

He meant to talk with Sally once, before it should be too late—while he was able to speak freely all his mind. He would save her by extorting from her promises which she could not but deem binding when he was gone—when he was dead and gone.

But, from time to time, he deferred the favorable hour, looking for a moment when he should feel stronger to speak to his dear child on this hateful topic—a moment when his cough did not trouble him so much. Such a day as he was looking for never came. Such a time as he anticipated never yet came to a mortal. The weakness that had spared her so long, could not nerve him now to stand, in his dying moments, the stern opposer of what she might deem her destiny! Yet, maybe, after all, he was disquieting himself in vain! Perhaps there was really no occasion for this fear. Many a time Huldah had assured him that he did a right wise thing when he got young Savage out of Martindale, for it was clear now, if it had never been before, that the girl cared nothing for the foolish fellow.

But even Huldah was disturbed in her mind when she saw the fate of Sally's lovers, who, one after another, went they ways discouraged and dejected—only she could always aver this truth, that a woman has no right to marry a man when she can't give him her heart. She could never get over that belief of her young maidenhood—her own experience had proved to her that there's only one oracle to be heard in regard to these matters.

So Elder Green died, and was buried. He died thanking God for all his mercies, and praying Heavenly forgiveness on his earthly life. He died not in an extacy, with more pain than one is apt to deem quite suitable for a man of his virtues—he died with a mind more darkly overcast with doubt, more troubled, than those who knew his blameless life could well account for. He had reaped many thorns in his last harvestings—he could not look on the pure grain—thistles were too many—and he said:

"The blue sky seems to be covered with white clouds, made of thistle-seeds. Oh, what a crop there'll be!—for the wind blows where it listeth, and carries the seed with it!"

They remembered this with a sad smile, for the Elder's mind was wandering in his last days; and even in that state they would fain have had its delusions all peaceful and bright. But he was a mortal man, and passing through the valley of shadows—soon he should see clearer, and God himself would wipe all tears from his eyes.

Alas, poor man, a little care, a little less fondness, a little less free indulgence, and you would have been spared this vision of the thistle crop! No wonder it perplexed your last hours to know how all those seed, light as air, light as vanity, could be gathered in and hindered from baneful growth next year! The little one was not an angel when she came to you, it was yours to make one of her! Oh, what have you done? Prayed for her; worked for her; saved your money for her; had her taught in Scripture and catechism; sent her to boarding-school, and paid away so much money, and never got the secret of her life, nor controlled, as a parent may, the workings of her heart! That prison unvisited! that nakedness unclothed! *that* hunger unfed! that thirst unappeased! Nay, thou doest well to call on the mere mercy of God, when those standing round thy death-bed wonder that that dost not rather appeal, as to thy judge, thou holy man, to attest to thy life's integrity; "My record is on high!"

So he has gone out of this world—so the sod covers him. But shall I say that all his work, the sum of it, was to plant an upas tree! Nay, friends, let us be still—let us lay our mouths in the dust—it breaks the heart to think and to behold.

Yet, let us think! let us behold! and let us look for judgments until we learn to live. Let us expect to see honorable names all covered with shame—honorable records blurred and blotted with disgrace—darkness and the shadow of death, where should be light, and life, and gladness. Cursing where there might be benediction! hate instead of love! treachery in place of steadfastness! lying instead of truth! For the children are what their parents doom them to be—feeble, or idle, or false; selfish, tyrannous, base. Nothing grows in all God's world but the very thing that is planted. And there is nowhere a chance. Precisely what we choose for our children, are they predestined to be.

And it was nothing strange, incredible, or even monstrously out of order, but in the true order of this entire disorder, that from time to time Oliver Savage, in Australia, read the messages Sally sent across the ocean through his sisters. Nothing incredible that a ghostly hand could not hinder the lines she sometimes even penned to meet his eyes!

But when he answered the letter that told him of the death of Elder Green, and spoke of the evil effect he experienced from the climate, and that he had succeeded beyond his expectation, and longed to come home, thought it his duty to come, for it seemed to him every one in Martindale was dying, and he must see his mother and his sisters—Sally trembled.

She read a meaning of these words which even the family that rejoiced over them, believing that this was the true note sounding his return, could not read, and she dared not encourage that return. And when some sign was expected of her, as if she at least would share their joy, she gave no sign. She dared not rejoice; and from the day of this reading she avoided Oliver's family. She said to herself she would be innocent of any connivance! If he returned it should not be on account of her encouragement!

Was she, then, wholly influenced by the suspicion and the fear, lest her secret was not in her hands alone? By the doubt whether there might not be, here in Martindale, some guardian, unguessed, who would be quick to frustrate any plan that might be made for Oliver's return? On the last day of his life, her father had made many fruitless efforts to speak last words to her and others—death hindered him from speaking. He died without a sign. But before this time, what might he not have said, to whom might he not have confided? She was fearful, because doubting. And then *her* sense of duty also hindered her. For of course she had not all along sustained the exile's hopes! Of course she had not cherished expectations for herself that were dearer, because secret and forbidden!

Esther Green had now retired into the dotage of her grief, for she had outlived her idol; had stayed on earth to see her son go down to death; had lived too long. So she shut herself up in the house. The outside world had never given her much; it now could give her nothing. For years she had lived through the Elder; he had been her pride through life; and now that he was dead, there was nothing more of summer or of winter, of seed-time or of harvest, that she could desire.

Huldah, on whom the conduct of the farm devolved—for the Elder, with an honorable trust, had confided that management to her—strove in vain to interest the old body in her plans and doings. Work, by which she kept her mind and body well, work—active sympathy, if any like the expression better—the resource of Huldah, the widow, had no isterest, could no longer absorb poor Esther. She sat by the fire in winter, and in her own bedroom in summer, and her knitting work and Bible occupied her time. So she seemed to dry away in the weariest and saddest manner of departure mortal body could devise.

Sally did not fail in duty to her. Between her and her mother, seven walls with double-locked gates could not have effected completer separation than was accomplished by the workings of the two distinct antagonistic natures. She is the Elder's daughter, Huldah was forever reminding herself; and she could never have lived through a day in peace without that reminder. For it was rare that Sally said to herself with anything like self-rebuke—she is my father's widow; she has been a faithful wife to him and a servant to us all.

But towards old Esther Sally did exhibit, day by day, such womanly tenderness and consideration as she had to bestow. And if Esther could do nothing more for her, she could nourish the family pride that was having in the daughter of the house a demonstration so unlooked for. King Cophetua may wed where it pleases him!

Sally's devotion to her grandmother was that of the ascetic, whose one virtue shall cover a multitude of sins. Of Annanias and Sapphira, those base speculators who brought their offering and risked it on a venture. Wall street never saw a more disastrous operation. The chances were not against Sally—but there was scant virtue in her sacrifices to age and infirmity, irrascible and exciting though it might be. Old Esther had the advantage of those compunctions with which Sally remembered wherein she had failed of duty to her father; but the service, in itself considered, was void of virtue as the unfortunate pair alluded to above.

Sally and Miranda saw very little of each other in these days. Randy's duties kept her busy, mind and body, in a healthful activity; and the prospect of retiring from her post was not a near one. The great peril in which Junior's wife had lain through many a month, passed finally, but the need of the skill and diligence which had made so new and strange a place of the Jobson home, public as well as private, seemed to be greater than ever now, when the wife's recovery had opened the way for Randy's departure.

Junior's wife, a weak and feeble woman in her best estate, full of dismal forebodings, saw all things falling back into the state of ruin from which Miranda, at the cost of so much time and such hard service, had recovered them. It was her prophesying, which Randy dared not gainsay; it all seemed too probable; that detained her in the blacksmith's house when the cause that brought her there seemed urgent no longer. This, still more than the fondness of the little children for her; this, still more than Junior's gratitude; this, still more than Senior Jobson's praise, uttered by him without constraint or ceremony, as if merely her due, of which he was the last man to defraud her.

For, though she might go from Martindale, and possibly find a home for herself where no old ties should disturb the service she designed to render Heaven; though elsewhere she might find some missionary work to engage in that would occupy her day by day, as her work did here, with the advantage that no one then could mistake her purpose; and her heart might act with a freedom which seemed impossible here; though this might be done, still, here was this house and family; children growing up who needed more than *their* mother's care and government; and an Eagle somewhat wild yet. Just now it might be well—the end of her reflections on the matter kept her where she was.

The last time that Sally and Miranda discussed Mr. Collamer, they came to an understanding of each other that seemed to be quite new. It happened thus:

Miranda was walking toward the grave-yard one bright, still Sunday afternoon, attended, as it chanced, by only one of Jobson's children, the youngest, a little girl, two years old. And the child had tired of the long walk, for the grave-yard of Martindale was nearly a mile from the tavern—it lay upon the hill-side, a bright spot of verdure, lovely in this season, for the fragrance of the thousands of sweetbrier roses in blossom, but for nought beside. When the little one began to complain of the long way, and was not to be pacified or allured over the rough road any longer, but stood still and cried, Randy took her up in her arms and carried her, for she longed to go and sit by her father's grave, and think in silence on him and the heaven where, to-day, he was rejoicing in the glory of his youth.

But the silence and the exaltation were not for her in this place; for as she went up the hill, toiling along slowly, for the day was warm, and "the baby" lay a dead weight on her shoulder, having now fallen asleep, Randy met Sally Green, who had walked past the grave-yard, and was now returning without having entered, though when she set out from home she had said she would go and see if the willow tree they planted prospered yet.

"Are you going in?" she asked of Randy. "What a heat you're in! Do put down that child."

"She was so tired," said Randy, wiping her face, "and now she's asleep. Yes; I'm going in. Come with me, will you?"

And so they walked together up the grassy path, and Sally was glad of this company; now the place was not so gloomy; she felt more assured; the hopping and singing of the birds, and the breeze coming through the pines on the brow of the hill would not startle her, as these slight sounds had done.

Randy was the first to speak as they walked among the graves. The dead were all around her; a greater number of her friends had their names written here than could be found now upon living records. Reverence and tenderness filled her speech with their spirit; but her gravity was not that of hopeless grief; it was the still composure of one whose hoping beheld fruition afar off. "I shall be with you soon," she looked and said, in a speech that had no words for Sally ear.

"I'm a pilgrim and I'm a stranger,
  I can tarry, I can tarry but a night!"

It was the conviction that took the sting from her sorrow and filled her soul with serenest anticipation

"It's the first time we have walked here together since," she said. "But we used to come very often. It was before we had lost any friends that we hunted strawberries on this hill! For your own mother died even before I can recollect, and you were only a baby."

"If she had only died before I was born—or if I had died with her," said Sally, "what trouble would have been got rid of!"

"It does all seem so strange," answered Randy. "Both gone. If it wasn't easier to bear pain than to cause it, one might wish we had gone first, instead of living on and losing all. But your father was so fond of you! And you were such a comfort to him—and to the old lady too!—it ought to make the sorrow easier to bear, as mine is lightened too when I remember."

Sally did not reply; but a glance of sharp questioning flashed from her eyes. No—how could she have suspected that Randy was conscious of the recollections, bitter and accusing, which this manner of consolation would revive?

The graves of the old neighbors were directly opposite each other—they lay on either side of the narrow path—friends in life, in death not far divided.

"Do you think that, when it is all over, we shall sleep so nigh each other? So near, it seems impossible they should not know it?"

"No," said Sally, "it isn't likely. You will not always be living in Martindale; neither shall I, I hope. And so it seems to me. What difference does it make where one's buried, if he's only well done with this life? That's the main thing. But it isn't living to stay here in Martindale."

"But I hope," said Randy, who, contrary to Sally's expectation, did not answer these words with reproof, though it was evident they pained her. She began to speak now in a way that commanded Sally's attention, and by her speech seemed, for the time at least, to control the unquiet spirit of the girl, who, from much thinking of herself, began to question, as she looked at her old friend, "What has happened to Randy? How quiet she looks. How very handsome she is!"

"I hope," said Randy, sitting down by her father's grave, with the sleeping child still in her arms, "I hope at the last that I shall lie just here, close by my father's side—there's room now. But the grave-yard fills very fast. I wouldn't wish to be far away from him, even in death—though I know that, when all is over, I shall see him again. He is lying in Abraham's bosom. Oh, Sally, if there *should* be a gulf between us! Blessed Savior! keep us safe and bring us to our dear ones! I have so many things I long to say to him—so much I've thought of since he went away, I want to be forgiven for—and I know a word would set all right. But then I know all *is* right when I remember his last words, and the great peace of those last hours we spent together. It seemed to me, when he was dead, I could only thank God for it, he suffered so much. And I had no tears for my loss as long as I could think of the happiness of his release, for his work is all done, and his debts are all paid, and his rheumatism is all over. When I thought, as I sat alone in the house afterward, of how he was himself in the presence of Jesus, whom he loved so dearly, I could n't but be glad. But the sight of him was precious, and my time came for grief when I felt I should see him no more. It returns upon me often—when I expect it least sometimes. I used to strive against it. But now I think better. Why should I wish to forget that I have met with a great loss, and that I am alone on this earth? That is the road by which I always come to see that I must be the better help to others who need help; for there's nothing to hinder me giving my time and my strength. And it's sorrow that humbles us best, and makes us gentler and kinder, and more earnest in doing with our might what we can."

"There's nothing to hope for or live for," said Sally. "You make it out all misery, and I don't know but it is. Is that all you're in the world for? To be made wretched, so you shall come to be a help to other wretched folks? It's a queer world—I'm tired of it!"

"There's nothing but God to live for—God is love," answered Randy; and Sally might have searched the words in vain to find reproach in them—there was no reproach, but there seemed to be some anxiety; fain would she have Sally to know the deep peace that had come to her by submission.

"To please Him, Sally, think of that!" said she, with a brightening face. "Why what is everything beside! If we have only the great trust for that! To please Him! not to be with those who despised and rejected Him, and made Him acquainted with grief. Oh, to give the Savior some joy! not to make him sorrow over us! It takes the bitterness from sorrow, believe me, for I know it; only to look up and see Him standing there, watchful and guarding, able and willing to save!"

"Are you going to stay at Junior Jobson's the rest of your life, Randy?" asked Sally, abruptly, after a silence which Randy had thought would bring forth something very different.

"I don't say anything to myself about that," she answered. "Junior and his wife like to have me there—and the children like me, and I am fond of them. So, just now, I am staying on."

"Why don't you marry Senior, and make a Christian of him?" asked Sally, at a venture. She had heard some idle speculations on this point, but she merely asked the question to make sure of changing the course of Randy's meditation.

"It would be to no good purpose."

"But you are so anxious to be used by other people, why not? There's a chance for a missionary! Convert Senior, and you might afford to fold your hands the rest of your days. I think I see it done. But you are ambitious, Randy, and you can't deny it—I wonder you don't undertake it."

"You're joking, Sally—don't do it. I never shall forget to pray for a change in Senior Jobson, but I have no right to trust myself to a kind of life that has been too much for one poor woman. It's ruined Junior's wife."

"Junior's wife is a drunkard out and out, and every body

knows it. Don't compare yourself with that woman. I wish you were out of Martindale, safe and sound. It's a dead waste for you to be living here. Where's Mr. Collamer in these days? I wish he would come and carry you off. You ought to marry him. He was made for you. I'll own it now, but I wouldn't once."

"He is good as married already," answered Randy, stooping over the child to screen her from the sun, it seemed. "I could have told you of that long ago. To a very beautiful woman. I have seen her likeness—prettier than Mrs. Carradine."

"Mrs. Carradine! She is a beauty, to be sure!"

"I think so. But not like Miss Grey. It seemed to me when I saw her face, as if it couldn't be that there ever was such a one. But may be you have seen such. I haven't seen much of what's in the world, to be sure."

"Randy, you ain't what I thought you was!" said Sally, thoughtfully. "I'd like to know how you took it when you knew he was going to marry her."

"I wish him a happy life. May she be as good as she is beautiful. God bless them both."

Sally looked at her old friend and did not answer. Presently the silence became oppressive, and she rose up from the grassy mound.

"Come, let us go," said she, and Randy followed her. She followed with a hope; she hoped that, if Sally had any secret trouble on her mind, as it seemed she must have, they might come near to each other; and that this trouble, or this burden, might be eased by sharing. And Randy was saying to herself that, if Sally should ever confide in her, she would give her true advice, and help her, as became a woman and friend. As they walked along the road together, she said:

"You are not really thinking of going away from Martindale?"

"What ever put that into your head?" asked Sally.

"You said something about it, as if you thought we shouldn't, either of us, be living here always."

"But I think you will, now! I've changed my mind. I think, now, you'll marry Senior. After a while you'll be quite famous for a landlady. I see it all. I can prophesy as well as another. You weren't meant to settle down in any quiet way, like common people. That's the reason I thought you would marry Mr. Collamer. As for me, I don't expect to live here all my days. Mother Green and I could live, if it was out of each other's sight, I reckon."

"There's few like Huldah Green," said Randy.

"I hope so. Suspicious and prying, and looking after me as if I couldn't be trusted out of sight."

"That's for your father."

"No it isn't. Did he ever watch me so? He—trusted me! He knew I could take care of myself."

"I wish you could see it different. It seems to me I can understand how Huldah feels—don't laugh—but it has seemed to me, lately, as if I could tell how everybody feels; as if I'd a key that opened all their hearts. She loves you, and she's anxious for you, more than if you was her own born child, just as I feel about Junior Jobson's children."

"You think I'm as unfit to take care of myself as Junior's wretched wife is to take care of her housefull!" exclaimed Sally, half angry, yet laughing. "Thank you! I'm in no danger of taking to drink and letting my responsibilities run wild like savages, as those children were doing when you went to the tavern."

"You don't understand—you can't see it! How she came to do it—worked to death, and sick, and getting a little dreadful strength out of drink, to keep her up and help her on. But she's a cured woman, Sally! She's a cured woman, and it seems to me we shouldn't be harder on her than her husband is. Even Senior Jobson is as kind to her, and always was, as if she was a daughter to him. And it was a good deal for him. Tavern-keepers don't like to have that sort of person about after they've sold their liquor; but they've tried to keep her up and about, them two brothers, as she tells me, and never give her a word of blame when things were at their worst—Senior never did."

"He didn't care, I suppose," said Sally.

"It isn't one of the kind o' things he'd be indifferent about. He cares—and he did care, but he pitied her; and it's brought him to the point, more than once, of shutting up the house and going off."

"Why don't he keep a temp'rance, then?" asked Sally.

"Pity he hadn't long ago!" Then, as Randy did not at once reply, she went on. "You think you know how Huldah feels. I think you don't. She's afraid now, Randy, that I am going to be inveigled off somehow, and some worthless fellow is to run through father's property. She's dreadfully anxious to marry me to some good man, that would look after me as my father would! That's exactly what she said when we got into a talk the other day. Now did you ever hear of a girl wanting to marry a man like her father!"

"Don't talk so, Sally."

"I'm not joking. I shall not marry an old man or a rich man. But I'll marry for love, if ever. But I never shall marry at all."

Nothing could have been more swift, nor indeed more keen, than the glance with which Sally now endeavored to possess herself of Randy's secret thought. Said Randy:

"You may change your mind; nobody can tell. But oh, I trust you may have a light to your feet when you do walk that way, Sally, because—"

"Why then? I suppose you see a special need of it, as well as Huldah!"

"Because you're a woman that—that—I'm afraid to say it!"

"Don't then. Yes, say it; a woman—what else?"

For yet a moment longer Randy hesitated ere she said,

"A woman that will be just what her husband is."

"There you're wrong."

"There isn't blame in it. It should be so. It ought to be, it would be—"

"No, I should—"

"Direct him? Make him what you knew he should be? No, you would not; you would not do that. You would love him as he was, and come to see no sin in his sinfulness, and go down instead of up; and all for love. And so—oh, I hope, how I hope! it might be some strong, good man, like some we have known. I wish it might be the best man I have ever known."

"You think I would be led, and not lead."

"I think you would believe that you led him, for that's your nature, Sally. Yes! but I think you would really be influenced by him most. Yes, that's what I think about it. And so, I'm anxious. For that reason I used to be afraid it might be Oliver Savage you would set your heart on.

And I never thanked God so heartily for anything as I did for his going away. It would have been such a dreadful marriage for you, Sally."

"Do you think so?"

"Yes," said Randy. And she spoke with power, as one who has gained time and opportunity for speech of inestimable importance; and thus she went on. "If you had married him, he would have shown you how you deceived yourself, trusting him, and then nothing but wretchedness all your life; or else, or else he would have persuaded you against your own knowledge, and you would have preferred him to all the world."

"And what if I had?"

"Then you would have gone down instead of up, as I said before."

"Of course you're thinking I'd choose the worst of any two things that offered."

"We're not ourselves entirely, Sally, when we love another. Remember your dear father. Don't think that you can go against his will and prosper."

Struggling against the suspicion and alarm Miranda's words excited, Sally answered, indignant,

"What do you mean? What has set you into this way of talking? Do you wonder that a woman, free to go where she chooses, should think sometimes of flying away, out of reach of such preachers as you and Huldah Green?"

"Oh, Sally, it might be going beyond your friends' reach. It is only a friend who would dare to pain you so."

More quietly, but not with less displeasure than her former speech had testified, Sally answered,

"I have been looking over the map of the world, and I can find Butler county, but no Martindale. Count the people worth your knowing; two dozen may be. It's stuff you talk; contentment here is a sin. I'll not stay here forever. And I am not afraid that I cannot find friends wherever I go. I could at school—plenty of them. I don't like this being lectured. I wish you hadn't such a sense of duty. I wish we could take a journey together. I wish we could do something that conscience hadn't got a single word to say about. If I hear too little to it, you hear a deal too much. When I marry Oliver Savage, you shall be my bridesmaid. Don't look so solemn. His mother likes me better than

Huldah ever did. I'd like to be loved a little. And the girls—aren't they pretty girls?—they don't care more for each other than they do for me. You might think I was their sister! They show me all their dear boy's letters home. When he sent back a lock of hair they wanted to share it."

"Sally, don't talk so. It seems to me I see you standing on the edge—"

"Oh, yes, that's true preaching style—on the edge of a precipice. Make the most of me, Randy—I may go over before you know."

Some strange pleasure she seemed to find in drawing from Randy these expressions of anxiety. She was only testing her—only probing the extent to which her knowledge of these matters went.

"You're not the only one to be considered," said Randy. "You don't know what you may put it into Oliver's head to hope for. His mother too. You ought to think you may be laying up great store of pain and disappointment for her and the girls. For, of course, it would be a great thing for them to have Oliver married to Sally Green."

"Well, what if I really did it?"

"Then, you must reap what you sow. Nothing can hinder that."

"Good-bye, Randy—you're poor company. Do you see that road? I wouldn't take it, except to rid you of me."

"Don't leave me—come this way, do!"

"No indeed—enough for one day, Randy. But don't look so solemn over it. I don't believe you would have been so hard, but you're tired carrying that great baby." Sally's voice softened a little, speaking these last words, and she went off with a smile on her face.

Striking into the road that led directly homeward, Randy met Senior Jobson. He had come out to meet her, and seeing that she looked tired and heated, he took the sleeping child out of her arms, at the same time giving her a letter.

"That's from your minister, I guess. I put it into my pocket because I wanted to ask you a question."

Randy took the letter, looked at the address, and then at Senior.

"Yes," she said, "this is from Mr. Collamer. The first letter for a long time."

Senior, who had not removed his eyes once from her, appeared to discern in her composure a sign of encouragement, for he spoke now more cheerfully.

"Then you ain't in quite such close communion? I thought, by this time, it must be all settled."

"Settled! What? It *is* all settled."

In her startled exclamation, her confused questioning, and the struggle with which she compelled herself to speak the last words, Senior Jobson seemed to receive a confirmation of a fear.

"I thought it was the minister that cut me out," said he.

That he had ever come to speak thus to her proved too surely that he had never really resigned his hope of Randy. It proved as much to her.

"You are mistaken," she said. "He is my friend, I hope—I like to think he is—I must think he is. But it was not he that came between you and me." Yet, as she said this, she looked at Senior as if under some sudden conviction; then she added, with a changing voice, "That could not have been his work. It was not his wish. He loves another woman. So you see that—that, in the way you think, he could not have come between you and me."

"Then it was some of his deuced nonsense that set you up to thinking what wasn't kind of you to think of me. The devil isn't as black as he's painted, Randy. I'll say that till you understand. Them eagles I've set up on the sign are eagles, not angels. I never set up for a saint. But if I was your husband, I should mind I didn't offend you; not willingly; I'd be careful. There! I've said what I agreed with myself I never would. It isn't like me to be urging a woman; but you've made yourself of such service to us, I don't know how we're ever going to get along without you. I've had a mind to sell out and go off, all for thinking of it. You're nearer to me than anybody. And it appears to me that you might see it was right so, if you would."

"If I could I would," she answered.

"Then I'll try to make you see it."

"No you could not. Don't try it, Senior; don't make it any harder for me to live. I haven't any heart to give you!

I haven't any heart to give to any one but God! I'm willing to stay in the tavern. I'll try my best to make it all comfortable to you. I'll look after the children, but don't ask anything more; don't think anything more. And I will not even ask God to take me out of the world as long as I can be of any use or comfort."

Senior was himself too much disturbed by her words, and his secret comments thereon, to observe how greatly distressed Randy was. If he heard the appeal she made, an appeal words could not frame, it moved him to say:

"I won't keep you to your promise then, Randy. It may happen you'll live longer than you think, and change your mind about staying. It's curious—maybe you won't believe it—but, seeing how you feel, I'd give you to the minister as if I was your father. I won't trouble you any more. I'll never think again that maybe you've changed your mind about me. There! I'm sorry; you're too good to be bothered so. But it's the devil's reign, I'm thinking."

"Don't say that, don't think it! *He* shall reign until all enemies are put under His feet! It only shows how weak we are when we are tempted. But out of every temptation He provides a way of escape. Give the baby to me, Senior. See, she wants to come."

The baby had wakened, and, finding herself nestled in so unusual a resting-place, seemed to have made up her mind to cry. Senior passed her over to Randy's arms; and, after she was thoroughly awake, she wanted to walk, so Randy set her on the ground between herself and Senior.

When he spoke last, Senior had a vague hope or expectation, that his words would excite the woman's pride, once an eminent quality; but she had attempted no such self-exoneration. That she had loved vainly, according to his apprehension, was a fact with which her pride had nothing to do. Senior would respect her secret; perhaps it was nothing to regret that he had discovered it. She had nothing more to say on that head.

Nothing more to say at all, it seemed; or else too much to say which must remain unsaid. So they walked on to the tavern, mindful chiefly of the child's step and the child's talk.

The letter Randy carried home with her had some passages which she read over and over again. It seemed to be a farewell letter, by which, taking leave of all the past, the minister addressed himself to his work with a new energy. The pastoral year had again expired, and his new appointment would carry him still further from Martindale, yet he held fast to the recollection of her friendship, and it was a consoling remembrance to him. He spoke of his experiences among the people from whom he was about to depart, as in one sense disastrous. Only Love had failed him! His labors had been blessed; he had been able to do much for his church and people; and, after all, he was able to say that his faith in man and woman remained firm.

He told her that, if she wrote to him again, the letter would not come amiss. Of her prosperity in this life he should rejoice to know. He thanked her for the encouragement he had found in her words many times. The subjects of her thoughts and prayers could never fail to interest him. A sad letter, on the whole, which brought Randy to her knees to pray a prayer in his behalf it would have startled Mr. Collamer to hear. Tell him the subject of her prayers! How should mortal make report for human eyes or ears of that which has been left with tears before the throne of the Almighty?

CHAPTER XLIII.

OLIVER'S RETURN.

It is more than a year since the death of Elder Green. Huldah, in the homestead, leads a rather sad and lonely life; much troubled when she thinks of the Elder's daughter, between whom and herself barriers wider than were ever built of stone seem to have arisen.

Time goes on, Time all comprehending; Sally endures it without much complaint; but she aims at nothing, and is nothing troubled. She is merely waiting.

She says to herself, "Oliver is coming home." And she says that to his mother. To these two with a difference. To soothe the latter, for it is long, it is months now, since any letter came from him.

She says it to herself. Whenever she hears any swift driving past the house that stands on the corner, sentinelled by poplars, she runs to the window and looks out. (And in these days she wears a ring.)

She says it to herself when she lies down at night, and when she rises in the morning. She is ever restless. She is restive, too; impatient and longing. She looks often— yes, often in the past months she has looked at, the marriage certificate, and on a roll of blue ribbons that figured on a time.

She is calculating what she shall do in a momentous future, which perchance may be ushered in to-morrow. It matters not to her she must leave the house where she was born; that pleading looks of dead and living follow her. Dead and living, alike, have mistaken. Who should counsel her as her own heart? Who should understand this place as well as she? She can forgive her father—she can forgive Huldah. But she must fulfil the vow she made to Oliver when he said she could save him.

And must we call this love? It is at least a passion powerful enough to transform and color all things. Powerful enough to compass sea and land, and defy earth and heaven.

Huldah Green has taken her knitting work and gone to sit with Junior's wife and Randy; she finds the long bright afternoons so lonely, for in the afternoons Esther is always dozing—poor, feeble, childish Esther—and Sally never comes to sit with Huldah, choosing solitude rather than such society, when she occupies herself with any ordinary woman work.

A lonely life the widow leads. She often goes to the grave of Elder Green, and she finds it a small consolation for a lonely heart to be left "well provided for." To be the Elder's widow, with "her thirds," and the use of the homestead as long as she lives, is not to occupy the summit of felicity, she thinks. The little man who sleeps under the sod was very dear to Huldah. The weariness of his slow speech and the rigor of his piety are remembered no more against him.

If, now, she could only come near to his daughter! If Sally would but see what was living in her heart! If Sally would only consider!

So, finding the house lonely and time long, Huldah has gone to sit with her friends; she can speak freely to Randy, who seems to understand so well when she lingers over her memories of her first wedded years, and of the last words of tenderness, the last cares of love. Randy, who knows so well how to listen and to soothe; the woman without whose presence and sympathy, it seems, the town of Martindale could not sustain itself!

Sally has given up the afternoon to a duty set apart for this time. Last night her new dress was sent home from Brighton—a pink dress of some fine thin material; barege, doubtless—a pink dress, flounced to the waist, six full flounces, edged with lace, and the basque likewise ornamented. She has curled her hair and prepared herself elaborately, out of deference to the new garment, whose "effect" she is curious to know.

Her mourning dress is lying on a chair beside the table,

as she stands before her glass you would not dream that she had ever mourned.

The house seems strangely quiet. It is not strangely so, but so it seems, for Sally is not quiet, cool and undisturbed in this work. She need not fear an interruption. Grandma is asleep; Huldah is gone out; the kitchen girl is attending to her business.

Sounds travel far to-day. The rumble of wagons is to be heard as they pass to and fro on the cross roads; and any vehicle approaching on the main road, from either direction, gives a warning to the house screened by tall poplars, on the corner.

Suddenly, while Sally fastens a bracelet around her wrist, a gold band whose clasp is a serpent's head, with a jeweled eye, there comes a sound of carriage wheels, and, true to her habit, she is at the window looking out. Who passes? Who passes, indeed!—the light carriage has stopped before the door—reins are dropped, and whoever has come is already out of sight—and there is a sound of footsteps in the hall below.

Some one calls her by name; then she repents the dress, and seems about to attempt its removal. It may be somebody from Brighton. It must be somebody in need.

And she goes down the stairs.

So they had decorated for each other! There they stood, those two, face to face.

As they met, they shed some tears. There were some broken utterances; some stifled sobbing; even a "thank God!" And all was forgotten except love—and all forgiven, perhaps even the dead!

Jaunty, and fine, and overgrown, Oliver returns to Martindale. He comes back in a sort of triumph.

Travel has made some change in him, and he was never a clown. He looks like a man—and a handsome man—a paragon to Sally.

By some extraordinary combination of circumstances, he had been successful beyond all expectation. But while he worked at all, Oliver worked hard, and he returns with a sense of merit, founded on that fact. He has his rights; he will drive straight to the Elder's house and assert them. He thinks that he and Sally have by this time proved each other! And in all the weariness and want of his banishment, this desire has been paramount—to proclaim himself, to be acknowledged in that town of Martindale, which has no name upon the map, though Butler county environs it, to be acknowledged there the husband of Sally Green. The Elder's son-in-law!

Yes, she has no objections; just as she is, she will go up with him to see his mother; will remain with him there; or they can return, and grandma will be easily reconciled. As to Huldah, it makes very little difference. She is glad that she put off her mourning—it was providential! She will go with him as she is—it will be a double joy to mother Savage. And Sally shows Oliver the ring. Is it not enchanting, this constancy? Does it not read like a romance? Lovers parting under such doleful conditions, meeting again in such blissful circumstances? Young, rich, handsome— valor on his part, condescension on hers! What could be rarer?

Bound, for sickness and for health; for poverty or riches; for better or for worse! Love dares it; and love may. For love can stand the tests of weariness, and watching, of pain; every seeming change in the dear person for the sake of the more precious spirit! It can endure the tests of want, of hunger, of all privation; of all that follows close on the loss of wealth or of reputation. Aye, love can endure it, for love is Love. But vanity! and world-pride! self-will! and tyranny! and dull ignorance! Poor Oliver! more pitiable Sally!

I perceive another driving than that of this brave afternoon, when two chat gaily past the grave-yard, the rein unslackened in the driver's hand, their voices still high and triumphant in their tone.

The way is steep and narrow, and the steeds are restive. A reckless hand is guiding them. Bystanders shudder at the risks they run—they can see better than the driver that the woman is alarmed, that she sees the danger! They see that her gestures are imperative, and that he heeds them no more than he heeds the rushing wind; that she attempts at last to save herself, when ruin is imminent, but in vain! It is too late; escape is impossible! Nothing short of miracle can avert the destruction before them!

Alas for the fine garments and the poor display! Alas

for Esther Green, who lives to see her pride laid low as the dust in which the worm trails! Alas for a hearthstone planted for no pure vestal fires, but for folly and untruth, for lust and shame, and the worship of the beast!

CHAPTER XLIV.

LIGHT IN THE VALLEY.

Can I say that, when Miranda Roy received the intelligence conveyed to her by the minister, she pondered the tidings with profoundest sorrow? What reader would credit the tale? There may be such a thing as perfect sympathy, but generally he who stands next the sorrowing will perceive that their sorrow falls something short of the absolute —that it has its mitigation.

Miranda believed that the person around whom Mr. Collamer had seen the halo that numbered her among the beatific visions, was not ordained to make his misery, and that, therefore their ways had suddenly diverged. And when she wrote to him she assured herself:

"He cannot mistake me. I can speak more freely, with a securer self-reliance than I could once. This woman has deceived him; but she has shown what sort of woman Mr. Collamer could love. Mrs. Carradine said the likeness was of a fashionable woman. I could see that, myself."

So she had written him the letter he looked for; kept him not waiting for it long. A letter weighed and measured, every word and line. It came short of what he had hoped for; it was not what he had expected.

But its deficiencies were not those of incompetence, he could well see, he did well know. Her letter pained him for that manner of sympathy in his sorrow of which he could never be patient. He would not surrender to any shape of human grief. His trust in the Divine love and protection was too firm and clear. And Randy's letter expressed more of Christian patience and resignation than Christian confidence and joy. When he looked into it he saw that this was not her spirit's natural speech. He saw it more clearly when he looked into her old letters; it was a brave spirit that spoke through them; quite a different spirit from that which now seemed to possess her. She endeavored to speak peace and comfort to him from the heavens, where she alone had found them. But of old her rejoicing was in the seen and the temporal, transfigured to her perception by the light of the Divine love!

By degrees the duties and the cares of his calling absorbed him again. His unfortunate, unhappy experience ceased to control him—it had no utterance, and it seemed to have no memory. The new charge and the new people were sufficient to absorb his time, and he gave to them his thoughts, and fought against the weakness of the drawing toward Martindale, which he had felt, at one time, to be almost beyond his resistance.

He closed and sealed up that experience of his which had shown him to *himself* a mortal, vulnerable man; a man to tremble for, hardly to be hoped for; capable of weakness, folly, guilt.

After this manner was his growth in wisdom; and so he stood among men a man who had been tried and tempted; who had yielded to temptations, and knew the anguish of repentance; a guide more competent because he had passed through the darkness, and danger, and terror of the way.

Humanity, the brotherhood of all Christ's servants, was now the constant burden of his speech; and men flocked to hear it as if it were a new evangel. The wisdom of experience was in his teaching; and he, in his bright youth, inspired the confidence which is the guerdon of old servants in the ministry. So that, still in his youth, his fame as a speaker extended far and wide, beyond the limits of his own church, and became a sort of public property, in which men, as men, might take an honorable pride.

Far off, Randy watched the rising and the shining of that star. Why was she not surprised? Why was no deeper emotion stirred? Senior Jobson observed her, and said to himself:

"She's the girl I took her for!" and a deal of consolation he seemed to derive from that self-assuring.

One Sunday morning, Jobson harnessed his horse, locked his bar-room, and drove down to Brighton. Junior and his wife had gone, a week ago, on a visit up the country, and Randy was left in charge of the house and children. It seemed to be a sudden purpose on which Senior acted. All the early morning his manner indicated that he had the day to idle in—and it seemed likely that he would spend it according to his usual habit, drinking little, smoking much, and napping in the bar-room, but not so soundly that he did not hear all that passed around him.

Perhaps some forgotten purpose was at last accidentally recalled, for he seemed to have conferred with no one when he locked the bar-room and went to put the harness on his horse. So Randy supposed; but the fact was he had heard that Mr. Collamer was to preach that day at Brighton, and all the morning Jobson had been saying to himself, "To go, or not to go; that is the question." To himself he said it; it was no part of his present purpose to take Miranda into his counsel.

Finally, having concluded to go, he went, and the consequences must look out for themselves.

The little church was crowded to overflowing, when, having left his horse at a neighboring tavern, Senior Jobson made his way through the multitude, until he came within hearing of the speaker's voice. To see him one could not have doubted that he came simply on an errand. But the very errand required that he should listen with respect— and with respect he did wait through a preaching, for the first time since he was a child.

If what he heard at all impressed or moved him, that was not apparent. No devotion, no anxiety, no serious interest even, was visible on his countenance. He saw the surprise he had excited in some familiar faces; and his recognitions were intended to convey the information that not even curiosity, but odd chances, had conspired to bring him into the midst of this audience.

But, disguise effectually as he might his secret convictions, Senior was not insensible to the power of the speaker, neither unmoved by his eloquence. And he was endeavoring to listen not entirely for himself; but as if he were a woman, as if he were Miranda. Martindale was not so far out of the world but many rumors drifted through it concerning that world. Mr. Collamer's experiences were, some of them, quite notable among certain circles, and to the ears of Senior Jobson had come the report of his entanglement in the fortunes of Miss Grey, and of his deliverance from them, when the world rolled as a tide between the woman of his choice and the man of God's ordaining.

Often he had been tempted to repeat these tales to Randy. But, gossip though he might be, he found that he had not the heart to do it. She would be sure to mistake his endeavor—and she was doing well—was living quietly in peaceful performance of her work—as well this manner of religious consolation served her as any rude discovery of Collamer's failure to make good a claim in her regard. And now he had gone to Brighton to see the man with his own eyes—to hear him with his ears. To see him with a woman's eyes and hear him with a woman's ears, it seemed.

When the congregation was dismissed, and the people began to disperse, Senior Jobson's conduct was contrary to anything his nearest friend could have anticipated. Instead of quitting the church he remained within, and let the people surge around and past him, as composedly as an island takes the flowing of a river. He never for a moment lost sight of the minister, who stood now at the foot of the pulpit stairs, in conversation with such of the brethren as rallied there to fatigue him with their praises and their hospitalities, and to cheer him with their thanks and sympathy.

Towards this group Mr. Jobson slowly approached when the church was so far vacated as to leave him a conspicuous object among the benches.

He had felt a little embarrassment and a little hesitation, some irresolution, while he stood waiting his time, but the instant he stepped into the aisle and advanced toward the pulpit nothing but purpose and directness was observable in him.

Mr. Collamer saw and recognized him, and advanced to meet him. He had looked about him in his preaching with a purpose to discover, and had seen no friend from Martindale. Last of all would he have looked for Senior Jobson.

He shook hands with him so cordially, and looked up into Jobson's face with such pure, friendly eyes, that Senior at once, assured in his purpose, said :

" I came down to hear you preach, sir. I've got my carriage with me. Come up to Martindell and spend the night. I've my reasons, sir, for asking it."

The minister reflected a moment.

"I must be in Brighton by sunrise—how could that be managed?"

"I'll manage it," said Jobson, with the air of a man who must not be put off. "You shall come back to-night, if it suits you."

"I am afraid my friends will expect me here this evening," he hesitated.

"I said I had my reasons," repeated Jobson, speaking still more earnestly, for he had set himself to accomplish something, and he was not the man to take up any project with spirit and drop it unaccomplished. "You have preached all day. You look as if it was killing work, sir. Give 'em time to think over what you've told 'em. And come with me!—there ain't a man among us needs you more."

"Is it so? Then I will leave the ninety and nine, Jobson. Where's your horse?"

"I'll have him at the door, sir, in five minutes."

"Very well; you will find me waiting in the porch."

Jobson turned away from the minister, put his hat on, pulled it well down on his forehead and walked from the church.

But, driving toward Martindale, Jobson's chief desire and aim seemed to be to annihilate the distance. The minister waited in vain for divulgence of the confidences he expected. He could not doubt that Randy was in some way concerned in them; but Jobson did not speak her name until, having asked after every other soul he knew, Mr. Collamer mentioned her. Then Senior opened his mouth and began to speak in earnest. Such a tide of words rolled from him as had rarely, except on the great occasions of his life, found vent. His heart and brain were full; and it seemed, as he went on, as if a new power of speech had been added, this day, to his by no means stammering tongue. The minister listened in silence to his rehearsal of Miranda's deeds, her daily life, her character. She seemed to have been the innkeeper's one study in these months, and he had proved her to a depth no other intelligence had done. How many times he had caught himself going from her presence, pierced by some arrow of the truth that she was living! How her purity of purpose, and her self-sacrifices, had shamed him in surrender to temptations! How he had lived as if in the sight of an angel whose " rebukes in blessings ended," whose firmness, and consistency, and steadfastness of faith, put to open shame his more pretentious, and more vascillating courage! She had been to him a " lively oracle," a " living word of God," he was free to own it. He did own it; and he told Mr. Collamer, in the end, that it wasn't for himself, as he may have supposed, that he was taking him to Martindell; it was because he thought it would please Randy to see the minister once more.

Nor did he conclude his sayings without openly declaring what had been his hope once in regard to Miranda. And how she had promised him; and how she had seemed afterwards to have a waking up, that showed her such a marriage was not lawful. That, for a long time, he had not seen it so, but now his mind was changed, not towards her—God bless her! —but in regard to his fitness for her! He had got over that sort of thing; he should never marry. But he hoped that Randy might. He thought that Randy should. If he could give her up to a good man she loved, if there was a man in the world she *could* love, it would be with all his heart!

And what he had to say, Senior had not quite made an end of when he reined his horse in before the *Spread Eagle.*

How did the preacher listen? As a man does before whom men and women are wont to unburden themselves of secret thoughts and deep experiences? Could he, with philosophic calmness, the assurance of Christian philosophy, refer all these matters from their beginning to their ultimate, and hail Sorrow as the purifier, and Duty as the gentlest of friends?

While they drove through the lovely country that Sunday afternoon, was it in his heart to clasp the driver's hand as the hand of a brother? Would he fain have hurried on yet faster? Were they going too fast? Did he hear more than Senior spoke? Had he anything to say to Randy worth a drive from Brighton?

See him greeting her! What is there in that greeting? They whom it concerns look in each other's eyes to see. And Senior has gone off and left them to a quiet talk, in this close of the quiet Sabbath, the first day of the week.

She was surprised! She had not expected to see him?

No, not yet. But a neighbor had stopped at the spring an hour ago, and he told her that Mr. Collamer was preaching in Brighton to-day. She thought that, perhaps to-morrow, he would come. Did not believe that he would return, when he had come so near, without visiting his friends in Martindale.

And now his visit must be brief; so brief! But there were hours of daylight yet; if she would go with him he would like to see the place where her father was buried—good old Elder Green too. Would she lead the way?

So they walked, talking of the dead and of the living. Along the lonely road, bordered by fair fields, meadow lands and orchards. Oh, night to stand alone in memory forever! Side by side; two in time; one for eternity!

From many things, he turned at last to speak of himself as he had never written. A speech of more significance than friendship could account for. Not to make light of, not to dwell bitterly upon the experience that had shown him to himself a man to be repented of; a man to be atoned for. He let her see the path by which he had come to a new possession of himself. For he could see that, though he was now here by the aid of Senior Jobson, it was not by the mere will of man! And in the end he said, stopping short in the lonely road :

"Miranda, Jobson brought me here by God's will, I believe. It is but just I should say again, what I have many times acknowledged, that, since I knew you, you have been my inspiration to every good work and labor of love I have been able to accomplish. I have told you all. Judge. With you I could do my best. While I was so infatuated, I believe that you were still my ideal, and the woman who frenzied me only represented you in another shape than your true and noble form. I love you; I have always loved you. I ask you to go with me, and share my work and bless my life, and let us see once more that it is a new world, as we did once; I know that we are living under a new dispensation!"

How answered she? Not as one in doubt, to be confused by a marvel.

"It is a new world. We are living under a new dispensation," she said, struggling into speech. "Yes, yes; you showed me the way of life once. I'll walk in it. God! —my God!"

So hard it was to drink "this wine of astonishment," so incredible to her seemed this rolling away of the grey shadows that showed Heaven crystal pure and bright!

He took her hand in silence; he drew her arm through his; he led her to the roadside, and they sat down under the great branches of a walnut tree; and fast their tears ran, and their words were few.

"He will complete His work. I seem to be lost in life—

"'The world recedes, it disappears!
Heaven opens on my eyes—my ears
With sounds seraphic ring!'"

"Blessed be God!" she answered. But she did not add, *I knew this day would come.* For with the recall of the conviction, which had indeed endured through years, came the recollection of doubt, and of despair and resignation; and that dreary wintry calm that held no presage of the tropical day.

"Is it indeed to go with you day by day, and care for you, and love you?—in your thought and in your heart?" she marvelled.

"The sunshine in my heart! The long calm summer season in which all that is good shall quicken and be perfected. My best sense, my most chaste will, my best source of inspiration."

"Because I know that you are everything to me, I would

not be less to you.   Only God above us.   God within us. All in all."

So stood he before her eyes most complete of all that live. So stood she to his vision, as an angel, fair and strong.

And their speech could no man understand, except the loving—and it befits well no audience except that of the unseen whose company is not intrusion, but blessing and honor.

On this Sunday evening a new hour has struck, whose soft echo rolls over the great deep of eternity. It blends with the divine harmony of God's own universe—a tone that never can be lost, absorbed or wrought into discordance. Oh, all ye loving, listen; you shall discern the sound, and smile for Randy's sake.

CHAPTER XLV.

A DAY OF THE LORD.

In October, Christian Peter Carradine was born. Rare event!

Perhaps ten thousand infants drew their first mortal breath on that same fine morning.

But he was Carradine's son; and what to Peter Carradine were the nine thousand nine hundred and ninety-nine that, under frescoed ceilings, surrounded by bare walls, pure white, smoke-stained, broken, in mud cabins, in the wigwams of red Indians, in the bungalos of natives, in barracks, on the ocean, in the tents of Arabs, in damp and dismal cellars, in the crowded city, on the lonely heath, amidst fearful confusion, in deep silence, and in death, in anguish, in shame, in pride, in holy thankfulness were born?

What to him nine thousand nine hundred and ninety-nine, of every shade of circumstance? Here, in his arms, he had held the son of Mercy—a silent, helpless creature, of whom they should make A MAN.

Carradine sat alone on the piazza of his new Home on the hill, on the fine evening of that day, sat there without smoking. He sat in silence, his arms folded across his broad chest; and he thought, with tearful eyes, with a heart humble and tender, of his childhood's home, and he vowed to God that he would honor Him in making happy the life of the child that slept on Mercy's bosom.

He saw in vision a little figure following his young mother in smooth garden walks—made smooth for childish feet. Running along the road that led down to the schoolhouse where his mother was once a teacher. A little lad hunting berries in the wood; driving the cows home night and morning; playing in the fields; sitting by his side when he drove the carriage down to Brighton; going away from home to learn what young men learn in High Schools and in Colleges; making the name of Carradine one of the names of the world.

Oh, strong paternal love! In that happy hour, as, by the release and the liberty of God, he took no note of disaster or of failure, of temptation or of death. No ruin was seen in his Eden—no serpent crept through its paths. It was all easy; all fair. In his strong love he saw no evil that could not be swept away by a hand-wave, by a word.

So, again and again, he went over the ground of that fair childhood and most noble youth. There were things which he alone could teach his son. Much of which the child's mother could alone be the teacher. He looked at all things, as it seemed, through a new medium. All things seemed to him transfigured. The most simple affairs were become endued with a new dignity by virtue of the young eyes that should come to knowledge of them; the pure young heart, the pure young life that should have to deal with them.

Doubtless in many homes loving men were thinking in his vein; enough so thinking that bright morning, to sanctify the world; enough to prove its continuance in the name, as by the power of love.

But—shall we dare enter the room where this one new life slumbers? Or enter the sanctuary of her thoughts, who, through sleep and waking, is to guard the child? Look with *her* eyes to the future, and see how *she* determines her son shall come to man's estate?

Who but she should prophesy the future of her son? In her will and in her heart it is an end decided. *From the foundations of this world, this being, its last day is determined.* Yes, who but she should prophesy? Who but a woman so presume? Who but a mother, through such fears, so trust? The all-cognizant mother!

A work to be done, moment by moment, hour by hour, day by day—a woman's never-ending work. God-like in this, that it could never *be* ended. So vast, so comprehending. It is the finite who dream of completion. But a mother's love, her aspirations have the nature of infinity.

Never for a moment was this burden she had lifted to be laid.

Alas for Mercy Carradine if she could not, having entered on this work find in its progress the consummation of all joy!

She was the child's mother. What must he, in his unfolding consciousness, come to perceive in her? Wisdom and strength, courage and tenderness; the whole being of love. How should she dare make a less perfect revelation to his eyes, who would look to her with growing expectation through these coming years?

Great men are the offspring of noble mothers. So had she read in many a record, with perpetual proving. What right then had she to give her son to the world bound in any faculty, in any manner impoverished or impaired? Nay, a free being must he be, with all the freedom of virtue.

It were much to follow her, as she, in fancy, fulfilled, hour by hour, her Holy Work.

Perhaps no vain labor, if but one who trusts that miracles will atone hereafter for ignorance and neglect could understand *how life is only discord, when it defies God's law.*

She had the consciousness that it was hers to make of this child what she would! And she had the surety in that consciousness that, if her doing was according to the will, it would be likewise with the certainty of God's own working. It being impossible that His blessing should be withheld where His pleasure is wrought; the blessing being involved in the working; the doing conveying knowledge of the will. * * * * * *

Why, she asked, and well might ask herself, why should any woman working in the fear of God for her children, never neglecting the work she has dared to engage in, constant in it as one who has come up to the dignity of the work that is for eternity, fear to ask the future what the end shall be?

How can it be other than triumphant? Is God the enemy of his creatures, or rather *is* "all love and all law." She, this mother, was not thinking of worldly gain, but of that which endures through mutations of time, and shall outlast "pillars of earthly pride" and "tenements of dust;" even virtue, integrity and love.

She was right—let it be said, though the praise seem to some impertinent; as if otherwise were to be overlooked—were to be forgiven! For, doubtless, if you educate a liar from the cradle, you shall have, oh woman, a mendacious manhood in your son! If you nurse a thief or any manner of moral imbecility, tyranny, or lust, or pride, anger, or vanity, or selfishness, "the mill of God grinds slow, but it grinds to powder," and "there are no fans in hell."

And could Mercy Carradine be so honest, now that one was in the world whom she must acknowledge, long as life should last for either, as her son, could *she* be so honest and so brave as to charge home the shame of this and every generation of civilized life, even as its glory also, back on the heart, let us not say the *will* of woman, as its source?

There may be some men who would lightly assent to, even as there are some women who will darkly resent, the hard saying. But neither in this world, nor in that which is to come, is there any real evasion of responsibility. Neglect of duty—enough of it.

Responsibility evaded—none!

The most perfect human life, the Divinest life, the heavenliest, was born of a woman; for the world's encouragement, as for the world's redemption. Mercy Carradine believed this in her heart. She saw something of the vast, all-comprehending truth. It has often enough been repeated. Ah, but think of the legions of women to whom this truth, sublimest of all, comes as a hard saying, who can bear it? As an incredible saying, who will believe it?

But—will God dwell with men? Behold, the *Heaven* of Heavens cannot contain him, how much less a woman's heart!

So we must have our images of life! Our slaves of every passion, our jails, asylums, houses of refuge. For prevention is not better than cure! And, in no sense conceivable, is the benevolence of this age a disgrace to the race!

Mercy saw the relation she sustained towards God's universe—the mother of a child. Alas, ye scoffing unbelievers, how do *ye* avouch the veracity of that record by which we *know* that, when Moses talked with God in the mountain, the people made their precious calf for worship; for their God, substituted a beast.

Do we read of ships loosed from the docks, in whose mighty planks some atom of a worm has lodged itself, atom that shall hereafter plunge a thousand souls into the ocean's depths? But science was at work here, science that was sacred, and would never yield to haste, or to haste's expediency.

So Mrs. Johnson said to Huldah Green,
"Here, look at the pretty creetur! Christian Peter! there's a name for you! It's got a voice for you, it has! and he's thinking such a thing never happened on this earth before. He calls it Bird, and Rose," said Mrs. Johnson, with a softened voice, " and you'd wonder to hear the questions that man asks. I've hit on an answer for short that I give 'm if I hear the sound of his boots after me. Says I, '*It's all right, sir,.*' but he put me to the blush once on that, and I'll own it to you, Huldah; says he, ' Then it isn't all wrong, Mrs. Johnson ? There's peace between you and me ? It's a child,' said he, ' brought peace to the poor world once, and by that token we'll keep it in this house.' "

The frank voice of Mrs. Johnson trembled as she spoke, and she ended her remarks with unexpected abruptness. Huldah wiped her eyes, and, smiling on the baby, kissed it, repeating as she rose to heights that loomed above her experiences,

" It's all right, Mrs. Johnson."

If the burden Mercy had to bear was great, love, she knew, could lighten it, and leave it not weighty beyond glad and proud endurance. The trust came to her as from God, and she said, " Behold the handmaid of the Lord."

So the house of Carradine became a temple, and sacred service was conducted there ! So " Heaven" lay around that " infancy !"

NEW BOOKS THIS FALL.

PETER CARRADINE,
OR
THE MARTINDALE PASTORAL.

By Caroline Chesebro'.

One vol. 12mo. $1.25.

BROKEN COLUMNS.

A Novel of great power and interest.

One vol. 12mo. $1.50.

(From Peter Bayne, Author of "Christian Life," "Essays," etc. etc.)

"I have complied with your request, and read "Broken Columns" *carefully.* I do not hesitate to pronounce it, in my judgment, superior to "Adam Bede." The plot is admirable, and the execution is a singular nearness to perfection. You must not hesitate to publish it. I am confident when it is read and known it will have an extensive sale."

HUSKS.

By Marion Harland.

Author of "Alone," "Hidden Path," "Moss Side," "Nemesis," and "Miriam."

One vol 12mo. $1.50.

CHRISTMAS STORIES.

By Charles Dickens.

An elegant edition on tinted paper, small quarto size, illustrated from designs by F. O. C. Darley.

One vol. 4to.

SHELDON & COMPANY, Publishers,
335 *Broadway, New York.*

Books Published by Sheldon & Co.

LIFE OF GEORGE WASHINGTON.

By EDWARD EVERETT, LL.D.

1 vol., 12mo. 348 pages.

With a steel-plate likeness of Mr. Everett, from the celebrated bust by Hiram Powers.

Price, in cloth, $1; in sheep binding, $1.50; in half-calf, $2.

"The last link of that golden chain which shall hereafter, for many generations, bind together the names of George Washington and Edward Everett, has just been fitted into its place. The unselfish labors of the scholar and statesman, of whom we are all proud, and whose successful devotion to the purchase of Mount Vernon has challenged the admiration of the world, are brought to a fitting conclusion in the compend of Washington's Life. The biography is a model of condensation, and, by its rapid narrative and attractive style, must commend itself to the mass of readers, as the standard popular Life of Washington."—*Correspondence of the Boston Post.*

"It is a nobler office to inspire one's countrymen with patriotic sentiments, with warm love and reverence for their institutions, than it is to take a conspicuous part in the movements of the governmental machine. Mr. Everett is rendering a signal and needed service in recalling attention to Washington, and teaching us to appreciate the reasons why he has been adjudged the greatest public character that has appeared in human history. * * * * *
Mr. Everett is unrivaled by any man of his time in the ability to give eloquent expression to the sentiment of patriotism."—*From an able editorial in the World.*

"Mr. Everett's name is destined to be indissolubly connected with that of Washington —not only by his exertions in behalf of the tomb of the *pater patriæ*—not only, even, by the just and eloquent tributes he has paid, in words, to the name and fame of the sage of Mount Vernon. Even in England, and among the scholars and historians and statesmen of the mother country, Edward Everett has come to be considered the fittest chronicler of Washington's history, and the fittest annalist of his character."—*N. Y. Express.*

"That it will be one of the most elegant, faithful, and charming productions of the day may readily be conceived. Probably no person in the country has studied the 'Father of his Country' more closely than the distinguished orator of Massachusetts. It will unquestionably be in great demand."—*Boston Atlas.*

"It will, doubtless, as it should, find its way into every household, as the popular embodiment of Washington, and be seen alike in the costly library, surrounded by thousands of other volumes, and on the humble mantel, where, in connection with the Bible and Pilgrim's Progress, it will form the entire stock of family reading."—*New York Examiner.*

"It is a duodecimo elegantly printed. It tells the whole story without circumlocution—clearly, fully, faithfully, and with the simple force and fluency the theme requires. It has evidently been a labor of love. Familiar as are the incidents, they read delightfully in Mr. Everett's diction, and are illustrated anew by many a fresh hint and idea gathered by his long study and great love of the subject. The work comes with singular propriety from his felicitous pen, as the orator whose eloquence has done so much to rescue Washington's domain, home, and sepulchre from desecration, and consecrate them to the nation. An excellent engraved portrait of the author, from Power's bust, and fresh material in the appendix, enhance the interest and value of this charming national souvenir."—*Henry T. Tuckerman, the distinguished Essayist.*

Books Published by Sheldon & Co.

LORD MACAULAY'S ESSAYS.

The publishers have now ready an entirely new and elegant edition of the *Critical, Historical,* and *Miscellaneous Essays* of the Right Hon. THOMAS BABINGTON MACAULAY.

With an Introduction and Biographical Sketch of the author.

By E. P. WHIPPLE, Esq., of Boston.

And containing a New Steel Plate Likeness of MACAULAY, from a Photograph by Claudet.

Six volumes Crown Octavo.

PRICE PER SET:

On tinted paper, cloth binding.......$9 00 | Sheep binding, white paper.........$12 00
Fine white   "   "   "   .... 7 50 | In hf. calf, or hf. Turkey, tint'd paper 15 00

The want of a complete, elegant, and accurate edition of Lord Macaulay's miscellaneous writings, containing all the author's later corrections, is universally acknowledged. All the American editions heretofore published have been printed from the earlier English editions, which were materially changed by Macaulay before his death. He expressed himself as not satisfied with any American edition of his works.

THE ADVANTAGES OF THIS EDITION.

1st. The Essays have been arranged in exact chronological order, so that their perusal affords, so to speak, a complete biographical portraiture of the brilliant author's mind. No other edition possesses the same advantage.

2d. A very full Index has been especially prepared,—without which the vast stores of his historical learning and pertinent anecdote contained in the Essays, can be referred to only by the fortunate man who possesses a memory as great as that of Macaulay himself. In this respect it is superior to the English editions, and wholly unlike any other American edition.

3d. This edition contains also the pure text of Macaulay's Essays. The exact punctuation, orthography, etc., of the English editions have been followed.

4th. The Portrait is from a photograph by Claudet, and represents the great historian as he appeared in the latter years of his life.

5th. The biographical and critical Introduction is from the well known pen of Mr. E. P. Whipple, who is fully entitled to speak with authority, in regard to the most brilliant Essayist of the age.

6th. The typographical excellence of the publication places it among the best that have issued from the "Riverside" Press.

7th. An Appendix contains several Essays attributed to Lord Macaulay—and unquestionably his—not found in any other edition of his miscellaneous writings.

Books Published by Sheldon & Co.

HISTORY OF LATIN CHRISTIANITY.

Including that of the Popes, to the Pontificate of Nicholas V. By HENRY HART MILMAN, D.D., Dean of St. Paul's.

8 vols. Crown 8vo.

Price in Cloth, cut, . . $12 00 | Price in Sheep, . . . $16 00
"   "   uncut, . 12 00 | "   Half Mor., gilt, . 20 00
Price in Half Calf, gilt or ant., $20 00.

"One of the remarkable works of the present age, and one in which the author reviews, with curious erudition, and in a profoundly philosophical spirit, the various changes that have taken place in the Roman hierarchy; and, while he fully exposes the manifold errors and corruptions of the system, he shows throughout that enlightened charity which is the most precious of Christian graces, as it is unhappily the rarest."—*Wm. H. Prescott, in a note in the second volume of Philip II., p. 500.*

In a private letter to S. Austin Allibone, Esq., written two years later, Prescott said:
"If it seems to you high praise, I believe no one who has carefully read the extraordinary work to which it refers, will consider it higher than the book deserves."

"BOSTON, October 11, 1860.

"*Gentlemen:*—I have great pleasure in expressing a most favorable opinion of Dean Milman's 'History of Latin Christianity.'

"Through the kindness of the author, I have been acquainted with the work since its first appearance in England. It is a work of vast research, conducted with judgment and discrimination among authorities of very diverse weight, and not seldom conflicting purposes, and always with a spirit of truly liberal inquiry.

"No one can deny to Dean Milman the credit of Learning, Candor, and a conscientious search after Truth.

"The Theological Literature of the modern English Church has, as far as I am aware, produced no more valuable work.

"I remain, gentlemen, with great respect, truly yours, EDWARD EVERETT."

"ST. GEORGE'S RECTORY, October 17, 1860.

"MESSRS. SHELDON & CO.:

"*Gentlemen:* I am exceedingly gratified with the appearance of your new edition of Milman's 'Latin Christianity.' It is a work equally remarkable for the extent of its research, the fullness of its material, and the eloquence and beauty of its arrangement and style. Its impartiality of statement and deductions is a very distinguishing feature of its excellence, and it will doubtless take its place among those histories which finally occupy their whole projected ground, and remain as permanent authorities among men.

"Yours respectfully, STEPHEN H. TYNG."

"UNION THEOLOGICAL SEMINARY, New York, Oct. 19, 1860.

"MESSRS. SHELDON & CO.:

"Dean Milman's 'History of Latin Christianity' is not only the ablest work of its distinguished author, but it also takes the front rank in English historical and ecclesiastical literature. Written in a liberal and impartial spirit, it presents in an attractive style the result, rather than the processes, of thorough investigation in a field almost unvisited by English Church historians. General and ecclesiastical history are here so combined, that the work is indispensable to every student. Your elegant and cheap edition deserves the widest circulation, and will, I doubt not, find its way into every good library, private or public. HENRY B. SMITH."

"The enterprise and usefulness of the Publishing House of Sheldon & Co., are exhibited in the continued issues of great standard religious works, such as the Christian student must have, and are valuable in all time. Among these books, and in the front rank of religious historical composition, we place the volumes which this house has now begun to publish, the first having just made its appearance. The rise, progress, and triumph of Christianity in the early centuries, constitutes the great epoch in the history of the world."—*New York Observer.*

Books Published by Sheldon & Co.

THE LIFE AND LETTERS OF
MRS. EMILY C. JUDSON,
(FANNY FORRESTER,)

Third wife of the Rev. Adoniram Judson, D.D., Missionary to Burmah.

By A. C. KENDRICK, Professor of Greek in the University of Rochester.

1 vol. 12mo., with a steel-plate Likeness of Mrs. Judson.

Price $1 25.

"The narrative is carefully and beautifully written."—*Commercial Advertiser.*

"This 'Life and Letters' must take a high rank among the religious biography of our country."—*New Bedford Mercury.*

"Not least among the many charms of this delightful bit of biography will be recognized several sunny letters from N. P. Willis, to his literary protégé, which present the *Home Journalist* in a most pleasing light."—*Cor. Boston Post.*

"It is a biography uncommonly rich with all the materials which a gifted and devoted woman could supply from the stores of her well-spent life. The world and the Church should both be grateful for these records of genius, and these triumphs of Christian faith, contained within the pages of this charming book."—*Christian Intelligencer.*

"Her correspondence is marked by frankness and an intensity of passion, and its perusal gives the reader an insight into her character, which he feels to be as truthful and positive as a personal acquaintance of considerable familiarity could afford. As a biography, the volume occupies the first rank. It is full of unpretending pathos, and will be widely read, valued, and treasured as a beautiful and thrilling history of one of the most talented, unselfish, noble, heroic, and devoted of women."—*Congregationalist.*

"In biography, this is *the* book of the season—and of many seasons. We confess to having always felt, in spite of our reluctance, an unpleasant degree of misgiving as to the fitness of 'Fanny Forrester' for the work of missions; but as Dr. Kendrick has portrayed her character and recorded her life, she carries our sympathy—our admiration—our reverence, by storm. Henceforth we place her among the heroines and martyrs of Christianity. Not because we forgive 'Alderbrook' for the sake of 'Bat Castle'—our old way of thinking was somewhat in that style—but because we see now how the spirit of unselfish consecration to the happiness of others runs through both, and makes them 'parts of one harmonious whole.' Her 'Life and Letters' are worthy of an immense sale, and will have it. How 'a digger among Greek roots' could write such a fresh, appreciative, glowing memoir of 'a sensitive child of genius and song,' passes our comprehension; and we can not forbear the remark, that Mrs. Judson does not rise more in our esteem as a Christian woman, than Dr. Kendrick as an author."—*Religious Herald, Richmond.*

"The correspondence is particularly attractive. Sweetness, simplicity affectionateness, and humor are its characteristics. The volume will raise even the high estimate which the public has formed of Mrs. Judson. The nearer it conducts us to the most secret feelings of her heart and most cherished convictions of her mind, the more genial, loveable, and noble she appears."—*Boston Transcript.*

"The letters of Dr. Judson throw new light upon his loving, genial nature, and show how thoroughly his last marriage was one of affection, and how happy it proved. For her faithfulness to every duty, her self-sacrificing generosity to her family, her devotion to her husband, the maternal love which knew no difference between his children and her own, and the ever-growing beauty of her spiritual life, Mrs. Emily C. Judson deserves a large place in the public heart."—*Boston Journal.*

FORTY YEARS' EXPERIENCE IN SUNDAY-SCHOOLS.

By Stephen H. Tyng, D.D.

Rector of St. George's Church, New York.

1 neat 16mo vol. Price 60 cents.

"As a matter of course the volume is in a measure autobiographical, which would alone secure general attention to it."—*Boston Gazette.*

"No one is entitled to speak about Sunday-schools with more authority than Dr. Tyng, and no one can read this volume without obtaining most valuable hints for the management of a Sunday-school."—*Southern Churchman.*

"In a literary point of view, they are marked by all the excellencies for which the reverend author is noted; while the amount of real, useful knowledge they convey in a brief and practical form, upon a subject the importance of which is little understood, is really surprising."—*Troy Times.*

"Every Sabbath-school teacher should read it; every pastor might profit by it."—*N. Y. Independent.*

"This will be a very welcome volume to Sunday-school teachers, and to all who are interested in Sunday-schools. It embodies the experience and the counsels of one who by his deep interest in the cause, and by a personal devotion to the work, even in its details, and by a success which has been rarely if ever equaled, is qualified to speak with great profit upon the important subject. We have often made mention of the school at St. George's church, as perhaps the largest in the country, and as exhibiting results, not only in the chief end of Sabbath-school instruction, but in the great work of Christian benevolence and Christian activity, which are delightful to contemplate. In these pages the author imparts, in a measure, the secret of this success. We are sure that the volume has a great mission to accomplish for good."—*N. Y. Observer.*

"Dr. Tyng commenced his Sabbath-school labors as a missionary in the town of Quincy, Massachusetts, in 1819, and ever since, in all his ministerial labors has given the Sabbath-school a prominent place, in later years, it would seem, almost the first place in his plans for doing good. Earnest, laborious, inventive, evangelical, and having in most of his career the amplest resources at his command, his experience can not but be worthy of the most attentive consideration of all who are interested in this kind of instruction. Considering the wealthy character of Dr. Tyng's church, we were hardly prepared for his statement as to the economy in the management of his schools. 'Years of experiment,' he says, 'have proved to me, that the whole cost of Sabbath-school management, on the most liberal scale, including question-books, Bibles, hymn-books, children's papers, libraries, and necessary printing, with the anniversary books added, may be brought within *two cents* a Sabbath for each scholar. Surely the Christian church can not ask for a more economical expenditure or more effective investment than this.' Where is the church that can not raise *two cents* a week for every child that can be gathered in?

"Though we would not follow Dr. Tyng in some things, yet we listen eagerly to what he has to say on all the important matters of which he treats. He has given us a fresh interest in the cause, and some of his valuable hints we mean to put into practice at once. We most earnestly commend the perusal of this work to pastors, elders, superintendents, teachers, and parents, assuring them all, that they will find it full of thoughts worthy of the distinguished author. It is perhaps the most important discussion of the whole subject that has yet been made in this."—*The Presbyterian, Philadelphia.*

Books Published by Sheldon & Co.

ABBOTT'S AMERICAN HISTORY.

A Series of American Histories for Youth,
By JACOB ABBOTT,
In Twelve Volumes, each volume complete in itself.
Illustrated with numerous Maps and Engravings, from designs by Darley, Chapin, Herrick, Perkins, Parsons, Stephens, and others.

The Series will consist of—

1. ABORIGINAL AMERICA. (now ready).
2. DISCOVERY OF AMERICA. (now ready).
3. THE SOUTHERN COLONIES. (now ready).
4. THE NORTHERN COLONIES.
5. THE MIDDLE COLONIES.
6. REVOLT OF THE COLONIES.
7. BOSTON IN SEVENTY-FIVE.
8. NEW YORK IN SEVENTY-SIX.
9. THE CAROLINAS IN SEVENTY-NINE.
10. CAMPAIGN IN THE JERSEYS.
11. BURGOYNE AND CORNWALLIS.
12. THE FEDERAL CONSTITUTION.

It is the intention of the publishers that this Series of Popular American Histories shall fill a place long vacant in the literature of our country, a task which no author is so capable of performing as Mr. JACOB ABBOTT. The utmost care in the mechanical execution of the books will be used, it being their intention to make them as attractive as they will be entertaining.

Each vol., 16mo. Price 75 cents.

From the Boston Traveller.

"Sheldon & Co. of New York have commenced the publication of a new series of popular American Histories for Youth, by Jacob Abbott, the best living author of juvenile books. The series opens with an elegant volume (16mo, 288 pages), entitled 'Aboriginal America,' giving a lively and reliable account of the country as it was when Europeans first reached it, and of the modes of Indian life. It has seventeen maps and illustrations, beautifully executed, from designs by the first artists. The series will be completed in twelve volumes. Judging from the plan of the work, and by the opening volume, we are confident that this series of juvenile books will be found, in all respects, the most excellent publication of the kind ever undertaken. In point of execution, the volumes are to stand at the head of their class, the printing and illustrations being admirable, and worthy of the highest praise."

From the New York Examiner.

"The Rev. Jacob Abbott and Messrs. Sheldon & Co. are doing an admirable service for the young people of America. The former is writing, and the latter are publishing, a series of volumes, the object of which is to narrate, in a simple and intelligible manner, the leading events of American History. The first volume of the series—'Aboriginal America'—is just issued, and it is so beautifully printed, so tastefully illustrated, and so pleasantly written, that we shall expect to hear that the sale is reaching a very high figure. Just such a history of our country was a necessity, and we are thankful that it is to be so well supplied."

From the Boston Advertiser.

"This is the first volume of an American History in the course of preparation by Mr. Abbott. The object of this history is to give, in a clear, simple, and intelligible manner, the leading events connected with the history of our country from the earliest periods down, as nearly as practicable, to the present time. The natural history, the plants, the native inhabitants of the country, are treated of in this first volume. The several volumes are to be illustrated with maps and engravings. The illustrations in this volume are well designed and executed."

Books Published by Sheldon & Co.

THE HOUSEHOLD LIBRARY.

A Series of Choice Biographies by Distinguished Authors.

In Eighteen Volumes. 18mo. Muslin. Uniform style. Price of each vol., 50 cents.

Vol. I.—LIFE AND MARTYRDOM OF JOAN OF ARC. By Michelet.
Vol. II.—LIFE OF ROBERT BURNS. By Thomas Carlyle, and others.
Vol. III.—LIFE AND TEACHINGS OF SOCRATES. By George Grote.
Vol. IV.—LIFE OF COLUMBUS. By Alphonse de Lamartine.
Vol. V.—LIFE OF FREDERICK THE GREAT. By Lord Macaulay.
Vol. VI.—LIFE OF WILLIAM PITT. By Lord Macaulay.
Vol. VII.—LIFE OF MAHOMET. By Gibbon. With the Notes of Dean Milman and Dr. William Smith.
Vol. VIII.—LIFE OF LUTHER. By Chev. Bunsen. With a Spiritual Portrait of Luther by Carlyle, and an Appendix by Sir Wm. Hamilton.
Vol. IX.—LIFE OF OLIVER CROMWELL. By Lamartine.
Vol. X.—LIFE OF TORQUATO TASSO. By G. H. Wiffen.
Vol. XI. ⎫ LIFE OF PETER THE GREAT. In two Volumes. Compiled by the
Vol. XII. ⎭ Editor.
Vol. XIII.—LIFE OF MILTON. By Professor Masson; and an Estimate of Milton's Genius and Character, by Lord Macaulay.
Vol. XIV.—LIFE OF THOMAS À BECKET. By Dean Milman.
Vol. XV.—LIFE OF HANNIBAL. By Thomas Arnold, LL.D.
Vol. XVI.—LIFE OF VITTORIA COLONNA. By T. Adolphus Trollope.
Vol. XVII.—LIFE OF JULIUS CÆSAR. By Henry G. Liddell, D.D.
Vol. XVIII.—LIFE OF MARY STUART. By Alphonse de Lamartine.

NOTICES OF THE PRESS:

"The story of the 'Maid of Orleans' has often been told, but never with such thrilling pathos as by Michelet. All the incidents of the heroine's life are invested with new interest, and her cruel and barbarous execution receive at the hands of the eloquent and indignant historian, the condemnation which it so well deserves. The volume is got up in beautiful style."—*Philadelphia News.*

"The 'Life of Socrates' is from Mr. Grote's splendid History of Greece. It is very complete, and will serve to introduce the great Athenian philosopher to a better household acquaintance in this country."—*U. S. Journal.*

"Carlyle's beautiful essay is one of the finest compositions of the kind ever written—and every admirer of the genius of Robert Burns, as well as all literary students, will find it to be a volume both of interest and value."—*Boston Bulletin.*

"This series is peculiarly calculated for school libraries, and they should find their way into all our common school and Sunday school libraries. We are confident the 'Household Library' will secure a widely-extended circulation."—*Christian Ambassador.*

"The romance of history is so much better for the young than the romance of fiction that we are always glad to see such books appear."—*Congregational Herald.*

"The plan is to present, from the very best authorities, biographies or episodes of history, admitting of separation without injury."—*The Century.*

"All the volumes of this series are deserving a large share of popular favor, as they are calculated to promote a familiarity with the great spirit of history and literature, tempting the reader to their study when the sight of more ponderous tomes would drive them back in despair."—*Evening Saturday Argus.*

www.ingramcontent.com/pod-product-compliance
Lightning Source LLC
Chambersburg PA
CBHW022118290426
44112CB00008B/725